COME TOGETHER

Trades Councils 1920–50

COME TOGETHER

TRADES COUNCILS 1920-50

MICHAEL BOR & JETHRO BOR

The Book Guild Ltd

First published in Great Britain in 2024 by
The Book Guild Ltd
Unit E2 Airfield Business Park,
Harrison Road, Market Harborough,
Leicestershire. LE16 7UL
Tel: 0116 2792299
www.bookguild.co.uk
Email: info@bookguild.co.uk
Twitter: @bookguild

Copyright © 2024 Jethro Bor
and Michael Bor

The right of Jethro Bor and Michael Bor to be identified as the author of this work has been asserted by them in accordance with the Copyright, Design and Patents Act 1988.

All rights reserved. No part of this publication may be reproduced, transmitted, or stored in a retrieval system, in any form or by any means, without permission in writing from the publisher, nor be otherwise circulated in any form of binding or cover other than that in which it is published and without a similar condition being imposed on the subsequent purchaser.

Typeset in 12pt Minion Pro

Printed on FSC accredited paper
Printed and bound in Great Britain by 4edge Limited

ISBN 978 1915603 685

British Library Cataloguing in Publication Data.
A catalogue record for this book is available from the British Library.

Dedicated to the Shrewsbury 24 of 1972 in their victory over a miscarriage of justice, victimisation, and against the state interfering in legitimate trade union activity, 50 years on; to Maisie Carter (1927–2023) Communist Party, Labour Party, NUT, Merton and Sutton Trades Council, CND activist and family friend; and to everyone who has ever inspired us.

Our thanks to Stanley Rice, militant shop steward, who influenced this book; initial cover designer Max Lom-Bor; all those who filled in the questionnaire and shared their annual report for chapter 10; those trades councils who contributed photographs of their banners; Harry Robbins who helped format the book; to Lindley Owen, Shaun Doherty, Glyn Oliver, Simon Hester, Ken Muller and John Adams for reading and comments, and to all at the Book Guild for their patience and support. Any errors are ours to own.

Man's dearest possession is life, and since it is given to him but once, he must live as to feel no torturing regrets for years without purpose; so live as not to be seared with the shame of a cowardly and trivial past; so live, that dying he can say: 'All my life and all my strength were given to the finest cause in the world – the liberation of mankind.'
~ N. Ostrovsky, as featured on the CP membership card

The purpose of life is to be useful, responsible, honourable, compassionate... to stand for something, to have made some difference that you lived at all
~ Leo Rosten, quoted in John Roger and Peter McWilliams, Wealth 101: Wealth Is Much More Than Money (1992 edition), p279

Kant said that life's three great questions are: What can I do? What ought I do? What can I hope for?
~ A.C. Grayling, The Heart of Things. Applying Philosophy to the 21st Century (2006 edition), p98

When I give food to the poor they call me a saint. When I ask why the poor have no food, they call me a communist.
~ Helder Camara quoted in Steven Gauge, Political Wit, 2011

To pursue the popularisation of history throughout the Labour movement, giving historical perspective to every part of the struggle for the achievement of Socialism... Knowledge of history must be used to strengthen the confidence of the workers in their own powers... and a clear understanding of the Party's historical roots in the Labour movement is one of the best ways of overcoming sectarianism and feelings of isolation.
~ *Marx Memorial House CP Historians' Group Statement, January 1952*

To see ourselves in the light of history is to restore our connection to the consolations of our ancestors and to discover our kinship with their experience.
~ *Michael Ignatieff, On Consolation: Finding Solace in Dark Times, 2022*

A people or a class which is cut off from its own past is far less free to choose and to act as a people or class than one that has been able to situate itself in history.
~ *John Berger, Ways of Seeing, 1972, p32*

CONTENTS

Abbreviations	xv
Trades Councils: Who They Are and What They Do	xix
The Key Players	xxi
Foreword	xxxi
Introduction: Historians' Assessment of Trades Councils	xxxiv

PART 1
TRADES COUNCILS IN PERSPECTIVE

Chapter 1: Trades Councils in Society

1.	A Different Take on Trades Councils' Histories	3
2.	Trades Councils' Personalities	6
3.	The Communist Party Critique via Trades Councils of the TUC	12
4.	Different Visions for Trades Councils	16
5.	Trades Councils in the Trade Union Movement	19
6.	Individual Trades Councils' Functions	25

Chapter 2: Sketching Trades Councils' Histories to the General Strike

1. Trades Councils Before 1926: Changes in Organisation — 35
2. Radicals vs. Rulers: Daring to Dream 1920–26 — 42
3. Trades Councils in 1926: a Survey — 49
4. Assessments of Trades Councils in the General Strike — 58

Chapter 3: Trades Councils and Trade Union Leaders 1924–39

1. Trades Councils and TUC Emerging Structures 1924–29 — 67
2. Priorities of Recruitment 1929–32 — 76
3. Campaigning Against Fascism and the Cuts, or Recruitment Agencies 1933–36 — 81
4. Opposition to War 1936–39 — 88

Chapter 4: Trades Councils in the War and its Reverberations 1939–50

1. Local Representation 1939–44 — 94
2. Post-war Reconstruction 1944–47 — 106
3. Reality Bites: Problems with a Labour Government 1947–50 — 115

PART 2
TRADES COUNCILS AND THE COMMUNIST PARTY

Chapter 5: Communism vs. Labourism:
Communists in Trades Councils 1926–39

1.	Trades Councils' Readjustments 1926–32	123
2.	The United Front and TUC Circulars 1933–39	137

Chapter 6: Communists in Trades Councils 1939–43

1.	The Soviet Union's Impact upon Trades Councils 1939–41	159
2.	The Communist Party at War 1941–43	173

Chapter 7: New Possibilities and a
Labour Government 1943–50

1.	From War to Peace 1943–46	191
2.	Planning the Future 1946–48	200
3.	The Cold War in Trades Councils 1948–51	207
4.	Overview – The Communist Party in Trades Councils 1920–50	224

PART 3
TRADES COUNCILS ON THE MARCH

Chapter 8: Mass Unemployment in a Capitalist Society

1.	An Old Encounter Renewed 1920–26	236
2.	The Miners' Marches and the First Unemployed Associations 1926–31	239
3.	The Means Test, Unemployed Associations and the National Unemployed Workers Movement: Trades Councils Turn to the Left 1931–32	253
4.	The General Council Intervenes 1933–35	261
5.	Diminution of Mass Unemployment 1935–40	264
6.	War Employment for Trades Councils 1940–45	272
7.	A Vision of Full Employment 1945–50	277

Chapter 9: Women in Trade Unions

1.	Women in Unions 1875–1914	288
2.	Leaders	291
3.	Women in Unions 1914–45	295
4.	Working Women After the Wars	298
5.	Striking Back for Equal Pay (1916 Onwards)	300
6.	Women Trade Unionists Since the 1970s	303
7.	Women's Union Organising Today	305
8.	Conclusion	306

Chapter 10: Trades Councils Yesterday and Today: In the Movement, Of the Movement

1.	Political Inheritance: The 1984-85 Miners' Strike and After	310
2.	The 2022-23 Strikes and the Signs of a Recovery	314
3.	Composition and Re-orientation	317
4.	In Contemporary Society: Industrial and Political	321
5.	Historical Sketches	331
6.	Prospects	333

Closing Remarks 338

Appendix 1:
Conference Chronologies 357

1.	Annual Conferences of Trades Councils 1925-50	357
2.	TUC Annual Conferences 1926-50	358

Appendix 2:
1923 and 2023 Comparisons 360

Bibliography:
Texts and Events Referred to in the Book 362

1.	Newspapers, Journals, Magazines, Programmes, Handbooks, Manifestos, Manuals, Online Sources and Books	362
2.	ACTCs, CP, LP, MM, TCs, UAs and other Annual Reports, Conferences and Committees	383
3.	TUC and TCJCC	391
4.	Letters, TUC Files and Archives, and LSE Library	400

Endnotes 404

ABBREVIATIONS OF ORGANISATIONS, EVENTS, ACTIVITIES AND PROCEDURES

ACR	Annual Conference Report
ACTC	Annual Conference of Trades Councils
AEU	Amalgamated Engineering Union
AR	Annual report
ARP	Air Raid Precautions
ASE	Amalgamated Society of Engineers
ASFCs	Anglo-Soviet Friendship Committees
ASWs	Anglo-Soviet weeks
AtR	Aid to Russia (funds/weeks)
BAME	Black and minority ethnic
BLM	Black Lives Matter
BoGs	Board of Guardians
BSP	British Socialist Party
BUF	British Union of Fascists
CBE	Commander of the British Empire
CC	Central Committee
CI	Communist International (aka Comintern)
CND	Campaign for Nuclear Disarmament
COP	Conference of the Parties
CP	Communist Party of Great Britain
CPSU	Communist Party of the Soviet Union
CSCA	Civil Service Clerical Association
CWU	Chemical Workers' Union
DWUC	Daily Worker Unity Conference
EC	Executive Committee
ELFS	East London Federation of Suffragettes

EPL	Equal Pay League
ETC	Edinburgh Trades Council
ETU	Electrical Trades Union
EUC	Electoral Unity Conference
FBU	Fire Brigades Union
GLATUC	Greater London Association of Trade Union Councils
HfRF	Help for Russia Fund
HoC	Hands-Off China (Committee)
HoR	Hands-Off Russia
IFTU	International Federation of Trade Unions
ILP	Independent Labour Party
ISEL	Industrial Syndicalist Education League
JPCs	Joint Production Committees
LEA	Local Education Authority
LGBT	Lesbian, Gay, Bisexual, Transgender
LP	Labour Party
LRC	Labour Representation Committee
LRD	Labour Research Department
LSE	London School of Economics
MCDA	Manchester Council for Democratic Aid
MFGB	Miners' Federation of Great Britain
MP	Member of Parliament
NATO	North Atlantic Treaty Organisation
NATSOPA	National Society of Operative Printers and Assistants
NCCL	National Council for Civil Liberties
NCL	National Council for Labour
NCLC	National Council of Labour Colleges
NEC	National Executive Committee
NEU	National Education Union

Abbreviations of Organisations, Events, Activities and Procedures

NFTC	National Federation of Trades Councils
NFWW	National Federation of Women Workers
NHS	National Health Service
(N)MM	(National) Minority Movement
NPVC	National People's Vigilance Committee
NUDAW	National Union of Distributive and Allied Workers
NUGMW	National Union of General and Municipal Workers
NUM	National Union of Miners
NUR	National Union of Railwaymen
(N)UW(C)M	(National) Unemployed Workers Committee Movement
NUWSS	National Union of Women Suffrage Societies
NVS	National Voluntary Service
OMS	Organisation for the Maintenance of Supplies
PAC	Public Assistance Committee
PLP	Parliamentary Labour Party
POEU	Post Office Engineering Union
PPPS	People's Press Printing Society
RILU	Red International of Labour Unions
SDF	Social Democratic Federation
SL	Socialist League
SLP	Socialist Labour Party
SMA	Socialist Medical Association
SMAC	Spanish Medical Aid Commitee
SP	Socialist Party
SPC	Sheffield Peace Conference
SUTR	Stand Up to Racism
SWMF	South Wales Miners' Federation
SWP	Socialist Workers Party

T&LC	Trades and Labour Council
TC	Trades Council
TCJCC	Trades Councils Joint Consultative Committee
TD&TU	Trade Disputes & Trade Union Bill/Act
TGWU	Transport and General Workers' Union
TU	Trade union
TUC	Trades Union Congress
TUCJCC	Trades Union Councils Joint Consultative Committee
UA	Unemployed Association
UAB	Unemployment Assistance Board
UCU	University and College Union
UPOW	Union of Post Office Workers
URAB	Unemployment Research and Advice Bureau
USC	Unemployed Services Committee
WEA	Workers' Educational Association
WFTU	World Federation of Trade Unions
WN and V	World News and Views
WSF	Workers' Socialist Federation
WSPU	Women's Social and Political Union
WTUL	Women's Trade Union League

TRADES COUNCILS

Who They Are and What They Do

(from https://www.tuc.org.uk/trades-councils-who-we-are-and-what-we-do, accessed December 2021, abbreviated with permission from the TUC)

Trades union councils promote working-class solidarity in local communities. They are local groups of trade unionists. They are elected from trade union branches whose members live and/or work in the area. Trades union councils are often referred to simply as trades councils (TCs). TCs promote effective solidarity in disputes, joint campaigns on issues such as health, education, welfare and transport, and, in general, provide the vital link between the workplace and the wider working-class community. Trade union branches affiliate to their local TC on the basis of a small annual fee per member. In turn, TCs support, and can themselves affiliate to, local and national union campaigns for social justice.

TCs' activities are guided by an annual programme of work, determined by their annual conference. This can include campaigns to defend the NHS, promote public education, transport, the welfare state, and support benefit claimants, women, ethnic minorities, gay and transgender people, youth and the disabled.

TCs promote effective solidarity in disputes and joint campaigns on various issues.

TCs are the local trade union movement. They can be called upon by any trade union branch for strikes via picket lines, media publicity and financial appeals. National trade unions can promote issues more effectively when local TCs assist with publicity, leaflet distribution, recruitment, and public speakers. When TCs respond to issues in local communities, they can report to the Trades Union Congress (TUC) at regional and national levels.

THE KEY PLAYERS

Highlights of leading political figures

(see www.spartacus.educational.com, Wikipedia and TUC files)

Clement Attlee (1883–1967), Fabian Society, Stepney ILP, Stepney mayor, Stepney TC, Labour MP 1922, Deputy Labour leader to 1932–35, LP leader 1935–51, War Cabinet 1939–45, PM 1945–51, Lord Attlee 1951–55.

Tom Bell (1882–1944), ILP 1900, SDF, SLP, helped form Clyde Workers' Committee in 1915 with Willie Gallacher, Arthur McManus and David Kirkwood, on the Clyde Emergency Committee, the national secretary of Scottish LP, founder CP member 1920, editor of *Communist Review*, on National Council for Democratic Aid for Spain from 1936.

Ernest Bevin (1881–1951), Dockers' Union, general secretary of TGWU 1922–40, TUC General Council 1925–

40, Minister of Labour 1940, MP, Secretary of State for Foreign Affairs 1945-51, accepted Marshall Plan, NATO and nuclear weapons.

Margaret Bondfield (1873-1953), secretary Women's Labour League, Women's Peace Crusade, National Council for Adult Suffrage 1916, LP MP 1923-24, and 1926-31, parliamentary secretary to Minister of Labour 1924, Minister of Labour and Britain's first woman Cabinet Minister 1929-31, TUC Council from 1918, TUC chairman from 1923.

J.R. Campbell (1894-1969), BSP 1912, Military Medal, Clyde Workers' Committee 1918, CP founder member 1920, editor *The Worker* 1921-24, EC of CI 1928, editor of *Daily Worker* 1939 and 1949-59.

Walter Citrine (1887-1983), ILP 1906, ETU, secretary of the Federation of Engineering and Shipbuilding Trades, 1924 assistant-general secretary of TUC, TUC general secretary 1926-46, 1928 established Mond-Turner industrial talks, President of IFTU 1928-45, on National Coal Board 1946, Central Electricity Board 1947-57, Lord Citrine from 1947.

Joseph R. Clynes (1869-1949), Lancashire Gasworkers' Union, Fabian Society, ILP, LRC 1900, secretary Oldham TC, LP MP 1906-31 and 1935-45, vice-chairman of LP 1910, LP chairman 1921-22, Lord Privy Seal 1924 and deputy leader House of Commons 1922-32, Home Secretary 1929-31.

G.D.H. Cole (1889–1959), EC Fabian Society, guild socialist, *Self-Government in Industry* (1917), reader in economics at University College, Oxford, founder of Society for Socialist Inquiry and Propaganda 1931, Socialist League's *Forward to Socialism* (1934), hunger march 1936, Oxford University professor 1944–57.

A. Conley (1881–1952), TUC General Council from 1928, TUC president from 1934.

A.J. Cook (1883–1931), Baptist preacher, ILP, SWMF, Industrial Democracy League, Syndicalist, '*The Miners' Next Step*' 1912, CP founder member 1920, ILP, executive of the MFGB 1921, NMM from 1924, MFGB general secretary 1924–31.

Arthur Deakin (1890–1955), TGWU trade unionist during WWI, full-time official from 1919. National secretary of the General Workers National Trade Group within the TGWU 1932. TGWU acting general secretary from 1940, TGWU general secretary 1945–55.

Charles Dukes (1881–1948), secretary of National Union of Gasworkers, Warrington branch. BSP founder member, BSP national executive 1914. WWI conscientious objector. LP MP 1923–24 and 1929–31. National Union of General Workers District Secretary. General secretary of the National Union of General and Municipal Workers 1934–46. CBE 1946. TUC president 1946–47. Bank of England director 1947. British representative on UN Commission on Human Rights 1947, helped draft Universal Declaration on Human Rights. Made baron 1947.

Vic Feather (1908–76), Bradford Co-operative Society, TUC from 1937, TUC assistant-secretary 1947–60, TUC assistant-general secretary 1960–69; TUC general secretary, 1969–73, president of European Trade Union Confederation 1973–74, Baron Feather 1974.

Arthur Greenwood (1880–1954), author *The Reorganisation of Industry* (1918), secretary and founder of the Research and Information Department, LP from 1920, LP MP 1922–31 and 1932–54, Deputy Labour leader 1935–45, Minister without Portfolio 1940–3, LP leader in House of Commons 1943–45, an architect of the NHS.

Wal Hannington (1896–1966), CP co-founder 1920, NUWCM co-founder and leader 1921–39, imprisoned 1925, AEU leader from 1939.

E.P. Harries (1888–1963), secretary, later president of Pembrokeshire County LP. From 1929 worked at the TUC in London. Secretary of the Organisation Department of the TUC (Trades Union Congress) 1932–48, CBE in 1948, retired from TUC 1948.

Betty Harrison, (dates unknown) first woman vice-president of Bradford TC, CP member from 1940.

H.N. Harrison (died 1947), active on Liverpool Trades

Council, in the NUGMW and the Confederation of Shipbuilding and Engineering Unions, of which he was president for two years. TUC General Council 1937–47. TUC delegate to the American Federation of Labour in 1943. Helped form the WFTU.

G. Hicks (1879–1954), SP founder 1904, Operative Bricklayers' Society general secretary 1919–21, Amalgamated Union of Building Trade Workers 1921–41, TUC General Council 1921–41, TUC president 1927–28, LP MP 1931–50.

A.E. Hobson, Sheffield T&LC TC secretary 1936–54.

Arthur L. Horner (1894–1968), ILP and NUM member, at Irish Easter Rising 1916, CP founder member 1920, NMM general secretary 1924, president of SWMF 1936–46, helped create International Brigade 1936, president of NUM, 1946.

Imprisoned Communists for seditious libel, inciting mutiny, 4 August 1925 included Wal Hannington, Tom Wintringham, Harry Pollitt, Tom Bell, William Rust, William Gallacher, J.R. Campbell, J.T. Murphy, Ernie Cant, Albert Inkpin and Arthur McManus.

Mary Macarthur (1880–1921) and **Sylvia Pankhurst** (1882–1960): see Chapter 9, section on 'Leaders'.

Tom Mann (1856–1941), on the London TC, helped form the Workers' Union (later TGWU), founded ILP 1894, formed Australian Socialist Party 1910, Amalgamated Society of Engineers (ASE) president 1919-21, joined CP in 1920, NMM chairman 1921-29, and the ISEL.

Arthur McManus (1889-1927), SLP, editor *The Socialist*, Clyde Workers' Committee 1915, conscientious objector 1916, CP founder 1920 and chairman 1920-22, EC of CI 1922, imprisoned 1925, at League against Imperialism 1927.

Herbert Morrison (1888-1965), ILP 1906, No Conscription Fellowship 1914, Mayor of Hackney 1920-21, LP MP 1923-24, 1929-31, 1935-45 and 1945-59, Transport Minister 1929-31, LCC leader 1934-40, Minister of Supply 1940, Home Secretary 1940-45, deputy leader of the Labour Party 1945-56, Foreign Secretary 1951, Lord Morrison 1959.

William James Munro (1873-1948), ILP, founded BSP 1911, CP, on Manchester & Salford TC from 1920, vice-president 1922-23, president in 1924-25, and treasurer from 1926. Resigned from the CP. Elected TC secretary 1936, and LP member.

J.T. Murphy (1888-1965), Methodist preacher, SLP, Sheffield Workers' Committee 1914-18, CP 1920, RILU 1921, on Praesidium and Comintern 1921-22, EC of CI, NMM from 1924, Socialist League member 1933-37.

Horace E. Newbold (born 1900) AEU, Barrow ILP, CP, NUWCM, 1928 TGWU, Manchester & Salford

TC secretary 1944–69, Manchester & Salford TC joint secretary 1969–74.

R. Palme Dutt (1896–1974), pacifist, International Secretary of Labour Research Department (LRD) 1919, CP founder and member 1920–32, *Workers Weekly* editor 1922, founded the *Labour Monthly*, CP Executive 1923–65, Comintern member, editor *Daily Worker* 1936, CP general secretary 1939–41.

R. Page Arnot (1890–1986), University Socialist Federation founder with G.D.H. Cole 1912, LRD 1914–16 and 1919–29, conscientious objector, CP founder 1920 and CP CC 1927–38, CI 1928, Northumberland and Durham Strike Committee 1926, founded *Labour Monthly* with R.P. Dutt and W.N. Ewer, first principal at Marx Memorial Library 1933, *Fascist Agents Exposed in Moscow Trials* (1938), LRD EC 1938–76, LRD honorary president 1976, *MFGB 1945–1975* (six volumes).

Willie Paul (1884–1959), SLP, joint editor *The Socialist*, No Conscription Fellowship, author *The State; Its Origins and Functions* (1918), CP 1920, editor *Communist Review* 1921–23, Aid to Soviet Union 1941–45, Derby Peace Council 1946.

Harry Pollitt (1890–1960), in WSF 1919, CP founder member 1920, NMM general secretary 1924–29, imprisoned 1925, CP general secretary 1929–39, resigned 1939, reinstated 1941–56.

Arthur Pugh (1870–1955), on Parliamentary Committee of TUC 1920, replaced A.B. Swales as chairman of TUC's Special Industrial Committee 1926, secretary of Iron and Steel Trades Confederation to 1937, on *Daily Herald*, and Economic Consultative Committee of the League of Nations, knighted 1935.

A.A. Purcell (1872–1935), CP founder 1920, TUC General Council 1921, IFTU president 1924–28, Labour MP 1923–24 and 1925–29.

Tom Quelch (1886–1954), BSP member, joint editor of *The Call* from 1916, CP member from 1920; author *Report as to the Communist Movement in Britain* (1920); delegate to Second Congress of the CI; author *The Trades Councils: The Need for the Extension of Their Scope and Work* (1922); *The Importance of Trades Councils* (1926), foreword to *The Militant Trades Council: A Model Constitution for Trades Councils* (1926).

William Rust (1903–49), CP member from 1920, executive on Young Communist League 1923, Fifth Congress of CI 1924, CI in Russia 1928–30, editor the *Daily Worker* 1930 and 1939–49, CP representative in Moscow 1932, International Brigade, Spain 1936.

Emanuel Shinwell (1884–1986), Glasgow TC 1911, LP MP 1922–24, 1928–31 and 1935–82, Secretary for Mines 1930–31, Minister of Fuel and Power 1945–47, Secretary of State for War 1947–50, Minister of Defence 1950–51, PLP chairman 1964–67, Baron Shinwell 1970, In the House of Lords 1970–86.

Thomas Sitch (1852–1923), Labour MP, supported women chain-makers when on strike in 1910. Chainmakers' and Strikers' Association founder and its general secretary for over 30 years.

Herbert Smith (1862–1938), formed MFGB in 1889, ILP member from 1897, ILP councillor 1903, president of Yorkshire Miners' Association 1906, in Triple Industrial Alliance 1914, president of MFGB 1922, resigned as president of MFGB over miners' hours extended 1931, Barnsley mayor 1932.

C.G. Spragg, (dates unknown) Birmingham TC president 1937–39, Birmingham TC secretary 1940–44.

A.R. Stewart (1877–1967), ILP 1895, Cape Town Trades Council, No Conscription Fellowship, CP founder member 1920, Scottish CP organiser, British representative to CI 1923, opposed Nazi–Soviet Pact 1939, wrote memoir *Breaking the Fetters* (1967).

A.B. Swales (1870–1952), ASE 1890, ASE EC 1920–35, TUC president 1925.

Vincent Tewson (1898–1981), TUC organisation secretary 1925, assistant-TUC general secretary 1931, TUC general secretary 1946–60, knighted 1950.

Jimmy Thomas (1874–1949), Society of Railway Servants Union, LP MP 1910, 1924–26 and 1935–36, general secretary of NUR 1916–31, led railway strike 1919, Secretary of State for the Colonies 1924, Lord Privy Seal 1929, National LP MP 1931, Secretary for the Colonies 1932–36.

Ben Tillett (1860–1943), Christian Socialist, Dockers' strike leader 1889, with T. Mann *New Unionism* (1890), Fabian Society, ILP founder, LP, SDP, National Transport Workers Federation 1910, *Daily Herald* 1912, Labour MP 1917–24 and 1929–31, on SMAC 1936.

Alfred M. Wall (1889–1957), BSP, LP after WWI, CP, secretary of HoC 1927, secretary of London TC 1926–38, vice principal of SMAC 1930s.

Tom Wintringham (1898–1949), Royal Flying Corps, barrister, CP in 1923, ed (with R.P. Dutt) *Workers' Weekly* and *Labour Monthly*, edited NMM's *The Worker*, founded *Left Review* (1934), wrote *The Coming World War* (1935), central role in Spain International Brigade 1937, expelled from CP 1938, military correspondent for the *Daily Mirror* 1940, wrote *People's War* (1942).

FOREWORD

> We need to know more of these anonymous men and women who swelled the ranks of the trades councils.
> ~ S. MacIntyre, *A Proletarian Science: Marxism in Britain 1917–1933*, 1980, p65

This book is a celebration of the activities and politics of trades council members and their contribution to British society, 1920 to 1950. *Come Together*. This was the title for a song famously written by peace campaigner and Beatles musician John Lennon, inspired by far-out psychologist Timothy Leary's slogan for a campaign to become governor of California. Leary never became governor but the song was an inspiration – popular and often covered, its central idea of *unity* a key notion for the working-class movement in trades councils.

Michael chose to study TCs in 1980 and his findings are unearthed here, alongside recent insights. The text has been re-energised by Jethro during and after the Covid lockdown of 2020–22, with two freshly researched and written chapters

(9 and 10). In the book there is a focus on trades councils (TCs) and the British Communist Party (CP). Why? Because it is our ideological inheritance and we need to know where we are coming from to understand our past and to move forward. The book provides a useful overview for all people politically engaged in their localities. It is not an in-depth academic study of any individual TC (which can be read elsewhere). It is about the many not the few! We hope it encourages readers to delve into their own local histories, and ongoing efforts seeking justice through organisation and compassion for the less fortunate and marginalised.

As we write, Europe is experiencing a war, its largest conflict and humanitarian tragedy since 1945, following the Covid crisis, which, as well as a global pandemic, has been the most challenging collective domestic trauma since 1939–45, with fundamental inequalities exposed. Overcrowded, multigenerational households and those working on the front line, an often-multi-ethnic population, bore the brunt, as the UK's disproportionately deprived. The war rumbles on; but a saviour for the pandemic, mass vaccinations, has been co-ordinated through the NHS nationally and locally, an organisation in which public trust has resided and is secure (in the face of malignant incursions of the profit motive).

TCs from 1920 to 1950 represented part of such a *collective voice*, flowering alongside an emergent welfare state, a safeguard to help workers cope with socially inherited depredations and insecurities. TCs provided local support to help all workers survive turbulent crises, particularly in the 1930s, which culminated in the partial healing process enacted by the redolent Labour government from 1945.

Conclusions are rarely stated upfront, but drawn from

the study. The systematic marginalisation of the Communist Party (CP) is investigated at length to communicate the intensity and magnitude of the witch-hunt they endured. The text is overlapping and not always linear to further a deeper understanding of the various themes that we explore.

Working-class politics was about belonging to local communities, loyalty in safeguarding working conditions, defending the rights of the vulnerable to protect themselves, reasoned criticism and the practice of accountability. It meant campaigning for union representation to offset bureaucracies that pursued 'economic efficiency' at the cost of decent living standards, and striving to maintain community cohesion against 'divide and rule' strategies by management and media. TCs dealt with a plethora of challenges: the prolonged impact of mass unemployment, opposing fascism in Britain, protecting civil liberties and workers' conditions in World War II, and political conflict between communists and the status quo. And the key question remained, as it has ever since:

> 'But what will you put in Capitalism's place?' ~ A familiar question to any Socialist… and a formidable poser… to think of replacements for unemployment, racialism, war, poverty, exploitation and oligarchy. But, we'll probably think of something.[1]

Although the authors have been warned by one of the publishers we approached that local activists 'don't read books' such as these, we hope you prove them wrong.

Michael Bor and Jethro Bor, 2024

INTRODUCTION

Historians' Assessment of Trades Councils

> We hear little… about the history of those who have reason to protest at their subjugation by the rich and powerful. An alternative history… would tell of the long, painful struggle of the majority to escape the heel of the minority, under which… the majority mainly languishes.
> ~ A.C. Grayling, *The Reason of Things: Living with Philosophy (2004 edition), p106*

Trade unions are a central feature of British industrial and political life. Trade union membership in Britain was at 6.25 million in 2022, 200,000 down on the previous year. However, TCs, the coming together of trade unions, have been marginalised by historians. Despite alluding to their significance in the 1926 General Strike, critics claim that TCs became increasingly harnessed to emerging union centralisation. The classic reductionism was given by Sidney and Beatrice Webb, who referred to the crowded meetings of tired workmen, unused to official business, with knowledge limited to a single industry, useless as a court of appeal, ineffective as joint committees of the local trades, and with no recognised authority in the trade union world.[2] The argument runs: without national leaders or an official programme or any precise work, TCs indulged in wild, inconsistent resolutions and fitful and erratic action. If they had any uses for the Webbs, it was to organise and educate local unionist electors, carry out instructions received from the Trades Union Congress (TUC) Parliamentary Committee, watch and criticise the action of parliamentary representatives, and supplement and supervise local councillors' activities.[3]

TC delegates have been labelled the 'rank and file', although they only represent a small section of it, while TCs had differentiating geographical, industrial and social identities and represented old established unions and emerging new ones. The ties of work, friendship and recreation provided some internal cohesion but also made TCs manipulable, as we will witness. They had their own traditional rules and formats and internal hierarchies for engaging with local problems and offering solutions. However, despite all the resolutions and manifestos emanating from individual TCs, they were rarely unified or politically mobilised. Most retained their form from the labour movement pre-World War I.

Historians have emphasised TC uniformity and downplayed their remarkable *diversity*. The best study, by Alan Clinton,[4] suggested that TCs made audible the voice of the non-articulate, but TCs were producing *contradictory* messages. Clinton argued that history showed rebellion appeased by responsibility, but this depends on how one defines the polarised aspects of 'rebellion' and 'responsibility'. Certainly for the TUC, the advent of the Communist Party of Great Britain (CP) as an organised group in TCs, prompted new TUC strictures.

In the years 1920–50, union leaders complained that TCs did not reflect the whole interests of their affiliated membership, yet they were constituents of a movement relying on *local initiative*. Some were quiescent in this, others outspoken. TCs reflecting tensions between acceptance and revolt begs the question: acceptance of what and revolt against what, as individual TC officials and delegates responded in diverse ways to industrial and political questions. But how? And why? That is what we will explore.

*

Motivations for being a TC representative varied from the idealist to the careerist, political affiliations from conservative to communist, petty bourgeois alongside Gramsci's 'organic' working-class intellectuals.[5] If dissent had not been contained in TCs as a safety valve it could have exploded onto the streets. So much energy, idealism, and rhetoric went into these years in TCs! References to TCs in union histories imply that they had lost most of their importance as industrial bodies, because local unions were absorbed into national ones, negotiating national agreements and regulating the methods of dealing with disputes. The residue of functions left included conducting campaigns for union membership and pressurising municipal authorities, public contractors and employers to secure wages and conditions. However, to assume, as G.D.H. Cole does, that TCs confined their activities to propaganda, organising and discussion, or affiliating to the divisional Labour parties to retain contact with the political side of the movement, omits TCs' emerging roles.[6]

The TUC General Council perceived TCs as local representative agencies of trade unionism, but less than half the total union membership were affiliated to TCs. Where union finances were centralised, contributions to TCs were usually paid out of the central funds. Only small affiliation fees were possible and these went mainly on costs of management and propaganda, and only a few large TCs could afford full-time secretaries, so most relied on voluntary workers and often had no office or paid staff. For Cole, TCs constituted local *trade union parliaments* fostering the spirit of trade union solidarity. If adequate resources had been made available, TCs could have played a much larger part in organising new trades in which unionism was weak or non-existent.[7]

Were TC activities restricted by lack of funds? As voluntary bodies, much of what they did was unaffected by such considerations. In fact, a TC with little income could sometimes be as active as one with enough to employ a secretary, an appeal for a campaign capable of raising as much in a week as affiliation fees in a year. But TCs were dependent upon windfalls and sometimes provided ineffective help (when the TUC decided upon a campaign) because of lack of finances. The TUC used such arguments for dissuading TCs from involvement in unofficial strikes or CP-led united front organisations, and no one in the TUC General Council advanced TCs' claims for Congress representation. But, by the 1920s, it had become essential to have local bodies that could appoint representatives to serve on committees.

With the elevation of union leaders in both world wars and Labour governments, by 1949 M. Turner-Samuels found it difficult to define TCs' status or explain their function in union organisation: they had no 'organic nexus' with the TUC or with any union, yet were employed by the TUC and co-ordinated deliberations of local union organisations as 'local agents'.[8] For Turner-Samuels, in the 19th century, TCs had been gradually marginalised between the political and industrial working-class movements and so declined as instruments of industrial cohesion, but in the 1930s and 1940s TCs were active in linking union branches and canalising the general views of unions and workers through this. He retained a romanticised picture of a local consensus of industrial criticism and opinion being obtained and divergence in local action thus avoided. As local agents of the TUC, TCs were supposed to forward regular reports of labour proceedings. In practice this occurred sporadically.

TCs were compelled to support policies in the making of which they had *not* participated or been consulted, so it is not surprising that they appear often as merely links of co-ordination of local trade union action and the channel of correspondence. The rationalisation was that there could not be two policy-making bodies, so the General Council set out limited duties to which TCs should adhere. Necessarily, TC activities widened with the growth of the welfare state. A. Flanders recognised TCs' main activities as local representatives of members' interests and nominating to local employment, insurance, advisory and hospital management committees,[9] a central theme being *co-operation* between TCs and local Labour parties based on mutual respect for their separate spheres of activity.

However, confusion and controversy remained between the TUC and TCs because the latter's resolutions were not binding upon the former, the mediatory Trades Councils Joint Consultative Committee (TCJCC) was only advisory, and TCs did not readily accept the role cast for them as policy-executing (not policy-making) bodies. A geographical rather than purely industrial analysis of union opinion on economic and social policy would have been helpful to the TUC in determining its attitude to impending legislative or administrative action. Any suggestion canvassed in 1945 that the TUC should open regional offices, each with a full-time official with TCs, would have been blocked. The total paying membership of TCs by 1952 had fallen to 3 million members (compared with a TUC membership of 8 million) totalling 531 TCs with 15,561 union branches affiliated, income from affiliation fees being c.£60 per TC, totalling £32,000, around £1,135,000 in today's money.

The typical characterisation of a *Trades Council* by 1950 is as a meeting place for local union delegates, weakened because they represented union branches, not districts, where the real local authority in industrial matters rested. Except in an emergency, they had no say over local industrial policy and, if they became involved in strike movements, it was usually at the cost of the TUC General Council's displeasure. TCs' value was seen in their provision of a valuable centre for learning about the wider problems of the movement. Many union leaders, having served apprenticeships in them, did not want to be faced with any alternative focal point of unionist sentiment and power that would unsettle centralised national collective bargaining, and, they believed, since the advent of the Soviet Union and the formation of the British CP, their suspicions were confirmed.

Another argument was that maintenance of national unions cost nearly all the money unionists paid, leaving very little for local work. These evaluations of TCs made them peripheral and subject to far closer control by the General Council than national unions, which could still choose CP officers, affiliate to proscribed organisations and send CP delegates to Congress. H.A. Clegg surmised the considerable powers over TCs were largely because national unions wished them 'kept in their place' and TCs' diminished importance was because they only co-ordinated action on issues unlikely to arouse interest outside their own area. Clegg cited personal interests and local feuds or rivalries disturbing TCs' harmony, with TCs making resolutions that bound no one to anything.[10] During our time frame, this view negates the true value of TCs, rooted in communities, and overestimates national unions' representation of the interests of all workers.

L. Bather's *History of Manchester and Salford Trades Council* noted TC delegates providing services to branches on industrial, civic and educational matters, increasing union membership, making TUC policy widely known, and nominating representatives to committees and tribunals. By the 1950s, TC objectives included monitoring the social rights and interests of labour and, before endorsing a strike, considering whether a collision could be obviated, either by its own mediation or by an arbitrative body agreed upon by employer and employed.[11] This was a few steps back from the possibilities envisaged in the early 1920s (which we will explore). E.L. Wigham maintained that if TCs served 'some minor useful purposes' as local TUC agents, co-ordinating local union views and making the voice of the movement heard on a range of local committees, they could not spend money on *political* activities and the annual conference could not impinge upon the policy-making prerogative of Congress[12] (an issue we shall likewise assess).

In 1956, B.C. Roberts described TCs as the TUC in miniature but insisted they had always represented a problem, fitting uncomfortably into the structure of the movement. He noted that TCs varied a great deal, only 17 having an affiliated membership of more than 20,000 and 256 having fewer than 4,000 members.[13] He did not draw any conclusion from this data as to their heterogeneity in action but asserted that their representative functions had considerably increased since 1945. He applauded TC work as 'the very stuff of local democracy', much depending upon it if the rise of bureaucracy was to be avoided and the schemes of social welfare were to be conducted in the spirit in which they were conceived. However laudable such aspirations, local democracy was being sidelined and by 1961 TCs were being treated as the poor relation of the labour movement, Flanders asserting that it was TCs' fate to pioneer, with the aid of very limited means, activities subsequently taken over by other bodies within the movement.[14]

In 1962, H.A. Turner returned to the notion of TCs providing a natural platform for radical and militant criticism of official union policy, from which would-be rivals to established leaders could advertise themselves. For organised oppositionist fractions, the Joint Shop Stewards' Committees at the workplace and TCs in the locality offered the basis for an alternative system of labour organisation to that of national unions, particularly adapted to mobilising class rather than sectional labour sentiment.[15] Such fractions might rarely be able to gain the leadership of a national union but a command of inter-union bodies might enable them to influence and, at critical moments, dominate industrial events; Turner concluded that TCs had been largely deprived of industrial functions and rebuked for assuming political ones.

*

TCs operated within the complex and shifting *dialectic* in unions between national and local leaders, active rank and file and professional bureaucracy, a *strategic point* within the working class, transmitting impulses from leaders and society, absorbing influences that altered workers' outlooks, and reflected changing moods and aspirations.[16] Such transmissions, absorptions and reflections are difficult to gauge when one lumps TCs together as having a dynamic internal life, which some TCs palpably lost after 1926, but TCs exemplified the tensions between acceptance and revolt in the movement. This requires elucidating in terms of their major interests: unemployment, housing, public health, collectivist social policies and campaigns on international issues. Heightening workers' expectations and affecting working-class consciousness is difficult to measure, as is even whether TCs were a medium whereby the interests of various groups of workers were brought to bear on state activities in social and economic policy. What influences TCs had were diffused regionally (as we will reveal).

TCs responded to events and rarely initiated them. They were primarily *defensive* organisations, with their Annual Conference of Trades Councils (ACTC) producing long speeches from TUC leaders who sought to use TCs to regulate local union conflicts. This was an empirical, remedial approach that prized administration and sectionalism enhancing TUC control. TCs squabbled over areas of jurisdiction – could they support this struggle? Were they allowed to perform that work? – while the confidentiality necessary in arbitration or negotiations integrated them into established local government and welfare services. With politics and economics compartmentalised, the more radical or militant TC delegate was usually overwhelmed by industrial 'rationalisation' and union centralisation.

There is a notion that an enfeebled working-class movement emerged after 1926, followed by a paucity of radical ideas in the 1930s, and that disparate origins, affiliations, funds, local traditions and clientele dispersed their relevance. Was TCs' diversity symptomatic of declining or emerging local industries? What was the effect of the numbers of unemployed, TC/local council relations, traditions of militancy and dominant union personalities? The truth is that TCs exhibited a *structural ambiguity* that often resulted in vociferous demands being met by union leaders' containment. The mass of local TC histories reveal that TC delegates might criticise union leaders for short-sightedness but delegates rarely successfully countered TUC hegemony. It was not so much that they were happy to be recognised with a share in a very limited area of decision-making as that they were denied a choice, radical activism frozen out. Nevertheless, to posit that the Labour Party constitution and TUC reorganisation left no room for local work is not borne out.

In this retrospective, 20 regional TCs, small and large, and throughout the UK have been selected on the basis of the continuity of records from 1920 to 1950, a cross-section of TCs in new and industrial areas, with reference to English, Scottish and Welsh TCs. Apart from official TUC publications, more is gleaned from annual reports, officials' private correspondence with head office, files on the implementation of 'black circulars'[*] and on the Minority Movement (MM), the National Unemployed Workers' Movement (NUWM) and unemployed associations (UAs), TUC circulars to TCs, and TUC files on communism (all in the TUC archives).

The results of TUC heresy-hunts created local confusions, lasting recriminations, subterfuge, accusations and disunity, with regional variations, but TCs were throughout more than merely transmission belts of orders

---

[*] 'Black circulars' were TUC rulings designed to exclude CP members from becoming dominant in TCs. They were introduced 1933–39 and then extended under a different name.

from leaders to the rank and file. Regarding independent opposition to Mondism,[†] UAs, TUC knighthoods, black circulars, anti-fascist demonstrations, conscription and responses to the outbreak of war in 1939, co-option of TUC leaders into the state apparatus, and support for the National Minority Movement (NMM), the NUWM, hunger marchers, reception committees, the united front, or unofficial strikes, TCs were surprisingly divergent in their responses.

In many ways to be presented, they ignored TUC admonitions. Following the General Strike in 1926, there were new functions including recruitment of women and youth, opposition to Bedaux schemes,[‡] support for industrial disputes in clothing, textiles and cotton industries, and action on courts of referees, local employment committees and unemployment assistance boards (UABs). We have alluded to new functions in the 1939–45 war and under the third Labour government. TC delegates often resented the limited say ordained for TCs, which were local voices made relevant in an era of mass unemployment, local fascists, peace campaigns, united fronts, developing social services and partial nationalisation.

With union leaders Walter Citrine, Vic Feather and Vincent Tewson, controversies with the CP were magnified to present union leaders' respectability in the eyes of governments. In practice, TCs' functions did not alter

---

[†] Based on the views of Alfred Mond, Mondism was introduced from 1927 by W. Citrine, TUC General Secretary, advocating co-operation between employers and union leaders in industry.

[‡] Bedaux schemes were incentive schemes in which the standard time for the completion of a job was fixed and the rate per hour defined.

dramatically despite legislation such as the Trade Disputes and Trade Union (TD&TU) Act, and the *Model Rules*. TCs mostly remained radical interpreters of TUC and Labour actions and policies, the local conscience of the movement, although most lost ground as significant pressure groups by 1950, paradoxically because of the success of national unions becoming integrated into government, thus pre-empting amplifications of TC functions.

In the UK 1920–50, only a few TCs advanced the militant unionists' voice, but, while the variegated political affiliations of TC delegates persisted, the ventilation of wider political debate on all issues reveals a significant contingent of communists. If TC delegates were the touchstone for the mood of the movement, they were also affected by, and some reflected, the co-option of the union leadership. In relations with local councils, the problems of local industries and government legislation, TCs sustained their official local voice, although the sometimes-hostile local press trivialised or marginalised their role as local democratic participants.

TCs faced structural encounters associated with union centralisation, CP activities, the war economy and welfare state administration. In these, the relationship between TCs and union leaders rarely presented a unified response, after the consciousness-raising General Strike clashed with the reaffirmation of diminishing independence. TCs *were* in a position to lessen sectionalism by *uniting* disparate unions around common causes, but they were harnessed between unions and TUC leaders (in the four main areas we analyse). Firstly, the relationship between TCs and union leaders; secondly, TCs' roles in 1926 and the subsequent reorientation by the TUC, TCJCC and local union leaders; thirdly, CP involvement in TCs via the NMM, the NUWM, the black circular controversy, and war and Cold War years; and, fourthly, the effect of mass unemployment on industrial politics including the impact of the NUWM, UAs, hunger marchers and union policies. Then we shall offer an overview highlighting women activists in trade union politics and briefly assess the functionality of TCs today, noting continuities and changes. Key questions arise: Have TCs been solely local debating and administrative centres or has overt *political* action been a possibility?[17] And could TCs have a *political* dimension sparking the embers of local activism?

PART 1

Trades Councils in Perspective

CHAPTER 1

Trades Councils in Society

We do not want to return to the narrow limitation of the trades councils of the past. We do not want trades councils to be purely strike committees. We cannot afford to neglect political action, the development of our co-operatives, independent working class education. A trades council today is really not a 'trades' council in the old restricted craft sense. It is a council of workers' representatives from various working class organisations – industrial, political and co-operative – met to consider how conscious working class action can be taken in regard to every sphere of activity.
~ A.B. Swales, at the ACTC, 27 February 1925

1. A DIFFERENT TAKE ON TRADES COUNCILS' HISTORIES

Throughout our period, the production and distribution of union information was an essential element for relations between the TUC and TCs. Objective TUC analyses of events were structured and interpellated to *create* a reality in which unionists were constrained in funds, debates and thus functions. At the ACTCs, the mediatory TCJCC set the agenda and always invited a leading TUC member to address the conference, within which parameters the linguistic arguments ensued. This fostered a predictable conformity, relegating interjections perceived as offering foreign heretical imports or irrelevant eccentricities regarding the quotidian matters on the agenda.

Seasoned by lurid media-constructed suspicions of Soviet practice, this ethnocentricity and British union chauvinism was buttressed by self-censorship. TC delegates understood the *guidelines* for discussions on union issues, which rendered most debates repetitious. The TUC, Labour Party and CP all declared that they used *facts* and the opposition used *propaganda*, propagating doctrines, practices, associations, actions and plans to spread opinions and principles, to effect change and reform. Within that interpretation, the TUC used explicit propaganda to link fascism with communism in the 1930s, while CP members in TCs used it during the 'Imperialist War' phase (1939–41) to taint Labour leaders as proto-Nazis. In actuality, every organisation, union or party used propaganda to advance its cause. TUC leaders exhibited a set of values that upheld the status quo in the union movement as they perpetuated myths/truths about communists (which the latter partially reinforced through their own tactics). Union leaders had precedence in the media over rank-and-file unionists, the TUC itself the 'official source' operating within the confines of a constructed economic, political and industrial system. The form and structure of conferences and committee meetings were an integral part of that message. Leading TUC and TCJCC members hosted the ACTCs, determined the style (and length) of debates, extracting the radical sting from them or intruding with the 'official version' of events. Occasionally, their role *was* challenged, but uppermost was *unity, loyalty* and *discipline*. This was about the democratic process as defined by union leaders, who presented themselves as the guardians (conducting the shadow-boxing), convincing delegates that they were always representing their interests to employers, to government and/or on national committees.

Some attempts were made to stimulate TCs in direct participation in major political or industrial events but this could get out of control with incalculable results, undermining the TUC's burgeoning national prestige. This product was masked within an ingrained mythology about 'democratic participation'. Hence the TUC perpetuated that ordered, well-organised package conceived by its leaders, any challenges demonised as disruptions, unofficial actions or interventions by the compromised 'outside bodies', while union leaders presented themselves as impartial.

The specific terminology union leaders, the CP and TC officials used is starkly suggestive in terms of crude attempts at manufacturing opinion. The TUC presentation was to create a picture of an ordered trade union world, with any opposition belonging to a lunatic fringe. In this, the opposition on *any* issue was never the result of TUC incompetence or misrepresentation but negative and disturbing the natural order, adumbrated as 'extremists versus moderates'. Such language was ritualised and rhetorical and circumscribed participation or produced reductionist reportage, shorthand journalese which trade unionists seemed particularly prone to mouth. The result was supposed to leave those elected to proceed with the minimum of interference.

Thus, the TUC presented the 'real facts' of any issue so that delegates rarely felt capable of influencing events. Communists were sidelined and responded in like manner. Hence the militaristic metaphors of 'rank and file' and 'the General Staff' (the TUC), although they become crude frames of reference for exploring internal relations within the labour movement. Designation of TUC leaders as 'the bureaucracy' was sometimes an unhelpful shorthand, even if the career structure, authority and legitimacy of full-time union officials differentiated them from most TC delegates. To envisage a crude coercion or manipulation in TC/TUC relations cloaks the underlying accommodations between union leaders and TC officials, which date back to the skilled workers of the 1860s and 1870s, when many TCs were formed to gain union representation and elevate collective bargaining. Furthermore, TCs highlighted through their practice the artificial division between industrial and political issues, and exemplified the complex internal differentiations of the working class and its potential but unrealised resilient unity. Their history is thus a prism in which to analyse the history of Britain from 1920 to 1950.

2. TRADES COUNCILS' PERSONALITIES

The first four volumes of the *Dictionary of Labour Biography* mentioned exactly 100 TC delegates who had their active life before 1950.[18] From an analysis of these it transpires most emerged from poor, working-class backgrounds; they began work when very young; there was a disproportionately high number from one-parent families; a few were orphans; most were self-educated; many were Liberal or Labour voters and later the backbone of local authorities as aldermen, mayors and justices of the peace. One of the most prominent TC secretaries was the socialist **A.A. Purcell**, who epitomised the qualities of a trade unionist, exemplar of a life dedicated to the amelioration of the working class. As fellow socialist **W.J. Munro** described him:

> whatever phase of activity he was dealing with, whether Industrial, Rents, Unemployment, Politics, Art, Travel, he imparted… a bristling challenge to the entrenched Conservatism and Stupidity that barred the way to the progress of his class; he possessed High Intelligence, Sound Common Sense, Stupendous Courage… marvellous optimism, a great fund of good humour… you were propelled along by his breezy manner.[19]

President of the TUC Congress in 1924, Purcell returned to his position as a TC secretary in 1929. He became an authority on rents, mortgages and housing, organised a People's Congress in 1931 with 21,000 delegates, and continued his long record as a union negotiator.

Most TC officials were not of this mould. There were careerists and idealists, Conservatives and Communists, Liberals and Labour activists, as well as local 'characters'. A famous trade union leader who began in a TC was **Ernest Bevin**. From being a delegate to Bristol TC he became the Labour government's Foreign Secretary; from socialist roots he became part of the establishment, giving

NATO Labour endorsement in 1949. **George L. Perkins** was a pioneer of the labour movement in Bristol and with Bevin established the TC on a sound footing, yet few know about Perkins. **John Hodge** and **Alexander Wilkie** of Glasgow TC opposed the General Strike of 1926 as an unconstitutional break with union traditions, the former remaining a patriotic Tory working man. Pragmatists like **Samuel Shaftoe** determined to make Bradford TC not only a useful institution but the representative head of trade unionism, while **William S. Mycock**, a working-class artist, was one of the finest public speakers and debaters Swindon T&LC had ever known.

Another feature of TC membership was the family connection. **Frank Jackson**'s father was a founder of Coventry TC. Frank became the organiser for Tottenham TC in the General Strike and for the NUWM later, began the *New Builders' Leader* in 1935 and engaged in life-long CP work.[20] The ideal is presented in **J. Goodfellow**, made a life member of Deptford TC because of 'the perseverance and straightforward manner in which he has always placed the welfare of the members before personal interests'.[21]

Long service in any TC was celebrated. Castleford TC had two stalwarts in **Jess Dowding** (secretary) and **Mark Bairstow** (president). Services to the community were honoured when the TC secretary, chairman and vice-chairman were elected mayor in successive years. This TC saw **Herbert Smith** (miners' leader in the General Strike) emerge after eight years as its president, later promoted to serve on the TUC General Council.[22] TC service also appears for **Samuel Reeves**, active in the Liverpool labour movement for over 40 years, and **Henry Hucker**, for 45 years secretary of Walsall Number 2 branch of the Amalgamated Society of Railway Servants.

TCs possessed many fine orators and organisers, often featuring the 'practical type' who had little time for political theories. Take **Thomas Sitch** from Newcastle, who felt as an MP his ideals of personal service would suffer by being too remote from his constituents; **George Hawkins**, the first Oxford working man elected to the Bench; **Thomas Lewis** of Southampton TC, who served on the Borough Council for 60 years, on the TC for 50 years, an excellent speaker, ruthless in debate and a socialist pioneer who married his ideals to practical purposes, with uncompromising principles (and, unusually, a teetotaller and non-smoker). He received a CBE for his public service.[23]

These TC officials show a solidity to TCs, representatives of a lifetime of commitment. **Arthur Eades** became president of Birmingham TC at 32 and was associated with it for 40 years; **Charles Gibbs** believed that the immediate practical ends could be better obtained as leader of West Bromwich TC, and eschewed the party struggle. Established trade union leaders such as **Robert Applegarth** began campaigning for legal recognition of unions and was made a life member of Brighton TC. He had a lawyer's gift for argument and persuasion, his activities not guided by specific theoretical principles so much as a broadly conceived ideal of working-class co-operation.

Most TC officials were only known in the local area because they excelled in daily union duties, such as **G.D. Kelley** of Manchester & Salford TC, who acquired a £50,000 loan (a fotune in today's money) from Manchester Council for local relief works. TCs could be a formative education: for **Tom Williams**, learning to prepare and deliver reports in his local TC, he became a privy councillor and Lord Williams of Barnburgh, while **Charles Sitch**'s success as a union organiser provided the basis on which his political career was founded as a Labour MP.

TC delegates politically could range from anti-fascists to Empire patriots, rebels to conformists. Communist and International Brigader **George Brown** of Manchester & Salford TC was killed in action in Spain aged 31 in 1937, while **James Seddon** had backed the British Empire in 1914. **Joseph Deakin** of Walsall TC never sought public office but was responsible for opening the way for working-class representation in Walsall's civic affairs, his propaganda work through the local press an inspiration, while Brown's colleague on Manchester & Salford's Executive Committee (EC) **Richard Coppock** was knighted.

TC delegates' attitudes to leftists varied. Some TC delegates disowned the hunger marches as a CP stunt (such as **Frank Sheppard** of Bristol TC) or opposed the NUWM and United Front for similar reasons (such as **W.M. Rogerson** of Walkden T&LC). Others retained their initial enthusiasms whatever high office they attained. **Robert Smillie** of Glasgow TC, later on the General Council (1920–26), was deemed a man of dignity and integrity, the first prominent personality to bring a socialist outlook into his union work among miners.

Typical TC delegates, though, were moderate and diplomatic with little interest in doctrinal disputes, always prepared to give general support to labour leadership, with little sympathy for overt radicalism. **J.E. Sutton** of

Manchester & Salford TC was one such figure. **Arthur D. White** of Romford and Hornchurch T&LC, a forthright, clear and persuasive platform speaker, excelling as a committee man, was another. The description of **T. Williams** could apply to many TC officials: 'an excellent administrator, of the more authoritarian type, strong but fair, outstanding as a chairman, a formidable opponent in argument, deadly logical as well as pugnacious'.[24]

The diversity in TCs could range from witty conversationalists, like **Montagu J. Blatchford** of Halifax TC to the unpredictable fiery propagandists like **Peter F. Curran** of Barnsley T&LC, to the stalwarts like **William H. Drew** of Bradford TC, who put the TC on its wider basis, paving the way for the full-time work of a secretary and beginning the TC Year Book annual report.

Of the few but notable women TC leaders was **Mary Macarthur**, who was in her time the only woman delegate to the London TC and founded the National Federation of Women Workers; **Betty Harrison**, the first woman vice-president of Bradford TC, was, as a communist, battling the witch-hunt in the 1940s and 1950s, while **Amelia Hicks** represented women rope-makers on the London TC. (Women's historical role in the workers' movement is explored further in Chapter 9.)

Apostasy was not forgotten in TCs. Two TC delegates exemplify this. Firstly, **Ben Tillett** (supported by Bradford TC), who from a childhood of extreme poverty became the dockers' famous leader who urged militant direct action, became an MP, but opposed the General Strike in 1926, preferring the status and social life of a public figure to that of union organiser. Secondly, **J. Havelock Wilson**, delegate to Sunderland TC, aligned his Seamen's Union with the government in 1926, the union becoming a faithful servant of the ship-owners, Havelock Wilson characterising the strike as a vast CP plot.

This brief synopsis of TC officials offers a glimpse into their contributions. TCs rarely spoke as one voice. Delegates were local people, sharing parochial experiences, confronting specific local issues, accountable to their union branches. Union pragmatism, self-advancement, TCs as a stepping-stone, TUC training courses for officials, were challenged by a minority of activists, often thwarted by local and national traditions and committee minutiae. Few delegates had the time or inclination to produce theoretical analyses of the role of TCs. Most were, indeed, pragmatic, long-term unionists with a sturdy local reputation and long-standing service to the area. Such people were rewarded by the TUC for loyalty, but most names in annual reports are little-known and long since forgotten. The secretary, chairman or president had the central roles, keeping head office informed of local activities, and they appear in the TUC files and the local TC histories, just as most delegates articulated local grievances but left workers, managers and local authorities in their respective positions, as often happens with pressure groups distanced from major decision-making.

3. THE COMMUNIST PARTY CRITIQUE VIA TRADES COUNCILS OF THE TUC

Over our 30 years (1920–50), witness the cavalier use by all groupings of the well-worn labels 'dictatorship', 'bureaucracy', 'democracy', 'representation', 'discipline', 'loyalty', 'traitors', 'sinister nuclei', 'block votes', 'cynical tactics', 'sabotage', 'disruption', 'scheming', 'camouflage' and 'wrecking the movement'. Observing this linguistic ritualism, two distinct versions of democracy and participation percolated through TCs: those of the General Council and that of the CP.

Social Historian Raphael Samuel had a reading of the CP as operating in a profoundly serious moral universe offering a complete social identity. Here, he deduced, was a principle of *collectivity*, an ideology of fair shares (not selfish interest and private gain), the struggle of the many versus the few, the people versus vested interests, the working class versus big business. CP members were usually self-taught and erudite, propounding Marxist texts as ambassadors of hope about controlling political/ economic forces and not being victims of circumstance. The struggle was internalised as ennobling, a unity of theory and practice.[25]

CP members imagined themselves as a proletarian clerisy, energetic in direct action, rational, disciplined, the dynamo of the left. It was about planning and foresight ('organise' was the CP buzzword), hence CP actions in hunger marches, realists who knew their union rule book, tested theory in practice as self-appointed mentors in TCs (with clarity on a par with correctness), training working-class leaders as conscious protagonists, the class memory bringing knowledge to identify *key* issues and central tasks with a long-term perspective. An elite of the working class, introducing the leadership principle into trade unionism, bearing a torch of enlightenment in working-class communities, the CP produced orators, authors and organisers. Historical materialism was their proletarian science challenging social democracy, the labour lieutenancy of the capitalist class. The CP brought a new lexicon of debate, with deviationists pathologised as bourgeois, opportunists and sectarians.[26]

The CP counterposed working-class militancy and direct action to a capitalism unable to solve the unemployment crisis; the system would compel labour to work for lower wages with less industrial and political rights and lead to future repression. In this analysis, it was delusory for the labour movement to support a liberal democratic state that would sap the militancy required for dynamic changes. Within TCs, the CP posited working-class power versus repressive aspects including unemployment and wage reductions. Labour and TUC leaders in turn positioned themselves with the binary 'democracy against disruption' approach.

From July 1935, the CP predicted that capitalism in crisis would lead to fascism in the UK. Hence, leading the mass movement on an anti-fascist platform was fundamental. The CP dovetailed relations between the capitalist economy and the political order, deducing that labour leaders would buttress fascism in some form. Central to this foreboding was the concept that the political order was a slave to the capitalist economy, the capitalist bourgeoisie dominant, controlling proceedings through all its institutions. The CP had a binary analysis of the state; the bourgeoisie's hold on the monopoly of political power had to be fought. TUC leaders were patently evolving a bargaining relationship with industrialists, integrated to extract minor concessions. The extent of CP influence in TCs can be gauged by resolutions concerning the economic crisis deepening everywhere, this interpretation being upheld by CP founder T.A. Jackson, who sought to overcome any vacuous terminology used.

Communists within TCs maintained radical class consciousness could be TCs' historical destiny, driven by the same forces as the state of consciousness claimed to be in operation in the Soviet Union. The pejorative labelling of Labour and union leaders (and of some leading TC officials, particularly between 1929 and 1933) as reformists, opportunists and petty bourgeois exclusionists was coupled with the notion that union leaders were corrupt *because* they were leaders. This perspective hindered a more nuanced understanding of the union movement and TCs. Assessing TCs as a site for unity between the political and the economic was advantageous, but would be some feat, given the entrenched Labourist origins of TCs.

The CP's holistic approach clashed with the partial vision of the TUC and Labour Party, the CP tailored to the notion that revolutionary political consciousness could only emerge from an understanding of socio-economic relationships. In reality, TCs were largely voluntary pressure groups, defensive and economistic under TUC blandishments. For the CP, in the course of the struggle, TCs had only developed a provisional, incomplete class consciousness, fragmented and Labourist, unless, hopefully, CP activists could capture major roles in the TC. The CP's class politics and economic critique clarified why workers needed to challenge TUC hegemony. Hence the CP's dialectical mediations between contradictions at the level of economic structure and socio-political forces, failures ascribed to the treachery of union leaders, the ruthless cunning of exploiting employers or government intervention and minimising varying regional economic conditions. Ultimately, could the genesis of strategies, which the CP proclaimed the Soviet Union (the 'Socialist Sixth of the World') was operating, prove to be transferable to unions in the UK, contained by employers and TCs' circumscribed objectives?

4. DIFFERENT VISIONS FOR TRADES COUNCILS

At the end of World War I, TC members envisaged a more egalitarian society. Surely, some form of social services would transform the structure of economic and social relations in favour of the majority of workers? Most TC delegates to the National Federation of Trades Councils (NFTC) and the ACTC retained their faith in the Labour Party. Occasionally a figure such as A.A. Purcell or Tom Quelch would advance theoretical/political analyses as to TCs' potential role, alongside imperialist/reformist problems to be overcome. However, generally there was resistance to abstraction or ruminations about TCs' potentially broader functions. Why? Because they were rooted in the traditional labour movement mentality and mainly reflected a Fabian commitment to evolutionary change.

Here, the TCs' structural context is essential. This is what the CP challenged: TCs' subsidiary role *vis-à-vis* TUC leaders and the Labour Party. That is why TUC/TC relations were characterised by endemic conflict, with TCs required to perform inflexible instrumental functions, appeals from above being based on considerations financial (shortage of funds) and ideological (opposing totalitarian regimes). Witness TCs being internally fragmented on support for/opposition to the NUWM or any forms of direct action.

Within each TC were radical and Labourist aspects of consciousness, both drivers of TCs' organisational loyalties and industrial strategies. TCs could mirror local differentiations: class consciousness did not automatically emerge from within traditional working-class areas. (Lower-middle-class white-collar workers in Brighton could be more radical in outlook than Labour Party stalwarts in TCs in heavy industrial areas in the North.) TUC hegemony inhibited alternative perspectives in their connection with the Labour Party; this power base was embedded and emerges from the TUC and the Labour Party as conveyers of messages to TCs to stifle militants (recalling the origins of TCs from the skilled unionism of the 1850s and 1860s). Hence that evolutionary path biased in favour of the distribution of power towards 'responsible' TUC leaders.

TCs were preponderantly masculine environments with a narrow frame of reference for union activities and emphases on established institutions. Most delegates lauded the administrator, the rules, procedures, regulations, constitutions and practical localised activity as part of the history of what was deemed 'popular democracy'. The CP offered alternative proposals, reassessing lost rights and TCs as *local working-class parliaments*. But most delegates comprehended union interests in an unproblematic manner and what they experienced of social injustices was projected onto their 'common-sense' judgements. Behind the rhetoric and rituals, TCs *were* minorities, not the whole working class but a conscious, politicised active segment, and *might* be envisaged as sites for the proto-politics of the masses. Delegates themselves mirrored the fragmentation in their experiences within a capitalist social stratification and were divided by parochialism.

*

In 1926, economic necessity, political practice and ideological struggle were momentarily fused in the General Strike, although soon the memory of those events became refracted through the traumas of the strike's failure, increasing unemployment, and Labour Party and TUC national allegiances. To TC delegates, theirs was the centrality not of theories but of local knowledge of economic consequences. Their rarely enacted resolutions at the ACTCs validated their empiricism, and much that passed for conflict within TCs was about which strategy was most appropriate to modify the effects of capitalist activities in the locality. Comfortable capitalism. What CP members hoped to develop in response was a radical populism, relevant to confront rising unemployment, oppose local fascists, expose the economic and social inequalities and thus galvanise the union movement.

The CP challenged the notion that the Labour Party and TUC represented the working class. TUC hegemony exhibited the processes by which conformity was sought and accepted, but it was a complex process to elucidate and transfer this to TC delegates. The TUC offered a *structure* for TCs (regardless of some TC delegates' alternative resistances) and solutions to apply in their specific locality. This incorporated oddly contradictory responses: support for the Soviet Union 1941–45 at the same time as opposition to CP members on the TC. So, there were particularist interests in TCs (local industrial and social issues) and general perspectives, such as class domination and subordination, which were sometimes signalled in a CP format but mostly adopted within the confines of Labourism.

Most delegates applauded free collective bargaining by the TUC because they wanted to be equal contestants *vis-à-vis* employers, and this was how the TUC allotted TCs' specific defensive roles in the economic struggle. TCs' activities became defending workers against the Bedaux system, redundancies, social inequalities and unemployment, and wages and conditions governing the sale of labour power.

5. TRADES COUNCILS IN THE TRADE UNION MOVEMENT

In the local community, TCs had to combat a local government structure that diverted workers from class identification. Adequate representation legitimated the status quo so that actions were channelled through existing institutions, and although TCs were incorporated as local representatives, micro-politics exposed the issues contained in the electoral representative arena and what was, as noted, defined as 'participatory democracy'.

TC delegates presented local issues in terms of inequalities and, despite the amorphous uniformity incorrectly attributed to them, showed distinct variations in their 'unifying' role in the battles within local councils for limited financial resources. This extended their possibilities from organising in the workplace to direct involvement in municipal politics, a development encouraged by union leaders. However, between 1920 and 1950, a gradual reorientation occurred between TCs and union leaders, as the TUC general secretaries elevated the administrative machinery of local unions, led the negotiating teams at the national level, and were chief spokespersons for the union movement via the media. Union leaders committed TCs to the process of negotiated agreements.

Leaders tended to become distanced from the rank and file and gradually identified more with management as bargaining expertise became a priority. Such leaders lacked explicit theories, had a professional eclecticism and a range of interpretations for economic solutions, but little theoretical exposition of political processes. The role of the TUC was to encourage any economic revival in a democratic context as TCs had to contend with socio-economic changes for workers in burgeoning trades, companies increasing salaries during TC recruitment drives, with loyalty bonuses to non-unionists. This weakened the hold of that vision of an alternative socialist society held by TC militants; TC letters to the TUC reveal the constraints placed upon TCs, having to come to terms with restricted, immediate, parochial grievances. In offering remedies to tackle the underlying *causes* of socio-economic issues, union leaders consolidated their own oligarchical control.[27] Most TC delegates condoned this. While union leaders enjoyed privileged positions, information and an instrumental approach to TCs regarding services, few objections were raised publicly about this.

The TUC's pluralist approach to industrial relations was managerial in its priorities. Union leaders determined TCs' purpose as loyalty to TUC policy, solvency, administrative efficiency and absence of dissent, which undermined TC endeavours on behalf of the NUWM, NMM, unofficial strikes or criticism of the 1945–50 Labour government's wage freeze. At ACTCs, union leaders sanctified procedures almost as ends in themselves, as organisational requirements, and ritualised these in rhetorical conference speeches to TC delegates.

Therefore, TCs reflected the General Council's priorities, apparent in organisation, financial solvency and a nebulous unity within which the main query was whether TC activities were industrial or political.[28] Direct connections with (or incorporations within) local Labour parties promoted compromises, sometimes blocking TC aspirations for local interventions and questioning TCs' autonomy. Local union leaders kept TCs separated by refusing to allow them to circularise to each other.[29] Union leaders managed them, estimated their local contribution, instructed, sanctioned, blamed, decorated, immortalised, silenced, deputised for, observed, examined and surveyed them.[30] Despite such strictures, the small and close-knit TCs (*gemeinschaften*) were rarely in conflict with the TUC, an enlarging bureaucratised, impersonal and anonymous union aggregation (*gesellschaften*). Union leaders had by 1950 co-opted TCs into the attainment of short-term economic gains and consolidation of their own managerial status. In the early 1920s, TCs in the labour movement had potentially offered a form of extra-parliamentary activism specific to the working class that might have combined economic and political struggles, but this soon reverted to more limited, factory-based organisation.[31]

One recurring theme in TC/TUC relations was the mystification surrounding the definition of 'union democracy'. With formalised structures and negotiating procedures, TC officials accepted the meticulous legalistic approach towards the rule book. Hence, the increased separation of leaders, with their access to government information plus control over communication to TCs through journals, conferences and circulars, and *deregistration* of dissenting TCs (which intensified divisions within TCs themselves). Full-time union work overcame the voluntaristic, amateur nature of most TC delegates, while union journals became mouthpieces for official policy with the occasional TC secretary or chairman being invited to contribute a piece on his/her TC.[32]

At ACTCs there were TC majorities to change the election procedure for the TCJCC, to have election addresses for ACTCs, and a two-day conference, but these majorities were ignored. Centralisation of media outlets and unions' consequent self-projection sidelined TCs and, despite vociferous opposition at ACTCs to TUC policy on occasions, the presence of the TUC general secretary or chairman ending the conference swung votes to the General Council, especially if they mentioned, in a frequent ploy, that negotiations were in a 'delicate state'! Anyway, the ACTCs were *advisory* and could not enforce its resolutions; they were only a gauge of TCs' opinions.

Fellow feeling or solidarity for TC requests for particular actions diminished with the emergence of permanent salaried officials chosen for perceived managerial acumen and negotiating capability. While TC delegates had little experience of politicians, businessmen or civil servants, there was little compunction for national union leaders to question the neutrality of the state. They operated within it and the information they gleaned from employers during negotiations enabled them to gain that authority and specialised knowledge (unavailable to rank-and-file TC members). Such union leaders were eventually co-opted as government consultants in the formation of economic policy and committees on economic planning (and wage restraint) from 1947. Articulation of any rank-and-file grievance was dependent upon their conjunctural position at the point at which conflicting pressures converged.

A TC's work was aligned to the experiences of its constituents. The TUC guided this through Trades Council Secretary Training Courses, which explained the structure of the movement, how to interpret agreements and how to use procedures for settling disputes, and imbued TC officials with an outlook embodying acceptance of the established system. When, after 1945, union leaders *collaborated* with the government in the wage freeze, this left a vacuum for workers' political views. The focus shifted from head office and TCs to the shop floor because union constitutions resulted in more provisions on members' obligations than on members' rights. Fiction became reality: 'It's an old trick, stealing the captains from the army of labour... how many of its leaders have been bought out?... it is cheaper to buy a general than to fight him and his whole army'.[33]

In the history of TCs, the essence of membership had been organisation not the particular skill. From the 1850s, TCs had been the basis for reform agitation, for working-class representation, but for 1920–50 this was gradually transferred to local Labour parties. Governmental committees, on which unions sat, rose in prominence as union leaders enjoyed their newly acquired privileges, zig-zagging from centralisation to decentralisation, giving TCs responsibilities, then removing them when local initiatives became challenging; accommodating TC unionists to a budgetary concept of their role in which instrumentalism was a source of attachment and the dominant vocabulary of collective bargaining gave priority to industrial over political concerns. This was prevalent in grievance procedure, arbitration and joint consultation whereby TC delegates had to acknowledge these TUC aims, which rendered TCs receptive to a hierarchical movement and a cult of union leaders, resulting in extensive biographies about their 'magnificent' careers!

Therefore, at a micro-level in TCs, there were ritualistic conflicts between the political divergence of delegates with a Marxist concept of a class exploitative state and those with a Fabian version of the neutral state. TCs were used as instruments for TUC policy *and* utilised as forums for the expression of radical sentiments, sounding boards about the direction of trade unionism. It remains a misreading of their history to assume that TCs retreated from questioning how local communities were run or limiting their analyses to local community issues. Repeatedly, new generations saw in TCs more potential for democratic participation. TC delegates maintained interests outside everyday union business and led different groups of workers to engage beyond bargaining about wages and conditions, especially in debates about collectivist and international issues.

However, responses of individual TCs to the increasing centralisation of the union movement was muted, their individual prestige and status dependent upon being acknowledged as local TUCs, not autonomous interpreters of union policies. Far from unifying TCs, constant TUC invigilation divided TC activists from constitutionalists (loyal pragmatic styles fostered quiescence). At the same time, the mediating TCJCC inhibited TCs' actions by nullifying oppositional resolutions. As a result, TCs tended to become observers of *fait accompli* decisions, as the General Council sought to define what issues were relevant and determined general knowledge through journals which dealt empirically with each issue and adjusted to economic crises in an *ad hoc* way. By 1950, most TCs represented pale shadows of an older world of dissent and were now integrated into guarding welfare state arrangements and extricating, for workers, implications of the labyrinthine contortions of local government recommendations.

6. INDIVIDUAL TRADES COUNCILS' FUNCTIONS

In 1925, a TC was, officially, a body formed by the voluntary association of union branches in a given locality to promote the interests of affiliated organisations and strengthen trade unionism in its area.[34] Declamatory aspirations for workers' control subsided in the 1940s, with joint consultative procedures and union leaders becoming 'establishmentarian reconcilers, dousers of conflict, disseminators of official pieties'.[35] By 1948, the definition of a TC had become a local organisation of union branches whose object was to co-ordinate union activities and provide information on trade union matters generally in the locality, functioning under the auspices of the TUC, which was responsible for recognition and registration.[36]

Officially, the objectives of a TC in 1925 were to promote the interests of all affiliated organisations to secure united action on all questions affecting those interests, to help promote educational, social and sports facilities for workers, to establish relations between its affiliated organisations and the TUC, to improve economic and social conditions and to promote the Industrial Workers' Charter and TUC schemes. These objectives were incorporated in the *Trades Councils' Guide* (1948), with the exception that TCs were now required *not* to promote the charter but to support and work for the policy of Congress. The voluntary nature of TCs implied that they had *consultative* powers but no official right to direct action to the unions they represented. TCs exercised an informal, *moral* authority but this was rarely invoked. TCs could compel no one and had to refer all measures to unions to be ratified.

The number of unionists represented by a delegate could vary from 25 to 150; a TC could have between 10 and 300 delegates present, with discrepancies between 20 per cent and 80 per cent attendance. Branches did not always decide upon their own delegates because this could be circumscribed by TUC restrictions as to political opinions, while the numbers of TCs in existence ranged from 580 in 1922 to 350 by 1950 (there were *c.* 150 in 2023.) . Apart from a few full-timers, secretaries, chairmen, presidents and treasurers went unpaid, the sole source of income from affiliation fees (from 2*d.* to 4*d.* per head per annum) supplemented by appeals and funds for strikes.

This highlights TCs' idiosyncratic, manipulable nature.

In this study we use a representative cross-section of large and small TCs: Sheffield (formed in 1858), London (1860), Birmingham (1866), Manchester & Salford (1866), Bristol (1873), Newcastle (1873), Oxford (1877), Brighton (1890) and Southampton (1890). Others specifically referred to include Liverpool (1848), Glasgow (1858), Leeds (1860–62), Edinburgh (1866), Leicester (1870), Bradford (1872), Huddersfield (1885), Ipswich (1885), Nottingham (1890), Swindon (1890), Blackpool (1893) and Hackney (1900). Their official histories and annual reports explain how TCs performed their innumerable tasks in their history, shaped by changes in the economic, political and industrial context. Meetings took on the character of a lively local debating society for some unionists, much to the vocalised annoyance of others. Delegates learned what members of other unions and the TUC had to say, and a TC often received more publicity for its actions than any local union branch, and, as noted, could be a training ground for future leaders, MPs, mayors and aldermen. Officials welcomed the recognition given to TCs by the General Council (in 1925), especially their role as Labour correspondents and circulating agencies for TUC publications.

TCs were also a battleground for conflicting views, between those who welcomed, for example, the Mond–Turner industrial negotiations and those who wanted no compromises with employers or their government, those downplaying any class struggle versus those convinced unions could be vehicles of radical action only if power were wrenched from the advocates of conciliation. For example,

Brighton TC once agreed that its function was to help protect workers from the worst excesses of the capitalist system since sectional unionism was unable to combat this encroachment. M. Carritt claimed for this TC that not one issue affecting workers had been neglected, their rights and interests had been stoutly championed, and in all matters the TC had spoken fearlessly for Labour.[37] In all TCs, national collective bargaining and increasing centralisation of authority reduced the scope for local initiative because TCs (linking workers in various unions and different industries) cut across the lines of authority in individual unions. Here are further examples of how different TCs operated.

A TC might be an arbiter, such as **Bristol TC**, where members strove to maintain themselves as the voice of the city's unionists on matters that were not the immediate responsibility either of individual unions or the local Labour Party, while maintaining close relations with both. The idea was a TC concerned with the *total* environment and with *expert speakers* addressing its meetings.[38] For **Southampton TC**, the main task was simply protecting workers' standard of living. **Sheffield T&LC** combined industrial with political functions but was hardly a unified organisation of all labour interests. From 1926 the industrial EC met less regularly and was less active than its political counterpart, the Labour Party. This T&LC's influence declined in industrial relations and, despite the CP's interventions, its main sphere became local government and administration as a recruiting agent for the Labour Party. The T&LC saw itself as the spokesperson of the working people of the whole city. It endeavoured to use its influence with the Labour group on the local council to sponsor policies, to provide a comprehensive service before tribunals, ministry offices, Labour MPs or direct approach to ministers themselves, but representations did not necessarily produce significant reforms.

A socio-economic class perspective in TCs is usually implicit. In **Oxford T&LC**'s case it could be explicit – that the division between those who lived by working and those who lived by owning was the one inevitable consequence of the capitalist system:

> we live in an age of material plenty, not of scarcity and famine; the right policy… is not to curtail production but to increase the consumption of the working class… by demanding… the raising of wages, better working conditions and shorter working hours.[39]

These were popular remedies that no trade unionists would deny but it tallied with the TC's secretary's belief that 'in trade unionism lies the only solid hope for the present and future'.[40] The question was: whose trade unionism? What security for trade union rights? **London TC**'s J. Jacobs asserted:

> Our history shows that the trade union movement must fight capitalism unceasingly if we would enjoy these things… the London Trades Council has realised that the fight for peace and against Imperialist oppression is an integral part of the struggle for better conditions and a secure future.[41]

This was stretching the net widely but such aspirations were voiced frequently in TCs. Tom Quelch viewed **London**

TC as the logical centre of London's industrial population in the working-class sense, the centre of its industrial organisation about which workers ought to gather to concentrate their strength and power as the determined subjective factor in industry. It was the centre that should give expression to their needs, aims and aspirations.[42] In practice, London TC was a political battleground and was disaffiliated in the early 1950s.

Nevertheless, TCs included the most engaged workers in local industries and services and Quelch highlighted this, arguing that all this power, if sensibly organised and intelligently led and used, would be irresistible in improving living conditions and social standards. He did not factor in capitalism's ability to offer quietus in the form of material benefits or its capacity to distract and/or demoralise workers. Despite this, once there was acceptance of working-class opinion on local committees, TCs offered a wider basis of representation than any individual group.[43]

The key attribute of TCs here is that daily 'pragmatic' union representation was considered the priority. **Edinburgh TC** leaders affirmed that it was *not* a debating society, an economic class or a school of sociological philosophy but a machine: 'We are not schoolmasters, we are mechanics.'[44] (But why not both?) This formulation was at the core of internal tussles that were contested in these years in all larger TCs.

Frequently the self-professed functions announced by individual TCs did not tally with TUC aims. Witness **Liverpool TC**, informed by the TUC in 1948 that it was under a misapprehension as to its functions and responsibilities![45] According to the TUC, its purpose was to serve branches on *local* matters and to publicise and administer policy decided by Congress, *not* to decide policy on national questions. There could not be two methods of deciding such national policy in one movement.

Much of TCs' 1926–50 history was seeking recognition of unions or helping workers retain what they had won. The 1920s and 1930s did not prove favourable for claims for higher wages, better conditions or shorter hours in those areas where the surplus pool of labour put employers in a strong negotiating position. As clarified in **Ipswich and District TC**, the idealised picture of being quick to deal with changes detrimental to the working class and ready to note any infringement of freedom or democracy, was 'difficult to enact'.[46]

One of the dilemmas for all TCs was that, once elected to a town council, councillors tended to lessen their interests in TC matters. Also, the initiative for action was narrowed to defence against anti-union legislation, some campaigns for the unemployed or union recruitment drives. Tuckett observed of **Swindon TC** that delegates supported campaigns begun by others, however 'On several occasions some simple topic was ruled out of discussion as being "political" as though the clock had turned back fifty or sixty years'.[47] W.J. Lane of **Luton TC** provided an image of typical TC members – 'Straight from the workshop, the office, the shop counter or from their driver's seat on the bus, come our delegates to attend committee meetings'[48] – to present the TC as a local TUC with its monthly meeting as its 'General Council', a useful influence in local affairs. Gone from this depiction is the reality that TCs struggled in a traumatising period of industrial relations at the local level, the onset of the world economic crisis, a ruthless economic attack on workers' living standards, and coping with the miseries of the long-term unemployed.

TC officials were often slow to acknowledge, as Percy Hall of **Blackpool TC** did,[49] that the trade union movement had been transformed from a self-protectionist body of protest against a capitalist society which treated people as 'hands', to a responsible part of the body politic. Within this context, TCs' work, unfortunately, was laborious, often unexciting and sometimes tedious, even if their mission might have been to serve the multifarious needs of its members by presenting a united front. The ideal underpinning TCs was promoting the creation of a society where individual liberties were combined with economic security and social equality. This was always tempered by the aims (here presented by **Hackney TC**): to advance workers' interests and to secure union hours, wages and general conditions for all workers with Labour and socialist representation on public bodies.[50] Ideally, a TC could be that forum for inter-union branch discussion and the council of united action, a microcosm of the trade union movement in struggle. If TCs were ably represented on all local committees, they could make an effective contribution in local affairs. Only then could they become well-informed and carry out their functions as local TUC representatives; however, few had plans beyond being co-ordinators of various union branches.

G. Hicks for the TUC's General Council designated TCs' meetings as *the* voice of the local workers, the

TC the body by and through which workers expressed themselves as wealth producers and as citizens within the community.[51] However, setbacks in numerical strength hampered many TCs. **Leicester TC** had 48,000 affiliated members in 1926 but 36,000 in 1938, a reflection of the depressed condition of British industry. Then, post-war, with a Labour government and minimal unemployment, this TC soon had 80,000 members, rejuvenated by years of relative industrial prosperity.[52]

The local prestige of the movement rested largely on the way TCs carried out their many public tasks; they provided a safety valve. As G. Fovargue (president of **Peterborough TC**) exclaimed, the TC was the mouthpiece of unionists, who would seldom consider an approach to their city or county councillor to air their grievances. Their isolation would gradually diminish as the link with civic authorities was enhanced with TC delegates becoming candidates for local government.[53]

Between 1920 and 1950, most TCs had increased their affiliated membership. **Huddersfield TC** had 4,000 members in 1903, 10,000 by 1935 and 14,000 in 1960, and all TC histories laud their loyal service to the community, for a fair share of the amenities for workers, and local representation in political counsels. Huddersfield TC put it thus: only through 'combined co-operative creative effort can they reach a higher stage of human happiness and well-being'.[54]

This assessment of TCs' functions shows the *melange* of the practical and the idealistic, and queries the unimaginative conclusions that, in 1926, power was thrust upon TCs but dissipated as soon as it was assumed. TCs may not have been close to seizing significant political power, but nor was there a more deactivated working-class movement after 1926, only *different forms and strategies* in campaigns. TCs were not all content to be reduced to very limited decision-making. The largest TCs did not lose their independence and initiative, although by 1950 not a single TC operated outside the TUC, and in accepting recognition/registration they had to adhere to the *Model Rules*, theoretically forbidden to associate with or subscribe to the funds of any TUC-proscribed body, funds still not to be used for 'political purposes'. However, there was *always* room for manoeuvre in the labour movement, as we will explore in the next chapter.

CHAPTER 2

Sketching Trades Councils' Histories to the General Strike

'Do you remember 1926? The great dream and the swift disaster
The fanatic and the traitor, and more than all,
The bravery of the simple, faithful folk?'
'Ay, ay, we remember 1926', said Dai and Shinkin,
As they stood on the kerb in Charing Cross Road,
'And we shall remember 1926 until our blood is dry.'
Idris Davies, Collected Poems 1976 edition

1. TRADES COUNCILS BEFORE 1926: CHANGES IN ORGANISATION

The contribution of the TCs in the General Strike of 1926 was stunning and appreciating it requires socio-historical contextualisation. The TUC, in reforming itself in 1895, had demoted TCs, which had originally promoted a Congress. TCs included younger socialists from a range of organisations that the Parliamentary Committee sought to marginalise.[55] The less skilled were becoming represented on TCs so the 1895 decision helped union officials exclude 'agitators' and 'irresponsible busybodies' and centralise through national union executives.[56] Union leaders soon appeared on royal commissions, became justices of the peace, MPs, part of the state machinery, as TCs had created local conciliation machinery (and offered a basis for an alternative system of labour organisation), but had no financial sanctions and could not bind union members nor perform a central role in wage negotiations. What they did do was warn of encroachment on labour rights, arrange demonstrations, lobby councils and provide information on working conditions to employers and councillors.

In the 1910s, TC officials emerged as union general secretaries, aldermen and mayors, espousing state ownership, collectivist welfare services and state aid rather than philanthropy. They campaigned for female suffrage and self-determination in Ireland and India, and encouraged right to work schemes, but were wary of new labour exchanges (the cheap labour issue). TCs accepted the national insurance system, compiled local surveys, organised tenants' defence leagues and were an integral part of the administration of welfare services. Suspicious of the Unemployed Workmen's Act, they criticised compulsory unemployment insurance as attacking unionism.

Through welfare legislation, TCs were represented on administrative, social and educational committees, some at the Industrial Syndicalist Education League (ISEL) 1910, which, hostile to union officialdom, lauded militant unionism as the answer for TCs, which, for syndicalists, could be alternative municipal councils, *the* centres of union agitation for rousing class struggle. Syndicalists, including Tom Mann and Jack Tanner, who sought workers' management and control over the means of production, promoted a National Federation of Trades Councils (NFTC) to transcend union officials and borough councils, TCs envisaged as the embryonic organisation of a new system of workers self-organisation.[57] Excluded from TUC conferences, TCs had ceased any direct function in policy-making, significant on the political side only as T&LCs through which the Labour Party operated. Syndicalists were positing TCs as *centres of radicalisation* beyond unions' strict functions, challenging notions of what TCs could offer in response to technological changes in industry, shop floor organisation and industrial relations' conciliation and arbitration.

Then, in World War I, trade union internationalism was marginalised and TCs were utilised to harness workers to immediate war demands. They undertook practical tasks regarding food supplies, conscription (most opposed compulsory military service), and conscientious objectors' claims. Guild socialists hailed TCs as local democratic assemblies since they were adjudged to be the most imbued with 'the class spirit', and the shop stewards' movement added industrial unionism to the mix. TCs defended union conditions, protected civil liberties, rejected Whitleyism,* and lauded the 1917 Russian Revolution, with its local soviets and factory councils as a model of the proletarian state. TCs might be similar in form.

The June 1917 Leeds Convention had 207 delegates from T&LCs, and 49 T&LCs affiliated to the Union of Democratic Control, for pacifism, an end to secret

---

* Industrial negotiations involving joint consultation.

diplomacy, for a negotiated peace, and a League of Nations.[58] Were TCs any potential basis for local soviets when the Labour Party dominated them? During the industrial militancy 1910–20, TCs played a marginal role compared to the shop stewards' movement, which only collaborated with TCs on food shortages. J.T. Murphy commented in 1920 that TCs were not 'the nuclei of soviets' but two years on T. Quelch described TCs as:

> infant soviets like the workers' councils in Russia… the local central bodies of the working class movement… best fitted to bring complete local working class solidarity into being.[59]

The Labour Party constitution of 1918 had removed TC representation from the National Executive Committee (NEC) when 146 TCs were associated with the Labour Party.[60] By 1921, there were 563 TCs in which 3 million union members were represented, but separation between political and industrial spheres perplexed and divided TCs, unionists often confused as to their legitimate activities.[61] If effective co-ordination of union affairs was to be secured, wouldn't TCs' democratic machinery need to be connected to both the TUC and the rank and file? This would happen, but not in the way militants would have preferred.

The seventh of May 1924 was a key moment. The TUC held a conference of the General Council and 24 TC delegates, to bring TCs into 'closer relations with Congress'. Those TCs invited were described as industrial units (as distinct from political bodies), Bramley, for the General Council, observing that TCs' detachment from the national centre had given rise to misunderstanding and a division of effort, local policies having conflicted with Congress decisions. He insisted that the NFTCs of 1922 and 1923 had threatened to elevate TCs into challenging Congress's authority, so much so that TCs might become, as H. Tracey warned, 'centres of disaffection'.[62] The General Council created a Trades Councils Joint Consultative Committee (TCJCC) as an advisory body. TCs were to be circulating agencies, labour correspondents for the TUC (given statements on General Council activities, reports and circulars), the NFTCs to be under General Council aegis. This was the origin of the stumbling blocks in relations between TCs and the General Council henceforth, a precursor to many of the ritualistic debates, with hopes for TC representation at Congress nullified.

In the fallout, TCs had to acknowledge that it was not *industrial* matters but *political* ones that, in the early 1920s, attracted more engaging debates. TCs behaving as mere corresponding bodies was insufficient, regardless of Bramley's assertion that TCs were getting 'a larger sphere of action' through the TCJCC, the centrally controlled alternative to the NFTCs. On this reorganisation, A. Conley (TCJCC chairman) later, in 1929, proclaimed that TCs 'developing their usefulness as organs of unionism' had dictated the TUC decision for TCs to spread union principles and co-ordinate local propaganda and serve locally the same purpose as the General Council nationally.[63] Such 'unity' was designed to exclude or isolate *alternative* voices, the TCJCC a designated fetter upon individual TCs, the latter at least representing the local working class as a whole and not trade sections of it.

Such an outcome emerged at the first TCJCC in July 1924. TCs had been already involved in unemployment campaigns, councils of action and strikes, but what the General Council deduced was that TCs had no right to overburden Congress by *unrestricted* representation. Congress was twice as large as in 1895. The resolution for TC representation at the TUC was lost by 3,499,000 to 221,000 votes.[64] TCs would be labour correspondents, *not* co-ordinators of militant local action. Minority opinions would have no influence on the TCJCC (the six TC delegates were from London, Bristol, Manchester, Leeds and two other TCs), the chairman and secretary being General Council members, the latter ruling proceedings, in practice making some decisions without consulting TC delegates.

On 8 December 1924, the General Council members launched a Conference of TCs and 19 Industrial Conferences.[65] The TCJCC invited TCs to send a delegate to the first ACTC on 27 February 1925, as they obviated future NFTCs. One hundred and thirty TCs were represented, A.B. Swales (chairman) remarking on the debt owed to TCs and their glorious future 'if given the right direction'. According to Swales, TCs' influence was now 'tenfold or twentyfold' that of the 1860/70s, although they had given 'too much attention to political action' and had neglected the industrial side, so the 'right balance' had to be introduced. TCs could do yeoman service in recruitment and for the unemployed; no other bodies were so well placed to ensure working-class solidarity; hence the need 'to clarify our conception as to what a TC should be and its rightful place in the movement'.[66]

The next 25 years of these chairman addresses offered a

lot of 'hot air' and fervent hopes, but few tangible advances. Precedents circumscribed future ACTCs and debates were tightly confined to the agenda, TCs with no say in policy-making (a motion for 'unity with Russian unions' side-stepped). The NFTC, where TCs had met in 1922 and 1923, was buried, although not *all* TC activity independent of the official union movement came to an end[67] (as will soon become apparent). Some argued that TCs should remain 'the parliament of local labour'; otherwise, as Pennifold (Brighton TC) exclaimed, TCs, excluded from moulding policy, were 'in the position of lackeys'.[68] TCs were told to send the General Council lists on the rise/fall in local trade prosperity. Agenda limitations stultified alternative resolutions and broader debates, but, although the TCJCC specifically sought to keep TCs within prescribed limits, activities were not to be so circumscribed in practice. But in May 1925 the TCJCC affirmed TCs could not intervene in disputes without the authority of the union concerned, the *Memorandum on the Constitution and Rules for Trades Councils* reiterating this.[69]

W. Citrine, now TUC assistant-general secretary, proposed that shop stewards and workshop committees should be linked through TCs but acknowledged *that* required a 'revolution in thinking' because union executives were protective of their autonomy, and E. Bevin was particularly wary of TCs' encroachment.[70] Indeed, The *Draft Model Rules for Trades Councils* in November 1925 questioned whether a TC was a purely industrial body or operated as a T&LC in both industrial and political spheres. By February 1926, Tom Mann had analysed four years of industrial depression, wage reductions and sectionalism but noted the new lease of life for TCs: 'the best agencies to grapple with these problems',[71] because they had the capacity for organising all labour groups and could include guilds, shop stewards, unemployed committees and Labour parties in harmony with the General Council. At the ACTC March 1926, A. Pugh (chairman) perspicaciously surmised that circumstances might soon arise to test TCs, so internal weaknesses in organisation in the movement had to be eradicated. He was likewise prophetic: *'The walls of vested interest, class domination and social injustices will not fall to the sound of resolutions'.*[72] TCs would soon learn what central control implied. Resolution-making became the hallmark of TCs. The TUC always concluded that, as *funds* were limited, so were campaigns.

2. RADICALS VS. RULERS: DARING TO DREAM 1920-26

It is difficult for the bourgeoisie to understand the ideas that move the Russian masses. It is all very easy to say they [the Russian masses] have no sense of patriotism, duty, honour, discipline or appreciate the privileges of democracy. But... there is patriotism, an allegiance to the international brotherhood; there is duty... to the revolutionary cause; there is honour based on the dignity of human life; there is discipline, revolutionary discipline, and the Russian masses are inventing a whole new form of civilisation.

~ John Reed, quoted in R. Rosenstone, Romantic Revolutionary, 1975, pp279-80

The years 1920-26 were arguably the most effective in the history of the British Communist Party. Since its inception in 1920, the CP had an ambition – to democratise the TUC as a Parliament of Labour, including TC representatives, and it envisaged TCs as potential General Staffs of Labour in their localities. The CP promoted the Red International of Labour Unions (RILU) Congress of July 1921,[73] which 10 TCs had supported, but Labour's NEC judged the CP ineligible for local and national affiliation. London TC and Glasgow T&LC requests for a Labour Party/CP debate on this did not bear fruit.

The CP's approach to TCs was elucidated in 1922 by their own Tom Quelch, who perceived TCs developing working-class political activity in municipal affairs, and, because they were a fixed part of the labour movement, their position was assured, with the means to achieve workers' solidarity.[74] Yet, while TCs supported candidates for municipal bodies and Parliament, agitated for social amenities, rallied unions in disputes and sought reforms in the union movement, they lacked a long-term strategy. For J.T. Murphy, this could be overcome as they were the 'cream of the local working class', able to gather 3,000 as a local workers' general staff to be roused for a national strike.[75]

This refreshing notion meant that TCs' constitutions could include *all* working-class organisations. A TC (with limited industrial functions) was envisioned as a workers' council, superseding municipal town and borough councils, with more control than local authorities, an administration of workshops, factories, food distribution and house-letting. This was a vision of *comprehensive TCs*, political, industrial and co-operative bodies with an information bureau on landlords, capitalists, shopkeepers and 'blacklegs' (strike-breakers). These visionary functions, inspired by the Russian Revolution, included training workers in the management of local affairs:

> Under its [TC] auspices a new social milieu should be created by the workers for the workers themselves, thus through propaganda, education, social and cultural work, the Trades Council could offer a new outlook on life, a new class spirit, notably implanting feelings of self-sacrifice *like the workers in Russian Soviets*.[76]

The CP Congress in 1922 proposed that local unemployed committees affiliate to TCs to help the latter in 'co-ordinating the workers' struggles'.[77] Further TC support accrued for CP affiliation to the Labour Party as the British Bureau of the RILU launched 'Back to the Unions' conferences in major TC areas (London, Glasgow, Newcastle, Birmingham, Sheffield and Cardiff). The NFTC conference was convened by Birmingham TC's W. Brain (the TC's vice-president and an RILU adherent). Sixty-seven TCs were represented, the CP declaring that TCs were an invaluable means for propaganda, advancing the practice of 'fractions' (to prepare strategy before TC meetings), CP activities on TCs forwarded to the CP's Central Industrial Committee.[78] Major influence via a TC would make it possible to send CP speakers to affiliated bodies, the CP to be the first party to carry its policies into unions, at branch, district and executive levels, to prove 'a party of a new type' amalgamating political and industrial activities. This strategy was incorporated in *Communist Industrial Policy: New Tasks for New Times*: 'We must have Communist guidance… in the trades councils and must organise the election of Communists as officials or union representatives to positions on the local trades councils.'[79]

The NFTC 1923 conference included 71 TC delegates, with Harry Pollitt from the CP and R. Page Arnot from the Labour Research Department (LRD) prominent. However, the TUC General Council refused to engage with the NFTC or its resolutions, although the CP's industrial policy was popular and relevant, more so, in reality, than the TUC's cautious policies.[80] The July 1923 *CP Handbook on Organisations* contained a register for TCs' fractions (for elections and municipal committees), while the NFTC assessed TCs to be in a healthier position to counteract sectionalism and voice workers' demands – more than harassed officials at head office, blinkered by the needs of a specific union! For the CP, the General Council might be the head but TCs could supply the body and the life-blood.[81] With those militaristic metaphors ('rank and file', 'the working-class army', 'the battle'), the CP criticised the lack of interest in TCs from union district committees and resolved to engage within TCs to administer radical campaigns.[82]

The CP's R.P. Dutt observed that the Labour press had ignored the NFTC, which was the *only* national meeting of the rank and file. He contrasted the 'bourgeois influence' in the General Council, with the NFTC conference, an expression of the workers, an integral part of the movement not controllable by 'the TUC machine'.[83] The CP critiqued the Labour Party and TUC conferences, with their agendas bristling with constitutions, rules, amendments, affiliation fees and union structure debates, wasting time on niggling controversies, 'the throttling machinery we are out to break'.[84] Resolutions repeated annually and obsessions with union hierarchy and structure had to end. TCs held the vantage ground unique in the movement: 'many of the best, the keenest and the most practical of the active workers, the hopes of the movement... are centred on them.'[85] Such were the aspirations of the CP. The battleground in the labour movement was prepared for the next 30 years.

*

In the early 1920s, the Minority Movement (MM) drew attention to TCs' importance and possible transformation. Over 50 TCs (including Manchester, London, Sheffield, Birmingham, Leeds and Coventry) sent delegates to the MM Conferences (1924–26) as the CP's *Manual of Party Training* aided 'proletarian mass struggle', CP fractions detached from trivial squabbles, presenting approved tactics on hunger marches, exposing 'petty graft and wire-pulling' by local business interests, demonstrating the class character of the state (regarding housing, education and labour relations),[86] and studying disillusionment with the short-lived 1924 Labour government, which had inadvertently prompted direct industrial action.[87] Now the CP had an input in most unions through Minority Movements, with many TCs affiliating. By August 1924, in conjunction with the NMM, TCs and the unemployed had become centres for CP focus and influence. Methods employed in lockouts and strikes were on the agenda at the TCJCC industrial conferences in December 1924. Here the NMM claimed that, if employers saw the General Council as the head of the union movement, 'control from below' meant TCs being representative of the working-class movement.[88]

TUC proscriptions had complex repercussions. While united front tactics for union work was a dialectical necessity to the CP, the TUC labelled it 'manipulative wrecking', denouncing any explicit ideology in unions, or what was termed outside interference/dual loyalty.[89] And, yet, MMs proved most effective in industrial centres where TCs were significant (London, South Wales, Clydeside, Durham and Sheffield). In the NMM's *What the Minority Movement Stands For*, TC reorganisation was heralded as a principal task. TCs were 'the leading local organs of the class struggle' for strikes, lockouts, elections or unemployed agitations, creating 'the machinery of local mobilisation', hence dubbed campaign mobilisers.[90] It was to monitor any of this activity that the TUC had established the TCJCC, the ACTC and the *Model Rules*, certainly not to applaud the CP's *Sunday Worker* (which had, among the shareholders, 24 TCs represented).

Encouraged by Red Friday in July 1925, the CP helped to create local councils of action as holistic formations to co-ordinate working-class resistance (e.g. in Edinburgh, Doncaster, Glasgow, Sheffield, Liverpool and North-West London). Middlesbrough T&LC's Mr Hogg rebutted such notions; for him, the only useful function for the TC was to support strike action;[91] and, at Scarborough TUC, the General Council (including J.H. Thomas, M. Bondfield, E. Bevin and A. Pugh) scotched another CP request for affiliation to the Labour Party.[92] With 12 CP leaders arrested on charges of seditious libel under the Emergency Powers Act, protests about this ensued from many TCs; however,

CP members were banned from local Labour parties; some TCs disaffiliated from the NMM, while others stated that the CP was exploiting the unemployed 'for political reasons'![93]

The CP Programme 1926 included specific roles for TCs and workers' defence corps and urged party members to redouble their activities in TCs and establish councils of action. Under TC leadership, blacklegging had to be prevented and TCs had to confront defeatist union and Labour leaders and the state's strike-breaking tactics.[94] By February, just six years after their founding, the CP had 62 fractions in London TCs (1,560 CP members) and eight fractions in Manchester (680 CP members); Birmingham's 326 CP members had several TC fractions operating 'fairly well'; Liverpool's 576 CP members had six TC fractions and 19 CP members occupying official positions; Glasgow's 1,105 CP members had a huge CP fraction of 54; Bradford's 250 CP members had 'well-organised fraction work' and Sheffield's 1,200 CP members had one of the largest fractions on the local T&LC.[95]

The MM 'Conference of Action' in March 1926 included 52 TCs' delegates, all TCs receiving the MM's *Model Constitution for Militant Trades Councils* for training workers to reorganise the industrial and social fabric of the locality 'on a Socialist basis', with unemployed workers, factory organisations, women's committees, the Co-operative Movement, education through the National Council of Labour Colleges (NCLC) and a local workers' press.[96]… Then it happened.

3. TRADES COUNCILS IN 1926: A SURVEY

The strike of 1926 has been the only nation-wide general strike in British history (so far). To summarise: in July 1925, Prime Minister Baldwin declared that all workers had to accept wage reductions. The TUC began a national embargo on coal movements, the government instigated an inquiry and, with strikes suspended, a given subsidy was planned to end on 1 May 1926. The Samuel Commission report in March confirmed that mine owners planned to increase hours and lower wages. But 'not a minute on the day, not a penny off the pay', famously responded the Miners' Federation of Great Britain's (MFGB) Herbert Smith. On 1 May 1926, a TUC conference reluctantly announced a general strike in defence of miners' wages and hours. From 3 May, there were sympathetic strikes in major industries. General Council leaders' negotiations ensued with the government and mine owners, Labour Party leader MacDonald opposing the strike. *The Daily Mail* denounced the strike's 'tyranny' and 'unpatriotic' union leaders. Baldwin spoke of a threat to constitutional rights, and used the *British Gazette* and the BBC as propaganda weapons, plus volunteer strike-breakers. The TUC Negotiating Committee met Herbert Samuel with proposals to end the strike. It ended after nine days. The miners themselves remained on strike for several months, supported by various TCs across the country. For many TCs, these were heady days but the failure of the strike was humiliating. One devastating consequence was the notorious TD&TU Act 1927, which made sympathetic strikes illegal and limited picketing.

Retrospectively assessing 20+ TCs' activities and

pronouncements during the General Strike presents an astonishing variety of trajectories, a mixed tapestry, providing lessons for local activists today involved in major strike activity. **Brighton TC** had a *Unity News* and formed a council of action, much to the chagrin of local employers. As in most TCs, it was not prepared for the strike, although unionism had never been stronger. Eight thousand were affiliated to the TC and the stoppage was the most complete of any town in the south of England. E. Trory concluded that *all* that was needed was a mass revolutionary party to raise the slogan 'All Power to the Councils of Action'! However, the career structure of the Labour/union leadership was a hindrance and the CP too small and inexperienced to provide the leadership necessary to fully transform what was fundamentally an economic campaign into a political confrontation.[97] The Brighton TC 5 May meeting (a record 65 delegates) debated organisational problems. They discussed their main opposition, the local Conservative Party, joining the Organisation for the Maintenance of Supplies (OMS) as volunteers whose rationale was 'to ensure that the old Country… is not ruled from Moscow or by a lot of Red-Heads.'[98] The local CP produced *Punch* and the Council of Action *Stand Firm* to offset the *Brighton Herald* and *Brighton Standard* championing the government. The local Free Church supported the strikers, although a TC majority opposed a workers' defence corps as being 'too close to a Red Army'! The mayor warned that the strike was a step towards revolution. Afterwards, workers had to sign a pledge not to engage in union activity that would 'interfere with duties to the Corporation or employers, not to break any agreements of service nor compel workers to join a union'. Yet, 50 miners' children were found homes among union members and £1,500 collected for the Miners' Relief Fund.

For **Southwark TC**, the Council of Action became the nearest experience to local control and autonomy in its whole history, the Labour-controlled council and the TC contributing £7,000 to a mining village. For the renowned unionist Jack Dash, it was a revolutionary situation and a good political education.[99] **Hackney TC**'s response was part of its militant history, including connections to the local National Unemployed Workers Committee Movement (NUWCM) branch. It had a council of action in operation from March 1926 and, because it was CP-inspired, was disaffiliated from the Labour Party by September.[100]

Although **Lewisham TC** was left-wing and supported the MM, it had no arrangements with the NUWCM or Co-operative Party and, as in Brighton, its Conservative council operated with the government, which Deptford's Labour-controlled council did not. In 1927, Lewisham TC was disaffiliated from **London TC** for refusing to ban CP members, while **Deptford TC** became a focus for left-wing activity.[101] The London TC, an umbrella organisation incorporating many local trades councils, represented no miners, but had its own traditions of international working-class unity (welcoming Garibaldi, the First International, and the Soviet government). By 1924, it had 136,629 affiliated members and disapproved of union leaders' industrial truce during the first Labour government. The London TC's weakness was as a mobilising centre since it advised TCs to act on their own initiative. Post-General Strike it became the archetypal battleground between the TUC and CP.[102]

Birmingham TC retained vestiges of 'no politics for

unions', had a substantial section of Conservative trade unionists, although it hosted the NFTC conferences in 1922 and 1923, and had the local newspaper *Town Crier* as an outlet. It had a council of action with 'a new spirit of determination... an exhibition of greater unity among all ranks... the workers await "a lead".'[103] The specific industrial and political framework of the city resulted in intricacies, with industries difficult to unionise, paternalistic employers and a multiplicity of trades. TC officials advised strikers to make 'moderate' speeches (since CP leaders had been arrested for reporting dissension in the armed forces in the strike bulletin *The Birmingham Worker*). All of Birmingham's Trade Union Emergency Committee were arrested on 10 May for publishing a *Government Defeated in Parliament* report. Damage to morale, membership and finances ensued despite TC officials witnessing 'manifestations of loyalty to great principles... recognition of the holy bond of universal brotherhood'.[104] Affiliation fees diminished from £470 in April 1926 to £120 in 1929, the aftermath resurrecting conflicts between right and left in the TC. Eleven years on, the TC's campaign reported fears and humiliations from 1926, prevalent in a city notorious for sweated industries, and, although TC delegates in the strike had exercised decisions and control normally performed by employers or police and experienced solidarity, comradeship and revelations about how the state functioned in a crisis, few envisaged significant changes afterwards.

TCs' responses to the strike were shaped by relations with the local council and Labour Party. **Bristol TC's** president had also been the Labour Representation Committee (LRC) president. After 1918, the local Labour Party became the central body, the TC losing most of its political functions. By 1926, Bristol TC was ill-equipped and suffered shock, anger and dismay at the strike's failure.[105]

The only area that had none of the initial complications of other TCs was **South Wales**, where refusal to join the strike would have led to social ostracism. OMS emergency powers regulations were rarely employed, communities (such as Mardy) run by strikers, 'blacklegging' practically unknown. Control was exercised by the TCs here more directly than anywhere else in Britain. With defeat, after seven months' traumatic lockout, local TCs were fragmented for a decade, decimating economic assets and political confidence.[106]

For **Swindon TC**, the General Strike unified the local community, although the TC had no leverage to prevent Great Western Railway using volunteers. The aftermath saw many young people leave the area and the economy contracted as road transport replaced much rail, the TC never acquiring the same status again.[107] In **Manchester & Salford**, the local TC's rules in 1923 required 'courage, patience and self-sacrifice in the work of elevating the workers socially and intellectually'.[108] W.J. Munro, the TC's secretary, resigned from the CP in 1926 because of its critique of TUC leaders.

Liverpool TC after the strike lost membership and industrial influence. In 1948, W. Hamling averred that this TC's work was pedestrian compared with the 1926 experience, when the TC secretary, W.H. Barton, recalled a 'magnificent response'[109] despite imprecise instructions and minimal General Council contact. Merseyside had traditions of strikes in 1911, 1919 and 1921, with the

TC supporting the police strike of 1919 and favouring a general strike for miners in 1923. Liverpool was one of the few cities in which adequate preparation had been made, a culmination of local militancy and, as in Manchester, it had its council of action in 1925. The dockers were the backbone of this. Bob Edwards (ILP) assessed the TC as 'a marvellous institution... a massive forum. We used to debate every subject under the sun'.[110] Debating was its forte, and, although the TC majority perceived the strike as a purely economic, industrial struggle, the *Liverpool Daily Post* and *Liverpool Echo* were used to demoralise the strikers and, as in Lewisham, the NUWM was not allowed to affiliate to the Council of Action.

Blackpool TC found it difficult to transform a debating, advisory TC into an executive in perpetual session and, as a democratic organisation, eschewed the adoption of 'semi-military tactics' (meaning strikes).[111] **St. Helens T&LC** had the CP and other socialists prompting the formation of a council of action and a workers' defence corps, the local CP doubling from 30 to 60, while **Bolton TC** (like Blackpool) pleaded that no 'disorderly or subversive elements' must interfere, the maintenance of order and confidence in TUC representatives being the rule.[112]

Analysing these responses, we see that they varied according to the type of local industry, TCs' political composition, and any strike traditions. T&LCs also had specific tasks. **Sheffield T&LC** had been active since 1920 for industrial unionism to offset competing engineering, light metal, transport and building trades. In 1923, this T&LC's executive presaged T&LCs as the central bodies for resistance in disputes because wages and conditions had changed from local to national settlements, so should be linked to the General Council to confront employers' associations. By 1925, the T&LC *was* the local Labour Party and had a full-time secretary (like Manchester and London). As with most TCs, no preparations had been made for the strike. A central dispute committee was composed of industrial T&LC members, the T&LC secretary afterwards regretting the 'most magnificent display of working-class solidarity in support of a principle was... marred by the eagerness with which the strike was ended.'[113] Yet he deduced that it was unwise to 'assume functions not possessed by the T&LC'.

The year 1920 had seen the worst slump in Bradford textiles and in 1925 a complete stoppage in all textile mills led to unemployment rising to 15%. Thus inflamed, textile workers were solidly behind the strike. Like Liverpool and Manchester, **Bradford TC** had a council of action, with the *Bradford Worker* acting as the strike bulletin. Echoing Liverpool's dockers and the miners, Bradford's railwaymen, builders and printers remained out of work for some time, the TC demanding a general amnesty for those arrested and imprisoned, although the 'normality of relative apathy' returned to the TC within six months, and, as in Liverpool, Sheffield and Bristol, activities were preponderately channelled via the Labour Party.[114]

Dowding of **Castleford TC** recalled the strike in terms of 'the trouble with the Communists', whereas **Leeds TC** condemned the government for encouraging anti-working-class organisations (such as the OMS) for interference in legitimate union rights in industrial disputes.[115] **Newcastle TC** spent much of these nine days coping with strike-breaking and controlling food supplies, had prepared for a long strike, and organised a conference of 28 local councils of action and 52 strike committees. The *Workers' Chronicle* summed up the aftermath: 'Never in the history of the working class struggle – with the exception of the treachery of our leaders in 1914 – has there been such a calculated betrayal of working class interests.'[116] Within months, the TC's secretary was requesting direct TC affiliation to the 'betrayers' in the TUC (H.V. Tewson rejected the request as 'duplication'!). For the secretary, J. Yarwood, the TC became 'a very limp body', its meetings poorly attended, its business and policy generally inconclusive and purposeless.[117]

In **Middlesbrough TC** delegates opposed giving the strike 'overt political overtones' so soon after the (hoax) Zinoviev Letter had helped sink the Labour government in 1924. While 'terrific tension' exuded from the TC committee room, 'like a military HQ on the offensive', a few activists undertook the main tasks while the remainder 'waited'.[118] As in the case of Birmingham's CP member John Trotter, Middlesbrough CP secretary, Jack Bell, was imprisoned for 'sedition'. CP activities were monitored closely by local councils for anything inflammatory and they were the easiest targets under the Emergency Powers Act, it being less problematic arresting CP members rather than other strike leaders. In Middlesbrough, the local TC's centralised strike direction faltered because some delegates would not countenance CP interference with unions' domestic business.[119]

The only equivalent to South Wales was **North Lanarkshire**, which directly experienced the depression in the coal industry and increasing unemployment in ironworks. As in South Wales, the NUWCM and MM mobilised workers to confront sectional disputes, and, like Liverpool's dockers, the local Mineworkers' Union had that history of industrial struggle from 1894, 1912 and 1921. The MM promoted councils of action and warned about the OMS. Lanarkshire's Joint Committee of the Council of Action was formed before the strike created a workers' defence corps, eight of its 41 delegates being CP members.[120]

For P. Kerrigan in the great **Glasgow TC**,[121] the strike brought memories of Red Clyde, the Hands-Off Russia (HoR) campaign and shop stewards' class-conscious traditions, and the TC affiliated to the NMM in 1925. Then, on the eve of the strike, the TC debarred CP members. The future for most unionists was thus to be in the Labour Party. **Leicester TC**'s president underlined the ambivalence of all TCs:

> Those Glorious Nine Days revealed our strength; they revealed our weaknesses. I cannot attach myself to the 'Never again' school of thought. Circumstances must determine, although... strenuous and united efforts on the political field will, compared with the strike weapon, be more likely to secure and maintain the standards we aim at.[122]

Was this Labourism TCs' epitaph for 1926? Would adopting or intruding into the political field mean departing from the industrial? Couldn't economic and political industrial campaigns come together?

4. ASSESSMENTS OF TRADES COUNCILS IN THE GENERAL STRIKE

The strike in support of the miners was defeated by the combined efforts of the government, the BBC, the law, police, army, employers, union leaders, local councils, OMS, volunteers and students, leaving the miners to continue alone. The strike had suffered from wavering leadership. That TC delegates were confused as to their tactics and aims is apparent from the above regional survey. Far from believing at the time that they had 'the wrong leaders', TCs found themselves making vital decisions. They coped with distortions from government and the media including the 'threat to the constitution' intimidations. Councils of action were not envisaged by most participants to be embryonic alternatives to 'ruling class hegemony'.[123] As has been exhibited, TCs witnessed every aspect of central government in operation. They rarely envisaged any revolutionary situation, and the strike's supposed 'unity' hid marked divisions within nearly all TCs, intensifying the mythologies between conflict or consensual models of politics and society. In TCs, radicals proclaimed spontaneous social combustion as elitists searched for leaders, while many unionists thought the strike's failure was inevitable. Most TC delegates emerged as essentially Labourist, convinced industrial action to influence political decisions should only be made *within* the given constitutional framework.[124] Ironically, just when they were relegated by the Labour Party and TUC to a limited industrial role, some TCs became the local cog aiming to transform economic demands into the broader political struggle, although few delegates conceived their task as building a new leadership from below, and dutifully administered TUC policy.

Most TCs accepted the curbed parameters laid down by the TUC in 1924 even though the TUC's W. Citrine criticised TCs as 'not sufficiently disciplined' to obey the instructions from HQ.[125] How they were supposed to obey what were confused instructions he does not elucidate but the lesson was to cement the new reality that the General Council determined policy and retained exclusive authority.[126] TCs all witness that aftermath of disillusionment but this is not reflected in the TCJCC, recording the achievement in securing financial assistance from TCs to the miners. The first General Council report following the strike praises TCs for rendering assistance while noting enthusiasm led to some 'overstepping of their duties'.[127] CP member A.L. Horner inquired in what respect TCs had overstepped their authority. Chairman A. Conley responded that they had called out workers 'unnecessarily'. He offered no examples. Only in the final agenda to the ACTC 1927 did the General Council add that TCs' machinery and diligence had reflected great credit and proved the necessity for an efficient, well-informed local organisation. However, the General Council wanted no repetition of TCs as centres for nationwide strike action.[128]

*

Three years on, J.T. Murphy returned to the theme of revolutionary leadership. He assessed councils of action confronting local municipal authorities in terms of class rule, the first stage of dual government,[129] envisaging a worker's parliament alongside the central government, although few TC delegates at the time referred to this.

Despite this, councils of action were seen by Murphy as *transitional* forms of organisation, prevailing over the idea that the working-class must come to power *through* the established Parliament. But what Murphy omitted was that unionists turned to the Labour Party for leadership because improvised councils of action were few, underprepared and lacking experience. Permanent workers' councils, which utilised TCs' organisational ability, energy and enthusiasm, was A.A. Purcell's solution in 1930,[130] but his idea of TCs as 'class organs' became for many a fading dream, yet to be resurrected.

J.T. Murphy returned in 1935 to perceive councils of action as a structural answer to problems in an age of mass strikes and the altered relationship to the state, extrapolating to the form in which a new political authority could arise out of class conflict.[131] However, this did not chime with a generation of TCs' experiences after 1926. Fabian historian G.D.H. Cole lauded the strike as the 'hour of glory for the trades councils', but his reasoning was to posit that TCs showed reserves of competence, skill and efficiency and then post-1926 returned to the humdrum functions of everyday life.[132] This trivialises and minimises the later work of TCs.

For the CP's A. Hutt, TCs 'kept the Socialist flag flying' when unions were becoming fused with the state machine, accommodation, and collaboration with monopoly capital,[133] not that this was the intention of many TC members. However, to claim, as L.C.B. Seaman does, that TCs ignored the nation, the constitutionally elected government and even the community to 'concentrate on their own class' is to miss the vital fact that they worked *within* national, constitutional, community-bound horizons. For TCs, the strike had been a *defensive* movement against wage reductions with a minimal reformist objective. Substituting one social order for another was not on the agenda (except for W. Churchill, who castigated 'the revolutionaries'). CP members did not control TCs or councils of action, TC unionists did not question the TUC hierarchy at the time, and few were planning anything beyond a fair deal for the miners.

As Chris Harman elucidated, CP unionists hoped union leaders like A.A. Purcell and A.B. Swales would stealthily transform the General Council, but they formulated no definite plans for action, apart from workers' defence corps.[134] The CP slogan until 1926 was 'All power to the General Council'; moreover TCs attempted to ensure General Council instructions were administered, not flouted. The TUC Strike Organising Committee actually inhibited local activism[135] and feared left-wing elements might take control and conduct the strike as a political affair, but the police and army did their work for them, TCs also often censoring themselves. Harman deduced that after the strike's defeat workers lost faith that they could challenge the 'powers-that-be', although he downplayed the victories of direct action in the 1930s.

Most TC delegates thought government and union leaders' compromise and bargaining meant that unionists would perhaps not need to challenge authorities to receive fair treatment. Few questioned whether unions should be run by a few 'union bureaucrats'; only communist TC delegates castigated union leaders thus. TCs defended themselves against a police operation that, for the supposedly neutral state, was 'maintaining services for public safety'. TCs were caught within the rubric of capitalist economics, and, for many, any hopes that they might have had that TC decisions would be implemented by the TUC evaporated when TC affiliation to the TUC, for NMM affiliation or for a TUC campaign against the 12 CP leaders' imprisonment, had failed. The CP offered the rationale that the more hesitant the General Council became, the more resilient the TCs, yet, for TCs, what actually transpired was a decreased level of political consciousness and class confidence combined with an awareness of their experience of economic struggles.

TCs presumed that the General Council would negotiate economic reforms within the existing political and industrial structure and that the Labour Party would serve their needs in Parliament. The General Council's role for TCs (from 1924) as 'propaganda agencies' was nebulous. If the majority of TCs were moderate, the radicals were locatable in central Scotland, South Wales and East London, which had composed the majority of 52 TCs at the MM conference in March 1926. The moderates predominated in councils of action and strike committees because they represented the majority of local unions. Where trades were well-organised in industrial centres, TCs had the highest morale; in isolated areas, lack of finances and threat of dismissal had affected TCs' performances in the General Strike.

*

The fire of activism can heighten consciousness but an extinguished flame can result in dislocation. After the strike, a sense of diminished influence occurred. TCs now had to face local government organisations and councillors with their own perception of local politics. TCs had begun to perform some of the tasks of the local municipal government, but lower wages, longer hours, victimisation and loss of seniority (pension and union rights and cuts in living standards) propelled TCs onto the defensive. As late as 1930, London TC was campaigning for reinstatement of unionists who had participated in the strike, and in 1932 Westminster TC was protesting against derogatory remarks made in a BBC news programme on the strike.

The year 1926 was a watershed for TCs' working-class heroes. They had for decades centred on miners, engineers, dockers and transport workers to furnish their main affiliations, but their future would incorporate white-collar unions in less cohesive areas. Just as the Russian soviets of 1917 bore little resemblance to their 1937 organisations, the British TCs and T&LCs of 1926 were unlike those of 1945 in affiliated membership. The Amalgamated Engineering Union (AEU), the National Union of Railwaymen (NUR) and the Miners' Federation of Great Britain (MFGB) had galvanised TCs in 1926 but by 1945 the National Union of Distributive and Allied Workers (NUDAW) and the Transport and General Workers Union (TGWU) were as relevant. No one put forward concrete proposals to TCs to administer their local communities (slogans from the MM and CP were rejected) and TCs soon accepted that the General Council was responsible for collecting funds for the miners.[136] Industrial solidarity with TCs at the centre was fleeting, the General Strike a representative example of the regional peculiarities in TCs during its few days.

Soviet responses to the strike's collapse exacerbated TUC relations with CP members in TCs. From the USSR, Losovsky blamed British union leaders, and Stalin spurned A.J. Cook and H. Smith as 'opportunists and reformists'. So, the CP began an exposé of the 'reactionary leaders', asserting it now had to politically educate the 'backward masses' and promote new *cadres* from the working class to leading positions in the movement,[137] although where these new leaders would emerge from was not spelled out. The CP's alternative perspective conflicted with the post-1926 TC practice of resolving issues within negotiating formulae propounded by the union hierarchy. CP proclamations to TC unionists for renewed direct action and a repeat general strike took second place to TCs' diminished finances and loss of affiliated membership, compounded by government hostility to strikes confirmed in the Trade Disputes and Trade Union (TD&TU) Act and a police raid on the Anglo-Russian Co-operative Society. The CP also had to contend with the government severing diplomatic relations with the Soviet Union, and union leaders' identification with the 'democratic apparatus' of the existing state and denunciation of those TCs connected to the NMM.[138]

Union leaders argued the strike had politically damaged the labour movement. The General Council was now shepherding TCs along safer channels that did not challenge union and Labour leaders, hence the imposition of fixed constitutions on TCs. This rendered them, in CP terms, 'docile, malleable and subservient', TCs now re-evaluated by the CP as being limited and reformist.[139]

The new *Model Rules and Constitution for TCs* gave TCs status and a uniformity of organisation, and they could not be weaned from Labour's electoralism. Soon the CP was maintaining that most 1926 councils of action had been controlled by 'confused, hesitating workers (mostly union officials)', and that the future task was to prevent the enforced separation of economic and political issues; exhibiting sectarianism alongside Leninist insight. The CP eventually interpreted the General Strike's defeat in terms of local union officials' hesitations and union leaders' individual weaknesses or betrayal, rather than an appreciation of the pressures to compromise inherent in their positions.[140] General Council officials countered such CP deductions in their own appeals for 'loyalty' to the movement against the CP's critique, its opportunism, and attempts at class-conscious unionism.

Post –'26 there was in TCs a generalised abulia, a loss of willpower to act decisively and ameliorate economic conditions. What can activists today learn from this historic, industrial setback from workers' past? Perhaps this: if the trade union movement was to again challenge the state it would have to be prepared, optimistic, organised, belief-driven – and united. To facilitate this TCs would need to act as 'councils of action', linking together rank and file union activists with other local organisations and public figures in ways that they failed to achieve in 1926. This would have to be proceeded by patient discussion and supporting solidarity actions. Next, we explore where the movement was heading post-1926.

CHAPTER 3

Trades Councils and Trade Union Leaders 1924–39

In 'Living in the End Times', Slavoj Zizek quotes an exchange between Spartacus (Kirk Douglas) and a pirate (Herbert Lom) in Kubrick's 'Spartacus' in which the pirate asks the slave leader whether he is aware that his rebellion is doomed... Spartacus replies that the slaves' struggle is not simply to improve their condition, but a principled rebellion in the name of freedom... their insurrection will not have been in vain... it will have manifested their unconditional commitment to emancipation. As Zizek remarks, 'Their act of rebellion itself, whatever the outcome, already counts as a success.' The price Spartacus and his comrades would pay for surviving without a struggle would be their integrity.

~ *Terry Eagleton, Hope Without Optimism (2017 edition), p110*

1. TRADES COUNCILS AND TUC EMERGING STRUCTURES 1924-29

To better comprehend the function and impact of TCs 1920-50 we need to create a more detailed picture of their structures and relationships, assessing interactions between the TUC General Council, the TCJCC, and the TC rank and file. The former used conferences and circulars to define and narrow TCs' perspectives and channel energies into union recruitment rather than ideological political debate or actions deemed *ultra vires*. TCs did not always accept restricted parameters, but were insufficiently prepared or consolidated to advance any unified counter-narrative. Nevertheless, TCs' determination, optimism and forbearance are constants.

We have directed attention to the ritualistic nature of interactions between TCs and the TUC, applied to union leaders' regulating mechanism for TCs via the TCJCC. Most TCs did accept the restrictions placed upon their activities, which had a deleterious effect on the rank-and-file movement. Trade union consciousness operated within conventions, a coded trade unionese, a language of significations, prioritising 'moderate' TCs and 'loyalty to the TUC' as crucial elements in this coding system. The TUC invoked its own version of the '3 Rs' – rules, regulations and resolutions. Between 1924 and 1939, evolving from the TCJCC and TC *Model Rules*, are moments of consent whereby union leaders garnered the support of TCs for gradualist union policies, bereft of radical viewpoints. TC/TUC relations were interpreted as part of a structure of declared *rules* so that the purpose of trade unionism is incorporated by TCs, delineated in the classification of industrial (i.e. legitimate) activities as distinct from political (i.e. officially illegitimate) work.

The arbitrary nature of this division becomes apparent through TUC correspondence with TCs and via union leaders' justifications announced at ACTCs, at which a semiological code of acceptable TC involvements is announced and then initiated. In the 1930s, TCs upheld the panacea of nationalisation as the TUC offered TCs as union recruitment centres and the gradual acquisition of status in this function. Within the categories of debates, resolutions, statements and then actions, a *structure* of conventions emerges. To elucidate how this was gradually instituted and the formulations to challenge this particular *modus operandi* is the objective here.

How did TC structures develop prior to the 1926 strike? Between 1910 and 1920, trade unionism, on the offensive, saw the TUC become a 'general staff of labour'[141] as old craft traditions were challenged by new forms of technology and utilitarian scientific management.[142] The TUC Parliamentary Committee recommended joint TUC/Labour Party offices in 1916 and a General Council to co-ordinate industrial action, inter-union settlements, and union administration through committees. TC/TUC relations were updated as the General Council organised general policy, national correspondence, Congress and circulars to TCs, a functional uniformity giving TCs a specific task collating information with local Labour parties,[143] to present union views to local authorities, MPs and the press, and a reduced political role implicit when the TUC acquired block votes at conference and a majority on the Labour Party's NEC.[144]

A few TC members openly espoused their guild socialist views (which bypassed orthodox union structure), but in 1922 TCs were seeking representation at the TUC and an annual conference for TCs. Since wages and conditions were being transformed through national settlements, TCs touted themselves as the central local organisations for the General Council, to uphold workers' living standards and confront the Federation of British Industry and Employers' Associations. The TUC initially ignored this, so TCs had created their own separate body, the National Federation of Trades Councils (NFTC).[145] It lasted for two years.

The character of the ties between the TUC and TCs would soon imply the separation of industrial from political, Birmingham TC echoing Sheffield T&LC in arguing that if TCs were to be the TUC's 'local agents' there should be direct representation on the TUC, so that TCs would have the opportunity to help formulate policy.[146] This would never be countenanced by the General Council. Instead, TCs were bequeathed the 'right' to be partly responsible for the 1923-24 'Back to the Unions' endeavours.[147] On defining 'propaganda work' in TCs, W. Citrine recalled in 1943:

> I first proposed measures to bring Trades Councils into closer association with the TUC 18 years ago. At that time the movement was in a state of... disrepair. Structurally it was neither one thing nor the other. Some TCs were purely political bodies, some were wholly industrial, some were both, with a confused idea as to where their political and industrial functions began and ended.[148]

This was the crux of the battle: how to compel TCs to perform the role of purely industrial bodies. Most of the subsequent disagreements were about this TUC definition, with the majority of ACTC delegates exhibiting a conformist view of the union movement, whose structure necessitated what were 'cinematograph leaders' (those who wanted to be in the picture) and an emerging oligarchy. This was not a problem in 1925, at the first ACTC, which debated those annual TC requests for representation at the TUC, as the formation of the TCJCC was considered a step in that direction. (The number of TCs rose from 329 in 1913 to 488 in 1924 and 480 in 1925, when it was 41% of union membership.)[149]

Then, with the advent of the General Strike 1926 (exemplified in chapter 2), TC activities suggest strikers did not expect to lose. The solidarity strikes were impressive. However, with defeat, TCs acknowledged the result would entail union and Labour Party leaders' style of conciliation and arbitration. Twelve years later, at the ACTC, the General Council proudly harked back to what the strike had revealed:

> the spiritual awakening of the organised forces... the whole movement went to the assistance of a section of the membership which was being attacked, and during that period the Trades Council Movement played an important part.[150]

Hindsight blurred the divisions within the union movement. In practice, for TCs, their relationship with the TUC post-strike was coloured by TC suspicions as to the role enacted by TUC leaders in 1926. There was much talk in TCs of backdoor TUC negotiations and betrayal, especially after the TD&TU Act 1927. In her diaries, Beatrice Webb maintained that union leaders were 'bolstering up a fraud – pretending to the outside world that [they] are the leaders of the Social Revolution'.[151]

Disappointment was widespread. TCs were deeply troubled by the loss of union members (1 million by 1934) alongside the resultant compulsion to prioritise union recruiting and labour representation on borough councils.[152] There were no plaudits about the 'spiritual awakening' when the TCJCC on 15 June 1926 omitted *any* discussion or analysis of the strike, and prioritised TCs sending in lists of unaffiliated union branches.[153] The TCJCC had a defensive plan for financial assistance to the miners through TC area conferences: 'The object is to try to use Trades Councils as an organising centre and clearing house [centre of exchange] for all contributions'.[154] Henceforth, the TCJCC chose to gear TCs to TUC policies. Owing to the parlous financial situation of unions, conditions were not suitable for another 'Back to the Unions' campaign; TCs could discuss policy affecting affiliated members but strikes and finances were now considered the prerogative of union executives.

At the TUC conference September 1926, the new structure to be imposed upon TCs was announced. The ACTC had been created to bring TCs together, and the *Model Rules and Constitution for TCs* were installed to create homogeneity, so TCs would become the General Council's local counterpart 'with a similarity of constitution'.[155] Belatedly recognising TCs value in the strike as 'a powerful stimulus… for the establishment of the Trades Councils in a sector of their own on the united working class front'[156] was how this was sold. Few TC delegates at the time articulated the view that their union was oppressive or officials 'demagogues', a later inference by radicals. The overriding aims were to rebuild unions and improve internal administration,[157] Sheffield T&LC reflecting the majoritarians who denounced those who 'slandered' the Labour Party.[158]

All TCs after 1926 witnessed some union branches reneging on fees, accepting restrictions on activities, and a long-term TUC strategy to secure a national position in economic policy-making. Industrial efficiency or 'rationalisation' would gradually transform the context of TC/TUC debates. In 1927–28, strike activity halved, conciliatory industrial relations the dominant theme fostered in ACTCs in the late 1920s, based on aspirations towards a healthier economic situation. Trade unionists were still hopeful. Disillusionment did not manifest itself generally until the collapse of the Labour government in 1931.

Another aspect of reducing TCs' purview from 1927 was termination of the *Monthly Report*, substituted by the *Industrial Review*,[159] the General Council's official publication, especially for union head offices, district offices and branches. The distinction between political and industrial was then highlighted in a TCJCC communication to West Ham TC and Borough Labour Party: no TC could 'interfere' in the executive's constitution in its political section. But this was a problem for TCs, as Brighton's joint executive declared: 'How difficult it is to state where trade unionism ends and Politics begins'.[160]

TC frustration was apposite. The TD&TU Act undermined union rights and, in campaigns against it, TCs' weak finances restricted propaganda work. Perceiving the Act as 'the blackleg's charter' and a 'stone age measure' (Edinburgh T&LC), TCs began their new recruiting campaigns, some forming local defence committees. There were more TCs' joint meetings with Labour parties, which the General Council promoted, while loss of union rights furnished the TUC with an opportunity to isolate interference by communists in TCs with 'democracy versus dictatorship', 'industrial anarchy' and 'infiltration' themes.[161]

By May 1927, 565 union branches were unaffiliated to TCs, even though the TCJCC praised TCs' efficient machinery and helpfulness and estimated the previous year as probably the most memorable in union history with TCs having 'played their part well'. Trade union leaders were planning tighter controls. For ACTC chairman G. Hicks, a nagging problem was that TCs were only partially identified with the movement, 'much looser than I care to see'.[162] For Hicks, TCs ought to be the equivalent of the General Council nationally, the latter currently 'a head without a body'. He may not have realised why some TCs might be disaffected, when the substitution of the *Industrial Review* was without consultation with TCs and the ACTC agenda so constructed that TCs' opinions were minimised. W. Mellor of Manchester & Salford TC estimated that half a TC's time was spent reconciling divisions between competing unions, TCs being asked to do what the TUC ought to have been doing itself.

For the General Council, when the TD&TU Bill became law, 'Trades Councils will have their opportunity presently to resume their historic role'. Whatever that was, it seemed not to encompass councils of action. The ACTC 1927 withheld recognition from TCs affiliated to the Minority Movement (MM), union policy condoned 'in orderly and constitutional ways through the proper channels and not imposed by mischievous agencies outside'.[163] Union machinery was considered sufficiently democratic with adequate opportunity for minority opinion, and no room for hostile organisations controlled from outside by those who had no responsibility for executing policy. The TUC's panacea? Another recruitment drive: 'here lies the great opportunity of the Trades Councils', propaganda for trade unionism, union organisation TCs' central purpose.[164]

With the TD&TU Act enforced, TCs lost branches of the Post Office Engineering Union (POEU) and Union of Post Office Workers (UPOW) and the services of some long-term local activists. A flavour of its impact on TCs: the Act resulted in London TC's affiliation to the Labour Party being made impossible and Manchester Labour Party's fusion with the local TC unviable (despite its rules including 'watching over the social and political rights of labour').[165] Birmingham TC lost seven UPOW branches and three POEU branches (and £70 income per year);[166] Edinburgh T&LC separated industrial and political funds;[167] Ipswich TC experienced a severe blow to its already precarious finances; Camberwell TC was marked by a period of gloom and demoralisation; and Aylesbury TC had to change its constitution, continuing as a purely industrial body and confining itself to 'non-political' activities. For Leicester, Huddersfield and Blackpool TCs, the Act brought them closer to the Labour Party[168] as the industrial character of TCs saw T&LCs deleting '& Labour' to allay suspicions that industrial funds might be used for political objectives, legislation against sympathetic strikes nullifying TCs' unifying role.

With workers' wage reductions, union membership decreasing and finances strained, the TUC construed that the future lay in consultations with business leaders. G. Hicks offered the mantra that, if 'a fair bargain' could be achieved with 'business reformers' through joint conferences, all unions would gain.[169] TCs were expected to delight in this supposedly healthier philosophy of conciliation, as the TUC in September 1927 reiterated opposition to direct affiliation or representation of TCs at Congress.[170] Why? Apparently, it would make the latter too unwieldy, and give 'irresponsible persons' a right to make important decisions and rebel against the responsible leaders of trade unionism. Besides, 'the unions as a whole have weathered the terrific storm of the last seven years [1920–27] with extraordinary success'.[171] TCs were encouraged to fit into the stricter arrangements.

Within a couple of months of announcing TC recruitment campaigns, the decision was reversed; recruitment was left to unions. TCs were to engage only when requested by a union. W. Citrine claimed the TD&TU Act did not apply directly to TCs since if any money was spent on 'political objectives' it made the union and not the TC liable.[172] Besides, if TC delegates indulged in 'distracting criticism', the TCJCC could create *new* TCs (as in Bethnal Green and Hackney).[173] Only union-controlled recruitment and conciliatory methods in disputes were to be embraced, as J.E. Corrin of Birmingham TC acknowledged in April

1928. Meanwhile, Brighton TC's urge to 'stir the mass of the middle class and semi-retired people in Brighton and Hove into political consciousness'[174] was truly aspirational! At the ACTC 1928, G. Hicks pondered that too little had been said or written about the valuable assistance from TCs in 1926,[175] but TCs received no help when incurring financial liability for lost union branch funds. Recruitment drives via unions (for Wolverhampton, Doncaster, Portsmouth, London and Hendon TCs) became central and 16 other TCs were chosen as experimental recruitment centres in 1928.[176] Thus, we see how TC/TUC relations were restructured within two years of the General Strike, the TUC turning a crisis into an opportunity.

2. PRIORITIES OF RECRUITMENT 1929–32

With Labour's election victory in 1929 TCs' future may have appeared rosy. London TC could surely become the dominating factor in the city's industrial and political life? Affiliated membership had swelled to 240,000 and for the CP's T. Quelch it 'ought to be the London workers' Parliament',[177] while Sheffield T&LC's executive proclaimed its guiding principle 'to secure the worker the full fruits of his labour, industrially and politically'.[178]

Optimism was likewise reflected in the ACTC 1929 in June, during which B. Tillett (TUC General Council chairman) praised TCs' conscientiousness.[179] However, the notion that TC/TUC relations were flourishing was queried. The *Industrial Review* did not prioritise reports on or from TCs, which were no nearer gaining representation on the TUC (an issue that resurfaced in 2023) or funds from the TUC, nor of securing an upsurge in affiliations from union branches. Unperturbed, the TUC *Labour Magazine* saluted this ACTC as the most successful ever because, before 1924, TCs had been isolated units with no contact with each other (convenient amnesia about the NFTCs of 1922 and 1923).

Tensions were mounting between the TUC and TCs. In October 1929, some of the TC speakers were reprimanded (by the TCJCC) for indulging in 'general political appeals' rather than 'the intelligent use of collective bargaining'.[180] This included Manchester & Salford TC secretary A.A. Purcell, a socialist who argued that class-conscious workers could not merely transform a town and secure workers' industrial and political control but could affect radical changes nationally, workers dominating the industrial, municipal and political life through their organisations.[181] A central obstacle to such visions becoming a reality for TCs was that union leaders were not in the business for the elimination of private profit but led organisations seeking higher rates of pay, shorter hours and decent conditions *within* the existing structure. These were the constraints put upon TC activities and aspirations.

*

Other TC frustrations were encapsulated in the rank-and-filism of CP member Pennifold (Brighton TC's president), who assessed 'the evil of the present time' as the over-weighting from the top with the result that the initiative was removed from TCs.[182] And this 'evil' was a by-product of Labourist centralisation. Such critical analysis of TUC strategy was not formulated or acknowledged by most

TCs, the consensus expressed in Sheffield T&LC's official view that a TC should safeguard workers by supervision of working conditions and wage rates, progress meaning loyalty to the principles of the movement (however defined) and the development of team spirit.[183] TCs were so variable. In Mexborough, the TC secretary absconded with the TC's funds (not *that* unique in TC history), while many activists were uncertain when a 'political issue' appertained, illustrated when Birmingham TC recorded the unacceptable treatment of Indian workers and spoke for India as a self-governing British Dominion; at the same time, Brighton TC would not debate this because it was 'a political question'.[184]

During the enforcement of the TD&TU Act, the labour movement was industrially and politically handicapped and TCs justifiably blamed the TUC for tardiness. A. Conley, TCJCC chairman, retorted that TCs should be loyal to the Labour Party if they were to be an 'integral part of the structure of the movement':[185] 'If and when Trades Councils do become a definite part of Trade Union machinery… this is bound to have a definite effect upon national development,'[186] he added. The assessment that TCs had 'no political functions' concealed a myriad of political implications for TC's daily concerns.

Such analyses were related to union leaders' association with employers, culminating in the Federation of British Industry/General Council Joint Memorandum in August 1930 as TCs were invited to get busy with propaganda weeks and recruitment drives.[187] Shrinkages in older staple industries compared to expansion in new industries required that the former be compensated by recruitment in the latter.[188] So TCs were to prepare surveys of new firms: 'the work will be a monument to the invaluable role which can be accomplished by trades councils in rendering service to their and our affiliated organisations', insisted the TCJCC.[189] TCs were given three months to complete these surveys but they retained the broader horizons of the Oxford T&LC secretary: 'to put forward demands commensurate with our rightful share of the product of industry',[190] or, as the Sheffield T&LC president opined,

> employers, meeting at their annual dinners, and replete with the good things of life, call for economy and decry the growing amount spent on social services, knowing full well that whatever the state of the money market… their children will be fed, clothed and educated.[191]

(*Plus ça change.*)

TCs were now trapped in a movement on the defensive. As the economic situation deteriorated, they consoled themselves with the shield of trade unionism. The People's Congress prepared by Manchester & Salford TC in May 1931 depicted TCs battling wage reductions, social services' curtailments, and unemployment benefit reductions. TCs were well-positioned in the structure of the union and labour movement to witness and record socio-economic outcomes,[192] but this Congress had a sting in it for TC/TUC relations to demonstrate 'the heart-burning desire on the part of the rank and file of the movement for a real, healthy lead',[193] calling into question official notions of what 'healthy' unionism actually encompassed. In May 1931, of 147 TCs, 67 had increased membership, 38 decreased, 42 unchanged. The TCJCC's conclusion: to urge TCs to prioritise inroads into non-unionism, enabling them to concentrate on the industrial.[194]

With the collapse of the Labour government and realignment under the National Government, the political direction of the labour movement turned for guidance to TUC leaders, a surprise after the press and BBC old trope insinuations about the 'dictatorship' by unions over the Labour government (an echoing line). Some TCs openly denounced the apostasy of those Labour ministers who, in the words of London TC's A.M. Wall, 'besmirched their loyalty and betrayed their party'.[195] Wall's solution: TCs should obey union leaders. This was fundamentally at odds with A.A. Purcell's radical call for a dynamic 'class-conscious, aggressive political working class movement to counteract the baleful tide of the economy-mongers'.[196]

Clouding the separation of political from industrial, E. Bevin suggested unions could help the fragmented Labour Party, especially in the work of political education.[197] As the National Council for Labour (NCL) became the authoritative body formulating party policy, the General Council gained prestige. The larger TCs now enunciated perspectives on industrial reconstruction, affirming progress could only be achieved if the electorate comprehended the principles of the movement in the new battles over the Means Test (Newcastle and District TC), closure of clothing factories (Birmingham TC), campaigns for women unionists (Huddersfield and Southampton TCs) and resisting cuts in public assistance committees' (PACs) scales (Bristol and Brighton TCs) – all of which was carefully scrutinised and monitored by the TUC and TCJCC.

'It is a jolly gathering marked by good temper', remarked E.P. Harries (TUC Organisation Department) of the ACTC 1932, as he waxed lyrical over unions' 'cherished local autonomy'.[198] The TCJCC added that it would be 'a serious blow' if local political activities overshadowed industrial actions.[199] Some industrial stoppages had occurred, TCs proving their value when Lancashire cotton workers went on strike in August 1932, numerous TCs sending food parcels (for example, Manchester & Salford, Birmingham, Bristol, Oxford and Southampton TCs) and forming Cotton Fund Committees. The TUC General Council now recommended public corporations in managing socialised industries, with personnel appointed by the government with particular interests represented on consultative boards, the rank and file providing a *minor advisory function*.[200] The fruition of such an intervention would not emerge until a decade later.

3. CAMPAIGNING AGAINST FASCISM AND THE CUTS, OR RECRUITMENT AGENCIES 1933-36

TCs had numerous issues with which to contend in the mid-1930s. Their campaigns against wage-cutting, confronting reductions in insurance payments, and strictures in public services, all deserve commendation. However, they had little influence on industrial policy, and most unionists retained faith in the Labour Party's capacity to eventually solve production and consumption problems through planned reconstruction. This was how Sheffield T&LC Executive perceived the terrain. Meanwhile, Oxford T&LC's idealist C. Bowles determined that the labour movement would end 'this present system with its class hatreds and its hideous wars'.[201]

In the 1930s, contradictions abounded. Many TC delegates acknowledged the paradox of capitalism undermining itself by its own chaotic, fitful economic development while union leaders sought a place in the direction of industries.[202] For all their promotion of recruitment, TUC propaganda weeks fronted by TCs had to be cancelled for lack of interest; in 1933 union membership was below 4 million, its lowest level between the two world wars and half that of 1920.[203] With union leaders entering wage negotiations to mitigate pay cuts, and with collective bargaining as the lauded procedure, political orthodoxy legitimised a weakened unionism. The General Council differed from the more vocal TCs on the ability of the economy to recover, the strike as a political weapon no longer promoted as a viable strategy.[204]

TC/TUC relations were analysed by Brighton TC's chairman, Pennifold, in 1933. For him, the dead weight of tradition in the movement and a conservatism of outlook stood for Sick Club benefits, negotiation and a meagre funeral; too many unionists had the negotiation complex and the result of Mond–Turnerism had been wage reductions of £34 million in the previous three years. The opposite approach was neatly summed up by E. Bevin: 'Our work is eminently practical and it is to deliver the goods to our members and we know as leaders the absolute folly of putting up programmes that are not likely to be realised'.[205] This 'pragmatic' approach diverged from TC-voiced schemes and aspirations to wage the class struggle 'aiming at the full realisation of working class power in our communities'.[206] The problem of unity was, for this minority of TCs, to allow 'the sincere revolutionary elements, not the mere blatherers'[207] to have a say, but at the practical level in local TC surveys the adage was: 'trades councils, know your localities'.

Since the TUC instructed TCs that joint industrial councils for wages and negotiations in municipal services required TCs to adhere to union policy, the perennial debate continued: how were TCs to differentiate trade unionism from political action, especially in TC campaigns to restore wage levels? For Manchester & Salford TC, there was a coherent solution: 'every town a workers' fortress'; and, because capitalism could not satisfy the working class: 'we are in the period of the dissolution of the old order and the painful birth of the new order – socialism. Only a united working class can usher in the new order.'[208] Here, in that TC and Bevin's comments, were irreconcilable approaches within the union movement, the abiding theme for that generation of TCs.

*

TCs' anti-fascist politics in the 1930s has not been fully appreciated. TCs were united in opposition to some upper-class lauding of fascism and Hitler's early 'achievements', particularly against socialists and communists. Had the British Union of Fascists (BUF) embedded itself in the UK and succeeded, TCs probably would have been replaced, their political activities outlawed. Yet, TCs did not gain sufficient backing from the TUC against this threat or the tangible intrusions of fascist propaganda in many localities.[209] Instead, TCs were instructed to focus their energies in areas where new suburban housing developments and light industries were based.[210] Regardless, numerous TCs contended that the Incitement to Disaffection Bill had fascist implications: 'a measure capable of being used to suppress all socialist propaganda' (Ipswich TC), 'a violation of the traditional liberties of the British people' (London TC) and 'the logical expression of capitalism driven to extremes by its own contradictions' (Manchester & Salford TC).[211] The bill was enacted.

This did not cancel out TCs' given role to revitalise unions with 'a new vision, a fresh energy, and a concrete plan for immediate action'.[212] For the union leadership, the central endeavour for the movement was somehow to rid itself of schisms and factions. This elevated an alternative perception of loyalty and anointed union leaders, a process confirmed by the TUC president and ACTC chairman in August 1934. TC delegates were, as usual, treated to lengthy speeches by TUC leaders, which swallowed up much of the agenda. The General Council announced 'Weekend Schools for Trades Councils', the method instigated and promulgated to cement loyalty. The message was encapsulated in the title of two sessions: 'Some Problems of Trade Union Organisation' and 'Dictatorship: The Threat to Industrial Democracy'.[213]

It was axiomatic in TCs, as E. Friend, chairman of London TC/Labour Party conference espoused it, that the British were highly experienced in 'democratic self-government' and the trade union movement was *the* protection against fascism.[214] Presumably, the economic crisis would pass and a rising standard of living would be granted without any fundamental shift in the industrial structure, even if, for a few TC unionists, nationalisation was about more than a change in legal relationships.[215] Recruitment campaigns, proclaimed the General Council, had created an 'excellent spirit' among officers and local unionists, although the nagging question remained: what precisely did union leaders envisage for TCs? The result was *Circular 15* on 'Organisation Activities'.[216] Continuity rather than transformation?

*

TC members were not merely administrative officials, but active campaigners.[217] According to Reg Groves in *Trades Councils in the Fight for Socialism* (1935), they could have provided the means to organise combined political and industrial agitation; they were suited to becoming the *co-ordinating bodies* of the movement if they widened their remit to become trades, labour and co-operative councils; and TCs' future would be determined by the extent to which they dominated the life of workers in their district.[218] Such decentralisation of union power had long been sought. Perhaps war resistance could be extended locally by TCs, or as Oxford T&LC's secretary put it, the great common struggle against 'the National Government of fascism and war'.[219] Although, at this time, only 5% to 10% of union members had a say in votes recorded in their name,[220] repulsion at the emergence of fascism/Nazism in Europe and the government's appeasement strategy propelled many TCs towards a more defiant perspective.[221]

Union leaders now focused upon and criticised TC recruitment campaigns as being badly organised, targeting TCs for being unscientific in method. In a revealing analogy, a General Council memorandum on this explained that TCs had a service 'just like salesmen'.[222] In practice, in 1934, recruitment campaigns could have been utilised with permanent officers in TCs, but this would have brought friction between TUC staff and full-time union organisers. ACTC chairman W. Kean in 1935 echoed that the first duty of TCs was, indeed, recruitment, and then unity of purpose with the General Council: 'If we are going to succeed there must be unity and loyalty.'[223]

Arguments went back and forth, the TCJCC reminding TCs that they were not to counter local Labour parties even if they were centres of industrial action, with propaganda weeks, demonstrations for the unemployed, and fair wages campaigns. This was not how the Labour left, the Socialist League (SL), was depicting TCs by June 1935. It instructed its National Council to popularise them as the local unifying centres to be empowered to win unorganised workers to the cause and become the basis for 'local defence against Fascist violence'. Contrary to TUC designs, TCs were envisioned by the SL as the foundations of strike organisation, including a general strike.[224] But such notions had limited support, TCs becoming demoralised after Labour's worst general election result to date in 1935.

With controversies over unofficial strikes and black circulars (analysed in Chapter 6), TCs affirmed that such strikes arose officially because union leaders were unaware of, or deliberately minimised, workers' requirements. Moreover, behind this was a policy that deplored the strike weapon. For the TUC, TCs were 'peculiarly adapted' to promoting recruitment in newer industries with their 'experience, knowledge, organising ability, enthusiasm and leadership'.[225] TCs responded to this estimation of TCs' limited function by critiquing the acceptance of knighthoods by A. Pugh and W. Citrine. Years later Citrine justified his award as recognition of services 'valuable to the community': 'Even in a capitalist state of society there were some things worth doing and others worth preserving. I had followed a long and honourable line of predecessors in the trade union movement who had received honours'.[226] There lay the tensions: definitions of 'service' and 'community' – but who was serving whom? And what was 'honourable'?

In 1935 it was announced (as though it was a revelation) that TCs were being fashioned as local TUCs to administer organisational, routine work! No TC objected to this. Deliberations at the ACTC were on the *Memorandum on Trade Union Recruitment*, which confined debate to 'matters coming within the purview' of TCs as local recruiting machines.[227] However, TUC income and expenditure budgeting meant no financial help was forthcoming. Apparently, it was beyond TCs' function to debate international events, although the annual reviews show this to have been a major feature of local TC meetings. Anxieties about how to confront imperialist warmongers and a competitive armaments race[228] came from numerous TCs and financial aid was extended to victims of fascism. The Sheffield T&LC president showed foresight: with rearmament leading to industrial conscription, there would be a filching of civil liberties, and then war.

The catastrophic defeat of the Labour Party in the general election of 1935 prompted further doubts. Would workers ever recognise the futility of electing those who were opposed to their interests? W.J. Munro of Manchester & Salford TC heralded the struggle:

> against this unjust, inequitable and abominable system known as capitalism... We produce all the wealth, we belong to the same class, our interests are identical. Let us put away all those petty carping differences that makes for disunity. Let us gird on the armour of unity and march forward against the bulwarks of deceit, hypocrisy and privilege.[229]

Such political aspiration may have triggered the TUC to offer study courses on the history, structure, functions and policy of trade unionism, but would TCs remain militantly pacifist on rearmament?

4. OPPOSITION TO WAR 1936-39

In World War I, TCs had held open-air meetings for speakers to vent their grievances. By 1936, *committees* were considered more effective.[230] TCs were instructed by the TCJCC not to call conferences against rearmament or industrial conscription or to oppose government intentions to regiment industry on war lines.[231] A. Findlay's ACTC 1936 address overtly criticised those TCs devoting themselves to 'political work' when they should be pursuing recruitment. (In fact, the difficulty to overcome was not obtaining new unionists but retaining them.)

Despite that injunction, this ACTC voted for armaments for the Spanish Republicans and a united front against fascism, with numerous TCs offering funds and campaigning for the SMAC.[232] This was proof for the TUC of CP infiltration, as the General Council's stated position was to underpin the government's neutral non-intervention strategy. Underlying TCs' bubbling discontents was the perception of a TUC conference, unrepresentative, insulated from TCs' perspectives, with block votes and a compliant TCJCC. There never had been a consistent definition of the demarcation between matters industrial and political but each year the General Council reminded TCs of what they should do: devote income and attention to industrial activities and recruitment.[233]

What had to be acknowledged, whether industrial or political, ill-judged or not, was that the government's armaments policy was condemned by the more vocal TCs, who objected to 'concessions to patriotic appeals' and the surrender of union rights. If there was to be intensive union recruiting, it should be in the war industries. However, the previously mentioned foresight, that the armaments race would inevitably lead to war, was not adopted by the majority of TCs, which exhibited the same uncertainty as the TUC General Council.[234] At the TUC conference in Plymouth, E. Bevin, as he had surmised, repeated that the differences between the trade unionism of the 1920s and later 1930s was that 'those were the days of advocacy, ours are the days of administration'.[235]

*

In November 1936 the TCJCC published *Trades Councils – Their Functions and Activities*, a document updating and clarifying TC/TUC relations. TCs had become the local distributors of union propaganda and information: 'if a Trades Council is not an industrial body there is no excuse for its existence'.[236] For union leaders, any TC that subordinated industrial to political activities was 'duplicating the machinery'. Actions in support of Spanish Republicans were thus deemed peripheral, and this memorandum set the agenda for TCs up to the 1948 *Trades Councils' Guide*, as did *Circular 59* on 'Local Trade Union Recruitment Campaigns'.[237] E. Bevin, elevated as chairman of the General Council, warned TCs not to assume political changes could be achieved through industrial negotiations. The General Council was unaware that TCs did not perceive recruitment campaigns as particularly beneficial (of 370 TCs, only 56 actually had an ongoing recruiting campaign). Half the ACTC was spent debating this memorandum, and a two-day ACTC was again rejected.[238]

TCs were instructed to ignore aiding or supporting unofficial strikes. Yet, in September 1937, Manchester & Salford TC's £250 assistance to the apprentices' strike in local engineering factories had helped breach employers' resistance to union recognition, while Bevin's broader aim was for the movement to become an integral part of the state, utilising TCs as training for future union officials. 'The more authoritative information that they obtained, the better equipped they will become for their future careers',[239] a functional role for TCs as a professional stepping-stone. Such plans diverged from many TCs, whose intention was not merely personal but political aspiration: for a more egalitarian society.[240]

A socialist core was upheld among many local TCs, despite the TUC leadership. Sheffield T&LC had invited union branches to establish a Council of Action to work for 'the overthrow of the Government', which the TCJCC thought 'quite irregular'! TCs were only *advisory* bodies, so could be ignored even when they submitted memoranda on air raid precautions (ARP) or offered a representative on ARP committees.[241] Praise for TCs' activities was at the ACTC 1938, provided by Chairman E. Elvin, stating that TCs should aim to transform society through the organisation of industry. How this was to be achieved he did not elucidate, perhaps because the ACTC represented the movement not on the basis of trade or industry but on geography.

For the General Council, a successful, healthy, useful TC incorporated more branches and conducted regular union propaganda. When Leicester and Newcastle TCs complained about lack of union officials' support for their recruitment campaigns, W. Citrine insisted General Council endeavours were, at all times, to 'strengthen the power of Trades Councils'[242] and he could not remember a single occasion where it had not been used thus. Nobody had suggested TCs' functions had been diminished since 1926; some TCs had been disaffiliated for debating political issues and others demoted for undue influence by 'outside bodies' such as the MM. Concurrently, Sheffield T&LC contended that the capitalist classes aimed to wrest from workers their hard-won privileges, with huge amounts spent on armaments, little on shelters, ARP part of the capitalist war machine assisting conscription, so it was the duty of TCs to *politicise* unionists.[243]

In the approach to war, the invitation to the TUC's General Council to help with the Schedule of Reserved Occupations for National Service and representation on local committees gave TCs the opportunity to nominate participants. In February 1939, Brighton TC refused this offer and Croydon TC debated and questioned whether or not the General Council had a mandate to define policy on National Voluntary Service (NVS).[244] Many TCs specifically resisted industrial conscription. Birmingham TC reiterated the need to 'stave off this deadly peril to our hard-won liberties', but, by April 1939, 257 TCs had forwarded nominations to NVS committees (and 66 had not).[245] A few TCs challenged the Conscription Bill and insisted that the government had introduced conscription to *hinder* the anti-fascist forces. Birmingham TC contended the voluntary system could defend democracy, while 'compulsion' aped the fascist and Nazi states.[246] The TUC's own 'fascism/communism/dictatorship' formulation from 1933 re-emerged, as South Shields TC and Bradford TC reflected TC reservations, commenting that the General Council had become a recruiting agent for the government. Most TCs now sought to be on NVS committees and did not contend that national defence as constructed only implied defence of private enterprise and dividends, and they were not taking seriously any proposal for a general strike against conscription.[247]

What TCs *were* effective in doing was drawing attention to democratic ARP administration (as in the election of wardens) and for deep, bomb-proof shelters, articulating anxieties that the Conscription Bill would result in wage reductions, intensification of labour and loss of civil rights. However, the General Council gauged the pulse of patriotism in 1939. W. Citrine later recalled: 'It would have been mad folly to have awaited the outbreak of war before providing the trained manpower to handle the weapons which had been produced'.[248] TCs had raised the alarm about exploitation of non-unionised workers in factories under the Special Areas Commission as 'co-operation with the boss classes' (as a Camberwell TC delegate put it in May 1939)[249] just as this was to be put into operation. TCs recognised that the division of labour in the movement was as real as division of labour within the factory, despite *Circular 116* on 'National Voluntary Service Representatives on Local Committees'.[250] War would transform relations between TCs and the TUC and offer TCs new tasks in their localities; but in 1939 no TC could envisage what administrative powers union leaders would achieve during or following World War II.

CHAPTER 4

Trades Councils in the War and its Reverberations 1939–50

> The typical form of organisation is the trade union, a hierarchical and generally bureaucratic form... that [takes] for granted the reproduction of capitalist domination... Trade union struggle is an economic struggle that needs to be complemented by political struggle.
>
> ~ *John Holloway, Crack Capitalism, 2010, pp157–8*

1. LOCAL REPRESENTATION 1939–44

In *Goodbye Britannia* (2021), Sylvie Bermann, former French ambassador to the UK, commented that Britain was psychologically stuck in the patriotic discourse of the 1940s. Without retorting with the *Simpsons* skit about French 'surrender monkeys', we can recognise that there *was* indeed a paradigm shift in the UK from 1939. Workers were about to experience *agency* in their war contributions and social-democratic safety-nets in workers' lives.

Government war necessities were accompanied by popular yearnings for updated communitarian structures after the interwar class and North v South divide, as well as the fragmentation of civil society.

In the necessary conditions for a cohesive society, a moral project was possible: shared values, genuine equalities, inclusivity; stabilisation through a national endeavour and not just market-based incentives. By 1945, the state was no longer to be a business of market exchange based on cost-benefit analysis but one about the *whole* nation's welfare. This outlook re-emerged in the populace during the 2020s pandemic (see chapter 10) and reminds us that questions of life and death, and civic duty, were at the forefront of people's minds in 1939–45. In this chapter, we will question to what extent Britain existed to protect the Empire, democracy and workers' rights, and what was prioritised. We assess the impact of TCs as the country developed a centrally controlled war economy for national survival and provide evidence that confirms Kenneth O. Morgan's verdict that the British class system itself was not fundamentally transformed during the war years.[251]

*

When war was declared in September 1939, some TCs suspended meetings in the mistaken assumption that they were forbidden. Co-ordination in unionism on wartime essentials soon caused a resumption. The Military Service Acts, war relief funds and welfare of armed forces' dependents stimulated TC vigilance committee work.[252] Coping with the bombings became a TC prerogative, although Sheffield T&LC's president exemplified TCs' anti-fascism and *distrust of the Establishment*:

> The international tragedy has at last broken forth upon the world, thanks to the folly and class prejudice of capitalist politicians throughout Europe. The criminal Nazi regime has been strengthened in the past and millions of innocent people are today paying the price of the policy of their governments.[253]

Meetings in TCs turned to the immediate issues to be dealt with: evacuation arrangements, rising costs of living, and the problem of food distribution. The TUC harnessed all TCs to the war effort and invited them to nominate members for food control committees,[254] but TC wariness towards government strategies did not suddenly diminish. Edinburgh TC EC expressed this criticism of Conservatives and imperialists who had, overnight, become enthusiasts for democracy and liberty after years of condoning fascist aggressions, now alarmed at fascist challenges to their own authority. Nevertheless, all TCs were now supervising conditions in local industries that were reverting to war production, with TC representations to local authorities for provisions for evacuees.[255]

Sheffield's T&LC accentuated the centrality of defending civil liberties, given the memories of 1914–18:

> It is imperative that our political and industrial organisations should be maintained and strengthened. The experiences of the last war demonstrated their inestimable value and they stand as a bulwark against

injustice, profiteering and the attempts of unscrupulous elements in our midst to attack our liberties and living conditions.[256]

TCs' representation on local committees burgeoned as they faced their own 'war on two fronts': mobilising resources *and* defending workers' standards. This required improving ARP and shelterers' sanitation, aiding evacuees, campaigning for women defence workers to be paid the same as men, and being cognisant of the accretion of government emergency regulations, particularly objecting to the Emergency Powers Act, which gave the government *carte blanche* on regulations.[257] Birmingham TC's secretary commented on the tragic mistakes of British diplomacy in the 1930s, while offering wild, unsubstantiated conclusions:

We are cursed with our own would-be dictators who seek to regiment us under the cover of National Emergency… who are ready to adopt fascist or Nazi methods in dealing with the workers.[258]

This was not how union leaders enjoined TCs to respond. They could, however, endorse Manchester & Salford TC's evaluation that war difficulties over food production were exacerbated by private land ownership, as the trade union movement was now being perceived to be a 'civil service' boosting war production.[259] This did not inhibit TCs expressing disapproval when workers were compelled to do 12 hours' *voluntary* duty per week to secure employers' property! However, the TUC General Council had little trouble justifying its new national role and announced conferences arranged with TC federations on 'Trade Unionism During War'[260] as TCs' seats on Citizens' Advice Bureaux gave them a new status. Prompted by their new tasks, TCs structured demands for joint production committees (JPCs) with union rights guaranteed, and government control of industries associated with war materials, placing contracts with firms that employed union labour. TCs voiced apprehension that safeguarding workers' conditions was taking second place to military and industrial conscription.[261] One result of this was for a significant group of TCs seeking advice from the CP's Labour Research Department (LRD) and National Council for Civil Liberties (NCCL) for help on wartime defence regulations and pay negotiations.

Union leaders were questioned by TCs because, with mobilisation of the workforce, unions were pressured by employers and the government to meet specific production targets. Not only that; they were supposed to educate civilians into a patriotic brand of citizenship.[262] Notions of the common efforts of the people (a rhetoric of unity) did not reduce TCs' resentments about unequal food supplies' distribution or inadequate bomb shelters. Further strictures were imposed by the TUC for the sake of 'national unity', prompting the Darlington TC delegate to remark: '*The Trades Council movement was the father of the TUC and the baby was getting a bit unwieldy*'.[263]

The TUC assented to the government's directive preventing strikes, the TCJCC's E.H. Parker in July 1940 bluntly announcing that the ACTC was not the place for academic discussions about capitalism: 'their job was to stand… with the General Council'. The national mood had transmogrified, illustrated by Camberwell's TC chairman, charged under the Sedition Act (for talking politics to a soldier), serving a three-month prison sentence. Should TCs not mention massive profits being made by monopolies and cartels? (Not during a war, apparently.) On recruitment, Birmingham TC's C.G. Spragg estimated that, of 14 million employed, only 5 million were in unions: 'To remedy this was one of the functions of the trades councils'.[264]

*

The TCJCC had not relinquished any supervision of TCs and hounding associations with 'disruptive bodies' remained high on the agenda. Those culpable (for example, Hendon, Enfield, Watford and Mexborough TCs) were reprimanded, while the majority of TCs prioritised patriotism and national loyalty above anything else. Manchester & Salford TC's president expressed the mood as it proclaimed that all TCs should support the TUC General Council:

> If we believe in Democracy, we will loyally carry out the carefully considered decisions arrived at and help to bring about that Unity... we are all in the front line and the result of this international conflict against the powers of Darkness and Despair depends upon the workers of this and all freedom-loving nations.[265]

London TC added that workers' representatives on committees should not be 'hand-picked yes-men chosen by the management'.[266] Throughout the war, TCs retained and professed the notion that private ownership of industry handicapped war production, and TCs were cognisant of government wages policy relying upon union leaders' *moderating* influence.

Nothing was more valued in the trade union movement than *loyalty*. E.H. Parker insisted:

> When a well-organised Trades Council like Bristol, with a tradition of well over 60 years, appeals year after year for loyalty from its affiliated societies, it is unfair if those concerned do not respond... in such branches there has sprung up a feeling of direct antagonism to... the official policy of the trades union movement. This has the effect of undermining Comradeship.[267]

Any hesitations or conflicting views on loyalty and comradeship ended after the German invasion of the Soviet Union in 1941, as almost all British workers rallied behind the war.[268] Internal divisions in the CP evaporated, literally overnight, communists in TCs becoming militant advocates to 'win the war' now that the supposed workers' state was under attack. Regardless of this astonishing *volte face*, at the 1941 ACTC, G. Gibson was adamant that the bulk of unionists ('the solid, loyal body') were not accurately represented by delegates; it was easy for something to be designated 'policy' at a branch meeting that would never be adopted on a referendum. For Gibson, *production* was the number one priority and TCs must focus on that.

Nevertheless, under wartime conditions and after a generation of TC resolutions, the TUC was prepared to welcome fraternal delegates at Congress from TCs because, 'in the event of invasion', communication between HQ and local organisations might be disrupted. Less than half the union membership was connected to TCs, which were now planning 'to aid our Russian comrades in their heroic resistance to Hitler and his hordes [because] Russia's fight is our fight, Russia's victory will be our victory'.[269] TCs now interpreted JPCs as a vital new centre of the war effort (see Brighton TC), a new designation for TCs suggested by Birmingham TC's C.G. Spragg: 'Trades Councils as Watch-Dogs': 'The Chamber of Commerce of the industrial wing'.[270] TCs for Spragg were the local guardians of social legislation and 'forcing ground' for future industrial legislation with 'continuous organising', the proviso not to usurp local Labour Party functions. A suitably patriotic view came from T.W. Smith of Dover TC: 'Do your damnedest to ensure the highest possible turnout of tanks, planes and guns and so ensure a victory which the workers can claim as their own'.[271]

To TCs, future nationalisation of industries was essential since JPCs' terms of reference covered discussion at every level to improve production. Now, for the first time since 1917–18, a smidgeon of 'workers' control' appeared on the horizon.[272] Co-operation in production was reflected in conferences convened by Manchester & Salford TC and Glasgow TC in January 1942, but, contrary to TCs' estimation, JPCs inhibited and restrained wage demands at the same time as TC delegates enjoyed a new status on committees:

> We have been invited to serve on many important bodies… showing our ability as a movement to be

capable of producing men and women who can and are prepared to shoulder heavier responsibilities with civic pride and dignity.[273]

TCs urged the government to requisition property and wealth immediately in the national interest. This was echoed at the ACTC 1942, where methods associated with Stakhanovism (rewarding maximum productivity) were advocated with the aspiration that workers could have a greater share in the management of industries. In practice, the TUC bypassed TCs when it established war emergency committees[274] (to act for the movement in the event of invasion). It would not transfer the right of nomination from unions to TCs, who continued to raise the crucial question whether post-war economic reconstruction could be left to private enterprise.

TCs were also frustrated at the procrastination over the promise of repealing the TD&TU Act, union rights having been surrendered in labour conscription.[275] London TC at this time denounced as 'fascist' a statement by 200 industrialists calling for a halt to the rationing of fuel.[276] There was not yet any sign of a production plan, and TCs' initiatives were not appreciated by TUC leaders. As Birmingham TC formed a production liaison committee in August 1942, the TCJCC insisted this was a matter for unions, not TCs.

At least, regulating women's hours on fire-watching (Birmingham, London, Manchester, Brighton and Sheffield TCs)[277] was endorsed by the TUC. Apart from that, TCs had little influence on the government's national wartime policies. War defence exigencies necessitated TCs on local committees but they were carefully scrutinised and monitored, and were not to transgress union prerogatives. If TCs strayed from their allotted role, a letter of complaint would be made to the TUC and the trespasser sent a reminder of lines not to be crossed. The TUC General Council warned that, in view of employers' weariness, any TC that helped to form Joint Works Production Committees was in fact trespassing on unions' purview. Alternatively, by October 1942, the London TC secretary was voicing exasperation that, in the cause of national unity, the TUC was 'giving way' to the government on every issue; the rationing scheme for the coal crisis had been withdrawn, directly from a vested interest, in the name of 'national unity'. The London TC secretary informed TC delegates of the worst possible scenario and 'not to put their socialist principles in cold storage because of the war, because they had to prevent the reactionaries in the capitalist world from driving us down to the level of slaves'.[278]

This undercurrent of wariness at the incorporation of union leaders was not confined to CP delegates. Numerous TCs condemned the TUC chairman when he projected an all-inclusive anti-German sentiment; delegates spoke instead of future co-operation between German and Allied workers 'to establish a socialist Europe'. In fact, Birmingham TC characterised anti-German sentiment as 'race hatred' and deduced that capitalist interests distracted workers from the economic chaos that had produced Hitlerism and the war. This TC even sent fraternal greetings to anti-Nazis in Germany, for 'the common people's peace which only Socialism can realise'; a lonely view in wartime Britain.[279]

Following TCs' local anti-fascist stance throughout

the 1930s, TCs exhibited pro-Sovietism from 1941, and compared TUC leaders' ensconced at the high table of government with:

> the tremendous force created by a free people in the only country controlled by the workers which victoriously held the fascist hordes and rolled them back with terrifying losses after the fascists had swept through Europe'. (Birmingham TC)[280]

Aspirations emerged in Sheffield T&LC:

> There appears a glimmer of light on the distant horizon; it is as yet faint in the dark leaden skies… but nevertheless it heralds a new era for mankind… Let there be peace… Yes, the clash of material arms will cease but this time we must not sheathe the sword of justice until every vestige of class distinction has vanished from our midst.[281]

As the Soviet Union was thought to be a workers' model abroad, the Beveridge Report on social security symbolised TCs' egalitarianism at home. They had campaigned for decades for a safety-net and for state collectivism in economic and social affairs, and the report presaged a minimum level of security for all.[282] TC aspirations for class distinctions 'being removed' or the existing order being 'doomed'[283] were not yet realisable. Writing in 1943, philosopher Bertrand Russell opined that the success of socialism, at this time of war and dictatorship, was an ideal as distant as the return of Christ![284] Yet Southampton TC's vision of 'planning a world for all nations to live in security and peace without fear or want'[285] resonated throughout TCs. Such inspiration sustained members when working overtime on civil defence duties and voluntary union recruitment activities. More conventionally, J. Marchbank posited that 'A Trades Council which could not find enough industrial questions to fill its agenda must be neglecting its job.'[286]

In wartime, visions of a classless future, whatever that encompassed, were deferred, while TCs' experience and knowledge of factories and workshops, and as centres of education in the principles of public service, were highly valued. For the TCJCC and the TUC, TC membership implied being a good committee person, with 'sound judgement, courtesy, common-sense, lack of bias, and a knowledge of the world.'[287] As for Civil Service Association problems, TCs were instructed not to bother: the priority for TC personnel was to be 'heavily engaged in war-work of every kind.'[288]

London TC continued to state that this was not only a war to defeat Nazism; it was the opportunity to remove 'inequalities in Britain' so the TUC should counter the government's 'feeble sporadic attempts to tinker with bits and pieces of reconstruction instead of envisaging a bold and comprehensive plan.'[289] Accordingly, TCs considered reconstruction through housing plans and offered recommendations to local authorities. Before the TUC or national unions encouraged it, TCs were working on local post-war planning committees and were the first to demand war pensions commensurate to the service of those in the Forces. (The disablement pension was then the same as that paid to victims of the 1899–1902 Boer War.) TCs had also been among the first to call for the Second Front, for TD&TU Act repeal, and to oppose conscription of conscientious objectors in the mines.[290] Such TC contributions have been undervalued alongside their consistent anti-fascism in their own towns and cities.

2. POST-WAR RECONSTRUCTION 1944–47

Debates on post-war reconstruction and Beveridgism dominated TCs' gatherings in 1944, more than soldiers' pensions or 'free expression of opinion in the Forces' debates. Beveridge began from the notion of *society* rather than the economy; the state could provide social welfare by legislation, regulation and enforced co-ordination, and J.M. Keynes had theorised economic circumstances in which Beveridge's policies could be applied.[291] TCs were also exercised over bringing Oswald Mosley and other leading fascists to trial, and opposing the secrecy shrouding advisory committees and appointment of JPs. However, a TC deputation to a minister on a national matter would not be tolerated and could only produce 'chaos', according to the TCJCC. Sheffield T&LC highlighted those political and union rights for the Forces 'lest they be filched away from us overnight'.[292] This, when a third of the male working population was in the Forces, war industries had expanded at the expense of civilian food, goods and services, and Whitehall ostensibly controlled labour prices, retail outlets and raw materials.

TCs rejected the idea that the Beveridge Report was just 'a capitalist bribe'.[293] On the contrary, it was a valuable reform and a significant stepping-stone towards an NHS.

For E. Smith, president of Lancashire/Cheshire Federation of TCs, the future role for TCs was a coherent, practical one – to ensure full employment, reduced working hours, new housing estates and community centres, augmenting TCs' utilitarian provision of information on fire-watching and the Home Guard.

In *Trades Councils and Policy*, March 1944, the TUC's General Council claimed to have enhanced TCs' legitimate activities.[294] No TC remarked publicly upon the wartime elevation of union leaders' status, but they expressed their worries in the delay in implementing Beveridge's recommendations. Typical local campaigns proceeded on rents for farmworkers (Salisbury TC), conferences on production (Wolverhampton TC), rationing regulations evasions (Westminster City TC), post-war reconstruction (Brighton & Hove District TC) and mines' nationalisation (Orpington & District TC, and Welwyn Garden City TC).[295]

In popularising the Beveridge Plan, secondary education, the NHS and regenerative housing plans, TCs articulated the sentiments of all local unions. However, they could not join the Socialist Medical Association (SMA) in conferences on industrial health: the TCs' *alter ego* (the TCJCC) argued that industrial health was the TUC's responsibility and prevented the SMA from inviting TCs. When TCs pursued heavier penalties for employers who breached essential work orders (*c.*2,000 workers had been imprisoned under these and no employers had been imprisoned), the TUC's V. Feather responded that it would require unacceptable alterations to the judicial system. In the florid style of the TCJCC's H.N. Harrison, one should instead foresee 'the downfall of the sunless hovel, the lifting up of the stunted child' without that 'narrow, undisciplined, sectarian element'.[296] So, 'academic chatter and idle theories' would be circumvented.

Pre-war TC criticisms of union leaders' strategies had not been forgotten. Now there was a renewed attempt to isolate those TCs who were 'never happy unless they can find something wrong'. For Harrison, a 'normal' TC took up a problem to get it rectified, but a few hoped nobody would rectify it so they could 'trot round to find some other point of grievance'.[297] He depicted such delegates labelling TUC leaders as 'scheming old men or mugs' when TCs' protest against the shelving of the TD&TU Act repeal 'embarrassed' the TUC. The TCs' 'Equal Pay for Equal Work' resolution had been rejected because a royal commission was 'in progress'. On such issues the TCJCC responded directly to TCs such as Hatfield TC, characterised in its dispute on the rural council over a report on its work, condemning them as 'a damned nuisance'.[298]

There had been numerous campaigns for TCs during wartime on the housing situation. Norwich and London TCs queried implications in the Town and Country Planning Bill, which suggested it was designed to protect property interests and burden local authorities' finances. Union leaders were again 'embarrassed' by this, and by TC priorities of future 'democratic control of the NHS' (Portsmouth and Chorley TCs enunciated this view). Housing shortages brought TC recommendations for local councils to use direct labour to recondition all bombed property (Willesden TC and Nottingham & District TC). For London, Birmingham, and Manchester

& Salford TCs, post-war planning was a concomitant of workers' achievements in the war.[299] For those prominent TCs, capitalism had led to mass unemployment, and a democratic planned economy would prevent a repetition. In this, TCs could become the channel through which workers, *shaping their own lives*, could find expression. Comprehensive memoranda had been formulated in TCs on local industry and housing, which did not take the form of blueprints from Whitehall. The participation of TCs' – '*the people on the spot*'[300] – in adapting reconstruction plans to workers' requirements, was part of that process. But union leaders were adamant. In *The TUC in Wartime* (April 1945) they pronounced restrictions and complained that 'It is a foolish waste of time for Trades Councils to seek to duplicate the work done by the Labour Party'.[301]

'Political' activities indulged in by TCs would soon be redefined under the third Labour government. TCs were *ipso facto* an important consideration in the electoral machinery since it was considered their duty to explain what any government would offer union members. Most TCs now worked in co-operation with local Labour parties, some epitomised by the local press as 'socialist-minded and revolutionary'.[302] It is not clear how a 'revolutionary TC' could escape censure by the TUC but the image of the decade for TCs was Manchester & Salford TC's May Day programme, which illustrated a father and two young children walking towards the sun, entitled '*International Socialism*'! In contrast, in Battersea TC, when some delegates advocated a meeting of industrial workers to oppose local Conservatives, the TC majority decided the meeting was 'political' and that the Labour Party must call it. Finally, J. Benstead (TCJCC) admonished TCs: 90% of the ACTC's time was distracted from industrial matters, he wailed, and E.P. Harries (TUC) reiterated that TCs had to 'sell their value' to union branches.[303]

TCs sold their value on their own terms, objecting to the government relinquishing controls over certain factories and arguing that premises should be retained for peacetime production under state control. Factories had been built from workers' taxes so the government should give workers a share in administering them, with essential goods for the many rather than luxuries for the few.[304] Such designs preceded Labour's epoch-making election victory: 'to ensure the elimination for all time of the causes of war and to open up possibilities of creating a world of happy and joyous people.'[305] Such utopian notions were a bold expression of the relief felt by millions who had survived six years of daily fear. TCs were, indeed, brought closer to government than ever before (or since). Elation was expressed by J. Madin of Sheffield T&LC on the reconstruction of the economy, a national health service, new towns, full employment and nationalisation. But, with such objectives, TCs were instructed to avoid 'muddying the waters' by aiding unofficial strikes.

*

Edinburgh T&LC declared the post-war Labour government the most memorable in the world's history, especially for trade unionists. F. Thraves, Sheffield T&LC, espoused TCs' fidelity:

You are entering on the first year in the history of this country when labour is in power in Parliament, and however the Conservative Party with its powerful press and propaganda may endeavour to ridicule and hamper our efforts to build up a new economic system, it will come if WE inside the Party are loyal.[306]

Edinburgh and Sheffield T&LC's veneration was understandable. Seven-tenths of Labour Party funds came from unions. Transformation from privately-owned industries to public corporations would surely bring genuine redistribution of wealth and possibly some form of workers' control of industry. Union leaders now consulted on nationalised industries, TCs in tune with that, Blackpool TUC conference foreseeing TCs taking their place among influential public bodies in cities and towns.[307]

The exhilaration of 1945 has been captured in many histories and temporarily camouflaged tensions between capital and labour. The philosophy of the Labour government was instinctively integrationist, welding legitimate working-class demands onto existing power relations within British capitalism.[308] No TC debated the burgeoning of a centralised state as a threat to egalitarian social formations (until the ACTC 1947). The TUC had been promoting production-boosting exercises as TCs engaged in applying their government's legislation. Overt criticism was anathema:

Every man and woman in industry is responsible for the building up of a sound, planned economy; if we permit sectional interests to divide us and fail to accept our full share of the burden which lays heavy on our nation, then the labours of the early pioneers of our movement will have been in vain; old prejudices and suspicions must give way to reason, sound judgement and a faith in each other.[309]

This was from Sheffield T&LC's annual report for 1946. Echoing E. Bevin's observations on the mid-1930s, Manchester's H.E. Newbold acknowledged TCs now had greater responsibility since they were moving: 'from purely agitational activity into the sphere of administration'.[310] Extended representation on committees helped TCs' prestige blossom and, by May 1946, 27 conferences through TC federations had outlined TUC policy on reconstruction. And, at last, repeal of the TD&TU Act resulted in more unions affiliating to TCs as post-war reconstruction could produce trained, competent unionists to take control of nationalised industries.[311]

However, restrictions pertained. All this came with the proviso that TCs were not to invest in the CP's People's Press Printing Society (PPPS) or the *Daily Worker*: TCs' income was *limited*: always the clincher in arguments. This was clarified in the TUC's *Details of the Method of the Election for the TCJCC*: 'It does not help the representations which the General Council make if it can be pointed out that trades councils have surpluses available for investment in a newspaper competitive with the *Daily Herald*.'[312] TCs were not allowed to ballot on whether they should invest in the PPPS, nor the single transferable vote in elections for the TCJCC (endorsed in three ACTCs). Could they democratically elect their representatives? No. Details of candidates' qualifications would lead to 'undignified window-dressing' (of which union leaders had considerable knowledge!).

According to the trade union leadership, union leaders were no longer on the doorstep; they were on the inside. H.N. Harrison lauded that 'refreshing wind' blowing with TUC policy on reconstruction 'the new blueprint of the new Britain', creating social equality through public ownership, to which he added his traditional call for loyalty and discipline: 'We are no longer petitioning for a place in the counsels of the State, we are the State.' Union leaders were on industrial consultative committees and boards of nationalised industries: 'We are on the threshold of a new society... which will assure a just reward for all those who enrich that society by their labour.'[313] This sounded promising, but in actuality TCs were henceforth peripheral to this decision-making process.

Between 1945 and 1947, one-fifth of the economy was taken into public ownership.[314] However, it would soon transpire that nationalised industries would not in practice radically transform workers' subordinate status, their welfare, the paucity of new housing, slackness in requisitioning empty properties or rent increases for council tenants. Birmingham TC expressed trepidation: 'We do not expect such treatment with a Labour Government in office.'[315] This refrain was mirrored in other TCs. Lambeth TC perceived that here was a Labour government using the state to victimise squatters. Others, such as Wolverhampton TC, were appalled to witness government defence of private property interests. TCs exposed the extensive black market in food distribution in a time of national rationing. A condition for any surge in production for Manchester & Salford and Bristol TCs was the joint consultative machinery, as CP members in TCs objected to production boosting *per se*. H.E. Newbold (Manchester and Salford TC) encapsulated the *zeitgeist*:

> The old Britain of pelf and privilege must go and in its place we must have a planned economy in which the industrial experience and resourcefulness of our organised workers may be drawn upon for more efficient management of industry... We are at the crossroads... free enterprise (so called) with its past record of industrial neglect, badly underpaid workpeople and unemployment... and a socialist policy determined to establish democracy in every part of our industrial life and in co-operation with other countries in Europe where economic planning has been developed, we can produce and exchange the goods to satisfy the urgent needs of our people.[316]

By 1947, public ownership was carried through in the Bank of England, cable and wireless, civil aviation, coal, electricity, and road and rail transport, gas, iron and steel.[317] Yet, the ACTC acknowledged shortages of raw materials were a handicap, denied wage increases caused inflation, and expressed concern that nationalisation processes would overcompensate former owners. Portsmouth TC concluded that workers were capable of organising industries but were 'strangled by bureaucracy'.[318] Debates on the economy highlighted the 'community of interests in the productive process' but contradicted the government's functional divisions between management and labour. Was there unity in the labour movement? There was not.

The main union leaders had no intention of replacing public boards with any form of industrial democracy, let along workers' control.[319] The TUC was relieved that TCs dutifully deplored unofficial strikes, which 'harmed the national economy', and the 'harm' thesis about strikes has not diminished via the mainstream media ever since.[320]

3. REALITY BITES: PROBLEMS WITH A LABOUR GOVERNMENT 1947-50

After the war, more industrial cases were being brought before courts where magistrates had little knowledge of industries (or of workers' lives) and TCs sought to have more say on *who* became a justice of the peace. Now some TCs openly questioned the origins of the price rises and who was making profits. Time to play the 'loyalty' and 'faith' cards: G.W. Thomson (General Council chairman) averred that the solution to economic difficulties depended upon TCs' loyalty, and H.N. Harrison threatened TCs that were encouraging participation in 'unofficial disputes'. For Harrison, setting aside the machinery of joint negotiation showed a lack of faith in union leaders. Industrial negotiation was a skilled job, so 'Is it too much to ask for loyalty to trade union constitutional practice?'[321] A pertinent question as always.

TCs safeguarded workers' interests as a financial crisis and nationwide rationing led to a government programme of pay cuts. Yet the whole TC movement only had one representative at TUC conferences, a delegate with no right to talk or vote (a ceaseless issue). TCs' emerging distrust of the precise representation on nationalised industries' boards was voiced by the Midlands' Federation of Trades Councils in October 1947.[322] TCs were monitoring local food subsidies, price controls on consumer goods, and employers' profits. The TUC response?

This came with *The Registration Scheme for Trades Councils* and a new *Trades Councils' Guide*. Instead of merely being 'recognised by the TUC', 'registration' now indicated a more precise relationship and acceptance of the *Model Rules*.[323] Each TC secretary would have an authorised, personal credential to facilitate contact with representatives of government departments and local authorities. TCs were the centre for the exchange of information with rank-and-file unionists. The *Trades Councils' Guide* strove to fortify TC/TUC relations. It was produced as a response to requests from '*numerous* Trades Councils' (evidence not forthcoming) and was composed of a selection of conference decisions on TCs, their specifically constrained and minimised role and legal proceedings defined. There had been 120 changes in TC secretaryships in 1947, which for the TCJCC proved TCs' 'unreliability'.[324]

The *Registration Scheme* and *Guide* were utilised from 1948 to offset TC dissension from or querying of the government's social and economic policies. As a result of 'several unfortunate experiences', TCs were commanded yet again not to intervene in any industrial dispute without a union's National Executive consent. 'Safeguarding' became the *raison d'etre*. Unions' 'sophisticated negotiating machinery' was perceived as *far* better than all but the largest TCs. If TCs wished to secure a settlement of a dispute between unions, it should not be ventilated at TC meetings.

Union leaders warned of 'grandiose schemes' by delegates 'without the necessary knowledge or background to carry them through successfully'.[325] But was such an approach anything more than a vehicle for marginalising dissent?

TCs were now publicly critiquing the intentions of the 'productivity drive', which was not just about a balance of trade but economic planning by exhortation. A TC delegate who challenged 'wage restraint' was denigrated by H.V. Tewson (TUC general secretary) as a 'sectarian, irresponsible, uninformed, partisan, a threat to the nation's survival'.[326] Such labels echo down the decades. Observing thus, between 1940 and 1948, working in the 'national interest' was a conceit used to justify TUC condemnations of any TCs' industrial actions which might have political implications. Furthermore, some have subsequently concluded that the 'public ownership of industry' was basically a *managerial* revolution with no attempt to restructure the internal organisation of industries, nationalisation, a utilitarian, Fabian concept.[327]

Tewson denied 'irresponsible talk' about the General Council condoning a 'wage freeze': 'The people who use this term... use it for their own purposes', he cryptically retorted.[328] A majority at the ACTC refused to accept his insistence that wages had to 'be controlled' when profits were so high, arguing that, if the country could not afford widespread social services, it could not afford vast military expenditure (a robust perennial).

Relations between the TUC and the rank and file were becoming increasingly strained. The former was not going to ask the government to withdraw any White Paper, given union leaders were enjoying extensive new powers and social distinctions. Union leaders, to overcome productivity problems, were striving to keep Labour in office, and were surprised to experience no rapturous welcome at the ACTC. The mayor of Derby tried to calm the atmosphere: 'management and men must get together and do their best for the old country'. Sir Luke Fawcett's was a conciliatory position: 'Trades Councils were workshops of ideas and centres of action... most suited to give dynamic energy to increased production'.[329] He ignored a TC resolution denouncing the 'warlike attitude of world capitalist interests', and deemed Birmingham TC's conference (to organise public opinion in defence of world peace) as 'trespassing on political territory'.[330] The uncompromising, interventionist CP-style of TC resolutions galled union leaders, and the latter showed little warmth towards a *soupçon* of republican fervour from Deptford TC, which, referencing the huge amounts spent on royal households and estates, insisted those incomes be reduced.[331] Between 1947 and 1951, there were *c.*8,000 unofficial strikes in the newly state-owned companies, a 30% increase in production 1946–48, but no wage increases.[332]

TCs criticising a Labour government was not to be tolerated. In 1948, Stockton & Thornaby TC convened a May Day meeting during which the TC representative challenged the government. The outcome was that 11 TGWU branches affiliated to the TC withdrew their membership on the grounds that TC speeches had to represent union opinion as a whole, not that of a small minority. The TC's conduct had to be 'proper to an agent of Congress'.[333] At the same time, many TC delegates praised Birmingham TC Executive's critique of the TUC, accused of tying the movement to the Anglo-American Joint Council on Production. This critique was, of course, outside 'TCs' brief.'

*

On balance, we can deduce that TCs were at the heart of a war effort that fought simultaneously for maintenance of the Empire *and* democratic values, while civil liberties and workers' rights were being challenged. Prime Minister Churchill was dedicated to retaining the Empire, as the pro-war TC delegates, involved in wartime production, confirmed their investment in democracy to quell the fascist tide. Regardless of the sacrifices and constrictions of war, TCs were resolute and optimistic about the future. In 1948 Manchester & Salford TC's annual report encapsulated that positive message:

> Our workers are becoming more confident of their own potentialities [with] a growing desire to bring about a change from the capitalist form of production for profit to the planned socialist order of society based upon production to satisfy the needs of the people.[334]

In practice, in TCs, a small minority dubbed 'ideologically-motivated sentimentalists',[335] who sought to propel TCs towards socialist outcomes, were being brusquely marginalised. Who were they? What did they want? Would they succeed? We turn to the fascinating intervention in

TCs by the small but influential Communist Party of Great Britain. That industrial *and* political struggle 1920–50 is what we shall explore and investigate in the next three chapters.

PART 2

TRADES COUNCILS AND THE COMMUNIST PARTY

CHAPTER 5

Communism vs. Labourism:
Communists in Trades Councils 1926–39

> CLR James argued that, rather than facilitating the self-organisation of workers, labour unions facilitate their alienation and subjugation, disciplining and punishing workers rather than giving free scope to their political potential.
> ~ David Austin, Philosophy Now, February/March 2022, p46

1. TRADES COUNCILS' READJUSTMENTS 1926–32

Early trade unions in the 19th century had a radical political outlook as a response to being treated as illegal, and as workers' countervailing defence. Post-1926, the new problem affecting TCs was to what extent the unions' role now was to influence the nature of the state.[336] The few communists in the UK tended to dominate the numerous debates and activities in many TCs around Britain because they were conscious of TCs' strategic importance, were driven by a bold vision for TCs, could rally their members with experience in unions, and found in TCs an arena in which to circulate CP views when other platforms were closed, noting that the TUC General Council had no intention to 'challenge the Constitution'. While there is a seed of truth in C.L.R. James's view presented above, the CP, throughout our period, sought to *confront* such strictures in TCs and unions.

CP activities proceeded with instructions to create 'fractions' (CP members) in TCs to offset being constantly under suspicion and scrutiny for 'infiltration'. In July 1926 a Labour Party circular utilised a government *Blue Book of Communist Documents* to expose how the CP fractions and nuclei operated. To this, the Labour Party attached the London District CP instructions to the London TC. Henceforth, claims of 'disruption' would be used to expel communists from unions. R.W. Robson (for the TC and CP London District Committee) was advising fraction leaders whom to elect, what to vote for, and what resolutions to propose at the TC.[337] W. Citrine would not tolerate CP interventions and informed the Bournemouth TUC conference 1926 that instructions to communist delegates were discovered, giving orders as to who should intervene in debates and 'the line' they were to take.[338] In fact the CP was quite transparent about fractions' tasks and tactics, as T. Quelch clarified:

> I especially desire to urge in regard to fraction work, the importance of strong fractions on the TCs. They hold the key positions in the localities as far as the organised working class movement is concerned. They provide a gateway into and a means of influencing all the affiliated organisations.[339]

The British CP, founded on 31 July 1920, and the Chinese Communist Party, founded 23 July 1921, were both inspired by the Bolsheviks of the USSR. The Bolsheviks were a new type of party, revolutionaries who exhibited discipline, organisation and dedicated observance of party rituals, with adherence to the classical traditions of Marxism–Leninism. They had an unshakeable faith ('We are the political party of the working class' – Bukharin) that devotion to the cause would, they hoped, bring victory and justify the party's centralism. Exposing capitalist machinations gave the party 'moral eminence'.[340]

However, years of political and military isolation and civil war, entrenched by a change of leadership, diverted the trajectory of the USSR. With V.I. Lenin's death in 1924, Joseph Stalin led a diversion where 'wreckers' were to be eliminated and gradually the Old Bolsheviks, who had made and sustained the Russian Revolution, were murdered under the pretence they had lost 'faith' or were 'counter-revolutionary'. Meanwhile, in the UK, the British CP channelled its efforts in unions and decided to inject its distinct fervour to re-energise, transform and remodel TCs. In so doing, the CP deliberately set out to challenge the separation of powers in the labour movement (between unions and the Labour Party) and planned to deploy TCs' cohesive union function to tackle societal inequalities. CP attempts to join the Labour Party, on the advice of Lenin, failed every time the CP applied but it seized, in 'Little Moscows' in South Wales, a moment in history. In Chapter 2, Section 2, we explored the CP's burgeoning role in TCs up to and including the General Strike 1926. What came next?

At the post-General Strike Bournemouth conference delegates questioned the General Council's decision not to permit unions to join the National Minority Movement (NMM), a united front in trade unions created by CP members and other leftists who sought to spread radical ideas and activities. (Amongst its members was MFGB leader A.J. Cook.) For A. Conley, representing the General Council, if TCs allowed requests for NMM affiliation, within a short period the Minority Movement might become the Majority Movement![341] This was an outcome many union leaders dreaded. The CP, at its own Congress, characterised Labour and union leaders as 'lacklustre reformists', pointing to the difficulties inducing union officials to work under TCs' guidance, and noting the Labourist tendencies in most TCs. For the CP, contributions in TCs had to be very precisely galvanised: 'Bad fraction work inside TCs would do more to damage the CP than most members realised'.[342] It proposed TCs form Hands-Off China (HoC) Committees (reminiscent of the earlier Hands-Off Russia (HoR) campaign), and the HoC conference organised by London TC attracted 29 TCs; by February 1927 70 HoC Committees had been created, almost solely the result of CP initiatives.

The General Council now reissued the document that required TCs accept TUC authority and ignore NMM links. Some TCs were all prepared to challenge this ruling, when suddenly the CP and NMM accepted it, in order not to be isolated.[343] This demoralised much of the resistance, although Manchester, Glasgow and Sheffield TCs/T&LCs prolonged opposition to the ultimatum. For union leaders generally, industrial action of a political character had been firmly rejected after the General Strike in favour of a Labourist separation of industrial and political spheres of action. In this strategy, NMM and CP influences in TCs were to be shelved.

At the Conference of Trade Union Executives, TUC leaders were aware that the CP blamed the General Council for subsuming the strike weapon within an 'industrial peace' agenda. The TUC in turn was planning a strategy to counter that faith in the politics of class struggle, especially general strikes, drawing 'pragmatic' conclusions about unions' new role following the 1926 defeat. The CP stance on what TCs could offer had not changed. They were to be endorsed as local centres of the workers' struggle *vis-à-vis* TUC strictures, in co-operation with the NUWCM – a CP-led united front dedicated to the challenges faced by the unemployed – and the NMM, part of the CP strategy to revitalise and bolster unions in wage campaigns.[344]

The General Council decision to reject TCs' affiliation to the (N)MM had been in response to identified CP fraction work. In January 1927, an illustration of the CP's tactics in its *Handbook on Local Organisation*[345] disclosed in detail how to organise fractions in T&LCs, how to elect CP officials and how to adjust rules and constitutions. Herbert Morrison had unearthed that bulletin from the London District CP Committee to fraction leaders, which posited: 'Organised fraction work is the keystone to success in the many activities before us in the localities. In particular does this apply to Trades Council and Labour Party work.'[346]

The General Council would not tolerate communists organising in its TCs, and it instructed TCs that unions had the right to refuse affiliation fees to any TC utilising them for NMM affiliation or delegates' expenses to NMM Conferences. Reports from 'several TCs' (as usual, unspecified) had highlighted the difficulties when trying to support official policy. The evidence from and nomenclature of these TCs (or what had transpired) was never produced. The General Council spoke of ample opportunity for the ventilation of opinions; policies could not be the result of what it always labelled 'dictation by any outside and irresponsible organisation', however one defined 'dictation', 'outside' or 'irresponsible'. TCs were instructed (or dictated) to represent 'accredited local union opinion' and refrain from association with so called 'dissident organisations'.[347] Dictation from dissident, irresponsible, outside organisations became the mantra utilised to distance unions and TCs from the CP, NUWM and NMM.

The stumbling block here was that CP members were also obviously unionists at the very time TCs were given this ultimatum. They had until 30 April 1927 to disassociate from the NMM or be expunged from General Council records and disaffiliated from TC federations.[348] For the NMM, H. Pollitt observed that there had actually been no General Council interest in TCs before 1924, whereas the NMM had grasped TCs' potential and sought TC representation on the General Council and 100% union affiliation to TCs. Additionally, Pollitt challenged the General Council to show a single instance where NMM policy had 'injured or retarded the working class movement'. TCs were entitled to propagate any policy or become affiliated to any movement that had for its objective this empowerment. For him, it was the

General Council that was destroying these rights and imposing *its* dictatorship on TCs.[349]

As noted above, the CP sought to retain CP influence in the ACTC or TCJCC, and the NMM agreed to the about-turn (on TC affiliation to the NMM) to prevent the TUC dividing the left.[350] The CP and TUC in this spat illuminated how their positions diverged and manifested themselves over the semantics of 'democracy'. The CP had thus concluded that union leaders had taken the 'undemocratic step' of placing the MM under a ban, threatening to fragment any section of the organised workers who combined,[351] whereas, for TUC leaders, fractions and nuclei had Soviet resonances, the connotations of which were unacceptable in a British context. A further CP circular to its fraction on the London TC included the tactics for a TC meeting on 10 March 1927. This was again reproduced by Morrison to illustrate how non-CP delegates were 'forced to act for the CP'.[352] Morrison ignored the CP allegation that the trade union block vote (workers not consulted on the voting intentions of their representatives) was a tactic deployed by the London Labour Party to suppress the militant London TC. The latter was led by ex-CP member (now virulently anti-CP) A.M. Wall, who was elected by 102 to 82 votes, the NUWCM subsequently being disaffiliated.[353]

The NMM was nurtured in a London Industrial Council with a few TCs attached, although union leaders voiced their suspicions of this organisation. TCs renewed their queries as to the General Council's diktat on any CP members in T&LCs,[354] but by April 1927 196 TCs had signed the declaration for NMM disaffiliation. A. Conley reiterated to ACTC delegates that TCs should not waste time endorsing other organisations. He offered no reply to delegates who estimated that this would weaken TCs' status in workshops or the fact that most active TCs had been affiliated to the NMM. A.M. Wall endorsed Conley's viewpoint: TCs existed through union fees; if unions had no confidence in TCs they would disaffiliate; union work would not be embarrassed by foolish and misguided activities of the 'minoritaires' whose sole function was finding reasons for dissenting.[355]

But the CP did have confidence in TCs and their future – they wanted to further empower them. The CP sought updated versions of councils of action, TCs re-imagining 1920's possibilities, this time to protest against the TD&TU Act via mass demonstrations and connections between TCs and other workers' organisations. In May 1927, the London TC voted to exclude the CP from office (including most of the Executive!) and local TCs that had elected CP members were disaffiliated. Regarding the CP's 'cynical techniques', Wall characterised them as 'cliques that tried to tear the London Trades Council apart'. Subsequently, for Wall, the TC withdrew from a number of 'fancifully-named' organisations and rejected a resolution which doubted and questioned whether the TUC was 'successful' in its industrial negotiations. One of the results of these frictions was London TC's withdrawal from the reception committee for South Wales' Miners. Attempts to associate the London TC with the NMM had, in Wall's opinion, led to 'dislocation and sabotage'. Had it not been for the 'loyalty of unions', the London TC would have been rendered ineffective. For him, the newly created TCs were more representative; the

London TC had re-emerged stronger with these alterations to the rules; fraction work, designed to disrupt unions' policies, would not be tolerated. He justified these changes by using an analogy with the Stalin's Communist Party of the Soviet Union (CPSU) at this time banishing Trotsky for fractional work and 'oppositionist' tactics: 'proof that no party or movement could countenance actions designed to upset majority decisions'. A curious analogy indeed!

At the TUC conference 1927 it transpired that the circular on the NMM had *not* been sent to TCs because of any genuine difficulties over the NMM: only *one* organisation had requested advice. Nine CP delegates were there to hear Herbert Smith express the TUC's perspective, that there was no difference between the Minority Movement and communism as both were trying to 'wreck' the movement. This was based on an experience of a Glasgow TC meeting at 8pm, with the MM grouping at 7pm to determine their actions at the TC: an image of 'scheming'. Weighing in, J.H. Thomas designated it 'humbug or camouflage' to imagine the General Council suppressed *any* minority opinions.[356]

The TCJCC confirmed that it no longer recognised TCs disaffiliated by the Labour Party, nor would it support any Miners' March to London. A.M. Wall disclosed that the NUWM was organising this march and the reception committee included eight CP members. Ironically, the Labour Party's expulsion of 'CP-controlled TCs' (and promotion of rival ones) had resulted in the TUC facing *duplicate* TCs in four London areas (Battersea, Camberwell, Hackney, Bethnal Green). Naturally, the General Council promoted the new Labour Party-endorsed TCs, which

Sam Elsbury (chairman of the expelled Bethnal Green TC) berated as 'scab TCs'.[357] In its *Labour* magazine, the TUC reinforced the purge and, as adjuncts, was revising union constitutions, conducting 'disruption' inquiries, and expelling recalcitrant members. It was beginning to look like a witch-hunt, the intentions and purpose of which were about to be uncovered.

W. Citrine outlined his version of the conflicts for the next generation's debate. Entitled *Democracy or Disruption* (that Manichean polarisation), Citrine vexed over communist activities in unions and the history and tactics of the MM and the RILU. He highlighted the CP's disruptive tendencies and its intentions to capture the trade union movement and exploit it for a 'revolutionary subversive' purpose that required a minority dictatorship based on the 'suppression of popular liberties'. According to Citrine, unionists had been *deluded* into believing the CP member was somehow more militant, honest, resolute, and a better guide than elected representatives; communists were engaging in 'unscrupulous methods, grossest misrepresentation, vilification and imputation of the vilest motives'.[358]

For Citrine, the evolution of trade unions had been an integral part of the economic machinery and should not be turned into an instrument of social upheaval. As such, union leaders' calm judgement, integrity and sincerity had to be deployed to overcome CP 'innuendo, insinuation, dissemination of half-truths, distortion of facts and improper motives'.[359] For him, these 'adventurers' had a crude and faulty understanding of British conditions: their policies alien to traditions of British workers, they were an agency for misrepresentation and distortion of the true aims of unions. He contended that the NMM was undermining union solidarity, fostering suspicion, distrust, discontent, disloyalty, and bypassing majority rule in unions via fractions:

> With their cant phrases, the kindergarten knowledge of history, economics and sociology, the standardised abusive epithets... the meaningless references to "revolutionary situations and united fronts"... The Minority Movement offered fatuous and hair-brained [sic] policies prompted by the "Ring Masters of the Red International" for general strikes.[360]

Citrine's message to TCs for the next generation was contained in this embellished invective. The TUC leadership was to spearhead TCs in counteracting CP 'front' organisations, which for him operated solely to undermine confidence in union executives and officials, capture union posts, and overthrow the social system. The battle-lines had been clarified.

*

In 1928 unity between the established industrial and political wings of the labour movement was formalised: the Labour Party moved into Transport House (E. Bevin's TGWU abode) and Bevin himself became the ace card for trade union leaders smearing 'outsiders' in the workers' movement. The CP deduced that the TUC's function in this was to promote unions as the bulwark of the state; what 'democracy in unions' really meant in practice was the implementation of the interests of 'existing bureaucrats' (the latter a militant's code word for union leaders ever since). The CP now damned the NUGMW and the NATSOPA, which refused to allow any branch to belong to a TC that had connections with the NMM, as 'bureaucrats'. Accordingly, for the CP, TCs were being transformed into hunting grounds for 'careerists and political opportunists' (always damning indictments) and were being prevented from deployment as 'weapons of struggle'.[361] TCs, instead, were being used to oppose miners' marches and to form unemployed associations (UAs) to compete with the NUWCM, with TCs reduced to mere cogs in the TUC's bureaucratic machinery: 'The Model Rules made Trades Councils unpaid maids-of-all-work doing odd jobs as routine distribution channels of General Council propaganda.'[362]

W. Citrine's furious rebuke laid down markers for the Mond–Turner industrial negotiations. For the NMM, it was these negotiations that showed 'the bankruptcy of reformist leadership'. It is vital to add here that, from 1928, the CP's Third Period, the CP critiqued union officials and labour leaders as 'social fascists', with the TUC's 'pro-capitalist policy of the bureaucrats' hampering TCs.[363] 'Right opportunist deviations' included TCs that were no longer exposing reformist illusions nor union bureaucracy but becoming part of the capitalist apparatus. It is also worth noting at this juncture that CP membership was fluctuating dramatically. Between September 1927 and January 1929 it fell from 7,377 to 3,500, it then increased from 6,279 in November 1931 to *c*.9,000 by mid-1932 (before reaching 15,570 in 1938).[364]

The Mond–Turner talks had implications for all TCs in terms of union recognition, victimisation, rationalisation, and new industrial relations' machinery. This was exemplified in Birmingham TC's conciliation with employers and proscription of the League Against Imperialism and Friends of the Soviet Union.[365] In April 1929, TCs were also sent General Council stipulations about 'breakaway unions'. These were dubbed part of a 'wrecking campaign' fomenting discord and disloyalty in unions with 'calumny and misrepresentation'.[366] In response, the CP's espousal of the NMM as an alternative industrial base encouraged TCs not to be part of the 'sell-out'.[367] Significantly, at the time, a General Council poll on CP disruption found that, of 124 unions, 92 reported 'no disruptive elements',[368] as the new *Daily Worker* in 1930 honed in on 'pseudo-Lefts', Labour's deceptions and union bureaucrats.

*

J. McDonald in *Trades Councils* (1930) provided an analysis of TCs' potential development to administer in their localities as 'the parliament of organised wage-labour'. For McDonald, the c.500 TCs' had the potential to offer a genuine *alternative* to the municipal council as a political institution of union representatives.[369] This notion of TCs as alternatives to county councils and civic authorities had surprisingly little appeal in TCs, which did not run strikes, pay benefits or negotiate with employers, and did not duplicate local Labour parties.

Following McDonald, A.A. Purcell in *The Trades Councils and the Local Working Class Movement* (December

1930) spoke of an 'ideal TC' with political, industrial, co-operative and educational departments. He celebrated TCs as a united working class, rather than simply affiliated branches and municipal electioneering. TCs could be the leading local organ of the working class, the concentration point of *all* local power, incorporating workers' clubs, sports and drama societies: 'freeing the workers from the thraldom of capitalist influence'.[370] As it was, in 1930 TCs were a long way from being the guardians of class interests even if they could revive the demonstration habit, which serving CP members in TCs endorsed, in resistance to wage cuts, support for hunger marches, and anti-fascist protests.

Attitudes towards the CP always varied amongst TCs. In 1931 we can witness Birmingham TC's non-association with the NUWM (because 'it was a subsidiary of the CP')[371] and at the same time Brighton TC receiving an NUWM deputation for TC affiliation, the NUWM justifying its links with the MM since union officials 'thought more of the bosses than their own members'. Of the 200 local NUWM members in Brighton, only six were CP members, and, although several NUWM resolutions received TC endorsement, TCs had no authority to prevent Means Test inquisitions.[372] In Sheffield T&LC, Secretary F. Thraves ruled that unionists lending credence to the CP at municipal and parliamentary elections were unacceptable as TC delegates: 'The time has arrived when Labour must clear them out from positions in the counsels of the [Labour] party'.[373] Curiously and paradoxically, TCs displayed warmth towards Stalin's Five-Year Plan for the USSR while simultaneously excluding members of the CP at home. However, there arose another major consideration for TCs to grapple with: unemployment had doubled to 2.7 million, and, according to Clement Attlee, Labour had witnessed Ramsay MacDonald's 'greatest betrayal in the political history of this country'.

2. THE UNITED FRONT AND TUC CIRCULARS 1933-39

As intimated, TCs' annual reports for 1933 welcomed the Soviet Five-Year Plan, and also commented on the rise of fascism in the UK that had to be opposed – not admired, as delineated in some Conservative aristocratic circles. The London TC criticised the government for not developing relations with the USSR and for its embargo on Soviet trade. In March arrived the General Council's *The Communist Solar System* with the assumed nightmare of 'communists in disguise' embedded in the Labour Party and union branches. This pertained to the CP disclosing confidential information, discrediting union officials, intervening in disputes, preventing settlements and tampering with union officials' elections. In June 1933, the National Joint Council (TUC, LP, PLP) issued the notorious *Circular 124: Communist and Other Organisations*. Romford, Woolwich and West Ham TCs had apparently 'gone Communist'. T.E. Eaton, Sheffield T&LC, was furious:

> These people were permitted to come to our monthly meetings, which in many instances resembled a Tower of Babel, with Bedlam thrown in. They were thus enabled to become fully conversant with every detail of business and policy of the Trades Council… Instead of treating the business of the Trades Council as being in Committee, they were broadcast to the world at large, at

the Street Corner and in the pages of the *Daily Worker*. Everything possible was done to damage the prestige of the TC and to stultify its every effort.[374]

Political conflict between the communists and the right was now played out in TCs. Manchester & Salford TC had a demonstration for international solidarity and a campaign against war and fascism in July, and after a recent visit to Russia, A.A. Purcell reported back on the 'powerful socialist dynamic' revitalising everything; Russia had energy, ideas, plans and constructive work, he insisted, in contrast to 'those sabotage experts who sit in the office chairs in the union and Labour Party headquarters'.[375] But at the TUC conference in Brighton the trade union leadership was equating fascist with communist dictatorships, warning TCs that communism stood for a dictatorship just as ruthless to minority opinion as fascism, hallmarks of W. Citrine's previous compositions all over this document.

Then came the Seventh Congress of the Comintern (CI), the international organisation linking communist parties across the world. This, the CP held aloft as the best anti-fascist organisation, but in the UK their 'United Front', including CP members in TCs, made little headway. R. Pennifold of Brighton TC pleaded with the TUC to encourage United Front committees (UFCs) against fascism. This TC joined a local UFC, only to withdraw when union branches objected.

Likewise, in Manchester, the CP failed to persuade the TC to include CP members yet the CP recorded great success in Bradford, where the local TC had its union recruiting week and CP unionists offered their services.

The president of Bradford Transport Workers endorsed the United Front in the TC, and, from having one CP member, eight were elected. The TC overrode the General Council's boycott of the anti-war movement and sent a delegate to the London anti-war demonstration. CP members on the TC convinced the TC that the local NUWM should front the TC's unemployed organisation.[376]

On 19 October 1933 a headline blazed: 'Unions May Link up with Reds and ILP – Trades Council Alliance Move – Big Majority in Favour',[377] announcing Manchester & Salford TC's proposed alliance with the local CP and ILP, a left wing faction in the Labour Party. The TC's approach, boldly announcing that it was only antagonistic to the city council because the latter's purpose was 'capitalist administration', leading to a joint committee with 'the sincere revolutionary elements', the CP's Central Committee convinced that influence and work in the TC would revive the CP.[378]

A reassessment of TCs' functions required a flexible CP approach, with less demonising of 'reformist' TCs and their presumed restricted absorption in parochial issues. The CP now acknowledged union participation as the best working-class experience; new union comrades could introduce some wholesome proletarian efficiency into the party, 'a mélange of the Russian spirit of revolutionary zeal and the Americans' business-like practicality.'[379] In the Fairdale workers' strike in East London, CP members on two of the three TCs were able to call a conference within a week to create solidarity, while CP activity was divided into 'fronts' so they could 'go underground' if the CP was made illegal (as happened with the ban on the *Daily Worker* from

1940). CP fractions re-emerged in TCs, with the Labour Party and TUC detecting 'the Communist snake in the thick herbage of Pacifist propaganda'.[380] TCs were divided over whether it was poisonous, or to whom.

Prompted by 'disruptive actions' by CP delegates, Southampton TC compelled Hampshire Federation to insert into their rulebook 'the ineligibility of Communist or Fascist to trades councils'[381] and the TCJCC denounced Bradford, Barrow and Deptford & Greenwich TCs for associating with certain minority organisations.

Circular 120: Communist and Other Bodies[382] disclosed the proscribed CP 'front' groups, instructing TCs not to dissipate time, energy and union money on them. Debates swirled around TCs on this *Circular 120*. Some Southampton TC delegates objected to denunciation of organisations named in the circular. R. Chick (secretary of the TC) relayed to the General Council that their meeting had 40% CP representation; applying the circular might end with the TC losing its recognition. Echoing Chick, Alderman Lewis worried about disbandment: 'because CP members did not adhere to principles any longer than might suit their convenience.'[383] TC officials used the TUC arguments about 'dictatorship' including the erroneous notion that 'nothing was helping fascism… more than the Communist movement, whose isolation and militancy gave fascists an excuse for violence.'[384] In actuality, the United Front was established to isolate fascists, but the vote was 49 to 12 to apply the circular.

In Bradford TC, which had a delegate at the Bermondsey United Front conference that proved pivotal to a demonstration with Bradford Labour Party, CP, ILP,

NUWM and UA, the circular was taken as a disservice to all unions; the General Council would be better employed warning workers about the *real* dangers from capitalism and fascism. However, when Oxford T&LC adopted an ex-fascist in the municipal election, E.P. Harries for the TUC deduced: 'It shows that the contention is right that the psychology of Communists and Fascists are identical.' (Whatever that supposed mutual psychology, BUF membership in 1934 was *c*.40,000).[385]

At Brighton TC the circular arrived at the same time as the 'Friends of the Soviet Union' invited TC delegates to a conference in London! At this conference, eight branches opposed the circular, nine supported it and the resolution was passed 10 to seven for the circular's implementation. An amendment, that delegates were industrial representatives and *not* concerned with shades of politics, was lost by 11 to eight, the TC president being forced to resign.[386]

Communists had some authoritarian tendencies but they were not fascists. The CP had a vision of something far more progressive (particularly leading up to the general strike). Equating communists with fascists was in 1930s Britain an insult to enthusiastic unionists in TCs.

Understandably, *Circular 120* received mixed responses. Deptford & Greenwich TC refused to endorse it and, as a result, in August 1934, was disaffiliated. Sheffield T&LC reprimanded a delegate's 'CP line' but this was resolved on the grounds that TCs could not bar delegates just because they had a different opinion to the Labour Party. Birmingham, Glasgow, Leeds, Bradford and Manchester & Salford all acknowledged that CP numbers in their TCs had increased, London and Tyneside TCs noting a lessening of CP activities in theirs.

At the ACTC 1934, TCs' association with the United Front was challenged and counteracted. Anecdotes about 'disturbances by CP members' at TC meetings were reheated and regurgitated. The TCJCC again welcomed union branches who had refused credential cards to CP and NMM members. It required only one TC to report CP 'interference' to legitimise a ruling applicable to all. Given the platform, delegates eagerly regaled the grievances they had against the CP, the 'sabotage' and even the CI's 'iron discipline'.[387] R. Chick reiterated his disapproval of the local CP tactics of *interruptions* as A.M. Wall recalled how the London TC had assisted in a demonstration against the Incitement Bill, although the CP 'infiltrated' it. Further appeals to TCs to ban CP members were extended at the Weymouth TUC conference. Keenness to malign the CP was high on the agenda, Deptford & Greenwich TC's president relating how TC delegates represented their own political interests, and, with the TC disbanded, all its valuable work had stagnated.

The TUC and CP would never be reconciled. Unlike TCs in 2020s Britain, where trade union political conflicts are explored through the dialectics of debate, in the 1930s TUC and CP delegates were diametrically opposed to each other's organisations – and neither would compromise. TUC leaders could be vitriolic. W. Citrine later fulminated: 'With whom are we in the trade union movement asked to unite? A few dozen Communists who are telling the workers to place no confidence in the movement?'[388] And E. Bevin inveighed: 'If you do not keep down the Communists, you cannot keep down the Fascists.'[389] Meanwhile the CP helped foster discord between TC members and the TUC, convinced that reformist leaders' policies would *lead* to fascism, an inaccurate comprehension of union leaders' remit and without any historical basis. The CP equation of the TUC/Labour 'alliance with monopoly capital and Fascism' was an association as dismally unilluminating as the TUC's 'dictatorship equals communism'. R.P. Dutt's (CP) crude designation of union leaders as 'social fascists'[390] was incomprehensible to most TC members. Consequently, by October 1934, only 10 TCs were campaigning for the CP's (post-sectarian) United Front (Manchester, Bradford, Coventry and Barrow TCs particularly keen).[391]

The trade union leadership were unsparing in their war on the CP. A. Conley (TUC) asserted that 'disruptive tactics' only arose at conference when communists were sent from unions, so alteration of the rules was necessary if they were not to witness 'Communist influence more and more interfering with the TCs'. He added that TCs should make sure *no* communist was appointed to *any* office. J. Marchbank concurred; he reiterated that the only definitive solution was to debar CP members from occupying any position. Likewise, C. Dukes saw no difficulty in excluding any person who had 'disruptive purposes', however defined. He had experienced 'clearing CP members out', closing down branches and replacing them by 'good men' (there were few women unionists then.). Expel members when they followed 'Communist policy', stated A. Pugh, and, for Beard, any TC that included CP members or fascists should be disaffiliated.[392]

In October 1934, *Circular 16* had a huge impact on all TCs, yet it was surprisingly vague. 'Certain localities' reported 'disruptive elements' rendering the work of TCs more difficult; union delegates had avoided TC meetings because they refused endless discussions hindering the practical work of unionism and impairing the efficiency of the TC. One 'large TC' had participated with the CP in a united front in spite of a vote of more than two to one against; 'in some instances', delegates pursuing 'subversive tactics' were representing their own view on the TC and not reflecting union branches. Eventually though, *Circular 16* brought acceptances from 353 TCs, 80 did not reply, 11 dissented, but this ban was never fully implemented. While hunger marches against unemployment were encouraged by some TCs (against the advice of the Labour Party and TUC), enough TCs maintained that union leaders had been deluged with CP invective and abuse. The circular was not a 'knockout blow to communism' but tamed TCs, apart from muted protests that industrial delegates were entitled to discuss any politics which concerned industries.

*

In the TUC files for January 1935 there is a curiosity: the Reverend T.J. Fitzgerald's 'The Decline of Communism in Great Britain' in *Clergy Review*. It concludes:

> From time to time certain people with superficial minds cast aspersions and innuendoes on the integrity of union officials because of their apparent comfort and prosperity. No crueller libel could be uttered

against a body of honourable and devoted servants of the working class. The union movement opened up to workers of talent and ability, opportunities of combining honourable and lucrative careers with service to their comrades: thus, from the point of view of capturing unionism, the Communist offensive had lamentably failed.[393]

Failure is a damning judgement by the Reverend, but the communists in the UK were certainly rebutted.

The Scottish TUC General Council produced its statement on the United Front for Scottish TCs in February 1935. It claimed that the stability of TCs would be prejudiced by association with CP organisations, and the local expression of union policy and practice would cease. 'Well-disciplined and logical action without the suppression of individual opinion'[394] was the theme, updating TCs' *Model Rules and Constitution*, about no TCs co-operating with communist or fascist parties, or subsidiaries.[395] A frequently voiced query was: shouldn't unions and TCs have local autonomy? And wouldn't TCs' enforcement of instructions mean the withdrawal of branches as a protest against interference with what were *their own domestic affairs*?

Not troubled by communists as such, most TCs expressed resentment towards interference with the right of delegates' selection by union branches. A centralised authority was curbing their democratic freedom. Some TCs voiced the opinion that such circulars should allow them to form the 'right conclusions'. As A.E. Hobson (Sheffield T&LC) pondered: 'why worry because we have a few Judases in our ranks?'[396] The idea that TC members affected by the CP were dissipating energies was projected to divert attention from any united front fusing TC delegates and communists.

The complex practicalities of establishing such a policy emerged in Hackney TC (which had been re-formed in 1926–27). Initially the TC had been wary of CP members but then the united front gained ground because CP members had 'proved themselves' and had organised non-union factories, briefed speakers, and vigorously campaigned for strikers and the unemployed. 'Down with the National Government' was a slogan to which all sections of the TC subscribed.[397] CP members might disrupt TC meetings, but they were in the forefront building unions, gaining concessions from employers, and, in recruiting campaigns, were highly valued.

By 10 January 1935, 53 TCs had accepted *Circular 16*. Oxford, Bradford, Cowes, St Albans and Wood Green TCs were among those who in fact refused to operate it; while Wood Green TC's connections with NUWM local branches and 'Friends of Soviet Russia' groups led to disaffiliation. TCs requested that any disaffiliations be carried through unions and not TCs (as in Birmingham, Bristol, Yorkshire Federation, Manchester and Newcastle Staffs), while Wolverhampton, Barrow, Coventry, Leicester and Lincoln opposed any united fronts. (Brighouse and Runcorn TCs reported no disruptive influences and resented the circular.)[398] At the Thirteenth Congress of the CP in February 1935, sectarianism was theoretically abandoned; TCs were reconsidered and hailed as *the* centres of working-class life and struggle. All those prohibitions had reinvigorated CP interest in TCs' work. Its members were now back on board, remotivated and intending to get onto TC ECs, to enliven them.[399]

From March 1935, the TCJCC, pursuing TCs over *Circular 16*, refused them credentials to the ACTC if they did not reply. By now, Brighton, Bristol, Hackney, Ipswich, Leeds, Liverpool, Newcastle, Sheffield and Southampton were in the 179 for the ruling, Bradford and Oxford TCs in the 12 opposing, with Birmingham and Manchester & Salford TCs noting the unions' prerogative for delegates to be with whatever party they wished.[400] By April, 232 TCs had signified tacit support, only seven TCs officially refusing, while the CP remained angered by continued 'heresy hunting' and union leaders 'acting at the behest of the ruling class', typical of the 'bankrupt ideas' of TUC leaders. By May it had become apparent that, regarding CP work in TCs, the circulars had been a setback for any united front, and this made it difficult for the CP to reach out to Labour Party members on the TC. To transfer CP activities into factories might as contemplated before prove more fruitful.[401]

The General Council opposed the United Front when the NUWCM and the NMM were using such tactical platforms to rally opinion contrary to TUC policy, provoking TCs with affiliations to the League against Imperialism, Friends of the Soviet Union, International Labour Defence and the anti-war movement. In the TUC's *General Council Action Against Disruptive Bodies* in May 1935, E.P. Harries egregiously stated that communists were 'out to smash social democratic organisations'.[402] Numerous 'complaints' from (an unspecified number of) TCs had insinuated that, owing to the *apathy* of branch members, CP delegates were increasing, and, regardless of the circular, were indulging in more 'interminable discussions' on foreign affairs, which prevented TCs' central business. 288 TCs were now in agreement with the circular. Ten TCs opposed, and many remained affiliated to the LRD.[403]

At the ACTC 1935, the *'Communist and Other Bodies' Circular 120* was discussed. The NCL rejected a united front with the CP against fascism and war. The circulars had, it was announced, recorded TCs' 'overwhelming acceptance', even if *Circular 16* had resulted in the loss of active TC members. C. Dukes maintained that TCs were still being used as 'a dumping ground for a peculiar form of propaganda',[404] with CP and NMM delegates waiting until a meeting thinned out before forcing through policy which they knew was opposed by unions or the TUC. Yet, a number of TC delegates, even those who abhorred CP tactics, disliked the implementation of *Circular 16* because it depleted TCs' rights, and policies needed to be challenged to get the best results.

At each ACTC from 1935 to 1942 TCs accepted the rubric that, if they did not counteract disruptions, union branches would become a secondary consideration and the CP would take the initiative. TCs were invited to consider if it was unfair to ask branches to pay fees only to discover that delegates did not represent branch policy, but attended with specific instructions from the CP. There were oxymoronic repercussions, as John Sheffield in the June 1935 *The Socialist Leaguer* chided readers:

> to ban certain members from office because of their politics is the most dangerous step trade unionists can take... To impose political qualifications on members

as a condition of office is to transform the trade unions into political parties. That is a violation of their purpose and function.[405]

(Few would disagree with such progressive pluralism; banning fascists – who wish to destroy working-class representation – the exception to the rule.)

The CP deduced that the black circular was 'encouraging Fascism', an instrument wielded to debilitate workers' resistance to attacks by employers, remove genuine democracy from unions and, ultimately, dismantle trade unionism. Yet the CP's use of separatist and divisive tactics had contributed towards its own isolation, and its partisan manoeuvres alienated many union branches and TCs, thus it was doctoring the evidence for the CP to assert that TCs had 'refused to accept this dictatorial invasion of their rights', well-paid union officials sabotaging activity to protect their 'cushy jobs', labour leaders 'assisting Fascism to power'.

This 'social fascist' theme thus continued into July 1935 when Idris Cox, for the CP, offered the exegesis that CP mass work in unions and TCs had developed so much that the black circular could be pronounced an attack on the revolutionary union elements.[406] The CP endeavoured to make the most of the anaemic TC opposition to the circulars by categorising trade unionism anew as a *capitalistic institution* with middle-class officials, the TUC steamrollering policy through unions and TCs. The trade union movement had in the past recruited workers of different political opinions, who were given equal rights in standing for union office, a principle not affected by union affiliation to the Labour Party. Now the circulars would carry *political discrimination* into the industrial side of the union.[407] At its Thirteenth Party Congress, the CP noted no possible compatibility between communism and the fascism that had in reality destroyed trade unionism and workers' rights.[408]

Having failed to gain much support to overturn the circulars, the CP turned to local conferences on war, hopefully via TCs, bypassing the circulars by devoting attention to a single issue. The TUC onslaught on the CP was not suspended for a moment. On the plus side for the CP, in Bradford TC, the circulars had been outvoted with only four of 100 delegates supporting them, and a united front programme was accepted by this TC, which promoted the hunger march despite the official ban. The CP resolved that:

> our work in the trades council linked up with the struggles of the workers in the factory. The trades council can play a very effective part in developing working class unity in giving support for increased wages and becoming the centre of real working class activity.[409]

The outcome of such intentions would depend upon TCs' recognition of their status and precise functions.

*

The Margate 1935 TUC conference returned to the 'disruptive elements' in TCs. Of 420 TCs, 2/3rds had now endorsed the TUC position; only 11 dissented (Abertillery, Oxford, Dover, Pontypool, Hendon, Kingston, St Albans,

High Wycombe, Watford, Bradford, Welwyn). G. Hicks waxed lyrical about TCs' immense value as *recruiting agencies* but they had to be aware of factions 'constantly trying to pull them to bits'; control in the union movement was 'sacred and fundamental'; coteries formulating plans from outside were unacceptable; and, as formulated, the circulars were a tool for self-preservation.

While the CP facilitated significant united front plans and defended the empowerment of TCs locally to tackle society's inequalities, they and the TUC diminished each other's efficacy. Where one functioned through 'fractions' and 'cells' the other operated through circulars and rules. The significant factor by now was that the TUC possessed the status, finances and authority to isolate active TC communists. E. Bevin's hyperbole was apocryphal: 'literally hundreds of TCs, important ones like Manchester, Leeds and London'[410] were reporting continual obstruction, with TCs not able to proceed beyond the Minutes because of continual 'moving the reference back'. There was 'nothing in the circular about excluding Communist or Fascist as such', but he had 'proof' of money handed over to his union reps to get officials sacked. Such unsubstantiated vilification targeted CP secret meetings; rational arguments were immaterial.

Framing any debate as 'democracy versus fascism and communism' was C. Dukes's speciality. He averred that those contributing to 'the philosophy of dictatorships' were hiding under the umbrella of democratic rights. Then came the block vote on *Circular 16*: 1,869,000 to 1,427,000. The TGWU rejected it but Bevin's 600,000 votes in favour of the General Council turned the scales.[411] Miners, engineers, builders and railwaymen continued to elect CP members to TCs and the CP insisted it had been vindicated: that substantial vote against proscriptions was proof that when the TUC imposed political restrictions there would be repercussions. 'Trade union democracy' would enhance the CP's defence of militants against officialdom, and leading TCs London, Glasgow, Manchester and Bradford were not enforcing the instructions.

*

The CP persisted with its global adumbration. In a letter to unions on *The Communist Party and the Trade Unions* in September 1935, the CP heralded the Soviet Union as where 'the final and complete victory of Socialism had been achieved', in conjunction with the strongest trade union movement in the world. The CP added that it always accepted majority decisions and loyally instigated them in factories, branches, district committees and TCs.[412] Far from disorganising unions, the CP claimed to lessen union sectionalism in order for branch meetings to take on 'a real representative character'. Class consciousness occurred when the worker recognised being in conflict with the employer, TCs a political weapon, with CP members 'the vanguard of class-conscious workers'.[413]

However, by October 1935, 299 TCs had signed up to Circular 16, only four against. Yet TCs were continuing to elect CP members owing to the altered circumstances of the United Front, continuing mass unemployment, and a beleaguered Labour Party. The Spanish Civil War from 1936 also emerged as a monumental rallying cause on the left, with the CP the spearhead in that international confrontation with fascism. Numerous TCs sent funds for the Republican cause while honouring the TUC circular in the breach rather than the observance, ignoring its implementation in their rules. By March 1936, 353 TCs had formally adhered to Congress policy (again four TCs against). How did this operate? When Hastings TC's F.G. Philcox informed the TUC that a recruitment campaign had experienced 'CP interference', the TUC's A. Conley threatened that if there was any trouble about affiliations in TCs, C. Dukes would visit the TC 'to point out their duty'.[414]

The CP proceeded with its efforts to canvass for affiliation to the Labour Party during the 'disruptive bodies' review and Bradford TC, having convened a conference with the Labour Party and CP, continued to defy the rules. TCs would not always conform to strictures when popularising unions, tabulating unorganised factories, compiling lists of firms, shareholders, profits, production quotas, and comparison of pay with union rates uppermost – CP members often the participants, if not leaders.

When P. Allott (for the London TC)[415] lauded Russia with its planned economy as a beacon of hope, as well as acknowledging that 'a few young and over-exuberant self-styled Communists had adopted disruptive tactics', C. Dukes retorted that TCs could not have the advantage of recognition *and* disapprove of Congress; for him 'healthier' TCs meant no communist disruption. The NCL's *British Labour and Communism*[416] deprecated communists and the United Front, postulating that the CP was motivated to sell its newspaper in TCs 'to sow disruption' and that the NUWM 'exploited the unemployed'! This was a monstrous canard. In reality, both the CP and NUWM, as tribunes of the oppressed, sought to bolster workers and help the unemployed. Dukes had further views, though. He professed that CP fractions in factory cells and union branches negated union leaders' collective bargaining work and union ECs, posed with unofficial strikes, lost authority; and, if CP affiliation was accepted or allowed into a united front, finances would be made available 'from abroad' to consolidate communist inroads.

E. Bevin, W. Citrine and C. Dukes frequently wheeled themselves out to have their say on communists in unions. Citrine in particular launched a further attack upon the CP's 'frenzied incursions', 'ingratiating itself' with organised labour, having abused unions as 'pillars of capitalism', with resultant union executives' authority 'being usurped'. For him, Congress could no longer have TCs 'disrupted by CP intrigue'; accordingly, CP members did not accept democratic solutions, their tactics came directly from the CI; all was a devious plot to use TCs to gain respectability and cloak infiltration via this so-called unity campaign.[417] Of the London TC, J. Stokes recalled its 'little cliques propagating CP doctrines', even if the anti-fascist, anti-imperialist CP record had tacit acknowledgement in TCs (and in organising unemployed, in the Popular Front against fascists in Spain, and at the Battle of Cable Street, against fascists at home).

In November 1936, in *Trades Councils – Their Industrial Functions and Activities*, the TCJCC clarified that a TC should be the leader of the industrial movement in the district (regarding local authorities, chambers of commerce and employers). Devotion to *political* activities (or subordinating industrial to political), as always stated, 'duplicated the machinery'.[418] Of 370 TCs, only 57 had organised campaigns during 1935 and 56 in 1936, and too many TCs had settled into a state of 'semi-respectable inertia', while the CP's 'band of trained and informed propagandists' (was that detrimental?) were to be rejected. The TCJCC described TCs as representatives, the 'conning tower' of local movements, centres for local industrial surveys, collectors of legislation on factory safety, welfare and regulations on industrial diseases, checking the operation of the fair wages clause in contracts, and organiser for TUC-created unemployed associations (UAs).

Directed at TCs, *Circular 29: The Witchcraft Trial in Moscow* was another sideswipe at the CP. It focused on the notorious forced confessions and fictitious proof in the political show trials in Stalin's USSR,[419] and was transcribed to combat those TCs involved in the UK with unofficial disputes and the censure of union officials. Pressurising unions after a union decision had been taken was naturally touted as indefensible. At this stage, W. Citrine and H.V. Tewson recruited V. Feather to the Organisation Department specifically to hunt down any communist influences. He was assigned to TCs. Wherever there was 'trouble with the Communists', Feather was sent to smooth it over and/or prepare the ground for someone with local authority. His assignment against communists in trade unions and TCs continued for a generation.

Oblivious to this latest strategy, Don Melville for the CP in February 1937 projected the London TC as the new base, as it had included CP members in the latest hunger march and the CP offered its LRD services in 'Trades Council union weeks'. On the South Coast, what CP members on Portsmouth TC had to counter was 'suppressive procedure' (i.e. being ruled out of order) and officials' interpretation of standing orders. CP member F. Clay scolded comrades who neglected correct debating procedure; theirs had to be a professional approach, not 'the old crude subterfuge'; too often matters were introduced into TCs without reference to union branches; reports of TC decisions were not given in branches when such work was more important than reputations for talking; and, if the CP wanted to gain mass support, this necessitated contacts between a TC, the local Labour Party and factory workers.[420]

International and local events became entangled and caused confusions in TCs. Manchester & Salford and Brighton TCs' CP members counselled for the Soviet Union against Nazi aggression, but Birmingham TC was not persuaded. According to one delegate, 'the mad dogs of Communism and Fascism which have overrun other nations must not gain even a foothold here'.[421] For some, the TUC circulars were of 'untold benefit' to TCs in eliminating 'disruptive elements' to enable them to devote their time to 'purely industrial activities'. At the CP's Fourteenth Congress in Battersea in May 1937, TCs were celebrated as 'effective union-building bodies' in contrast to the Norwich TUC conference 1937, where the CP-inspired motion for a united front was defeated. For the TUC, J. Marchbank alleged (contradicting himself) that 'union apathy' had been *caused* by the CP's scurrilous attacks on union leaders and it was this that deterred union members from meetings, not any supposed disillusionment with union leaders, who were, of course, tolerant and 'allowed' freedom of speech.

One example illustrates the confusion. In Manchester & Salford TC in December 1937 the president demanded that the CP delegates leave, naming the three who were forced to resign. The new president then ignored *Circular 16* and other delegates (by 106 votes to 51) maintained that CP members were integral to the TC. This decision was then reversed a month later with nominations for four delegates to the Lancashire and Cheshire Federation of TCs, resulting in one treated as unacceptable because he was a communist. The new president replied: 'heated debates there may, but no evidence of disruption'. He pleaded for toleration for 'minority viewpoints' with a tribute to the late George Brown (a CP member killed in Spain).[422] (Could delegates only associate with CP members when they were dead?) The vote on *Circular 16* was won by 67 to 57, the ruling laxly enforced. TCs remained in a quandary about *Circular 16*. Brighton TC resolved to overlook it via a press statement: 'Let other Trades Councils and trade union organisations know of the new awakening.'[423] Birmingham TC officially refused communists, in contrast to the London TC, where the CP renewed its foothold to galvanise opposition to the government's rearmament policy.

The TCJCC expended so much energy hunting for and tracking down communists across the UK. In Manchester & Salford TCs the secretary, turned out to be a CP member, prompting some union officials to decline to participate, just as others withdrew from the TC because CP members had been expelled![424] Such conundrums were intensified with breakaway unions. The Chemical Workers' Union (CWU) was refused admission to Congress, so a TC that lined up with the CWU was courting trouble. Despite this, in 1937 four TCs campaigned for CWU affiliation and in 1938, 42 TCs did. (By 1939 this encompassed 73 TCs, 167 in 1940, 207 in 1941 and 317 TCs by 1942.)[425]

A CP member could be officially refused credentials by a TC but there was nothing in TUC standing orders to prevent that member being a delegate. The TCJCC aimed to rectify this anomaly.[426] When Croydon TC's unemployed association (UA) had a meeting the principal speaker was the CP's general secretary, so the TC was removed from the official list. The CP had battled with union leaders for 19 years, other TC delegates caught in the crossfire.

TCs now turned their attention to the National Voluntary Service schemes. What would be the requirements of the TUC's 'local agents' in the war? How would the CP, which reached its peak membership since its formation, 17,756, in July 1939, seek to influence TCs?[427] Would there be a wartime compromise between the CP and the TUC? Would this be a desirable aspiration for either organisation? War would re-situate all allegiances.

CHAPTER 6

Communists in Trades Councils 1939–43

Our consciousness is highly contradictory, a multiplicity of knowledges, of vague awareness of intuitions and reactions-against... To create rigidities and dogmas and 'we do not talk to them because they are reformists' and 'we will not co-operate with them because they are sectarian' is to reproduce the definitions and classifications and fetishes of capitalist thought... The issue is not one of degrees of radicalness but of touching nerves, of channelling angers, of finding resonances.
~ *John Holloway, Crack Capitalism, 2010, pp225, 257, 78*

1. THE SOVIET UNION'S IMPACT UPON TRADES COUNCILS 1939–41

John Holloway's ideological insight above could not be more pertinent to this chapter. In context, leading up to World War II, Britain ruled over one-quarter of the world's population and deployed a barely concealed imperialist perspective to vindicate its actions.[428] Within this at the local level the hundreds of TCs emerged as loose alliances espousing all types of politics. They were now to be challenged by fundamental issues including state intervention in industry, workers' safety controversies, British defences, and daily restrictions in social services.

After a 20-year feud between the CP and the TUC over what 'political debates' were on or off the agenda, TCs now had to rethink their functions within a wartime context.

Analysing CP involvement in TCs from 1939 illuminates the political traps and hazards. From 5,000 members in the early 1920s to the *c.*50,000 at its dramatic peak in 1943, the CP had agency far beyond its purported membership. Whether the TUC or TCJCC acknowledged it or not, with energy and political commitment, CP union members had become an integral section of many TCs. Indignation at the consequences of the economic crises and revulsion against palpable social injustices and staggering inequalities were foremost. Confronting fascism and fearing the consequences of another war compelled TCs to be anchored in the realities of local social life and the economic productive process. This was part of the gulf between organisers and organised, trade union leaders and the rank and file.

The most divisive event impacting upon TCs occurred with the Nazi–Soviet Pact on 23 August 1939, with confusing interpretations as to why it had been formalised. Was it a totalitarian stitch-up? A cynical division of Poland? A distrust of British and French government intentions? A tactical delaying war tactic? Or a melange of them all?[429] TC delegates mirrored those conflicting, divergent suppositions. Who grasped what was going on during that confusing time? The CP's heuristic expressed publicly on 2 October was that the war could be designated as 'imperialist aggression' and was a threat to the workers' state, the Soviet Union; the British government's policies were being formulated by the 'pro-Fascist class forces' that controlled the Cabinet, appeasing aggression abroad and encouraging reactionaries at home. The CP thus proclaimed a 'war on two fronts': one against German fascism, the other against the Chamberlain government, and hoped, simplistically, to somehow rally the trade union movement to ask the government to sign a pact of mutual assistance with the USSR.[430]

All TCs had publicly expressed revulsion at the prospect of another world conflagration. Now that it had come to pass, a few, as a gauge of CP influence, were openly sympathetic towards this CP 'Imperialist analysis'. The case of C.S. Darvill, Sheffield's T&LC president, illustrates what would transpire. He followed the CP's majority position in this, along with several on the EC. As a result, the Labour Party's NEC ditched Darvill.[431] Elsewhere, CP members in TCs, renowned for operating the party's disciplinary procedures, were conscious 'an error of judgement' could be construed as appalling 'betrayal'. They were divided over the 'party line' and over the notion of independence of thought. They tended loyally to champion the Soviet Union and convinced themselves that opposition to the party line had, at that juncture, to be vilified as 'deviationist' and 'opportunist' (i.e. 'Trotskyist').

This deduction trickled through those TCs in which CP fractions existed, especially in Stop the War groups and the opposition to Finland's war with Russia. Although there might be only a few CP members on a TC (as in Newcastle & District TC), there was an impression that they dominated TCs' outlook when they often merely reflected a small contingent of it. In the largest TCs (such as the London TC) the atmosphere of meetings had been *political* for years. Industrial resolutions were often relegated to the end of the agenda and, before the Nazi invasion of Soviet territory in 1941, CP members in the London TC were promoting the 'Imperialist War' designation of the international situation.[432]

All TCs were reacting to the war situation in both pragmatic and idealistic modes. In the 1930s CP members in TCs had experienced nearly every action as a defeat: unemployed campaigns, all those marches, united fronts, fractions, programmes and resolutions failed to make an impact on TUC, government or Labour policies and generated insufficient impetus to affect any substantial reforms. Now the war required urgent interventions. From September 1939, the CP, railing against the Emergency Powers Acts and lauding democratic rights in the armed forces plus improved ARP, encountered a TCJCC persistently removing 'disruptive personnel' from TCs. C.G. Spragg (Birmingham TC) probed as to whether a TC member could be a delegate to or take the chair at conferences organised by the CP's *Daily Worker*.[433] The TCJCC's definitive retort was that this was a 'war for democracy' against all others, including the *Daily Worker* which was banned.

Communists in TCs highlighted the wrongdoings in the government's decision to pay women defence workers a third less than men, insisting to unionists that they were *not* fighting the war to make Britain 'a profiteers' paradise'.[434] Meanwhile the TUC propagated the notion that 'CP intrigue' in the TCs was even more of a costly business in the war effort, especially when the TCJCC was wasting time having to ponder over transparently unacceptable anti-war resolutions from TCs. One such came from Manchester & Salford TC in February 1940. This determined that the government, in 'appeasing Fascist acts of aggression', bore equal responsibility for the conflict with Nazi Germany; British financial and economic interests were bound up with the 'continuance of capitalism in Germany'. A TC resolution for 'the independence of the labour movement' from the government was only just defeated by 63 to 60. Indeed, in numerous TCs the government was taken to task for undermining wages and working conditions during this vital national transition to a war economy.[435]

On 7 October 1939 a CP manifesto boldly formalised its assertions. The war was ostensibly *not* for democracy against fascism. Nor was it for small nations' liberties. Nor was it for the defence of peace against foreign aggression. The British and French ruling classes were manipulating genuine anti-fascist sentiments to prop up imperialism and its colonies. Only the Soviet Union was promoting peace.[436] That majority CP interpretation of events, during the implementation of the Nazi-Soviet Pact, was endorsed by some leading TCs throughout the first 18 months of the war. This was apparent as the CP pursued the idea of a peace conference when it denounced Labour and union leaders for underwriting government war aims. This CP stance was never subsequently forgiven by the TUC nor the Labour

Party, who derided the CP's call for 'militant struggle by the working class movement' as being unpatriotic.

Despite this, R.P. Dutt's characterisation of the war as a 'second imperialist war'[437] did not adversely impact upon CP members' work on tenants' defence leagues, food vigilance committees, evacuation plans, and spotlighting rent profiteering. Widening the gap further from the TUC, the CP Industrial Bureau on 5 November 1939 posited an end to any 'industrial truce'. It proposed to harness working-class democratic representation in the form of shop stewards' committees, with TC elements in a new 'united front from below'.[438] It likewise anticipated that the Finnish–Soviet War would signal for the British government the unleashing of anti-Sovietism throughout the UK.

TCs were invited to debate this scenario. Chichester TC's secretary chaired a conference in Brighton on 'Labour and the War Economy' arranged by the CP's *Daily Worker*. This upheld the depiction of the war as capitalist and imperialist.[439] A dwindling number of TCs still adhered to the CP's call for a cessation of hostilities, although the CP reported 'scores' of Labour and union organisations condemning the war as imperialist. These groups opposed Labour and union leaders' political truce and collaboration with the government, and continued to demand an immediate end to the war. However, such sentiments were recorded in only 15 TCs, with the famous and potent Glasgow TC planning a conference of working-class organisations for ending the war.[440]

In February 1940 another CP conference, this time on 'Labour and the War', informed TCs of the deleterious effects of rising prices and the specific impact of rationing. Labour and union leaders were now being blamed for dragging the labour movement into a war against the Soviet Union, as CP members in TCs began to focus their attention upon cuts in social services, the suspension of housing schemes, low wages, long hours, inadequate soldiers' allowances, monitoring overtime regulations and ARP plans. A CP resolution in Brighton TC 'protested against the Capitalist Government of France' (for deposing communist deputies), and reaffirmed that 'the capitalist class should pay for its own War'.[441]

However, by mid-1940 it was apparent that all TCs were engaged and active in war efforts in all localities. Significantly, they were tolerating inroads into and deleterious effects upon civil liberties, rights of association and living standards. Yet for the TCJCC between March and June 1940 the major focus was on the removal of communists from TCs. For example, Lincoln and Finchley TCs officially removed their CP members; Lambeth and Bermondsey TCs had their political sections dissolved, and, for the TCJCC, breakaway unions 'had the object of creating disruption within TCs'.[442] As noted, Bournemouth TC's chairman was revealed to be a communist; Oxford T&LC arranged a demonstration with a communist as speaker, leading to the termination of his secretaryship of the TC's UA; and Yeovil TC was forced to halt the dissemination of Anti-Fascist Relief Committee propaganda.[443] A TCJCC subcommittee was now appointed to eliminate these 'disruptive elements' from TCs.

W. Citrine synchronised TUC actions with the government to control industries. *En passant* he mentioned that CP connections with 'a Russia which had deserted the Peace Front and made a pact with Germany' had been a complete disaster.[444] He declared that the CP's agenda was to divide and weaken every grievance of unionists and to sway them to oppose the promulgation of the war. Rejuvenated actions to 'clean up' TCs ensued and were implemented. Fewer were listening to the CP's frequent denunciations that Transport House (the TUC) imposed a 'democratic form of dictatorship' on the movement with 'loyalty' and 'discipline' tropes used to scupper debates. All TCs' anti-war resolutions were ignored by the TUC even as TC activists pleaded for opportunities for minorities to speak. This was considered a 'big ask' in a war situation, as London TC's EC exemplified.

On this EC, those delegates, exasperated that the London TC was continually used by CP members as a platform for political resolutions, decided yet again that only matters affecting *industrial welfare* were henceforth to be on the agenda. Some delegates queried the old borderline, political/industrial, when the government was taking so prominent a part in determining labour conditions. Complete exclusion of political discussion was impossible to eradicate (especially given that inappropriate plaudits for the Nazi–Soviet Pact seeped into debates in TC meetings throughout 1940). On the exclusion of political discussion from the London TC, R. Willis (secretary) recorded that it was, as always, intolerable to have delegates dominating meetings who did not represent views of the union that sent them.[445] He was infuriated that CP members on the EC were well-drilled to say their piece while other delegates were often unaware of the subjects for discussion until they reached the meeting.

May Day 1940 occasioned further demonstrations against the war, an index of those declining numbers of TCs who stuck to the CP line *in toto*. Again it was Glasgow TC that called out the rival imperialisms devastating the world for capitalist profit and territorial expansion, honest labour degraded to produce weapons of destruction.[446] This CP position stood in contradistinction to the majority of TCs, which welcomed the new coalition with Churchill to secure 'equality of sacrifice', as the CP zeroed into those 'utilising the war for profits'. Only 10 TCs eventually came out in favour of the Soviet Union in its war with Finland[447] at the same time as the TUC Organisation Department suspended a CP member in Sheffield T&LC for giving information to the banned *Daily Worker*. Here, a new T&LC was installed and nine CP members were denied credentials. One, a Mr Wilkins, had never sold CP literature but distributed pamphlets for 'subversive organisations': 'a very acceptable man in many respects, [but] he did... always take the CP point of view'![448]

In June 1940 the CP's proposition for the removal of 'friends of Fascism' from the government was unlikely to have much leverage. Neither were recommendations for the immediate conscription of wealth, nationalisation of industries, workers' control committees in factories, and an end to armaments' production. The proposal to arm workers in factories would hardly delight the TUC, and close relations with the Soviet Union were particularly unviable given the Nazi-Soviet Pact still in operation. (Barnsley TC, with its CP delegates, was on board with the former CP recommendations!)

On 7 July a National People's Vigilance Committee (NPVC) was formed by Hammersmith Labour Party

& TC resulting in the Labour Party's NEC disaffiliating Hammersmith LP&TC for 'a policy indistinguishable from the CP'; the 'capitalist class' was not going to 'perish of its own contradictions' (not yet). The war was seemingly submerging class differences as it harnessed unions and TCs to war necessities. CP propaganda, with its baiting of sell-outs and petty bourgeois unions (and implicitly TCs) and its inexact 'stark alternatives' (the ruling class offering a fascist deal or imperialist war in the guise of 'defence of the nation'), proved unpersuasive and counterproductive.[449] The London TC memorandum urged abstention from purely political matters, although, in a war, industrial questions were incontrovertibly entangled with political ones.[450] Social legislation was trade unionism transplanted into the political field. Wages, hours of labour, working conditions and protection, were *ipso facto political* questions. Would union leaders respond to these as 'sabotage' during a world war?

*

Debates on the precise characterisation of what type of war this was turning out to be, continued. NPVC recommendations became resolutions in a few TCs. Complexities pertained. Manchester & Salford TC EC ruled 'out of order' a resolution condemning the 'Men of Munich' (pre-war appeasers), but the TC ignored the city council's ban on public meetings. Meanwhile, W. Citrine at the July 1940 ACTC renovated the 'CP sabotage' trope and took it to the ultimate level of threat in a war scenario, treachery. 'The trade union movement would defend any militant trade unionist but it would not stand by a traitor', he fumed.[451] W. Holmes (TUC president) added ominously that not all 'enemies of the working class movement' were outside it. TCs mainly ignored the NPVC's united front with its anti-war slogan.

In September 1940, during the Nazi invasion bombing in the UK, a particularly contentious historical moment, the CP mounted 'The People's Convention' (PC) for a negotiated peace.[452] TCs were in a quandary, especially when 'disruptive activities' were recorded throughout London, in Hampstead, Lambeth, Bermondsey, Islington, Stepney, Hammersmith, Paddington and Bethnal Green TCs. A further 10 TCs, it transpired, had 'CP associations'. All were theoretically brought into conformity under the *Model Rules*. TCs, with their long history within the local labour movement, were not about to throw this away. 'Infiltration' motifs re-emerged as it transpired that Southall TC's secretary 'winked an eye' at CP members on the TC! A General Council member was present. The TC was disbanded. The General Council's H. Harrison took the paternal route: TCs' reorganisation was because of communists who could not be delegates to 'any of *our* trades councils'.[453]

A few TCs did rally behind the CP stance on ARP as a potential flashpoint, 'a focal point of the class struggle',[454] proposing in terms of equality, that wealthy homeowners should accommodate air raid refugees. CP/TC work on tenants' associations and shelter committees raised political consciousness at a time when TCs had been restricted, if not regimented, and union branch life declined in the war. This was aggravated by the extensive 1940 air raids, labour transference schemes, postal services delaying TC correspondence, and enforced 'extended working hours', all of which diluted attendances. In such circumstances, the CP turned to workshop activity and shop stewards.[455]

In September 1940 W. Citrine conceded that all the TCs were coping with 'community problems'. As the government hooked local authorities into the war effort, TCs for the CP became the natural centre to prepare for the People's Convention. Unfortunately for the CP, most TCs followed the TUC lead. Manchester & Salford TC's W.J. Munro typified TC responses to the Manchester Council for Democratic Aid (MCDA). 'I have been fighting against the TC having anything to do with this organisation which I feel sure is another cloak for the Communist Party', he reported.[456] Time for V. Feather and the TUC to intervene. If this MCDA was in any way connected to the Anti-Fascist Relief Committee, it was proscribed. The TC meeting in November was spent on the NCL decision to proscribe the People's Convention, the TC voting against the latter by 60 to 41 and against the MCDA by 45 to 41, an index of the balance of power in the TC. Munro closed with an observation concerning those diverting the TC from its industrial function to the 'propagation of the Communist doctrine of Dictatorship' and for devoting misguided efforts to a tirade upon TUC/Labour leaders and 'indulged in mental acrobats, one day vomiting destruction of Hitler, the next collaborating with him'.[457]

The CP's 'Imperialist War' analysis, positioning and message – at a time when the mass of the population identified promulgation of the war with thwarting fascism – presented insurmountable difficulties. Just as in our recent pandemic, war-time air raids exposed inequalities over varying levels of protection from harm. This was of crucial importance for CP members to raise in TCs. TUC leaders, unsurprisingly, dubbed the People's Convention a 'Communist manoeuvre' and in December 1940 the TCJCC reported on those few TCs' signatories to the NPVC (now banned). E.P. Harries described the Manchester & Salford TC meeting on this as 'of a most unruly character'. When three EC members signed the appeal for the NPVC, W.J. Munro accused a delegate of being an 'open member of the CP'.[458]

TCs were forming ARP petition committees (for local authorities: 'embryo soviets') and the CP denounced Bournemouth Labour Party conference resolutions as 'capitulations to the class enemy' and concession to 'imperialist war aims'.[459] Munro was profusely thanked for helping to remove the disruptive elements and obstructionist tactics. Regardless, Glasgow TC arranged its anti-war conference and Cardiff TC had an even bolder idea – the overthrow of the government: 'the ruling class of bankers and capitalists opposed to workers' interests'.[460] An incomplete picture is gleaned from TC minutes in 1940 because it was officially 'out of order' for a communication from a proscribed organisation to be brought before the TC. But the People's Convention hadn't gone away. The CP saw TCs as being decisive for the Convention, 'sparks waiting to be fanned into flame', with a central role for shop stewards and union branch secretaries, whereas Labour leaders (E. Bevin, W. Citrine, C. Attlee, A. Greenwood and H. Morrison) had been 'built up by the ruling class'.[461]

The People's Convention stemmed from the 'imperialist war' thesis, but the CP mistook dissatisfaction in various

TCs with the way the war was being handled for hostility to the war itself as a 'capitalist war'.[462] The CP seemed to have calculated that, somehow, defeat of the British Forces would (as had occurred in Russia in 1917) provide opportunities in a war situation to make radical alternatives possible. With such an outcome, perhaps a People's Convention (PC) could extend CP influence? This was not on the radar; in fact, the CP's *Daily Worker* being banned illustrated (for the CP) that this government was afraid of public criticism about the impending introduction of the conscription of labour. CP members on TCs protested the ban, arguing that the *Daily Worker* was the only newspaper challenging millionaires and exposing profiteering, inefficiency and the production and distribution mayhem. But to add that Labour and union leaders 'embodied all the essentials of the Nazi system of labour organisation'[463] was hyperbole!

A news agency, Industrial and General Information, was begun by the CP. Perhaps volunteers supplying news from factories would be as effective as having CP members on TCs? The CP retained a genuine fear the war might be utilised to destroy the Soviet Union. In February, Manchester & Salford TC debarred the 11 delegates who had supported the PC, including President T. Brown. (£50 was sent to the Aid for Russia (AfR) Fund just as the TC was debarring CP members!) Eleven other TCs were reorganised by September 1942, the NCL concluding that the CP distracted the movement, deluded the public, and misrepresented the working class with its 'Innocents Clubs' fake projects, the People's Convention the latest diversion.[464]

From January to June 1941 the CP's crude branding of the government as 'British Totalitarians' did not square with TCs' common-sense knowledge and lived experience. The CP maintained that the rank and file represented true democracy and shop stewards were directing the advanced posts of unionism while a Labour bureaucracy was regimenting workers, stifling discussion in TCs and compelling them to follow an official line. Union leaders were disaffiliating TCs when they debated questions 'distasteful to Government'. For the CP, the stage was set for a rigid conscription of labour.[465] (A TUC circular was sent to TCs on 1 May 1941 about refugee organisations undertaking welfare work. This was labelled 'Communist-inspired and controlled'.) Of TCs retaining a connection with the PC, 11 were 'reported' for sending delegates, two were removed from 'recognised TCs', Coventry TC was reprimanded for having invited CP speakers to a May Day demonstration, and London TC announced it had sorted out 'disruptive, subversive elements'.[466]

2. THE COMMUNIST PARTY AT WAR 1941-43

Union leaders did not substantially modify these suspicions and reservations about the CP following the Nazi invasion of the Soviet Union, 21 June 1941, which the CP proclaimed 'Fascism's aggression', two words applied in the correct context at last. R.P. Dutt, for the CP, continued to denounce the leaders of social democracy who played into the hands of anti-Soviet reactionaries and friends of fascism and paralysed the working class.[467] As it panned out, the dramatically recast situation was a relief for all British communists, in and out of TCs. Tortuous justifications eased and TCs unanimously greeted the new ally of the Soviet Union. Pointedly, the TUC and

TCJCC did not amend their list of proscribed bodies, but Edinburgh TC, with the Labour Party and Co-operative Party, formed a joint Aid to Russia (AtR) campaign, held a huge demonstration, the TC greeting an 'everlasting' association between British and Soviet peoples. By 1943, Sheffield T&LC had raised £5,200 for AtR, the equivalent of almost £300,000 today.[468]

Abandoning anti-war strategies, the CP experienced the largest growth in its history in the first three months of 1942, membership increasing by 25,000. Enthusiastic war efforts in factories won the respect of more TCs and the perception of the Soviet Union as a 'workers' state' spread, with TCs commencing plans for a Second Front in Europe. Now the CP was all for promoting higher productivity and discouraging strikes, a surprising *volte-face*! The TUC's ambivalence was neatly encapsulated by J. Marchbank, ACTC chairman, who expressed delight that Soviet Russia was on the 'right side' now, even as it created for TCs 'some difficult problems of relationship'.[469] He explained how the trade union movement could note how communist policy had changed and how oppositional activity had transpired when People's Conventions and popular fronts were aimed at becoming 'centres of subversive activities'. What the CP now agitated for was a Second Front to all our 'Soviet allies'.

London TC greeted the new ally, the USSR, and had a referendum of its affiliated unions as to whether *Circular 16* should be honoured, voting 177 to 77 to retain the ban.[470] Unconditional support for the war effort and the promise that nothing should stand in the way of the Empire co-operating with Britain and Russia in defeating the common enemy, was now the CP position. The answer to the question 'who were the aggressors?' depended upon the Soviet Union. A CP appeal for the defeat of fascism maintained that it was an axiom of Marxism that the CP formulate its policies in accordance with the concrete situation: Churchill was now, for the CP, definitely opposed to fascism![471] (His earlier support of Mussolini did not enter the equation.)

TCs organised Anglo-Soviet Friendship Committees (ASFCs) as the war, for the CP, had become a 'just war of liberation'. Defence of working-class interests could now encompass CP expressions in favour of a trade union bond with unions of the USSR, an Anglo-Soviet Trade Union Committee created in September.[472] Birmingham TC pledged aid to the USSR in their 'magnificent resistance to the Fascist dictators', and congratulations were sent to Soviet workers as TCs began contemplating how best to increase production (further proof of CP accreditation). The CP's new campaign for *war production* included JPCs' involvement, although CP shop stewards in TCs were ambivalent about expanding production quite so readily.[473] TC resolutions for lifting the ban on the *Daily Worker* became a priority to aid civil liberties and rights, without endangering the war effort.

However, some disputes continued. For example, the CP understood essential work orders as part of the 'connivance of union bureaucracy to impoverish workers', a method of legally disciplining labour, blaming workers for delaying production: 'the reformist leaders... are supporting those [yard and pit] committees in the hope that they will be a counterweight to the militant shop stewards and miners' branch committees'.[474]

Just as the TUC had not subsumed its wariness of CP endeavours, the CP hadn't changed its outlook on union bureaucrats' policies, and simultaneously, in August, the TCJCC was eagerly pursuing TCs that had associated with the People's Convention. Stafford TC was under the impression that, since the USSR was now an ally, policy had changed, only for the TCJCC to disavow them of this mistaken assumption. Unless the CP member on the TC resigned, the TC would be deregistered.

TC officials frequently carried out investigations on behalf of the TCJCC. The Woolwich TC secretary informed the TCJCC that the TC had gradually become inveigled by CP members, and the London TC for its part confirmed that no CP members could be elected TC officers,[475] while J.T. Hargreaves, a Leeds TC delegate, evoked images of TC meetings devoted to political matters, industrial issues hastened through, meetings on AtR and the *Daily Worker* ban packed in:

> Many delegates to the Trades Council are… there with the intent of securing a political platform for proscribed bodies, such as the Communist, Trotskyist and Militarist parties… they were intent upon using the TC for their own ends. The CP is the prime mover of this.[476]

Whatever 'Militarist parties' were doing, the TUC carried on with its wartime plans. TCs were on the agenda at Edinburgh TUC conference 1941, association with 'disruptive bodies' and jettisoning the *Model Rules* uppermost. Apparently, officers had been subjected to a 'malicious and vindictive allegation' because of their support for current policy.[477] Twelve TCs were accused of breaches of the *Model Rules* (six of them in London). Marchbank (TUC) affirmed that TCs were being 'prevented from doing useful work' and that (in most cases) the request for intervention had arisen from the TC itself. He insisted that before June 1941 the CP had taken every opportunity to obstruct and weaken the national effort and demonstrate its irresponsible, unstable character, reason enough for the TUC not to sacrifice independence of judgement or allow support for the Russian nation 'to be prostituted by political opponents who might divert it to other purposes'.[478] Charming alliteration; however, the notion that the CP delegates in TCs had demonstrably weakened the 'national effort' was fanciful, as their work on local issues from 1939 to 1941 proved.

In September 1941, TCs enthusiastically participated in 'Tanks for Russia' week although the black circulars remained steadfastly implemented. CP members introduced Second Front resolutions and galvanised Anglo-Russian Friendship Committees.[479] TCs sometimes both joined these ARFCs *and* banned CP delegates (e.g. Brighton TC) with no sense of incongruity. They also had joint committees with Labour parties for the 'Help for Russia Fund' (HfRF). Establishing JPCs had emerged as a central activity for TCs. CP delegates and others inquired as to whether private ownership of factories could actually provide the war materials necessary or government ownership possibly lead to workers' control (the latter suggested by Birmingham TC). TCs were advised to avoid conferences under LRD auspices, although some TC delegates appeared at the LRD Conference on Production in September 1941.

Beneath the surface of wartime 'unity', old battles raged. The complexities and trivialities between the CP and TUC over TCs deepened with the prolonged saga over Percy Allott and the London TC. R. Willis (secretary) informed V. Feather (TUC) that *Circular 16* was in operation in January 1942. Feather confirmed that W. Zak and P. Sloan (CP members) should be removed, and H. Adams and Allott (associated with the PC) were ineligible.[480] Adams had resigned from the PC but was a member of the proscribed LRD. Allott had been a member of the People's Convention London Committee and was excluded from attending the Conference of London Unions on Trade Unions and Production in March. Allott intended to take legal proceedings against Willis but the General Council would only accept Allott as a delegate to the London TC if he was not a member of a proscribed organisation. Willis eventually received such assurances on 8 January 1943[481] (coinciding with world history-altering events in Stalingrad's finest hour).

TCs urged the TCJCC to revise the list of proscribed organisations. The latter responded by saying it would not reissue delegates' credentials to TCs if they, like Allott, had been involved in the PC. The TCJCC knew 'Anglo-Soviet Weeks' (ASWs) were held by local authorities and CP members, and had resulted in the reintroduction of fraction meetings, with the CP turning out the largest, most disciplined contingent for ASW recruiting opportunities; through TCs the CP was resuming old contacts. More CP-sponsored resolutions were passed for rescinding the *Daily*

Worker ban, culminating, in April 1942, in a CP pamphlet for TCs, *The Communist Party and the National Front*,† which denoted support for the government.⁴⁸²

The CP and TCs were now truly united in the war, an alliance with the USSR, and a campaign for those underpaid in the armed forces. Though the terminology was not uttered, TCs favoured what was to a certain extent a form of war communism, even if many TCs did not infer that support for the Soviet Union implied any contact with the local CP. Marchbank at the ACTC 1942 informed delegates that the People's Convention had dissolved, but warned that it might be revived as another new 'Innocents Club' (echoes of the NCL circular of February 1941) to further the interests of the CP. Nationally, the ACTC voted for a 'Second Front', while locally the small Spen Valley TC collected £620 for the Fund for Russia. However, LRD affiliation was off limits. G. Woodcock (TUC Economic and Research Department) contended that the LRD was proscribed because of its 'inaccurate statements'. He castigated the CP: 'Were people who changed their tune at every expedient to be relied upon to give accurate information?'⁴⁸³ LRD proscription was upheld, 81 votes to 57, another pointer to the balance of views among TCs.

The collusion and communication between TUC HQ and TC officials is illustrated in Birmingham and Southampton TCs. The CP Midlands District Committee planned to debate TCs' role and functions, the rich and militant history of these 'workers' parliaments' and invoked the TC for working-class progress alongside post-

---

† The united front against fascism, not to be confused with the 1960s-founded far-right party of the same name.

war reconstruction: 'but only in so far as it rises above the obstacles limiting its work at the present time'.[484] V. Feather contacted Birmingham TC secretary C.G. Spragg on proscribed organisations:

> Dear Charley, the Rules the TC sought to rescind could only be altered by Congress; a Trades Council cannot expect to have the rights which result to them from recognition by Congress and yet avoid the responsibilities which Congress expects.[485]

Feather advised Spragg to hold this knowledge and that of breakaway unions 'up his sleeve' when the resolution was moved in the TC, a typical ruse to tackle CP members in TCs, a patently similar tactic that the right would complain about when deployed by their adversaries.

In Southampton, TC secretary G.F. Tutt requested assistance from Feather, asking him to visit the TC to deal with TC delegates who were, according to resolutions in *Circular 16*, out of order. R. Chick (TGWU area secretary) confirmed in the TC meeting that the power of the TC lay in the TUC:

> If you want to smash the Trades Council, pass the resolutions and automatically it will be disbanded. The TUC would have no alternative but immediately to inform the secretary that you have altered your rules in such a way that they do not conform with the general policy and constitution of the TUC and as such it would be no longer recognised as your representative body in the district.[486]

He would acquire instructions to disaffiliate from the TC and the largest sum in TC fees would cease. For Feather, the movement would be foolish if it allowed an outside body, which he saw as 'unconnected' with the industrial or political movements, to foist its policy on the movement and disrupt the work that had been put in for many years.

Such tortuous wrangles in TCs over CP delegates always brought these same arguments and ripostes, similar to the ETU delegate who supported CP affiliation and considered the TC a very valuable weapon but 'it was in the hands of the wrong class.' Two points here. First, as CP delegates were engaged as TC activists how were they 'unconnected' to the movement? Second, if TCs were 'workers' parliaments', the CP wanted to know: why were they being overseen by TC officials or, for the matter, the TUC?

*

Back in Southampton, in July 1942, the local TC rejected CP affiliation. R. Morley (TC chairman) offered the traditional rationale that CP members in the TC would mean a break with past policy, and would weaken unions and the Labour Party 'the elected instruments of the working class movement'. According to Morley, the CP had, for 20 years, berated every responsible Labour leader, adopted 'wrecking and disruptionist tactics', failed to understand the national character and outlook of the working classes (he did not expound on what *that* was), and they were inconsistent, hence their complete turnabout over the war. H.E. Child in exasperation pleaded:

We are sick to death of the friction and endless controversy between the Labour Party and the Communist Party... We associate with our Communist friends socially and industrially, but we are not allowed by the rules of this obsolete circular of the TUC to associate politically as members of a trades council.[487]

The debate in Southampton TC was replicated elsewhere. TCs began to associate the post-1941 Soviet Union in the war with the civil liberties' rationale for lifting the *Daily Worker* ban. The constructive attitude of the CP in TCs was reflected in the Blackpool TUC conference debate on international relations and the domestic scenario. There, delegates queried the CP members' anomalous position as delegates who were 'not officially' in TCs! And yet, where CP members had rights, union membership had increased. Weren't communists the most outspoken anti-fascists? Wouldn't withdrawing *Circular 16* help the movement combine all anti-fascists against the Nazis?[488] P. Allott argued unionists were being blacklisted because of their opinions and the labour movement had always exhibited a tendency towards conservatism. Good unionists were presumed 'splitters, disruptionists, wildmen, Reds, subversive agents'.[489] Paradoxically, the disruptionists of yesteryear sometimes became pillars of conformity and responsibility – the history of the labour movement having many such exemplars (as noted above in Key Players and Chapter 1).

J. Marchbank asserted at the ACTC that the TUC was not a political party, yet communists always wanted to introduce into industrial affairs their political outlook. He continued: before Russia was invaded, CP delegates' destructive tactics in TCs had aimed to defeat the movement in the war's prosecution. Every TC delegate should speak for his union and not for a party 'outside the movement'. The ban on communist delegates being represented in TCs was upheld, 2,550,000 to 2,137,000. For CP member J.R. Campbell: 'A majority of the General Council... appear to be miserable victims of an anti-Communist phobia'.[490]

Such confrontations were not confined to the TUC conference. Tutt of Southampton TC renewed correspondence with V. Feather:

> We have had another battle royal over *Circular 16* and I think it is nearly time that these people should be reported to their respected [sic] Executive Council of their union. I am enclosing the list of names which consist of the Communist element. I am rather afraid that we shall be losing our stalwart if this element still continues. Bro. Morley, the President, is thinking rather seriously of resigning from the Chair and the Council through this continuation of the Communist obstruction.[491]

What to do about such 'elements'? Feather was relieved to be informed that the chairman and Tutt were able to get a majority for Congress but expressed concern that Morley might resign. Regarding CP members on the TC he said: 'it is very difficult sometimes to discover who are actually members of the Communist Party, for that Party... makes provision for what they term 'undercover' members'.[492] (Always a problem!) *Circular 16* was pursued, but alongside TC resolutions for a Second Front, to ensure a 'smashing defeat of the Hitlerite forces' (Manchester & Salford Industrial Committee) and 'to secure a speedy victory over Fascism in 1942'. (Brighton TC).[493]

Communists had been severely tarnished by the Nazi–Soviet Pact, but TC officials' disassociation between the British CP and the CPSU could be bewildering. While a fraternal resolution was forwarded by Birmingham TC to unions in the USSR on the twenty-fifth anniversary of the Revolution of 1917, C.G. Spragg of this TC conveyed to H.V. Tewson of the TCJCC his frustrations in implementing *Circular 16*. Each TC delegate was compelled to sign a declaration that s/he was not a CP member. Spragg was sure that some delegates were signing when they were actively working with and/or assisting proscribed organisations:

> This infiltration is now becoming quite serious and several friends of the Communist Party… have obtained seats on my EC… There will be a serious attempt to delete the declaration from the Agendas… unless something is done I shall have to face a CP majority on the EC next year.[494]

H.V. Tewson raised this conundrum at the next TCJCC gathering. It advised the General Council to send TC secretaries an up-to-date list of proscribed organisations. It had to add that there was no guarantee that a person would not make a false declaration! More undercover operations were afoot. Within a month, Birmingham TC removed the reference to proscribed organisations, ushering in seven years of left-wing policies in the TC, C.G. Spragg's communications displaying the style, range and scope of TC officials at this time.[495]

*

Sheffield T&LC's A.E. Hobson in November 1942 presents a moment when the CP was at its most effective.[496] A National Union of Distributive and Allied Workers (NUDAW) representative endorsed a Second Front as TCs operated HfRFs and joined the Anglo-Russian Fellowship and the Daily Worker League, after the ban was lifted. Now, a CP memorandum, *Trade Union Policy in the War Against Fascism*,[497] counselled for revitalised input into TCs, based on intensified war work in unions, recruiting campaigns (especially in newer industries and for clerical workers) and advice through TCs on social services, requiring material assistance. Accordingly: 'Trades Councils, like the workshop organisations, are the training grounds of the future cadres of the trade union movement'.[498]

Yet the TCJCC was training its collective mind on delegates' credentials, legalistically securing definitions of the *Model Rules* on proscribed organisations. The TCJCC reiterated that:

> The Trades Council shall refuse to accept the credentials of a delegate from an affiliated branch if the delegate in question is a member of, acting for and on behalf of, or associated with the Communist or Fascist Parties or any subsidiary organisation of these parties or an organisation proscribed by the General Council.[499]

Slough TC was disaffiliated at this time, its delegates admonished because, it was asserted, they had little concern for the prestige of the TC so long as they were able to 'hook' it onto the local CP.

Although many TC delegates warmed towards the CP post-1941, the Nazi invasion of the Soviet Union did not really affect the TUC's judgement on the CP and neither did Nazi defeat at Stalingrad in February 1943, as stated the turning point in World War II. After Stalingrad, 'Red Army Day' became the greatest declaration of Anglo-Soviet solidarity in history, fostered by AtR weeks, Stalingrad Festivals, and CP films on the Soviet Union for TCs' delectation.[500] Sheffield T&LC's A.E. Hobson, having a breather from his diatribes against the CP, offered high praise to 'the heroism of our Russian comrades', and requested:

> let us not drift back to the days of disruptive and destructive criticism; criticism is good, and we cannot live without it, but let us be constructive, and not waste time on petty and individual grievances.[501]

Despite the adulation, Red Army Sundays were inextricably mixed with internecine squabbles and those petty grievances re-emerged.

V. Feather and C.G. Spragg were deep in anti-Communist business in early 1943:

> Dear Charley... I think you are certainly right when you say that the CP are doing all they can to get control of your Council... You can be assured that every possible assistance will be given to you from this Office in your

endeavours to keep Birmingham in line with Congress policy.[502]

Spragg had problems:

> Dear Victor... the CP did remarkably well in the Elections of the Executive... and the Declaration was removed from the Agenda. My name has been 'mud' ever since in left wing circles... I tried to persuade my new President that the affiliation of the CP to the LP was no concern of any Industrial Body such as ours but he did not agree... I have about nine left-wingers on the EC now and... it is difficult to prove they are members of the CP. I have warned them that it may mean the reorganisation of the Trades Council, but without any effect.[503]

V. Feather attended a Birmingham TC meeting that debated the question of CP affiliation to the Labour Party (carried 56 to 24). Nothing quite exemplifies so aptly the contradictions as this following missive to 'My Dear Victor' in April 1943:

> I hope you have now returned from your marvellous trip to the USSR and I confess I envied you as I should like to see that Great Country and judge for myself this experiment in Workers' Control, that is, of course, if all we hear is correct, that Workers *are* in control... The local Kremlin seems to have a good grip of the EC but I cannot prove anything yet.[504]

Feather was 'glad that the sounder trade unionists are hitting back a little bit more to the Communists'.[505] He enclosed a draft pamphlet on the CP for C.G. Spragg's perusal and comments.

Even in the midst of this world war against Nazism, the prevalent attitude towards the CP at the TUC, the TCJCC and among leading TC officials was to be singled out as 'the vilest enemy'. And this was the summit of the CP's popularity in Britain![506] TCs were being disaffiliated for having any connection with the CP, including Anglo-Soviet Committees. Officials such as C.G. Spragg, A.E. Hobson and Tutt applied the pre-1941 denigration of CP members, contending that the latter's methods were in conflict with 'common decency' if not 'against the law'.

As the war rolled on, examples of this perplexing contradiction abounded. In Brighton TC, money was raised for the Russia Fund and the Anglo-Russian Fellowship but when a Mr Hirst 'confessed' he was a communist, he was voted off the TC (by 12 to eight).[507] In St Pancras TC, North London, a communist was informed that he could not attend as a visitor, and Slough TC was reinstated when all delegates signed a declaration ensuring they were 'not connected with the CP' and that no CP correspondence would be brought before the TC.

All this may have been difficult to square with J. Marchbank's ACTC 1943 avowal there had never been any disposition to circumscribe TC activities or abridge freedom of discussion![508] On it went. Nottingham TC raised thousands of pounds for AtR with the Labour Party. The latter then refused to join a joint consultative committee unless the TC disassociated from the ASFC (which it declined to do). At the same precise time, 'May Day' for Manchester & Salford TC proclaimed a unity of all sections of the local labour movement, an 'Anglo-Soviet Treaty' welcome, and £50 donated to the HfRF to pay for a new hospital in Stalingrad.[509]

On 10 June 1943 the EC of the Comintern dissolved the Communist International (CI). This, and the TUC withdrawal of *Circulars 16* and *17*, temporarily reconciled TCs to a CP whose policies for state control and extension of social services along Beveridge lines constituted a reformist component of the labour movement. CP leaders had begun to relinquish the nomenclature of factory cells, cadres and factions. The demise of the CI reinforced this, when the largest ever CP in its UK history was an upshot of the Soviet Union's war battles and triumphs. Consideration by the TCJCC of 'disruptive bodies' was deferred. At the Southport TUC, W. Citrine acknowledged *Circular 16* had been fitfully enforced but warned delegates that the General Council, as 'custodian of the movement', had to safeguard TCs against disruption and had to be convinced CP 'disruptive tactics' had been abandoned. As such, the General Council would protect the movement against 'hostile elements' (that foremost phrase). P. Allott again led the protest:

> The Circular had perpetuated malice, envy, hatred and uncharitableness, and had never been applied to anti-Socialist and anti-unionist, but to the militant and most active Trades Councils.[510]

Evidently, removing militants from the labour movement has a prolonged history. Meanwhile, the fascist menace had to be fought. At this juncture, 70 pro-Nazis had been convicted in the UK under wartime defence regulations, which could detain anyone believed to pose a threat to the war effort.[511] And, on the continent, a Nazi hierarchy was operating a grotesque radicalised version of capitalism, utilising time and motion studies and HR management to rationalise death factories on an assembly-line, industrial basis. However, few in the TUC General Council, TCs or the CP had any inkling of the scale of that monstrous Holocaust as they were digging in for the final war effort.

Blackpool

Cambridge

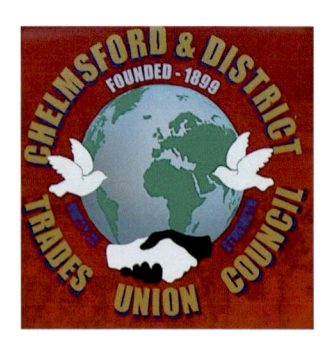

Chelmsford

Chesterfield

Chesterfield

Chesterfield

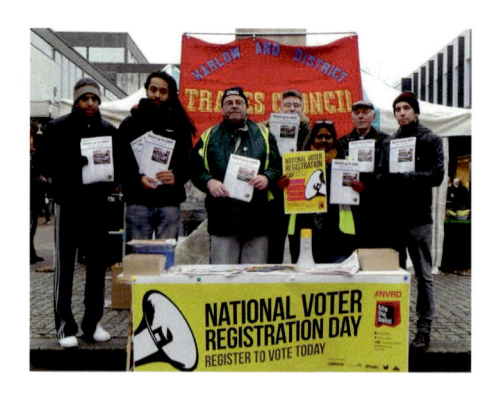

Harlow

Islington featuring Jeremy Corbyn

Islington

Lancaster

Portsmouth

Portsmouth

Wales

Wolverhampton

CHAPTER 7

New Possibilities and a Labour Government 1943–50

The Second World War was the largest and bloodiest conflict in world history… with the largest internal population migration in European history (90 million killed or displaced, 1939-1948)… the 27 million lost in The Great Patriotic War became the *key* component of communist legitimacy… war as a struggle of antifascist proletariats against fascist barbarians.
~ Dan Stone, *Goodbye to All That? The Story of Europe since 1945*, 2014 pp3-4, 26, 32, 36

1. FROM WAR TO PEACE 1943-46

By 1943, after the devastating purges of the 1930s, the Stalingrad military triumph had been reinvigorated by the use of professional generals. The subsequent brutality, valour and nobility of the time has been exhilaratingly captured in Vasily Grossman's *Life and Fate*.[512] And this monumental victory had the most electrifying *and* unifying effect across the whole of the British labour movement. Indeed there are few junctures in the latter's history when everyone was singing from the same hymn sheet. We nominate this moment.

To more parochial matters, after nine years of implementation, TCs officially withdrew their ban on CP delegates, although larger TCs were still ostensibly prevented from co-operating directly with the CP. TCs affiliated to the Labour Party kept the ban in place using Clause 14 of the TC *Model Rules* regarding subscription to communist or fascist parties' funds (viz. TUC's *Trade Union Structure and Closer Unity*).[513] Withdrawal of *Circular 16* was more a gain on a matter of principle. TC-affiliated membership would expand anyway. So the CP engaged in the campaign led by TCs and shop stewards to beef up union branch affiliation with TCs and carry out activities unimpeded. In November 1943 the LRD was removed from the list of proscribed organisations.[514]

Six TCs pleaded that the TC *Model Rules* should be applied to fascist parties' funds, not to the CP, while three TCs confirmed that they would not allow communists into their organisation. (A test case in Luton TC resulted in the TC's president choosing to join the CP!) The differing approaches to the CP can be witnessed in Sheffield T&LC, where President Madin registered that policies opposed to the Labour Party were being pushed through by 'an insignificant, noisy, Communist minority',[515] while Chelmsford TC's J. Young contrasted the Labour Party, 'an affiliation fee letter box', with the CP's 'tremendous union publicity'.[516]

During January and February 1944, 30 TCs contacted the War Office requesting that 'in the interests of democracy' (a gambit across the political spectrum), the *Daily Worker* should now at least have its own war correspondent (see Brighton, Manchester, Southampton TCs). Birmingham TC had a meeting on the subject of 'the Soviet Union', a discussion with none other than V. Feather (secretary of the TUC delegation to the Soviet Union) welcoming back old CP stalwarts J. Trotter and H. Shepperson! Undeterred, the bullish Feather wrote to his old mate Spragg about the Daily Worker Unity Conference (DWUC): 'It is all part of their political camouflage, and only people with politically undeveloped mentalities are deluded by this', the CP speakers (D.N. Pritt, W. Gallacher and W. Rust) categorised as an 'unimposing list of discredited dug-outs from the political graveyard'.[517] (Hardly harmonising, nuanced or inclusive language!)

CP members from numerous TCs attended the Daily Worker Unity Conference on 2 April 1944, raising money for the Stalingrad Hospital Memorial Fund Committee, Wolverhampton TC collecting £2,700 (*c.* £150,000 in today's money) from factory workers by June. The Second Front against the Nazis had enthralled and rejuvenated TCs. Swindon TC expressed the optimistic mood succinctly:

> The great allied offensive in the West will hasten the end of the War and in conjunction with our Russian ally and the oppressed peoples of Europe, bring speedy victory over fascism.[518]

With another year to go, in May 1944 the TCJCC's stolid anti-CP spokesman, H.N. Harrison, heralded 'our gallant Soviet ally', with their Soviet factories 'churning out great war machines to take such bloody toil of the contemptuous, sneering Nazis.'[519]

On the domestic front, the CP turned its attention to the inefficiency in the implementation of repairs to bomb-damaged buildings. Ideas for post-war planning were referenced in Birmingham TC, which considered the government's 'present puny measures' grossly inadequate, while Manchester & Salford TC was rebuked for sending 'synthetic Communist resolutions' to conference.[520] Birmingham TC was the paradigm for CP/TC relations between September and November 1944. The Midlands CP launched a Unity Conference, but, replacing C.G. Spragg's mantle, the TC's president, E. Haynes, wasn't having any of it: 'At no time has the question of co-operating with the CP been considered by this Trades Council.'[521] Accordingly, sending delegates to the Unity Conference *was* tantamount to co-operation with the CP. Haynes informed the TUC about the growing anxiety in Birmingham unions and the local Labour Party about 'a Communist Party caucus in the Trades Council'.[522]

This was confirmed to Haynes by NUDAW's A. Lees, who relayed details to V. Feather that the TC had spent too much time discussing *political* matters: 'The Trades Council was dominated by Communists, the prime movers behind this call to select the most suitable [general election] candidates'.[523] Mind you, in the middle of a world war, there had to be a little slippage into analysing the political ramifications of industrial policy. And 'political' did not just include the Labour Party.

In stepped Birmingham's Labour Party accusing a leading CP member, selected for a Midland constituency, of having 'rigged the selection procedure'. C.G. Spragg alerted V. Feather again that the TC was endangered and becoming 'a sub-committee of the Communist Party'. Feather replied to H. Baker on such crafty behaviour:

> The root of this trouble is the desire of a very small number of your branches to utilise the machinery of the Trades Council for political rather than industrial purposes... resolutions concerning electoral matters should not be included on the Trades Council agenda, but should be referred to the local Labour Party by the branch concerned.[524]

Withdrawal of *Circular 16* apparently made little difference one way or the other, in practice. For TUC and TCJCC leaders, communists would always involve themselves in undercover, devious, conspiratorial, and undemocratic stunts, overtly or covertly, through TCs. Of a meeting of Ruislip–Northwood TC in October 1944, of 30 members present all but one were communists. The one non-CP member, the chairman, ruled that none could participate! A Mr Glitz, from the London TC, proclaimed this was 'out of order'. The chairman demanded the secretary return books and correspondence belonging to the TC. Eventually, the secretary was 'struck on the jaw' by one of two mysterious delegates, and the whole rumpus ended up in the TCJCC Minutes of 28 November 1944.[525]

Elections were looming, but featuring TCs and/or communists in electoral unity conferences (EUCs) was deemed impermissible. Birmingham TC's internal squabbling was replicated in Southampton, December 1944 and January 1945, where the TC convened a conference of union branches for two Labour MPs for Southampton. CP district secretary M.J. Cohen offered a review of the CP's plan to challenge big business and monopolies.[526] Then a debate ensued over whether this review conflicted with the TC's constitution. When informed about these proceedings, V. Feather corresponded with TC secretary H.E. Child. Apparently, the EUC breached every rule: 'How could the Trades Council not be associated with the Communist Party when a breach of the Model Rules had been committed?'[527] There was to be no interference in the electoral machinery. The Labour Party's national agent, G.R. Shepherd, congratulated Feather on 1 February 1945: 'We are very pleased to note the line you have taken in the attempt to swing over a stunt engineered by the Communist Party.'[528] All this was symptomatic of TCs' complex relations with the CP and the Labour Party as the post-war general election came into focus.

*

A new world was being constructed. On 25 June 1945 *The Times* captured the *zeitgeist* with a quote from Labour Party leader (soon to be Prime Minister) C. Attlee, who trumpeted: 'public welfare comes before private interest'. This was in tune with TCs. At the ACTC 1945 six weeks earlier, Crewe T&LC launched a celebratory resolution for:

> a new order of society worthy of the sacrifices of all members of the fighting forces and the civil population who had suffered in the fight for liberty. It was about

not forgetting the years of poverty, unemployment and economic chaos, and in future making sure that uncontrolled private enterprise... shall not again be allowed to plunge people into misery and despair.[529]

(How this sentiment resonates into the 2020s.)

TCs' awareness of the Soviet Union's immense war achievements and sacrifices was inculcated in Crewe T&LC's aspirations. Huddersfield TC appointed a committee to aid 17 Red Army soldiers in a hospital, and Manchester & Salford TC messaged Kharkov in the USSR praising their valiant efforts of restoration. Vice-President T. Brown resigned from the TC when appointed as the general secretary of the National Council for Anglo-Soviet Friendship.[530]

The CP had been detached from parliamentary institutions and had previously avoided large-scale electioneering. Now, pre-election, its own members were 'spying on each other, each watching for a false move'.[531] What were CP members in TCs doing? Were they aiding the Labour Party? Supposedly they were. Yet, as some leading TCs were again becoming 'dominated' by very active CP members, they were carefully monitored by Labour and union leaders, the TUC prevailing upon those code words, vigilance and self-discipline, to be applied.

As previously acknowledged in Chapter 4, from 1943 to 1947, the whole labour movement had asseverated it could be united for economic reconstruction, nationalisation procedures and Beveridgism in a dynamic post-war Labour government, a shift in power relations between social classes a distinct possibility. A National

Plan for Industry could possibly, with major housing reconstruction and potentially egalitarian social services, instigate a movement towards 'common ownership'.[532] TCs' local social welfare activities could be part of this process. The challenge was to ensure a radical government was not reduced to palliatives with TCs merely restricted to and absorbed in committee work.

Communists in TCs kept alive a broader, more combative agenda, however inept their tactics or aversive their jargon. In July 1945 the TCJCC was interrogating five TCs that patently had 'Communist links'. As confirmed at Blackpool TUC, municipal elections were coming. TCs were about to be advised. Paddington TC was instructed to ignore a CP candidate, and the TCJCC characterised the CP the most oligarchical party of the age. TCs were reminded not to take shares in the PPPS or the *Daily Worker*,[533] but, as usual with pronouncements from head office, some TCs side-stepped this diktat. All of them were preparing to welcome the repeal of the TD&TU Act. Adding a widely held TC view, Julius Jacobs (London TC secretary and communist) observed that 'tying Britain to the USA's capitalist profit-making' bothered TCs.[534] Time for the Labour Party's position to surface in T. Wakley's *Communist Circus* 1946 pamphlet, which bemoaned: 'The Communist Party has a long-standing habit of instructing its members how to consolidate their vote in any other organisation with which CP members are connected.'[535]

The new Labour government and the Cold War reduced CP membership, but not its activities in TCs,[536] through which it sought to 'make Fascism illegal in Britain' (see Manchester & Salford, London, Wolverhampton,

Bath, Nottingham, Deptford, Battersea and Sutton TCs).[537] This laudable endeavour included a boycott of imports and exports regarding General Franco's Spain (e.g., Leeds, Nottingham and Lambeth TCs). Manchester & Salford TC held an anti-Franco demonstration, the TUC commenting that this had its origins in the CP. Similarly, in London, that huge TC prepared for a demonstration for May Day 1946 (the first since 1939). This would not involve the NUGMW Executive, which gauged London TC to be 'under the influence of Communists'. Indeed, the London TC, representing *c*.600,000 workers, had a CP secretary, a CP-dominated office staff and an executive with a CP majority, and was one of the CP's most effective outlets.

TC delegates articulated the conviction that the Labour government, with its overwhelming majority, would represent all their interests at last. Delegates argued that for many years their main activity had been to *defend* workers in coping with employers or local councils. After a Mr Torode awakened ACTC delegates in May 1946 to the reality that TCs must not lose sight of 'the class enemy', and other TC delegates (from Ealing, Mitcham and Gloucester) objected to the *Daily Herald*'s anti-Soviet stance, H.V. Tewson reminded them that: 'The Russian press did not hesitate to criticise Britain'.[538] Fortunately, with the election of a new government, the TUC and TCs were in the zone: the planning mode.

2. PLANNING THE FUTURE 1946-48

Political dualities within TCs impacted upon their pronouncements. TUC leaders adhered to a semi-planned, centralised state in which business executives, technicians and officials would 'take control', with unions' participation in Attlee's government.[539] All TCs knew this. In Brighton the TC was compelled by the local Labour Party to remove the two communists from local committees. Yet, this was the same TC unhappy with the 'anti-Soviet' local United Nations Association and sent a TC member to the CP district conference. The same dichotomous behaviour occurred in other TCs, as in Birmingham TC, which defeated a CP request to affiliate to the Labour Party, yet was dismayed when the General Council refused to sponsor its scheme to offer hospitality to Soviet trade unionists.

In Southampton, the local TC raised the issue of secrecy in scientific research.[540] This was of vital importance. Secrecy led to international suspicions. It stifled scientific development. And, for this TC, it did not help 'those democratic peoples' already working out 'Socialist Economic Planning'. This was transparently part of a CP defence of atomic scientist Nunn May, who was imprisoned for giving information to the Russian government.

TCs' admiration for the Soviet Union's planned economy was firmly ensconced by CP members in TCs, who helped underpin and galvanise anti-'Black Market' Committees.[541] They added their weight in those TCs that highlighted the abolition of independent unions in Greece and entreated the government to assist the Greeks in a government 'free from military and Fascist tendencies'.[542]

CP members in TCs also addressed the extensive delays in soldier demobilisation, which was owing, some CP members in TCs delineated, to the government's preservation of Imperial interests.

TUC leaders regularly toured the country on behalf of the government, and part of that touring included an endeavour to sideline communists engaged in TCs. Newcastle TC received visits from V. Feather and R. Boyfield to dissuade the TC from being attached to 'organisations whose policies were not enjoying the approval of the TUC'. This was a reference to the apparently unhealthy TC debates floating around in the post-war euphoria as to whether substantial economic changes could necessarily be achieved through constitutional means. CP members decided on a head-on confrontation against the TUC's wage restraint policy and its deleterious effects on workers' living standards. CP members encouraged TCs to be involved in every strike going, revitalising their 1930s approach, while TUC Assistant-Secretary Feather earned his Citrine-style TUC stripes, categorising the CP as a 'dictatorship with rigid discipline and Party instructions' as an offence against the TCs. He understood their tactics and techniques. They understood his. In *Vic Feather, TUC*, E. Silver quotes a unionist from the time: 'We knew Victor. He was the kind of man who caresses your back looking for the right place to put the knife'.[543]

*

This was the beginning of the Cold War (which is being revived in the 2020s). The CP's reach in the late 1940s was rumoured to be not only in TCs but extending into crucial sections of the state: in the armed forces, the press and cultural organisations. The TUC was fully cognisant of the fact that crucial for the CP in TCs was its National Industrial Policy Committee, an intermediary for CP fractions, which included organisers in unions and TCs. V. Feather and H.V. Tewson would have been relieved to discover that CP membership had decreased by 12,000, to 38,579 by June 1947.[544]

Regardless, what disturbed the General Council was the CP's positioning as the only organisation with experience, union members and a coherent class strategy. The CP critiqued the TUC's *Britain's Plan for Prosperity*, and now denounced the JPCs as moribund. In February 1947 it targeted Labour government failures to transcend existing vested interests. On the local level, Leeds TC's A.C. Lowcock wrote personally to Tewson, informing him that, while allowing known communists as delegates, CP members had no chance of holding office. He informed Tewson that he would not work with the local Leeds CP secretary, who was nominated for the post of assistant TC secretary: 'The chap may be a decent trade unionist but I claimed upon grounds of insufficient office space and equipment... that there was no need for an assistant.'[545] Lowcock and others like him, in their political acrobatics, used the very 'deviousness' they proclaimed to be exposing in the CP, while 'insufficient' funds was the 1930s perennial excuse for evading local activism, frequently reheated by the TUC.

Such trifling operated alongside TCs' genuine wariness and suspicions that a Labour government had harnessed its future to American capital and investment. Such a trajectory obviously came into conflict, and was juxtaposed to, TCs' affiliations to ASFCs. A number of TCs spoke officially of regret at the breakdown in British/Soviet trade talks, while prevalent communists on Brighton, Edinburgh and Manchester & Salford TCs were all for friendship with the Soviet Union and a national economic plan in line with 'the planned economies of Eastern Europe'.

The renowned aid, in the form of the Marshall Plan, tied Europe to the USA, a form of 'Empire by invitation'.[546] Adam Tooze has clarified that the Marshall Plan was the US's fabled aid programme, credited with kick-starting Western Europe's recovery and providing the material foundation for the era of liberalism in institutions that underpinned the post-war order, with ideological trappings entailing anti-communism, a Keynesian growth model and 'European integration'.[547] It was known as the European Reconstruction Programme (ERP), to enable recipient economies to grow more rapidly, with raw materials, fuel and machinery to consumers and investors, 3.2 billion dollars disbursed between 1948 and 1952 (1.1% of US GDP). It locked Western Europe into an alliance with the US, compelled the Labour government to square welfare introductions with investments, and consolidated the anti-Soviet front. Such governmental geopolitics was coupled with the TUC equating the CPSU with terror, oppression, a stultified media, rigged elections, suppression of personal freedoms – a totalitarian regime.

Despite this turn of world events, pro-Soviet exclamations persisted in TCs where CP activists dominated proceedings. The Marshall Plan was thus critiqued as an imperialist intervention. That bled into questioning the processes of 'increased production' *per se* and who were the winners in this, compared to wartime? Was this production drive at a time of a wage freeze merely creating more profits for capitalists, and thus, as the CP deduced, 'aiding dollar imperialism'? Those TCs who vocalised this viewpoint and summation were also championing 'unofficial disputes'. Inevitably this produced another ACTC 1947 ruling, not to intervene without the consent of union national executives.[548]

Birmingham TC, in a public meeting to celebrate the Soviet Union's thirtieth birthday, expressed the widespread TC yearning that co-operation between British and Soviet peoples was the best guarantee for peace and economic prosperity. Relations between the TC and Labour Party were depicted by the TC secretary as 'hostile', (the *mot juste* of the age!) a sizeable chunk of union members opting not to attend the TC. The result was predictable: the election of communists by a small proportion of union members.[549] In Bristol, the Labour Party dissociated itself from the TC's criticism of the government and noted the process whereby the CP used the TC 'politically' on this basis; by 92 to 57 the TC ruled out any political discussions. Unions were to forward resolutions on political matters to the Labour Party. To the uninitiated, Sheffield T&LC's president explained:

> Often under the shelter of the word 'democracy', the enemies within our [Labour] Party seek to weaken us. Within the shelter of the 'democratic right' to criticise, they seek to weaken the faith and confidence of the Party in its leadership... Criticism was a weapon we used when we were an opposition Party.[550]

The T&LC envisaged the future as binary, 'Totalitarianism versus Democratic Socialism', adhering to the government that was designed to implement 'Socialist Economic Planning without Political Tyranny'.[551]

By October 1947, TCs were projecting the following programme: no pegging of wages, diminution of the armed forces, iron and steel industry nationalisation, continuance of food subsidies, stringent price controls, constraints on profits, and a national economic plan with Eastern Europe, the latter obviously CP-originated.[552] In 1948 the TUC's General Council updated 'Communists and Fascists' in the new *Trades Councils' Guide*, rejigging *The Communist Solar System* from March 1933, as a diversion from the passionate opposition to the wage freeze. Under the section 'Communists and Fascists', TCs were again instructed to refuse both – as if there was an equivalence.

The wage freeze now took precedence in TCs' campaigns. Food shortages, rising prices and cuts in housing and education became the hot topics raised by communists in TCs and recorded in the TCs' annual reports.[553] Labour Party secretary Morgan Phillips enjoined unions to ban CP officials for 'sabotage', for fomenting discontent in factories, and aiming to undermine, and ultimately destroy, the labour movement. Manchester & Salford TC defied his judgement and sent delegates to the *Daily Worker* conference, its pro-communist EC rebelliously circumventing the TCJCC's 20 years of *Model Rules*.

Increasingly, more TCs began to reflect the CP's position on wage freezing (to name some: Battersea, Bath, Colchester, Sevenoaks, Pontypridd, Weston-super-Mare, Trowbridge, Rotherham and Bedford TCs).

Glasgow TC defiantly opposed the government's 'White Paper on Personal Incomes'. From Slough, Nottingham, Winchester and Dover TCs came similar protests. TCs all over Britain engaged in CP-inspired condemnations of the government's introduction of 'political discrimination' into the civil service. Funds, as we have reiterated, were made the central problem for the TCJCC: 'Very few Trades Councils have sufficient funds to carry out all the work they wish to undertake and the dissipation of funds in fruitless affiliations has the effect of limiting the useful work they do.'[554] (Seemingly, there was no magic money tree!)

In a preface to a history of Liverpool TC, E. Bevin accentuated the loyalty to the movement of the people for whom the TC had catered. For him, TCs, 'if properly used', had a great future. This, just as the TC's president had breached 'democratic procedure', after a resolution from the Liverpool branch of the Civil Service Clerical Association (CSCA) opposed the purge of employees and denial of union representation to the victims. Liverpool TC's EC prevented discussion of this, the local CSCA chairman furnishing H.V. Tewson with this fitting comeback:

> Inform me whether it is a fact that any decisions reached by the TUC are precluded from discussion by the trade union membership. If so, it would perhaps be desirable to abolish all Trades Councils and to set up offices in every town for the sole purpose of distributing all decisions of the TUC without any reference to the rank and file.[555]

(Probably not a good idea to offer this as an option!) Would this be the future? As one delegate at Margate TUC, with unconscious irony exclaimed, it was difficult for the General Council to secure CP members' rights because the latter would then have opportunities of learning how information was collected on CP activities 'prejudicial to State interests'.[556] Such were the oddities arising from the TUC's determination to marginalise the CP.

3. THE COLD WAR IN TRADES COUNCILS 1948-51

In October and November 1948, alongside the economic crisis and wage freeze (not as prolonged as under the five Conservative PMs from 2010), the TUC emerged with new circulars to deflate any enduring CP interventions. As was public in TCs, and alluded to above, CP members were continually discrediting the Marshall Plan and also any new rearmament plans. Some TCs endorsed this approach. And some also agreed with CP advocacy of a strike of clerical workers over victimisation of union branch officials.[557] A few TCs were deregistered following *Circular 18, Trade Unions and Communism*, which banned communists from union office, and the CP was likewise accused of obstructing the economic policy approved at the Margate conference.

The CP had declared its opposition, but H.V. Tewson extrapolated with the old rebuke that the CP was 'in servile obedience to decisions made by the Cominform, the new organisation linking CPs across Europe.[558] For Tewson, the 'pretended dissolution of the Comintern was a mere device to enable CPs to deny the charge that Moscow was interfering in the internal affairs of other States'. This was a peculiar criticism from a representative of the British establishment. Tewson insisted: CPs were 'acting on orders from outside when the Cominform opposed the European Recovery Programme'.[559] It was not necessary to argue about or try to verify this, but it certainly laid the path towards and forged an atmosphere for a legitimate proscription. The message for all TCs was that the CP and its acolytes had been ordered to oppose the Marshall Plan, to sabotage the European Recovery Programme (ERP), frame industrial demands for political agitation, magnify industrial grievances, and engineer strikes. A CP inspired refutation, which filtered through some TCs, scorned the TUC for upholding the sanctity of profits, foregoing wage demands, and co-operating with the 'master class' and American big business.[560]

Both the CP *and* the TUC here claimed to be representing workers' best interests. This encompassed resisting the employers' offensive, and striving to improve wages and living standards (at the expense of profits), thus strengthening trade unionism. It was evident to a majority of TC delegates that CP members *were* campaigning for better pay and working conditions, but this did not automatically imply that union leaders were always operating to hinder such advances. Conversely, blaming communists for the economic problems, explaining world history primarily in the stark terms of a 'communist conspiracy' and trampling on the mildest resolution as a 'communist trap' was as crude as accusing the TUC of not caring about wage levels or new social services.

The ritualistic barbs did not abate or mitigate these bruising conflicts. CP'ers in TCs would carry on. They would campaign to ban the atom bomb, advocate withdrawal of troops from Malaya, the expulsion of the US military from Britain, and promote Vyshinsky's United Nations' position 'in the cause of peace'. The letters would also stack up and pour into TUC HQ from TC and Labour officials about disruptive CP activities; it was ever thus since 1920.

*

In October 1948, F. Meade of *Labour's Northern Voice* contacted trusty conduit V. Feather. Manchester & Salford TC's EC was recommending the TC send delegates to another *Daily Worker* Peace Conference contrary to the TC's 'Rule 12'. The TC president had announced that, as the PPPS was not a proscribed organisation, the minute was in order. The ruling was upheld by 78 to 62 votes. Meade contended that the PPPS *was* proscribed 'because the PPPS was the *Daily Worker* and that was the same as the CP... the PPPS invited TCs to invest funds in it'. Feather was having none of it. He reduced this farrago to a continuation of the vain endeavours that communists had made for over 25 years to secure a footing and influence in the movement, which their policies did not command:

> Most Trades Councils had not been taken in by this deception, particularly as it had usually been accompanied by attacks on the Labour Government. Communist elements in some Trades Councils, however, contrived to create sufficient confusion of thought.[561]

V. Feather's rationale did not extend to any cogitation over the validity of anything the CP could offer. He did not entertain the CP's stated belief that TCs had never had a more important and vital role co-ordinating local experience and surmounting barriers between unions.[562] The TCJCC, as could have been anticipated, critiqued TCs for the peace conferences, and also when CP speakers and the CP's *Labour Monthly* invited TC contributions for the thirty-first anniversary of the Russian Revolution. J. Jacobs (London TC), W. Spencer (Coventry TC), D. Edwards (Newcastle & District TC), E. Butler (Ammanford, Llandebie & District TC) and even A.C. Lowcock (Leeds TC) praised Soviet achievements, as H. Baker (Birmingham TC) embellished the TCs' 'historic responsibility to the world working class'. Baker invited the TUC to inform the government, as it had in 1920: 'The masses of Europe and the world want peace. The inhuman imperialists and militarists want war.' TCs, as local watchdogs of the working class, had a role, to prevent a drift towards war against the 'Socialist States of Europe'. Baker further proclaimed:

> Ever since 1917 the workers in this country have refused to be duped by the dope of the capitalist press as to the real significance of the Russian Revolution, and have followed with pride the achievements of the First Workers' Socialist Republic.[563]

Placing the Soviet Union on such a pedestal was put to the test by the General Council's *Defend Democracy – Communist Activities Examined*.[564] This was intended to put the kibosh on the CP. It would expose their industrial committees, at last put a halt to 'certain TCs' being used to further communist policy, and was the most explicit statement on CP tactics in TCs and how to thwart them since *Circular 16* (1934), which was now partially reproduced.

V. Feather's depiction of CP intrusions in TCs was familiar, such interferences achieved by 'industrious, guileful and skilful tactics and single-mindedness on one side and easy-going apathy on the other'. Informers on TCs (or, more politely, communicators with the TUC) kept up a barrage of letters naming individual TC members who championed a CP candidate (rather than the Labour Party one) in a local election. Brighton TC was, claimed J.A. Evison, becoming 'a political arena' – yet again! A lengthy missive from Evison reached the eagle-eyed Feather:

> For your personal and private information I submit that the president, vice president and secretary are Communists or in the Communist band-wagon... Roland Mason, a most likeable man, is replaced by Gordon Cree, another avowed Communist... you and your colleagues of the TUC are being compelled to take action to defend yourselves (and we trade unionists) from the Communists... If you have to carry out a 'purge' it will mean exactly the same thing as that suggested in 1944, namely that the affiliated trades unions to the trades councils and the trade union branches will have to get busy... There is probably some straight-talking going on in high quarters but this needs supplementing by action... I have complete confidence in the part you are playing.[565]

Instead of dismissing him as a wearisome crank, Feather wished there were more TC members like him. He wrote:

> Maintain your vigilance and continue to 'open the eyes' of all trade unions with whom you come in contact to the great danger to which the democratic procedures of our movement are exposed from the attempts of the CP to impose policy upon the movement from without.[566]

How obsessed the TUC was about this 'great danger', how portentously they took CP unionists as a threat; but to what purpose? Blackpool TC acknowledged 'embarrassing actions' by CP shop stewards who had taken independent action in the name of the TC, but the TC added that an organisation that debarred the CP today might exclude unions tomorrow. This TC calmly informed the TUC that political conviction was a matter for the liberty of the individual, and democratic machinery allied with the intelligence of TC members was sufficient guarantee against 'disruption'.

Relations with the Labour Party in the combined Trades and Labour Councils could result in greater tension. A regular informer to the TUC General Council, A. E. Hobson, worried that a Sheffield T&LC general meeting would allow CP members to attend. Feather hastily replied that 'Clause 19' excluded communists, the CP (as always) undermined democratic procedures and relied upon alien and dictatorial methods. The TCJCC secretary had recorded that, in 1940, this very T&LC's Industrial Section had passed *appeasement* resolutions (in tune with the Nazi–Soviet Pact) that had received publicity on the German and Russian wireless (although Hobson admitted this had little bearing on the case he was raising).[567]

There is a curious anomaly with ironic overtones: the contents of decades of TUC/TC correspondence on communists' active contributions in TCs were not known about by TC delegates, who were themselves participating in spirited debates on *Defend Democracy – Communist Activities Examined*. The TUC projected a conviction that there was a ruse to suppress circulation and stifle examination of its circulars, and that the CP 'subjected Trades Councils to specious arguments' about the TUC and their circulars. A catch-22 was imparted here. The TUC's standpoint had the following logic: the fact that 'disruptive and undemocratic elements' might not have obtained a toehold within a TC should not lull the TC into 'a false sense of security', otherwise it might be 'caught napping' at a later date. The TUC was now investigating those TCs in which the CP claimed there had been opposition to the TUC: 'a typical distortion of the truth by disruptive bodies and their press'.[568] (A circular circular?)

The TUC often won this extenuated conflict by focusing TCs on the form rather than the content of TC activities. At Birmingham TC, T. Williamson (NUGMW) notified the TUC that the TC was 'very suspect' following the advent of CP resolutions. He enumerated those condemning withdrawal of the British delegation from the World Federation of Trade Unions (WFTU), organising a peace conference under TC auspices, overtly criticising British foreign policy and rejecting the TUC circular. He averred the secretary and chairman were 'hand in glove with the CP crowd', the 'responsible trade union element' absent.[569]

Congress policy did not go by default. TCs were frequently persuaded to accept CP-inspired appeals, their resolutions 'under the name of the TC' published in the local press. CP members prepared emergency resolutions, pushed them through TCs, and the *Daily Worker* reported them. All this happened as the TUC's *The Tactics of Disruption – Communist Methods Exposed* in March 1949[570] planned to further combat such 'infiltration and interference' in trade union policy.[571]

TCs' lived experiences were shared at the ACTC 1949. TC secretaries who were communists were questioned about their first loyalty (to TCs or to the CP). Others pointed out incidents quoted in *Tactics of Disruption* that were incorrect and without evidence. A majority of delegates judged that the union movement would be stronger if it discarded *Circular 16*. A. Eaton (Wolverhampton TC) encapsulated the general tone of this ACTC: he was proud to play his part alongside a communist 'but he watched him'.

V. Feather was present at this ACTC to air his long-held proclamation that those who loved democracy should be vigilant, not intimidated by a 'handful of fanatics' with 'totalitarian principles'.[572] Soon, the 'fanatics' had their trenchant say. The CP's *Defend Trade Union Rights* challenged him. Here were the TUC's 'carefully fostered misconceptions' of the CP, an organisation which had led a pioneering struggle in the 1920s for recognition of TCs and maintained, contrary to TUC statistics, that *Circulars 16* and *17* were upheld by a *minority* of unions. The bans had been lifted because union democracy had re-established itself and most unionists would not tolerate further discrimination against some of the best and most devoted representatives of the working class. A report to the CP EC in February 1949 advocated 'stronger Trades Councils' that would not rob branches of 'their right to determine policy'.[573]

*

Then came the Canadian Seamen's Union (CSU) fracas. In July 1949 Manchester & Salford TC saluted dockers locked out for refusing to 'blackleg' on Canadian seamen. The TC voted 81 to 46 for CSU representatives to be invited to the TC to explain the situation, but the CSU was not an affiliated body.[574] The general secretary of the Waterproof Garment Workers, F.C. Henry, contacted H.V. Tewson and A. Deakin (TGWU general secretary) in trepidation: the TC (particularly its secretary, H.E. Newbold) was 'very close to the CP'.

Tewson was at least relieved to read that within the TC there was a growing minority against the communist leadership. Newbold had been cited as a communist in the *Glossop Chronicle* in its own unique brand of serendipitous logic: 'If a man is sent to Russia by a Communist-dominated body and returns to tell us that Russia is a paradise, it is clearly improbable that he is a political ally of Mr. Churchill.'[575] It had done its research. Newbold *had* returned with glowing reports of Soviet 'dignity of labour', the 'full and free expression of opinion' and the singular notion that there was no time to organise a strike there 'because everything was settled before you could have one'!

Across Britain, the depleted CP faced daunting trials to overcome. For example, in Brighton, where the local TC was affiliated to the LRD, the TC protested (26 to 14 votes) when the town council prohibited CP meetings at the Dome. This was correctly diagnosed as 'an attack upon freedom of speech and assembly and the rights of citizens to hear the policy of a legitimate political party'.[576] However, at the TUC conference in 1949 priority was on safeguarding TCs; they had, as always, to be protected from becoming 'a vehicle for propaganda' directed against the democratic policy structure, the CP depicted as 'stabbing Congress and the country in the back'. The General Council report on this was upheld by 6,746,000 to 76,000. To rub salt into the wound, the WFTU was condemned as a 'communist-dominated international agency'.[577]

Resuming, this time in Liverpool, TC secretary R. Miller contacted R. Boyfield about 'trouble from Communists' on the TC. He targeted L.C. White (CSCA and communist) who refused to sign the declaration that he was/wasn't a CP member because he had the temerity to ascertain that it would be in breach of the Trade Union Act 1913, imposing a political test on membership. The CSCA was affiliated to a proscribed organisation (the LRD), although Boyfield had to acknowledge that the CSCA did not have a political fund. Exasperated, Miller retorted that the TC's meetings for years had been devoted to CP-originating resolutions on political issues, embarrassing the TC and the Labour Party.[578]

With General Election 1950 on the horizon, opposition in TCs to communist activities gathered. The tortuous controversy in Liverpool TC reverberated in Birmingham TC, with an interjection from the *Birmingham Gazette*, keen the TC could overcome its communist domination. Here, E. Rose (TGWU secretary) was wearying. Every TC discussion was 'coloured by CP bias'; the local CP's 'only propaganda outlet was the Trades Council', with discussions mainly of a political character, resolutions 'gerrymandered onto the agenda'. Rose felt uncomfortable that the TC had invited CP'er Wal Hannington as the speaker on 'The Midlands and International Trade'. T.H. Nimmo (ETU) was of the opinion that the TC had become a sounding board for the CP. Its president and secretary were 'helpless against the communist-controlled EC' and the CP voiced rank-and-file populist opposition to government stringencies.[579] V. Feather was adamant that Leeds TC was 'being told' to protest about the trial of CP officials in the USA. Accordingly: 'Trades Councils should not degenerate into debating societies discussing subjects *not in their terms of reference*'.[580] Feather contrasted the US trial with trials and death sentences in Bulgaria and Hungary, countries lacking 'free parliamentary institutions'.

Circular 46: Trades Councils and Proscribed Organisations[581] arrived in January 1950 after the circulars *Defend Democracy* and *Tactics of Disruption* were approved by the 1949 ACTC, the vote 180 to 83. *Circular 46* corroborated TCs' internal political divisions. There were rejoinders. Under the heading 'Trades Councils Defend the Rights of Communists', the *Brighton & Hove Gazette* construed Sussex Federation of TCs' statement on *Circular 46* (excluding delegates on political grounds) as an attack on all TCs. (The *Brighton Argus* wrote about the Communist threat.) Tom Parsons, Sussex trade unionist and Labour Party member, took a more measured position, that communists were 'merely mistakenly exuberant Socialists' reacting to social injustice and suppression by seeking to eradicate the 'disease of capitalism'![582]

*

The TUC ploughed on: official recognition had been withdrawn from seven TCs; they would not tolerate 'fifth columnists'. Hill (TCJCC) was alarmed that some TCs spent their time honouring Stalin's birthday. Back at the ACTC, nearly two-thirds (160 to 90) tacitly condoned the implementation of *Circular 46*, which reiterated that the CP was using the trade union movement as a 'cover' for its activities. Through the TUC lens, TCs were at least nominating more delegates on local committees, so what mattered was their representative industrial character. They could not spend time joining CP-sponsored ASFSs.[583]

Would proscribing CP members from TCs defeat CP arguments or benefit TCs' activism? E. Kavanagh (Leeds TC) now exclaimed that CP members had insulted TUC leaders when imputing they were 'arch-traitors'. 'Communists take you by the hand but eventually by the throat', he said, a phrase formerly used by V. Feather.[584] For F.R. Fermor of East Ham TC: 'The Communist had one God – Stalin; one Paradise – Moscow; and one policy – that dictated by the Cominform and in Russia the unions were dominated by the one-party state'.[585] CP tactics were about to be eviscerated. The CP was its own worst enemy, as Feather eagerly reaffirmed:

> Freedom of thought? Freedom of speech? The CP expelled members for the slightest ideological deviation

from the Party line. The Communist who refused to retract or who sought to justify the independence of his personal thought or to claim his right to freedom of speech was branded by Communist leaders as a renegade, a deviationist, a follower of Tito.[586]

He was only mistaken in judging that *only* communists misrepresented their branches. Countless delegates were guilty of this at some time, just as 'block votes' were misrepresentations. Similarly, it was not just the CP being guilty of what V. Feather termed 'furtive backstairs intrigue'.[587] As we have investigated, hitherto, no one was blameless on that account. Both the TUC and CP spoke of cloakings, facades, bluffs and camouflages. Eventually, Feather at the ACTC 1950 delivered a prolonged indictment, another diatribe caricaturing the CP's position in unions. A gauge of vocal CP sympathisers in the minority was apparent in the vote (191 to 75), the majority not to be discredited by the 'fractious political activity of a minority'. Yet, apart from the disastrous period in the war (1939–41), the CP's position had been consistent. The central thrust was to question the *motivation* behind Labour and union leaders' divisive tactics, the same appellation turned upon the CP.

CP member R. Stewart clarified this in July 1950. The CP had to endure sectarianism even in its own ranks, which 'tended to play the game of right-wing leaders by isolating the CP from the rank and file'.[588] And it resulted in confusion. In Newcastle & District TC, Secretary Edwards wrote to H.V. Tewson (when he requested a list of proscribed organisations), sighing that because the TC was inundated with literature it was almost impossible to keep track of the 'wheat from the chaff'. The TC had affiliated to the Britain–China Friendship Association and had a higher standing than ever before in the movement locally. Were the CP and TUC to be forever antlers locked?

*

By September 1950, a mounting list of TCs had altered their rules to exclude communists. Hackney, Stepney and Wood Green TCs were deregistered. More 'representative' TCs were to be formed there. The test case was the London TC, celebrating its ninetieth anniversary. Its application for registration was deferred, and in May the General Council put it bluntly to the TC about its use as a CP platform:

> A Trades Council should concentrate on the purpose for which it was formed and should not ignore these purposes or seek to duplicate the work for which other parts of the movement had responsibilities.[589]

At the TUC conference in Brighton, Prime Minister Attlee blamed some of the government's difficulties on CP-inspired actions, which had 'forced' more defence spending to be incurred. He added that CP methods had caused trouble all over the world by disruptive tactics and, in CP-controlled countries, unions had no independent life and were part of the police state and servile instruments of the ruling bureaucracy.

Despite this Labour Party snub, the largest TC, the London TC, retained a formidable CP platform within it, had increased affiliated membership from 664,687 to 688,396 by 1949, recruitment above all union leaders' criterion for a healthy TC![590] That did not dissuade V. Feather from maintaining that its proceedings were 'directed to propaganda'. (By 1952, J. Jacobs was the only CP officeholder on the TC, although, of 24 EC members, nine were communists.) Feather instructed West Yorkshire Federation of TCs to remove communist Bert Ramelson but it refused. Thus we see Feather's skills as fixer, propagandist and contact man for nearly two decades hounding communists in TCs, as has been illustrated,[591] which meant T. Quelch utopian visions of 1922 failed to materialise. TCs had indeed become a necessary part of TUC machinery, but not as Quelch had envisaged.

*

By 1950, CP aspirations for TCs' autonomy as independent local entities had been blunted. The major part of TCs' existence would for some time be as devoted representatives on local public committees, gathering consumers' views, publicising official TUC policy, recruiting union members – and not committed to Peace Congress propaganda campaigns.[592] We close this section on the anti-CP witch-hunts reaching risible proportions. There is one extensive illustration:

In November 1950, B. Kilgarriff of Brighton TC pleaded for assistance from R. Boyfield of the TUC: 'The Communist element is getting very powerful in this district and I find it increasingly difficult to move against them in their destructive propaganda.'[593] Branches that wanted to send delegates to the Sheffield

Peace Conference were 'locally Comm-controlled'. Boyfield decided to pay the TC a visit. He surmised that the International Brigade Association was also under CP control. Kilgarriff then dispatched another missive to Boyfield: 'The Comms were very concerned about the source of my information; on the point of order they were not enlightened'. Kilgarriff noted, with the 24 communists on the TC, an Amnesty of Greece meeting was to be convened with a CP delegate. Kilgarriff said he looked forward to Boyfield's visit at the next TC meeting but had not told anyone else.

Boyfield wondered about those TC delegates opposed to the TUC, who had decided not to contribute to the discussion while he was present, but noted the disagreement with the four official TC functions. Kilgarriff named a Mr Faulkner ('a reformed Mosleyite, now a Communist') as having been elected vice-president. Kilgarriff was the assistant-secretary so Boyfield would get the agenda and the latter was sent the lowdown – the EC included five socialists, two communists and two 'fellow travellers'. Boyfield imparted the obvious: he distrusted organisations that at first sight had useful objectives but which on closer acquaintance were CP-controlled:

> This was the 'front' technique where the CP hid behind a plausible facade when the fundamental aim was not improvement but propaganda and the undermining of the movement. They started on 'bread and butter' issues and developed towards resolutions on foreign policy or whatever was the Communist stand of the day.[594]

He requested further information after the next TC meeting. It was soon in the post. (There were two postal deliveries each day then.) Kilgarriff attended the famed Holborn Hall meeting about the strike at the South Bank and despaired that, although the speakers claimed that they were there in a private capacity, '50% of the delegates were active Communists'. He reported one delegate propagandising for the (political) strike. Kilgarriff shared with Boyfield further trepidations over the British–Soviet Friendship Society. Boyfield tarried not a jot: it was a proscribed organisation! Where to go? Such rigmarole was a central component in TUC strategy to undermine and marginalise communist influence in TCs.

Two final examples among myriads will suffice. In Southampton, the TC chairman informed Boyfield that a local candidate was a communist, as were the TC's secretary and assistant: 'There is great difficulty here in keeping an anti-communist bias. For two years we have been fairly successful in doing this but there appears to be a determined effort to upset the balance this year.'[595] Meanwhile, at Sheffield T&LC, A.E. Hobson informed Boyfield that for some years it had not been compulsory in TCs to refuse credentials to communists, although certain persons were ineligible to attend the ACTC. He ended his letter with *the* question: '*Was this charade the only way to discuss topics in a "democratic" organisation?*'[596] (Our italics). Let that query serve as the epitaph on TC/CP/TUC relations. Could these groups not arrive in what is termed the middle ground or enjoy the benefits of open, free and frank debate? How could anyone win out? In *Beyond the Fragments*, Lynne Segal asked: 'It *is* possible to create greater co-ordination and support between people involved in local struggles, and a militant trades council... could do just such a job'.[597] (Can today's radicals do any better?)

4. OVERVIEW – THE COMMUNIST PARTY IN TRADES COUNCILS 1920-50

From 1920 to 1950, CP delegates in TCs provided a running critique and radical narrative on the performance of trade union leaders. In this role they were alternately bolstered, challenged and restricted by workers' industrial and political traditions. When they secured positions on TCs as presidents, secretaries or chairpersons they used these to persuade/guide/cajole TCs to become crucibles for advancing particular causes. Optimum commitments were to the NUWM, the MM, hunger marches, anti-fascist campaigns, the Spanish Civil War response, conscription issues, the 'Imperialist War' thesis, against suppression of the *Daily Worker* and in defence of civil liberties', war production committees, and protests over the wage freeze. The causes highlighted here resulted in prolonged TC debates that, once the TUC entered the ring, would degenerate into stereotypes, caricatures and platitudes from all sides. The TUC frequently pointed out that the CP had another agenda. Plus, CP members would not always sensitise themselves to the viewpoint of non-CP unionists or incorporate how other TC officials had reacted. The unpredictable, sometimes unprincipled, vacillations of CP tactics and ideology inflicted its own damage, the wartime line 1939–41 the most pertinent example.

Distrust between CP and union leaders was omnipresent throughout these 30 years. The latter reacted to CP vilifications of 'reformism' by pledging eternal vigilance and CP plans for TCs were assiduously documented and monitored by the TUC, with the aid of TC secretaries' reports. Hence the continual revising and updating of TCs' *Model Rules*. Hence the mini-McCarthyite 'disruption inquiries' and the flurry of expelling recalcitrant delegates, disbanding TCs and creating new ones. From 1922 the CP initiated theories about the heroic potential functions of TCs as part of its broader industrial policies; it formulated a design as to the NMM's role for TCs in any industrial/political crisis.

Subsequently, the CP's diversification in tactics within the labour movement had mixed receptions within all TCs, revitalising some, stifling others, stimulating battles over industrial/political divisions in many. Numerous TC resolutions at ACTCs were patently CP-formulated. CP delegates surreptitiously planned their tactics before TC meetings and many of the resultant complaints from officials to the TUC were about this 'gerrymandering'. CP viewpoints were transparent in TC minutes in the constant paeans to the Soviet Union, refurbished in class-based terminology. Attending meetings with specific political agendas stretched TC/TUC relations yet injected a broader concept of TCs' role beyond TUC boundaries. Confidential exposés to the TUC Organisation Department notwithstanding, numerous unions objected to their TC nomination being removed 'for political reasons'.

The emergence during World War I of Councils of Workers' and Soldiers' Delegates had presaged a wider scope for TCs' activities with 'dual power' possibilities, and even as a potential counterweight to Parliament and the major parties. The CP was created on fertile ground. Those who had joined the CP from other socialist organisations motivated existing union activists in TCs, prompted by dissatisfaction and frustration with union officialdom, one of the reasons for the emergence of the shop stewards' movement.

The watershed for trade union and labour politics was the monumental impact on consciousness – faith in 'the First Workers' Government', Russia, 1917. That was surely, amazingly, the future? Wasn't this what workers in Britain needed to model themselves upon? This 'Socialist Sixth of the World', as the CP boasted, dovetailed into TC demands for councils of action and Hands-off Russia campaigns. CP members understandably latched onto aspects of this enervating post-1918 militant unionism plus the organisation of the unemployed begun by its predecessors, the SDF and the BSP, from which members of the CP originated and now flourished.

All TCs initially embraced any news of Soviet achievements for workers. As early as 1920, the London TC was invited to an international conference in Moscow to gather information on the economic position of Soviet workers, and TCs notably sought diplomatic relations with this new Soviet Union. The spirit of radicalism centred on the CP, whose members became the new dynamo in TCs, nudging Labour and union policies in a more radical direction. Acerbity towards an insidious CP, evident for Labour Party leaders at the national level, was not before 1924 (the year of Lenin's death) reflected in localities. The 1917 Leeds Convention and 1920 councils of action had merged industrial with political action, but the CP's applications to join the Labour Party (Lenin's instructions) were constantly rebuffed.

Essentially a revolutionary party in a non-revolutionary British situation, after 12 of its leaders had been imprisoned in 1925, the CP was soon compelled to explain in its trajectory the failure of the General Strike. Nevertheless, struggling to impress a new code of political action was its novel injection into TCs: the *politics of class struggle*. Many TCs, as the voluntary part of the union movement, abetted the new CP after Labour's A. Henderson had demoted TCs from being principal local agents for the Labour Party in 1918. Disheartened by Labour leaders (there had been no Labour government yet), TCs incorporated the enthusiasms and opportunities for workers (as witnessed in the young Soviet Union).

The CP was tracked and monitored by the TUC General Council because of the latter's post-1926 industrial relations' adaptations. Instigation of the black circulars resulted. Soviet defiance and immense sacrifices against Germany from 1941 to 1945, and subsequent CP support for JPCs, played a part in relaxing victimisation by three black circulars. TC representations on vigilance committees, war economy provisions and social services, and the peak $c.50,000$ CP members, contributed significantly. Communists extended their range in TCs with opposition to the Marshall Plan and the noteworthy wage freeze. Another set of *Model Rules* arrived, referring back to the 1920s when TCs had been viewed by the CP in Leninist terms as weapons to unify rank and file politics and economics. With retrospect we can see that the trade unions' role in the UK and the USSR was profoundly divergent. Where the absence of a reformist union history provided fewer barriers to revolution in Russia, in the UK reformist union traditions within capitalist society acted as a break on radical transformation.[598] During World War II, British union leaders were elevated to the centre of war counsels, but the subsequent Labour government consigned TCs' role to parroting the TUC in localities, and doing its bidding. CP plans for somehow marrying industrial with political aspirations outside the Labour Party were eclipsed.

*

Walter Citrine adumbrated his judgement on the CP in unions and TCs. He rebuked the CP for its simplistic analysis of a capitalism that implied workers' inexorable impoverishment; the automatic trajectory of 'stability' equated with treachery; and viably nurtured relations between unions and employers as 'detestable'; and the CP's contention the more frequent the strikes, the better for the morale of the worker. In 1964 he reflected upon these 30 years:

> Utterly unscrupulous methods, gross misrepresentation and vilification… were bound to follow my exposure of their activities. The laws of slander and libel were powerless against the subtle and malicious insinuations, accusations and innuendoes which were the stock-in-trade of the CP press and officials; the formation of subsidiary bodies to conceal [their] activities had become a feature of CP tactics… Generally speaking, Communists were a poor lot in discussion, their hackneyed phrases and stereotyped vituperation being easily anticipated… Communists knew well that it was due largely to my efforts that the union movement had

awakened to the danger of [them] gaining control of the trade unions.[599]

Such condemnations of the nature and character of the CP and its 'intrusions' monopolised debates in trade unions and TCs from 1920 to 1950 and beyond.

However, Citrine underestimated CP members' consistently useful and worthy endeavours in local communities (as spotlighted throughout this book), even if their efforts were marginalised and excoriated, and overshadowed by tomes glorifying the Bevins, Citrines and Feathers. Yes, the CP could be oligarchic in its style and strategies and that was inherited from being unreservedly, blindly loyal to 'the Moscow line' throughout. Union leaders were never slow in remonstrating to TCs about that. And yes, the CP dutifully followed the Moscow line of sectarianism in 1928–33 along with its members in TCs, and shockingly diluted the anti-fascist cause 1939–41, yet an intrinsic enthusiasm for applying the liberating 'Soviet idea' to be transposed in some form to Britain through workers' committees and 'extended TCs' was at the core: 'In the unions, of the unions, but not determined by their limitations' was how J.T. Murphy phrased it.[600]

*

Any potential expansion of TCs' remit was always at odds with the General Council and the TCJCC. Communist aspiration for politically conscious TC members committed to transforming local administration was not then realisable, not potent enough to shift the format of historically cumbersome, pedestrian municipal government. TCs were overwhelmingly trapped in the logic of Labour's reformism and union leaders' 'revisionism' despite the CP's techniques of industrial action intended to offer a *reorientation* in local politics. This entailed decades of the gradual processes of *demystification* that would marinate in TCs, and only emerge as economic, social and political events revitalised union consciousness. (This radicalisation can be witnessed in the major UK strikes of 2022 and 2023 after over a decade of austerity and wage freezes for essential workers.)

In the 1940s the economy was stabilised predominantly through Keynesian economic ratifications. The mixed economy and the implementation of Beveridgism included social security, council housing, the magnificent NHS, and state-funded secondary education. The Labour Party (and government) with the TUC in the 1940s redirected TCs into a world of union prestige, status and a hierarchy based on aspirational self-interest. Proletarian consciousness and the CP's class model competed with entrenched parochialism and deferential union members in most TCs. The TUC legitimised the rules, procedures and demarcations, and governed the allocation of resources; funds and allotted time for any debates were prescribed, restricting options outside designated tasks. TCs that followed the TUC rules consented to a lesser role, a preoccupation with union recruitment.

Exposing communist skulduggery in TCs became useful when the TUC General Council was forging those links with employers or any government (e.g. 1928, 1933, 1939, 1945–50). This gradual process of union incorporation within capitalist hegemony amplified that further dimension, when, from 1945, unionism centred on routinisation and union leaders' priorities in the first majority Labour government. To transcend the TUC's carefully nurtured alignment with the government and its wage freeze was an awesome task, especially when challenges were treated as an impertinence, as detritus. Post-1939–45 the CP observed and focused attention upon *how* TCs were being inculcated and coaxed into a fabricated model of 'participation'. Whenever TC initiatives were taken up (evident in hunger marches, anti-fascist campaigns, and lending credence to unofficial strikes), the TUC judged: 'not in the best interests' of the union movement, a waste of time, finances and resources.

Eventually the CP itself chose the easy option, to steer its own reformist path, the path of least resistance. It too advised its members in TCs to campaign for short-term economic advantages, workers' control of production now deemed a pipe-dream. As analysed, the CP operated in TCs as part of a union movement on the defensive, searching for new options while beleaguered by Labourist traditions in both T&LCs and TCs, which had, before the CP's inception, separated the *political* from the *industrial* life of workers. The CP had set out to unravel that false dichotomy. Its timely so-called 'incursions' into TCs occurred, when the Labour Party and TC links were fragile in the early 1920s, and then when many were discombobulated by the transfer of labour, conscription and evacuation during 1941–44 and the establishment of JPCs.

In these 30 years, via TCs, CP members strove to link workers' economic interests in the UK with what they purported was happening for Soviet workers. In any production campaigns, the tactic was to 'zero in' upon employers' inefficiencies, and promote the Second Front, the war effort, and anti-capitalist populist sentiments: to offer an alternative. It was what being a communist meant then. In a depiction of his mother, Minna Keal, Raphael Samuel averred:

> The [Communist] Party gave her a new social life where she could learn to argue and find confidence in herself, and it offered her a cause to believe in, fighting fascism, in a movement… for the betterment of others.[601]

Communist shop steward Stan Rice, whose militancy inspired this book, would have concurred with that sentiment. Conversely, as Arthur Koesther noted: 'In fighting the Communists one is always embarrassed by one's allies.'[602] On October 27th 1951, the whole of *Collier's* magazine was devoted to a graphic, hypothetical account of a third world war between the 'United Nations' (free world) and the Soviet Union. This period was evidently a searching one for Britain's young communist party.

In chapter 8 we shall explore how TCs, including the CP vanguard, ventured to protect the most vulnerable in a devastating interwar experience, two decades of mass unemployment.

PART 3

TRADES COUNCILS ON THE MARCH

CHAPTER 8

Mass Unemployment in a Capitalist Society

If you are able-bodied, you must prove your bona fides and submit to test-work just to see whether any further sign of activity exists within that frame that has been crushed in the ever-grinding mills of the capitalist system. If you don't submit then there is no relief for you. When we knock out this selfish attitude of our minds, when we realise that it is the coal miner today, the engineer the next, the railway worker the next, then we shall perceive a great dawn before us. The real truth will percolate into our rusty minds that 'an injury to one eventually means an injury to all'.

~ *H.E. Cushnie, Brighton TC, 'When Will the Workers Wake Up?', Unity News, March 1926*

The mad dance of Capitalism's unconditional spiral of productivity is ultimately nothing but a desperate fuite en avant to escape its own debilitating inherent contradictions.

~ *Slavoj Zizek, In Defence of Lost Causes (2008 edition), p190.*

1. AN OLD ENCOUNTER RENEWED 1920-26

'Homes fit for heroes' implied one area of employment for returning soldiers. A recent article on the 1921 census estimates that post-1918 more women acquired employment, with increasing numbers 'working as engineers, vets, barristers, architects and solicitors... The census reveals there were 1,096 women for every 1,000 men, this discrepancy being the biggest between 20 and 45... There were over 1.7 million more women than men'[603] and many men were in hospital, recovering from war wounds. Unanticipated were increasing levels of *unemployment*.

In 1920 TCs were sending deputations to town councils for 'more work of public utility', for the unemployed to be given any kind of work to fulfil social and moral as much as economic needs. As such, public works could provide a safety-net or at least a palliative, but TCs noted, in their annual reports, unequal distribution of wealth as the primary cause of unemployment. TCs historically had monitored local unemployment rates (Mansfield TC had begun its existence compiling registers of the unemployed).[604] In previous chapters we have enumerated the constant tussles throughout the interwar years within TCs as to whether, or to what extent, 'local militants' were representing, or being used for (as the TUC critiqued it), 'revolutionary ends'. Cogently, many TCs during these 20 years turned this argument on its head, deducing, like Edinburgh TC, the *systemic* source of mass unemployment as 'an ever-present feature of capitalist society... not to be satisfactorily solved until the capitalist system is abolished.'[605]

A central anxiety for TCs was that unemployment was being utilised to threaten workers' standard of living. Sheffield T&LC president E.G. Rowlinson put this demonstrably: unemployment was being used as a weapon to decrease workers' pay.[606] So, in TCs, union members of *all* political persuasions began to assess the bane created by what became labelled as the 'scourge of mass unemployment', and its onerous implications for the whole labour movement, for those in work or not.

The National Unemployed Workers Committee Movement (NUWCM) had been formed on 15 April 1921. In 1922, it organised the first hunger march, which gathered TCs' advocacy in many areas of the UK. At the NFTC conference in 1923 it was the mighty Glasgow TC that initiated the 'work or maintenance' resolution. The NFTC requested all TCs affiliate to local unemployed committees and endorse the General Council/NUWCM connections at that time.[607] Then, in June 1924, the NUWCM confronted the boards of guardians (BoGs) when the latter stipulated that all able-bodied men were to be 'work-tested'. This prompted TCs' to voice calls for relief comparable to unemployment benefit, with proposed marches demonstrating against the thousands being struck off the unemployment register.

By January 1925 the TUC General Council and the Labour Party's NEC had created a joint subcommittee on unemployment insurance and declared no useful purpose could or would be served in any joint committee with the NUWCM. In response, at the first ACTC that year, CP leading light and NUWCM co-founder Wal Hannington urged closer relations between the TCs and the NUWCM, stressing it was the NUWCM that had prevented the unemployed being used as 'blacklegs' (strike-breakers) in industrial disputes. Like Sheffield T&LC's Rowlinson, Hannington warned that 'the employing class wanted to use the unemployed as a lever to reduce the standard of living'.[608] TCs, he asseverated, should affiliate to local NUWCM branches. But the TUC ruled that neither TCs nor unemployed organisations could affiliate to Congress. So began the prolonged, divisive, mutually taxing battle in TCs between TCs and the TUC over the precise role, interventions and alternatives to the NUWCM, the key question: who was best able to represent and protect the unemployed, and help them find work?

As with all proscriptions, some TCs willingly enforced them, others ignored them every time or protested such impositions, while the majority of TCs (according to their annual reports) enforced some and ignored others, depending upon the prominence of unemployment locally and TC membership commitments. TCs' activities in conjunction with local NUWCM branches did not suddenly diminish or vanish. On National Unemployment Sunday in June 1925, demonstrations on behalf of the unemployed took place in industrial centres, with numerous TCs participating.[609] London TC planned a conference for as many TCs as possible to protest against the situation whereby the unemployed were being offered the choice to apply for poor law relief or accept lower-paid work.[610] The NUWCM-organised march to the 1925 Labour Party Conference was met by local TC members. A deputation was admitted to the conference platform.[611] Thrusting this campaign to centre stage would shake up the conflicting positions within the Labour Party, TUC and TCs *vis-à-vis* the NUWCM.

In December 1925, Middlesbrough TC was specifically publicly campaigning with the local unemployed and a number of TCs followed this with their own demonstrations of support. A joint conference of all TCs with the NUWCM was suggested to enable the TUC General Council to encourage unions to retain their unemployed members at a reduced contribution. As an example, Brighton TC affiliated to the NUWCM in January 1926 and an unemployed delegate was invited onto the TC. The new *Model Rules, Constitution and Standing Orders* for TCs promoted training centres for unemployed juveniles and extension of training facilities for adults during periods of industrial depression. However, the General Strike and its defeat and repercussions were about to readjust the political alignments that had been fostered to ease the burdens of the unemployed, as constructed over the previous six years.

2. THE MINERS' MARCHES AND THE FIRST UNEMPLOYED ASSOCIATIONS 1926-31

Following the rousing nine days of May 1926 and the strike's collapse, there was, as we have dissected, a pronounced shift to the right among union leaders.[612] With exploratory union/employer negotiations, fewer strikes, and CP incipient dominance in the NUWCM, the relationship between the TUC and TCs, on how to approach the dire situation for the unemployed, was reshaped. TCs convened conferences on the administration of Unemployment Insurance Acts, but there was no hint of a chance the TUC was about to entrust TCs with the task of organising the unemployed under the aegis of the NUWCM.

The official statement from the TUC was overtly and publicly to castigate the NUWCM as being under communist guidance. This was at the same time as TCs' collaboration with local NUWCM branches was apparent, and when labour exchanges were disqualified from giving benefits to strikers (on the spurious grounds that they had 'left their jobs without reason')! BoGs were handing out 'not genuinely seeking work' forms, and many unions were placed in a compromised position, witnessing unemployment increases as the price for securing the existing wage structure for those employed.

Into this mix, TCs found it difficult to lay aside or offer the NUWCM funds. By April 1927, TC rules did not officially allow their branches to affiliate and NUWCM connections with TCs were only allowable through mass rallies and hunger marches.[613] By now the humiliations and traumas of the returned 'war heroes' had become the TCs' most urgent problem to address. Unemployment was spreading – unevenly. What and where were the solutions to this national disgrace? In Birmingham the local TC recorded a 25,000 unemployed weekly average in the city, as traditional TC-representing areas of coal mining, iron and steel, engineering, shipbuilding and textile industries, particularly in the North, were severely affected by the downturn in employment outlets.[614]

A new phenomenon was introduced into the evolving dynamics of the TUC General Council as it was reformulating its priorities, above all in negotiations with employers. Unlike the NUWCM branches, it heralded a *new* organisation to be supervised and monitored by the TUC. It began in September 1927 with Bristol TC's inauguration of the first *unemployed association* (UA). Although this was not announced as such, the timing of this was not fortuitous. This local UA had been deliberately fashioned as an alternative to the local NUWCM. Manifestly, the intention was to steer the union movement away from NUWCM-style confrontations with the police. The objective was to plan deputations to the BoGs and the city council. Relief works to ease employment issues were begun, the BoGs recognising Bristol TC as an *intermediary* between itself and unemployed applicants. Through the TC, the city council created a superannuation scheme for council employees.

In November, Bristol UA's aims were widely commended and advertised through the TCJCC. They were not so at variance with the NUWCM's aims, except the UA functioned as an *official* auxiliary of the trade union movement. A membership card was to be interchangeable with a union card when the holder found employment. As a 'trade union' for the unemployed, the Bristol UA gained recognition from local authorities for its right to negotiate on their behalf. The TC soon handled hundreds of cases with the public assistance committees (PACs) and courts of referees. Having officially sanctioned this UA, the TUC now ratified the scheme and prepared to sponsor similar UAs through other TCs.[615]

Which should TCs prioritise or endorse: UAs or the NUWCM? All TCs were made aware of this question and some lived with it unresolved until 1939. Some TCs, it transpired, managed to achieve the impossible and strove to adopt a curious neutrality between the two. There were also those TCs that stayed on friendly terms with the local NUWCM branch without collaborating with it. It was the

TCs' duty to advance unemployed peoples' claims for better treatment to individual local authorities, as they persisted with deputations and protests against unemployed workers being hired for public works at less than union rates. NUWCM-style mobilisation of the unemployed endured beside the union leaders' new strategy, which negated any minor confrontations with the state on the issue of unemployment.

The TCJCC had researched the local situation: Bristol had an NUWCM branch of 250 out of 13,000 unemployed.[616] It was 'hopelessly in debt', and, from the official viewpoint (BoGs and local authorities), discredited. Therefore, Bristol TC had introduced a trade union structure into its unemployed organisation; the TC's secretary became the secretary of the new UA. An EC was formed from the TC, the Labour group on the city council, the BoGs, and the unemployed. The UA's membership leapt to 1,200 and speakers came, irrespective of political party or creed. The UA had become what TCs were now primarily about, according to union leaders, a recruitment ground for unions.

The General Council promoted this Bristol UA to coincide with the South Wales Miners' March to London. Before the latter, the General Council circularised all TCs in the UK to affirm it was unable to recommend that any TCs 'champion' this march; it recapitulated the undesirability of any participation in such 'unofficial activities', an already jaded trope for organisations attached to the CP. In fact, the TUC decision arose directly from the TCJCC reporting that the Miners' March was being 'exploited by the Communists'. In his inimitable fashion, W. Citrine, for the TUC, weighed in, arraigning the march as 'merely another expedient of the CP to bolster up its declining influence and to spread dissension and suspicion of the responsible representatives of the trade unions among the rank and file'.[617] Incorrigibly this gave him the opportunity to expose CP misrepresentations, the authors of whom sheltered behind 'a cloud of insinuations and innuendoes which are so framed as to make it difficult to bring them to book',[618] phrases echoed by others thereafter. For Citrine, no possible good could accrue from any TCs' joint activity with communists, only inevitable hardship, injury and disaster. Central for Citrine was staying within 'appropriate' parameters.

TCs cogitated about the proposed march. A.M. Wall, London TC secretary, alleged that the TC had been 'misled' into believing that the march was officially supported by the South Wales Miners' Federation (SWMF). He claimed to have discovered that it was actually organised by the NUWCM. Furthermore, the London TC reception committees were predominantly CP-constituted. A vote was taken, and by 153 to 77 the TC's representatives voted against attending. Reading TC&LP secretary A. Lockwood also cautioned against the march:

> In marginal constituencies like this, the intervention of such bodies of marchers is a positive handicap to the work we are trying to do and upsets plans which have carefully to be laid if we are to win seats in the next parliament. In the light of experience… these marchers do little good. They may or may not be an embarrassment to the Tory Government but they certainly are an embarrassment to the Labour Parties in the towns on the route.[619]

Not many TCs overtly followed this vote-catching priority or conveyed any awkwardness that marches on behalf of the deprived and marginalised were 'embarrassing'. Brighton TC sent a letter of admiration to the marchers. (No discomfiture there.)

B. Turner and W. Citrine of the General Council refused to meet W. Hannington, on the rather spurious grounds they had unearthed that he was not an 'actual working miner' (although he was on the Miners' March Control Council and had been invited by the Rhondda miners to organise the march). Citrine maintained his opposition, declaring the march the result of 'some Communist plot'! (The 'plot' unearthed 30 communists of the 270 marchers.) Spending limited TC funds on this became problematic. For Citrine, TCs should not spend funds on a march that had *no* support from Labour leaders, who would certainly not promote a march co-ordinated by any communists. In fact, the march had been sympathetically, even if in some towns surreptitiously, received by many TCs en route. Thereafter, for the CP, a nuanced approach would not do justice to the scenario: 'the bureaucrats got busy to stop it' with their 'vile handiwork' of 'the smug, complacent capitalists who take refuge behind an arrogant and callous Tory Government… the cowardice and funk of the Labour bureaucrats'.[620]

The spaghetti tangles about the miners' march resurfaced at the Swansea TUC conference in September 1928. The report stated definitively: communists had run the march. Davies (of the MFGB) denied this and thought the circulars to TCs showed its narrowness of spirit: 'The trades councils rallied around these boys, fed them, clothed them and inspired them' he said.[621] Citrine would not budge. The TCJCC concluded the march was controlled by the CP, which, in its well-known incursions, was indulging in its typical 'show and tell' that the trade union movement was indifferent to the unemployed.

*

For the TUC, UAs had to be formed across the nation. Since December 1927, the TUC, having severed its connections with the NUWCM, was now extending the reach of its own UAs based on the Bristol TC model. The TCJCC approved the constitution for Bristol UA and recommended a similar scheme be applied nationally. E.H. Parker (TCJCC member and Bristol TC secretary) recorded that the UA now had 1,500 members. Those fortunate to get a job had been transferred to a union, and relief works had begun.[622] In February 1928 the TCJCC recommended UAs in Bradford, Manchester, Sheffield and Newcastle-upon-Tyne, distinctly proposing them as alternatives to NUWCM branches not associated with the official trade union movement. The TUC sent out its circular in response to 'numerous requests' from TCs. W. Citrine explained to any sleepy, naive TC that might inquire about how widespread these numerous requests were that NUWCM policy was 'dictated' from quarters other than that of the trade union movement and, as such, the NUWCM was not recognised by the General Council.[623]

Soon six experimental centres for UAs were targeted. TCJCC secretary H.V. Tewson expected these TCs to prove satisfactory or amenable. They would cater for unemployed organisations under close TCJCC supervision.[624] On 18 May 1928 the TCJCC reported that Bradford and Walsall TCs had adopted the constitution; Manchester, Hull and Liverpool TCs were 'mulling it over'; and Leeds TC was added to the list of experimental centres. When Sheffield T&LC refused the invitation to establish a UA, the TCJCC secretary requested particulars on the local NUWCM branch.[625]

In August 1928 the General Council decided to ramp up its conflict with the NUWCM with malign insinuations. The General Council reported 'instances' where claimants to unemployment benefit, with cases pending, were induced to hand over the matter, the NUWCM obtaining subscriptions and recruitment for itself. TCs were asked to ensure that all appeals were dealt with by TCs: 'Warn your members in their own interests to have nothing to do with the NUWCM' exhorted the General Council.[626] Delegate A.B. Cohen raised his head above the parapet, naming this as a heresy hunt against the CP, MM and NUWCM. Simultaneously, a march in Scotland organised by the NUWCM in September received approval from Edinburgh T&LC.[627]

In November 1928 there was another NUWCM-organised miners' march. Again, the TCJCC requested the General Council advise TCs to abstain from any involvement with this as 'another attempt to exploit the unemployed for the propaganda purpose of the Minority Movement and the CP', plus there was the TCJCC's extolled humanitarian justification of the 'dangers attendant upon undernourished men making a long trek in the middle of winter'.[628] There was also that constant reminder that, if TC funds *were* used, unions would be indirectly assisting the MM. (And every TC member knew who inspired the MM!) On 10 December the General Council decreed, because the march did not have the backing of its affiliated unions, sorry, yet again it could not recommend it. TCs were in a quandary how to respond to the march. Sheffield T&LC gave money, food, clothing and shelter, and Oxford T&LC helped the NUWCM, whereas Birmingham, London, Leeds, Burnley, Peterborough and Southampton TCs opposed the march.[629]

For the CP, 'the right-wing trade union and Labour Party leaders will stop at nothing to defend their allies – the capitalists – from any threat offered by the working class'.[630] F. Rowland (in the minority on Birmingham TC) observed that rank-and-file workers' bolstering the marchers put the TCJCC's 'undernourished trekkers' and the General Council's objections to shame:

> These poor devils had been tramping for two and a half years and nobody had taken any notice of them. The General Council refused to lead the fight against capitalism and it has sabotaged and tried to prevent the revolutionary fighters and workers from doing so.[631]

The TUC wanted to be in control of the campaign to ease the growing crisis of unemployment. A. Conley, for the General Council, affirmed that if anybody wanted an unemployed march, it was for unions to organise it, not an 'outside body' imposed upon them. For TCs, the transfer of men from 'distressed areas' was the heart of the issue; firms had displaced workers and were recruiting from distressed areas with reduced wages. Plymouth, Southampton,

Portsmouth and Brighton TCs were already comparing notes about how their areas were particularly affected by this transference of labour.[632] And everyone was aware there was mounting unemployment aggravated by the failure to abolish the 'not genuinely seeking work' clause.

At the June 1929 ACTC the Bradford TC delegate reported that the local UA had been a failure since unions claimed that they were able to cater for their own unemployed, although Bristol's UA was flourishing.[633] At the Belfast TUC 1929, in the debate on UAs, a delegate asked, in view of the fact that no *substantial* steps were to be taken in the organisation of the unemployed, was it not time they got in touch with the NUWCM?[634] (No official reply to this query could be found.) Now TCs were coming out to protest at their exclusion from the reconstituted local employment committees (e.g. Brighton, Workington, Plymouth TCs). They were also seeking nomination of a workers' representative on the new Public Assistance Committee (PAC) under the Local Government Act, and TCs were truly embroiled in the administrative tentacles subject to employment exchanges, courts of referees and the dependence phenomena of the unemployed.[635]

In 1930, TC members were pondering and evaluating whether it was true (and, if so, why?) that the Soviet Union was 'immune' to the economic depression that was wreaking havoc on Western economies. Certainly, that was what CP members were planning to focus attention upon in TCs. In February the NUWCM organised a national unemployed march to London. The CP asserted, without any evidence produced, that the march had faced 'brutal sabotage' from TCs,[636] when it had actually secured substantial welcomes and aid support from several TCs (e.g. Bristol, Coventry, Loughborough, Macclesfield and Guildford). Birmingham TC had rejected an appeal from the NUWCM to help and Newcastle TC had refused the application for NUWCM affiliation,[637] yet there were Labour Party members who gave assistance to the reception committees who were subsequently expelled from the Labour Party! (There could be a thick book detailing expulsions from the Labour party.) All TCs assumed erroneously that the shackles of the TD&TU Act would be broken as they campaigned for direct labour to absorb the unemployed. As Labour and union leaders were working through BoGs and city councils for generous interpretations of the Relief Acts and direct works programmes (unions unable to influence government policy), TCs' local contributions reflected the defensive character of the whole union movement.

*

UAs could not function until unions gave their support. If unions were prepared to retain their unemployed membership, there was little need for UAs. The exception was, as noted, Bristol UA, which, by 1930, had a membership of *c.*2,000 (500 of whom had been transferred from the UA to unions). ACTC 1930 delegates were keen to have TC representation on local employment committees restored, while the TCJCC secretary proclaimed the Ministry of Labour could only work with TCs as purely *industrial* bodies.[638] (i.e without political interference). Where were TCs on employment matters under the short-lived Labour government? Some, such as Birmingham TC, proposed that overtime should be made illegal. Others, such as London TC, zeroed in on the exploitation of juvenile labour. In response to a British Chamber of Commerce report on unemployment (a preparation for lower wages in 'sheltered occupations', removal of union regulation, and curtailment of national expenditure on unemployment), Manchester & Salford TC produced an extensive analysis of the causes of and remedies for unemployment.[639]

TCs stood firm against the notion that international trade should be regenerated by wage reductions. For TCs, reducing unemployment relief would only deepen the industrial crisis; the past belonged to private finance, the future to public enterprise. Manchester & Salford TC deduced:

> public ownership and control of industry is the only logical method of bringing order out of this chaos… national and local authorities must assume greater control of all the means and instruments of work production and distribution. Capitalism had failed… Socialism – the social reorganisation and management of the means of life – must come.[640]

Here in 1930 a TC envisaged, through a Labour government, the post-1945 possibilities. CP strategy was to release the forces of production from capitalist ownership and lay the basis for socialist production. One practice to edge towards such an aim implied wide-scale demonstrations by the masses, but in its 'class versus class' phase the CP construed TCs' schemes to alleviate unemployment were merely paradigms of capitalist rationalisation, when what the situation required was workers' mobilisation and exposure of local officials as 'ruled by the social fascists'![641]

TCs upped their protests against the Ministry of Labour's cheap labour policy. Glasgow TC convened its conference critiquing overtime as the only means of countering rationalisation. And TCs *were* affected by the TUC plans for UAs. Middlesbrough TC appointed two representatives onto the Middlesbrough UA and the TC reported this UA was 'doing very good work'.[642]

TCs characterised the unemployment problem in 1930 as the cornerstone of the economic situation. Oxford T&LC exclaimed, 'unless united action of the workers is established, by the unity of employed and unemployed workers, unemployment is the means of dragging down the conditions of the workers generally'.[643] Birmingham TC noted that, if it had not been for improved social services and the amended Unemployment Insurance and Pensions Act, conditions would have been much worse.

By January 1931, trade unions had lost half their members (since 1920) and a Conference of the Unemployed[644] was convened by the NUWM. W. Hannington proclaimed that the latter had given the correct leadership in mobilising the country's unemployed workers, and Edinburgh TC's self-critical conclusion was not uncommon in TCs:

> that so little of a tangible nature has been secured for the unemployed must largely be the responsibility of the workers themselves. They have not learned the

lesson that all legislation is class legislation and if they will vote against their own class it is hardly possible for them to escape the consequences of their own action.'[645]

While defensive strategies predominated in TCs, the CP planned to broaden the NUWM's appeal through elected committees at labour exchanges, PACs and tenants' leagues. Under the leadership of the MM, the NUWM had been extended to elect representatives to committees and mobilise the unemployed in mass picketing.[646] TCs were partially involved in challenging the government's economy measures. 'Mass unemployment' may have been explained by some TCs as the consequence of the 'mismanagement of industry' but the initial remedy was at hand: Manchester & Salford TC's People's Congress 1931 advocated full maintenance until work was provided and unemployment pay to guarantee at least a basic living.[647]

The ACTC counselled all TCs to form UAs to help obtain work or maintenance for the unemployed as the TCJCC saluted political parties, religious bodies and philanthropic organisations offering to play a part in helping to form UAs. Thirty-four UAs had by now been created (with 24 TCs declining). TCs vocalised their impatience with the Labour government's lackadaisical treatment of the unemployed, while the implementation of the Means Test was about to create visceral opposition from TCs.[648]

3. THE MEANS TEST, UNEMPLOYED ASSOCIATIONS AND THE NATIONAL UNEMPLOYED WORKERS MOVEMENT: TRADES COUNCILS TURN TO THE LEFT 1931–32

By July 1931, TCs' activities included meetings at local labour exchanges, where new rulings for the unemployed, brought about by Unemployment Insurance Acts, were enunciated. TCs safeguarded applicants, upheld rights for economic assistance (when appearing before committees) and deduced that reductions to existing inadequate allowances to the unemployed were part of a deliberate policy of impoverishment and degradation of those who were most vulnerable. Was capitalism heading straight to complete chaos? [649]

Brought in to reduce expenditure and purportedly to ease the economic crisis, the notorious Means Test strictly assessed and estimated how much economic support unemployed workers would receive. TCs were outraged, propelling a few more towards association with the NUWM rather than UAs, and triggering the same TCJCC and General Council stipulations for unions to keep the lines of communication open with unemployed members 'to prevent their exploitation by outside bodies'.[650]

TC positions differed greatly. Birmingham TC reaffirmed its non-association with the NUWM ('a subsidiary of the CP'),[651] yet protested against government cuts in unemployment benefit. In contrast, Brighton TC affiliated to the NUWM in December 1931 and was addressed by NUWM speakers, several of its resolutions TC-endorsed; and even Bristol TC's UA flagship for the local unemployed had to acknowledge achievements by the local NUWM.[652]

Every TC joined in the protests against the Means Test, for restoration of unemployment benefit, and amendment of the transitional benefit system administered by the PACs. In December 1931 a memorandum was produced by London TC that outlined the theory behind the Means Test and how it affected workers. It explained how the administration of transitional benefit penalised thrift by taking into account union benefits in assessing means. Furthermore two-thirds of PAC members were nominated by the majority party on the London County Council, chosen not because of their knowledge of industry but for their 'social standing', with little knowledge of working-class life or conditions. TCs were attempting to salvage a more humane PAC administration, providing moral support to those appearing before the PAC, with a union representative present.[653] TC activist A.A. Purcell, designated the Means Test as 'perhaps the most degrading thing of our day and generation'. For him, the decline in social services and the transfer of public works to private contractors indicated the frenzied efforts of decaying capitalism to rehabilitate itself at the expense of the workers and the national welfare.[654]

*

Capitalism in crisis was a given; degradation because of the Means Test threatened TCs' *raison d'être*. In Hackney, where 11,137 had applied to the local PAC for benefit, 4,214 were 'disallowed'. Some TCs were damning another ruling that workers on assistance had to perform hard labour as *proof* of their willingness to take jobs,[655] while the TUC promulgated the view that the PAC was a neutral body that determined whether any applicant, while unemployed, was in need of financial assistance. It recommended TCs to convene conferences on PAC procedures and submit reports on the local operations of the Means Test machinery.[656]

UAs were not having the resounding success anticipated by the TUC. H.V. Tewson communicated that, although many TCs had been asked to form UAs, 'nothing much had resulted'.[657] Bristol UA proposed a delegate conference of local unemployed organisations to create a National Federation of Unemployed Associations and the TCJCC recommended that the General Council now promote union demonstrations with the unemployed in industrial centres to protest against the Means Test. Policy on UAs was controlled by 'responsible national bodies'.[658] TCs that retained their connections (including activities) with the local NUWM were threatened with 'withdrawal of recognition' as a consequence. One way round this was to do what Brighton TC did and disaffiliate the NUWM branch, but refuse to form a UA.[659] Or one could go the way of Southampton TC. It had been approached by the local NUWM to beef up the organising of the local unemployed; secretary R. Chick declared that the NUWM was *opposed* to the trade union movement. Thus the TC was restricted to conferences on unemployed insurance and sending anti-Means Test resolutions to the Minister of Labour.[660]

January 1932 witnessed the TCJCC advising TCs to form UAs until 'changed circumstances'. They had to avoid the impression of this being merely 'uplift work', just making the most of the situation. Threatened by the NUWM 'stealing' the genuine action to organise the unemployed over the previous decade, the TCJCC had to assess whether it could afford to see the NUWM making the most of opportunities to deploy the growing numbers of unemployed. As always with 'crafty militants', they came masked and disguised: 'In certain instances, we have knowledge that they are proceeding so carefully that it is not known in the locality that they are associated with the MM and the CP'![661] The TUC/TCJCC decided they wanted precise observations about which TCs were fostering NUWM branches and which were opposing the recently legitimated UAs.

*

By now, TCs' functions stretched to provide sports club facilities, equipment through the National Playing Fields Association, allotments from the Society of Friends, and education classes through the Workers Education Association (WEA) and National Council of Labour Colleges (NCLC).[662] This was praised by the TUC, which spotted a source of future union recruitment. Bristol TC had an epiphany: unemployed marchers were *more effective* than the TC had been, in swaying the council to delay the operation of the PAC relief cuts. And TCs became more outspoken, defiant. One TC secretary, posited a conspiracy linking unemployment, the Means Test and the pauper relief system, which led to demoralisation: 'Our rulers want a degraded, poverty-stricken, servile slum working class so as to make their domination certain.'[663]

UAs were not succeeding. They could not prevent cuts in PAC scales of relief and it was difficult to convince anyone that UAs were a viable alternative to the NUWM.

Oxford T&LC had created a UA and, just as it had become a 'real living force', most of the local unemployed joined the local NUWM. In Southampton the TC bypassed the TUC and created advice centres on unemployment transitional benefit, rents and rates. Despite all the dedicated work of UAs undertaken by some TCs, most of the latter acknowledged the hopes in Newcastle TC: 'That economic salvation lay in socialist reconstruction and reorganisation of industry as a public service.'[664] UAs were having minimal significance.

In 1932, the General Council somehow deduced it was the increase in unemployment (during the previous three years) that had 'impressed localities with the need to create some organisation for unemployed persons' – as if the NUWM had never existed.[665] The new Conference of Unemployed Associations, convened in Bristol, included 50 delegates. Here, A. Conley and H.V. Tewson declared that the General Council scheme would be expanded to all TCs. They did not like the idea of the formation of a national federation because it might insinuate that the unemployed could be determining policy when, as had been enunciated *ad infinitum*, all policies had to be TUC-initiated. When the UA conference went ahead and voted to form a national federation and requested the General Council recognise this, Tewson and Conley left the conference! The 'unfortunate atmosphere' was attributed to NUWM interference:

> with the exception of the delegates from London, the feeling of the conference was entirely opposed to the NUWM which incidentally had drafted organisers

from all parts of the country to Bristol to demonstrate against the formation of a national federation. They created some disturbance outside the hall which was strongly guarded by police.[666]

The NUWM was apparently up to no good but the TUC scheme was rejected; a national federation could not compete with the NUWM, nor could a united front of the unemployed be created out of this. The TUC had been negotiating with the Federation of British Industry, had assisted employers in imposing rationalisation schemes (which exacerbated unemployment levels) and, at this vital juncture, opposed strikes. (Another history could be written on which strikes the TUC has opposed!). It had created divisions within TCs by endorsing UAs against local NUWM branches, yet assumed and expected TCs to agitate against the Means Test, as appeared in its policy in February 1932, *Pauperising the Unemployed: The TUC Case Against the Means Test*. TCs complied, arranging conferences at which General Council speakers explained the regulations,[667] and in April the TUC delighted in the fact that few proposals had excited more interest in TCs than the circulars and draft model constitution for UAs! It was now claimed that 24 UAs had been formed; only nine TCs had refused.[668]

The NUWM were not cowed. On 19 April 1932 it sent a declaration for 'United Action Against Unemployment' to the General Council and the UAs. The Chancellor of the Exchequer had just declared that no reduction in unemployment could be expected in the next decade and the government had saved £29 million (almost £2.5billion today) through benefit cuts and the Means Test. Many TCs thus welcomed the NUWM's Eighth Conference 'Declaration For Abolition of the Means Test'. The TUC sidelined the idea of unemployed councils[669] and the TUC Organisation Department planned another 'non-collaboration with the NUWM' circular to be sent TCs. Attempts to keep TCs at a distance from 'contamination' by the NUWM continued into mid-1932.[670]

In April, although 16 TCs had declined to create the UAs, the latter made another effort at affiliation to the TUC, the answer was no. UAs *were* recognised under the Unemployment Insurance Acts as competent bodies to submit appeals, but H.V. Tewson warned that any National Federation of UAs would 'segregate the unemployed': 'There is no objection to demonstrations being held if they were for specific purposes and properly organised, but the unemployed should not be merely trailed around aimlessly from day to day,'[671] an observation utilised previously for any justification. For W. Citrine, though, TCs were the only organisations available since the NUWCM was 'hostile' to the trade union movement. He did not elucidate but the result was that TCs with UAs kept the local NUWM at a distance in Newcastle, Bristol, Birmingham and Leeds.

With the 1932 hunger march, some UAs (e.g. Leeds, Jarrow, Bath, Abertillery) embraced the marchers despite TUC opposition. Unemployment figures had reached *c.*3 million by August 1932, the employment rate 61%, the lowest rate ever.[672] UAs had been reduced to compiling registers of the unemployed and tabulating hardship cases, while the TCJCC was promoting the Lincoln scheme of workshops for unemployed workers organised by the WEA. By now, 58 UAs had been formed, 31 TCs declining,[673] the General Council claiming that the UA scheme had raised no objections from a single union.

H.V. Tewson continued his scorn towards the NUWM for marching the unemployed in demonstrations, where heads were smashed in clashes with the police and innocent marchers suffered. (Curious how the same arguments are utilised nowadays about protesters and strikers.) For Tewson, the NUWM pursued disruptive tactics, at a crucial time when the unemployed could not be asked to wait for the clarification of economic theories and he doubted the General Council would ever place before the trade union movement 'a plan for the new Jerusalem',[674] such plans presumably being *ultra vires*.

There were 70 UAs by October 1932, but this had minimal bearing upon TCs lauding NUWM activities in combating evictions via rent strikes and in hunger marches. (The Ministry of Health advised them not to be too generous with rations or blankets for marchers!) TCs, as usual, exhibited diverse responses to this particular hunger march. Swindon TC was not untypical. It opposed the march but welcomed marchers with a reception committee that offered food and shelter. In warning TCs not to become involved with this hunger march, in November 1932, E.P. Harries contrasted the demonstration's 'spectacular methods' with the 'quiet but useful work' of UAs. He cited Plymouth TC's UA with its 750 members, which had fought 53 cases before the Court of Referees, so much more effective than a dozen riots or unemployed marches: 'Simply breaking up meetings gets one nowhere', he opined.[675] Who was doing that? Harries did not acknowledge that the police broke up meetings, or that more TCs had empathy for the NUWM. As Birmingham TC propounded, most of the unemployed were 'decent self-respecting citizens and innocent victims of a vicious set of circumstances over which they have no control', Middlesbrough TC concluding that Ministry of Labour officials were using local PACs to pauperise people.[676]

4. THE GENERAL COUNCIL INTERVENES 1933-35

In 1932-33, 23% of the labour force were unemployed and public provision for social security was meagre. Having opposed NUWM demonstrations and instructed TCs to ignore them, in November 1932 the National Joint Council (the TUC and the Labour Party) at last considered a demonstration against government policy apposite. The TCJCC agreed to a march in London.[677] E.P. Harries designated TCs as the centres for organising this. For Harries, the UAs were purely industrial bodies 'as non-political as trade unionism' (the debate echoed throughout this book) and he countered the assumption that the TUC had declared demonstrations were taboo: 'This is very far from the truth. Where the need is felt for local demonstrations, it [sic] has been held.'[678]

Informing TCs of the upcoming march, the General Council stated it was a protest for a shorter working week. By January 1933, the 103 UAs (from 30 UAs in April 1932, 58 in August 1932, and 70 by October 1932) were planning deputations to the PACs, suggesting work schemes, appealing for funds from union branches, and gathering information on social and occupational services for the unemployed, with some TCs represented on mayors' funds committees. The TCJCC applauded those unemployed demonstrations organised by TCs as a tonic to the movement.[679] There were reservations. Sheffield T&LC's secretary F. Thraves posited that unemployment would increase as the latest technology was embedded; that would result in the displacement of manual labour by machinery. (90 years ago!) Minor social palliatives were not the answer: 'we have the most abject poverty and enforced idleness which an unintelligent Parliament grudgingly subsidises, obviously to stave off revolution'.[680]

Hopes for a fairer distribution of wealth coexisted with counsels of despair. At the ACTC May 1933 an NUWM delegate appealed for unity for all the unemployed, alongside fears of looming fascism in the UK:

> The attempt to impose bans upon organisations must be combatted and defeated. It represents a deliberate attempt to disrupt the forces of working class resistance and prepares the way for the general fascist ban of all working class organisations.[681]

While Birmingham NUWM's district committee did not receive the ACTC's endorsement, the Battersea TC delegate found the UA scheme useful for 'stamping out' NUWM influence. Other TCs challenged what they judged to be a scheme to lower wages, keep the unemployed below the poverty line, cripple social services and enforce a false economy. As Glasgow, Manchester, London and Sheffield TCs/T&LCs were nurtured as politicised pressure groups, smaller TCs now concentrated on their industrial role (e.g. Brighton and Southampton).[682]

Restrictions upon UAs were illustrated at the Conference of Unemployed Associations and the TCJCC in July 1933. W. Citrine now acknowledged that the TUC had been organising UAs to combat the NUWM, and the TCJCC secretary confirmed that UAs had not been given the status of affiliated bodies, because it would have made it 'very easy for other people to get in and cause a split'.[683] TCs' diverse responses to UAs proliferated: some for the local UA to affiliate, others unconvinced, some for closer links with the Labour Party, others for UAs to remain 'non-political'. And events did not all go in favour of the General Council. Brighton TC supported an NUWM leader who had been arrested,[684] Bristol TC joined the local UA and NUWM in a strike, Southampton TC high-fived the NUWM's critique of 'charity' implicit in the mayor's welfare scheme, and Oxford T&LC mirrored the NUWM's view on wage reductions.[685]

About 500 NUWM marchers descended upon the Brighton TUC conference 1933. This time there was no contact with the local TC. W. Citrine reiterated the NUWM was 'finding a propaganda means to beat the TUC and trade union movement'[686] although the NUWM's 1934 hunger march attracted even more TCs and ignored a UA president's suppositions that 'useless marching and empty gestures have no real effect'.[687] Glasgow TC welcomed the march, Birmingham opposed it, while the TCJCC lamented that by June 1934 only 25% to 30% of TCs were 'live bodies'.[688]

The following month, A.M. Wall's *Memorandum on Services for Unemployed Workers* queried whether these UAs could ever be capable of fulfilling any useful contribution to the solution of unemployment except:

> to prevent them falling under the influence of organisations whose aims and objects are not desirable…

Once a trades council usurped the functions of a union, it became absolutely dangerous... The Movement had to safeguard the nation from the economic imbecility of Fascism and the dangers of Communism.[689]

Looking forward with a more positive outlook, the Southampton TC president averred: 'the Trades Council can and will play its part in endeavouring to secure all that the increased productivity and efficiency in industry entitles the workers to'.[690] Mrs Rackham for the TUC intimated that instead of the NUWM the most apposite organisations to help the unemployed were PACs, courts of referees or the UAB, and warned: 'Too much of this work is left to the Communists, with the result that young people are apt to think trade unionism tame and to ignore politics'.[691] (Ignoring politics was not a CP trait!) By December 1934, it was estimated that, of 194 TCs charted, 60 were working with social service committees, 137 offered recreational activities, 88 were involved in educational facilities, 11 had occupational centres and 23 had training schemes. Birmingham TC announced a decade before the implementation of the Beveridge Report: 'If the present system cannot provide adequately remunerative work for those able and willing to work, then they should be properly provided for by the State.'[692]

5. DIMINUTION OF MASS UNEMPLOYMENT 1935-40

In January 1935 Manchester & Salford TC held a conference on the Unemployment Insurance Bill, which, if enacted, would give local authorities the right to draft those who were unemployed into 'labour camps' (cheap labour). The deleterious connotations surrounding German labour camps had not yet filtered into the British consciousness. Meanwhile, the TUC's Unemployed Services Committee (USC) report hailed the 140 UAs as having performed a useful task in securing rights under existing legislation for work schemes and PAC administration. About 200,000 unemployed were now attached to unions, those in UAs far exceeding those aided by any other voluntary organisation, it was asserted, in a sideswipe at the NUWM.[693]

The year 1935 was to be one of TCs engaged in combating UAB regulations, with union leaders critical of TC members' 'apathy towards UAs'. H.H. Elvin returned to his fixation: the CP wished to 'adopt tactics which would split the trade union movement... those holding positions in the labour movement must abide by the principles of the movement... Control by the CP could not be tolerated.'[694] This allegation and its remedy dovetailed into UAs' requirements to familiarise themselves with the Unemployment Act's regulations and umpires' decisions and assist those before courts of referees. TCs were instructed to study UAB scales, advise UA members before tribunals, and list practical jobs. C. Dukes reiterated E.P. Harries's critique of poorly attended and rather dull TC meetings. Accordingly, the TCJCC's March 1935 *Suggested Activities for Unemployed Associations* advised TCs to become social service centres with excursions, trips, social evenings and concerts.[695]

Tensions between TCs and the TUC General Council had not dissipated. Newcastle TC had organised a conference on what had become the Unemployed Insurance Act but the General Council sent an officer to a neighbouring conference where the union did not even support the TC! In Southampton the TC reprimanded the General Council for sending circulars on fair wages clauses to local Labour parties, who had taken action without consulting the TC. The polar opposite position came from Councillor N. McGretton of Gateshead, who was not prepared to concede 'that the unemployed is the particular pitch of the NUWM'.[696]

The crux of the matter was centre stage at the Margate TUC conference 1935, where Wal Hannington rebuked the General Council for damaging the cause: 'The setting up of Unemployed Associations in opposition to the NUWM and the exclusion of militants from office in the Unemployed Associations could have harmful effects on the struggle of the unemployed'.[697] For Hannington, UAs could only offer help if they were not used, as they palpably were, to prevent unions from working with the NUWM. The General Council was separating the unemployed into 'respectable' and 'unrespectable', a divide-and-rule tactic that can always succeed unless resisted by united action.

TCs were further discombobulated by the conference decision to take no action on the importation of labour from distressed areas, the General Council channelling blame onto the NUWM:

> faulty information is given to the unemployed by people who profess to cater for them better than the Trades Councils and Unemployed Associations. It often happens that people making those professions know very little about the subject and the unemployed are agitated and led astray with false and insufficient information.[698]

Moreover, the struggle on behalf of the unemployed required knowledge, experience and 'correct' information, and nobody could be in a better position than unions. Most UAs had been established in the industrial north, where unemployed workers turned to them to do more than supply them with sports equipment but TCs were suspicious of the uses made of training centres for unemployed juveniles.[699]

TCs provided assistance to the hunger marchers in the famous, widely advertised unemployed march to London, 5–31 October 1936 (known since as the 'Jarrow March' or 'Crusade'). More TCs than ever before participated, remarkably and intriguingly with no repercussions from the General Council. This likewise applied to Edinburgh's huge anti-Means Test demonstration before the Labour Party conference, with TCs attesting to people of all classes and political persuasions marching and notable involvement by Leeds and Bristol TUC-approved UAs. Although the TCJCC stated that the March required consultation with TCs before implementation, it glowed with enthusiasm: 'Marches have lighted a candle… and if many more such candles can be lighted then we may be approaching great changes in our political and economic life'.[700] TCs' achievements now included Bristol TC convincing employers to observe the fair wages clause in unemployment benefit, Manchester & Salford TC's conference on the UAB regulations and Brighton TC's campaign in the UAB to appoint more representatives on the UA. On UAB regulations alone, 30 conferences and 122 demonstrations had been organised by the end of 1936.

Then came *Circular 55: Trades Councils on Unemployed Marches* in February 1937. This was in the form of a questionnaire for all TCs. Nowadays, feedback has become almost a daily obsession utilised by all organisations in their interface with the public, but in 1937, in the union movement, this had a very specific function. *Circular 55* was searching for information as to whether TCs had been consulted about such marches and, if not, what inconveniences had resulted, and what expenses had been incurred. Oxford and Newcastle TCs' immediate response was to characterise the circular an impertinence![701] The TCJCC had its presuppositions: the marches were imposed on TCs, marchers had created inconveniences, TCs had been coerced. However, the ACTC 1937 recorded that 26 TCs had been consulted before the march, 26 not; 15 TCs noted inconveniences, 33 not; 39 said no expenses were incurred, 11 had paid out small amounts. Thirty-four TCs reported the efforts were justified – for propaganda value and the media spotlight on 'distressed areas'. TCs emerged with their enhanced reputations with an opportunity to distribute union information and arouse local sympathy and enthusiasm. Only seven TCs considered the efforts unjustified.[702]

Then, TCs' vocal protests about the derisory provisions in the national rates of assistance under the UABs bore fruit when the government forestalled the introduction of a new lower rate in April 1937. This was a victory for the whole union movement.

Yet, the debate on the unemployed at the ACTC 1937 unveiled the chasm between TCJCC officials and the majority of TC delegates. The chairman, contrary to the evidence presented, announced that only those who had no 'responsibility' were 'very enthusiastic' about marches, and besides (guess what?) funds were 'scarce'! A stigma was now attached to TCs who had participated, yet most had claimed the march had beneficial effects and regretted any impression that any TCs objected to providing hospitality. The frustrations were captured by Bethnal Green TC delegate: 'The TUC itself has not seen fit to organise a march and it turned down every constructive proposal; it was negation after negation from the platform.'[703]

It was calculated that 75% of TCs had by now left unemployed organisation to the local NUWM. Apart from UAs in Bristol, Birmingham and Leeds thriving, UAs run by TCs had minimal activities ~ individual hardship cases, children's excursions, Christmas treats, and 'men's suppers and teas for their wives'![704] All TCs were monitoring wage rates, pensions and unemployment allowances. A macro-perspective clarifies that:

> A major cause [of unemployment] ...is private ownership of the land and instruments of production; as such the latter is used as a means of massaging the economy. So, commercial crises are a permanent feature of our industrial system.[705]

This was recognised by TCs in 1937. However, this was not uppermost for debate for union leaders at the Norwich TUC conference 1937, where the General Council again expressed doubts about marches and demonstrations and informed the Labour Party that unless marches were 'General Council-endorsed', they should not receive TCs' help. *Circular 33: Trades Councils on Unofficial*

Marches concluded that such demonstrations were 'not worthwhile'.[706] Thus ignoring *Circular 55* of February 1937, whose feedback from TCs proved the opposite! Significantly, in its *Memorandum on Trades Councils' Unemployed Associations* in February 1938, the TCJCC did not mention the use of marches. Alas the window of opportunity had passed for Wal Hannington to seek union branches for affiliation to the Unemployment Research and Advice Bureau (URAB), through which advice on courts of referees, appeal tribunals, health insurance, pensions and compensation would be given.

In 1938, the General Council was pleased the NUWM's influence had been 'very substantially diminished', hence the latter's attempts to create the URAB. That useful fallback, finances, was the issue: 'the funds of union branches ought not to be devoted to supporting extraneous organisations, whose policy is avowedly *hostile* to the labour movement'.[707] (Full marks for consistency and reiteration of the General Council's choice word!) The URAB became another proscribed body. W. Citrine at the ACTC reassured delegates it would be interpreted as an attempt 'to stir up agitation' if Transport House organised marches. Revamping the 'infiltrator' notion, he castigated the usual suspects: 'elements outside the trade union movement trying to use and exploit the workers' grievances for the purpose of ingratiating themselves with the trade union movement'; the ACTC was not to 'go out of its way to give *carte blanche* to marches organised by all sorts of bodies'.[708] There were objections to this take. Some delegates took the view that, unlike negotiations enacted and paraded via the union leaders (who also opposed strikes), unemployed marches had been responsible for government policy leniency. TCs' voices also raised the issue, noted above, of TUC policy on the transference of juvenile workers to other centres, because if there was to be a great industrial boom (which could bring prosperity back to the North ~ an echoing theme of proposed 'levelling up'), areas would be deprived of the best of their labour.

At the ACTC 1939, the Lancashire UA delegate focused on 'TC apathy' to explain UAs' weaknesses. The ambivalence in TCs towards UAs was shown in the resolution (narrowly carried by 96 to 91 votes) for the General Council to bolster UAs with a full-time national organiser. For E.P. Harries (now TCJCC secretary) it was confession time: 'The General Council has always visualised Unemployed Associations as a feeding ground for the trade unions'.[709] It had always primarily been about recruitment (and side-lining militants). Meanwhile, the ACTC voted for those engaged in ARP work and National Voluntary Service to be paid at current union rates. Those previously unemployed should not be exploited. In June 1940, the UAs' demise prompted a despondent W. Citrine to acknowledge: 'the position of Unemployed Associations had been one of considerable difficulty; many have faded out entirely.'[710] TCs' campaigns now deliberated upon air raid shelters, building trade conundrums, working conditions (adjusted because of military service), the sudden influx of women into industry, and employment committees with TC representatives.

6. WAR EMPLOYMENT FOR TRADES COUNCILS 1940-45

There was, at last, a united endeavour among TCs on employment issues between 1940 and 1945, more than at any other time in their history. During wartime, requirements were such that unemployment temporarily vanished:

> This is a sad reflection on our system or lack of it that in peacetime we permit workers to be placed on the industrial scrapheap yet in wartime it is considered to be in the national interest to find work for everyone![711]

This sound observation from the Birmingham TC secretary epitomises TCs' extended obligations during World War II. Yet, also at this time, despite government subsidies to stabilise prices and rationing, a further increase in the cost of living transpired. All TCs became immersed in conferences on production. Wherever new factories were situated, TCs campaigned for (and argued about) those from 'depressed areas' having the first opportunities so that those unemployed could be absorbed into industry or civil defence work.

TCs became embroiled in the social security campaign. In May 1942 the ACTC acknowledged the TUC social insurance proposals before the Beveridge Committee.[712] New tasks for TCs arose. London and Manchester & Salford TCs argued that compulsory enrolment of women for fire-watching was secondary to women's contribution in industry. TCs encouraged part-time employment campaigns and legislation to release union representatives to attend government committees, and be appointed to local food control committees and unemployed workers' interview panels.[713] In Autumn 1942 TCs arranged conferences on social services in Newcastle, Birmingham, Manchester, Bristol, London and Bradford, and after the publication of the Beveridge Report, 20 more TCs held conferences on its social and economic implications. TCs' outlook, moulded by their interwar experience of the irrationality of capitalist economies and TCs' prolonged and extensive activities on behalf of the unemployed, made them responsive to the Beveridge recommendations, which, hopefully, could unify services and conditions for soldiers and civilians.

The Beveridge Report had an astonishing impact upon TCs. One of its aspects was to rationalise relief benefit contributions and administration *without* a means test. This had been an aspiration for TCs for a decade. Wary of the major insurance companies, TCs upheld the principle of the right to work.[714] *The Times* editorial of 23 January 1943 serves as a crisp summary of what this chapter has tried to illuminate:

> Next to war, unemployment has been the most widespread, the most insidious, and the most corroding malady of our generation: it is the specific social disease of western civilization in our time.

TCs studied the Beveridge Report. Glasgow TC recorded that it was not being welcomed by PM Winston Churchill. No matter. For TCs, who had always sought workers' employment opportunities, as they awaited a Ministry of Social Security, the Beveridge Plan was embraced as providing fundamental improvements for all workers.

The ACTC 1943 approved the Report's principles, as TCs' requests to organise nationwide demonstrations, 'Beveridge Sundays', was referred to the TUC Social Insurance Committee in December 1943 for approval.[715]

TCs had coherent objectives now. They held conferences on employment policy, to aid union members with help from departments administering social services. They took some time to recognise the contributory basis of benefit under Beveridge, which in fact dovetailed with private insurance interests where the free market was treated, in the last resort, as sacrosanct. State intervention was not to constrain the market but liberate it from previous obstructions.[716] Nevertheless, TCs succeeded via unions in getting service pay increased and equal pay for servicewomen, arguing that a rise in the cost of living index justified such increases; the corollary being courts of referees, employment committees and hardship committees should reflect workers' interests and provide a guaranteed minimum wage. The Lancashire, Cheshire & North Wales Federation of TCs in June 1944 summarised:

> The soldier of today will be the workman of tomorrow; if the wages and conditions of the working man were poor today, then our soldiers will have to accept those same poor wages and conditions when they return to Civvy Street. We have a responsibility on their behalf to preserve the sound heart of labour – the loyalty, courage and rugged honesty which are our heritage.[717]

TCs were now campaigning for increases in Forces pay, allowances and pensions – and broader objectives pertained. Leeds UA, in operation in 1944, commented on the UA's purpose:

> to understand the many contradictions in everyday society, the chaos and muddle, why they arise and finally why it had become necessary to change the present system to one which will ensure that fear, poverty and degradation have no place in a well-ordered and planned society.[718]

The planning strategy would emerge from a war that encompassed the total enrolment of labour with the principle of 'equal pay for equal work' for women and men underpinning TCs' objectives, part of their *raison d'etre* to end basic inequalities then, and 80 years later.

In July 1944 a small victory for TCs was achieved with the amendment of Essential Work Orders, so workers who won their appeal against dismissal would now receive a guaranteed wage. TCs exposed the use of Home Guard personnel as 'unpaid labourers', as they prepared industrial surveys critical of any exploitation of labour.[719] Exposés of employers' dubious practices were TCs' *forte*.

TC conferences on 'equal pay for equal work' led to a memorandum as part of the evidence to a royal commission. TCs condemned the Agricultural Wages Board for rejecting agricultural workers' minimum wage demands and TCs' industrial surveys throughout the UK tabulated wage scales and working conditions to aid a smooth transition from war to peacetime production. They requested the government publish post-war plans and consult unions and JPCs.[720] They also worked on behalf of demobilised war workers, stipulating a guaranteed wage until a peace production job became available.

In January 1945 Manchester & Salford TC applied its survey of industry to employment, and Glasgow TC's memorandum on post-war planning clarified the dependence on heavy industries in the west of Scotland.[721] TCs were being given status on industrial boards. They were keen to form 'full employment councils' in conjunction with local chambers of commerce and town councils and the British Legion. Conferences were now held by TCs on redundancy and paying workers at full union rates during the change to peace-time production. Croydon TC, in an upcoming light industry area, approached the Chamber of Commerce to form a joint council for a comprehensive plan for local industry and state retention of all factories. TCs proposed that JPCs should be given responsibility in the control of industry, Newcastle TC exemplifying TCs' awareness of redundancies when war contracts were ending.

The mantra of 'full employment' was put into context by H.E. Newbold, Manchester & Salford TC secretary who agitated over how full employment would transpire in reality: 'this talk of building a new Britain is all very well, but we must have something positive to put forward to show *how* it can be done.'[722] The Bristol TC secretary was practical:

> We have to face an unemployment problem when hostilities cease, but this may be only temporary if the city is allowed to handle its own factory development with a view to replacing war-damaged buildings and making provision for the actual expansion of its other plants.[723]

By 1945, a compelling, bold vision of the future, challenging the mass unemployment and inequalities of the past, was presented by the new Labour government. TCs were more optimistic about employment prospects than ever before, apart from the recent war years.

7. A VISION OF FULL EMPLOYMENT 1945-50

In rebuilding devastated areas of Britain, ending mass unemployment was at the core of government economic policy. Following the social security legislation, the range of local advisory committees and appeals tribunals were extended, TCs dealing with new areas of national insurance, assistance, war pensions and local and youth employment. TCs were informed that they were not permitted to 'interfere with Congress policy' on post-war reconstruction or the complaints' machinery relating to the National Arbitration Tribunal. Fruitfully, co-operation with the government would help maintain employment levels. The government would also be judged on its ability to restore industrial output in the shortest possible time, and TCs were cognisant of rapidly emerging geopolitical realignments. One example came from a devastated Coventry. The TC announced the local machine tool industry would benefit from trade with the Soviet Union and building on India's industrial resources.[724]

However, in February 1946, Newcastle TC recorded a growing number of the unemployed, and Southport TC sent a deputation to the Minister of Labour about a factory closure when the Air Ministry's contract ended. Leeds TC proposed a review of all wage rates and a basic minimum; Glasgow TC calculated 23,907 unemployed in May; Burnley

T&LC pleaded with the government for new industry to absorb the unemployed; and Kidderminster TC stated the overriding factor was not to rely on one particular industry, when employers had sited their factories for their own convenience. TC delegates applauded ACTC chairman H.N. Harrison when he proclaimed:

> The depression which followed the last war and which deepened into world economic disaster with its means tests, rising unemployment, UABs and increasing poverty and misery, will not be repeated, for we face this transitional period and a future with a great and powerful trade union and labour movement. Men who are trade unionists are at the helm of state affairs.[725]

TC delegates were reassured, with representation on the local employment committees, the main advisory committees to the Ministry of Labour.

Another issue that came to prominence was the right of a worker's appeal to an impartial body, necessary in the transitions from private ownership to state control, the process in which TCs placed their faith. This was blunted by the General Council's Luke Fawcett. He instructed TCs not to adopt such resolutions because the Minister of Labour had given ample notice that the Essential Work Orders would be withdrawn; these matters would be determined by each industry. The underlying relationship between the General Council and TCs was contained in his quip: 'The only impartial committee I personally respect is one that gives me my own way'.[726]

Compromise was embedded in the TCJCC report on the National Insurance Bill, part of a comprehensive plan for social security into which the industrial injuries scheme, family allowances, and the NHS were to fit. The TCs' resolution for Means Test abolition was put on the back burner. Belatedly it dawned upon TCs that government aspirations, in relation to the location of industry, were inadequate to ensure full employment. Most TCs had posited a planned economy in which a workers' government would surely decide where industries were placed and run. Local authorities were facing heavy costs to expand social services while TCs sought to ensure urban district councils' recognition for the right of workers to join their appropriate union and be paid union rates. TCs now faced the long-term problems of reductions in unemployment pay and the employment of non-unionists.[727]

By September 1946 over 50 TCs had approached local authorities on the issue of 'the closed shop' (workplaces with complete union membership), seeking to enhance membership among skilled workers.[728] At the Birmingham TC conference in February 1947 delegates spoke of being planned to assist the production drive during the winter fuel crisis, TCs warning of 'reactionary circles' using the crisis to undermine the Labour government.[729] Walthamstow and Luton TCs located the cause of the crisis: years of Conservative governments. TCs, as recorded in their annual reports were urging workers not to be swayed by anti-Labour propaganda. A Luton TC delegate exclaimed hopefully: 'we will never permit the present crisis to be used by unscrupulous employers to wring from us any improvements we have won'.[730]

Rooted in this politics of post-war Labourism were promises of full-scale nationalisation and equal pay as incentives to TCs, but the confidence embodied in H.N. Harrison's speech to the ACTC 1946 (quoted above) gradually waned in TCs. Brighton and Hackney TCs proposed the release of a million people from the armed forces to industry and a prohibition of inessential luxuries. TCs held conferences on 'production targets' and for JPCs in all industries (see Edinburgh T&LC, Bath TC, Stafford TC and Camberwell TC) and for rates of unemployment benefit to be raised to meet the rising cost of living. These activities were acknowledged in the TUC's observation in May 1947: 'Trades Councils now have an important part in production matters regarding full employment, location of industry, use of factory space and storage of government equipment'.[731] As never before, TCs (e.g. Cambridge TC, Nottingham TC, Uxbridge TC, Rotherham TC&LP and London TC) were now enthusiastically searching for ways to implement the production drive through which the government planned to stabilise the economy, but the same personnel who had owned private enterprises were responsible for workers' low living standards.

The year 1947 was the turning point. TCs were sharing their observations on increases in prices and profits compared to wages. (This has a resonance in 2024.) While accepting the shortage of raw materials as an inhibiting factor, delegates at the ACTC 1947 were convinced difficulties could be overcome by the extension of joint consultative machinery in each industry and planning boards owned by the government. As happens in times dominated by economic austerity, the burden of the economic crisis was falling on the working class, hence TC demands to place a ceiling on all company profits and dividends.

Such proposals had little effect; neither did TCs engaging with local councils over factory closures. Penrith TC affirmed: 'the idle rich who spent their time at Goodwood and Ascot' should have their rations curtailed! TCs had given loyal support to overcome the economic crisis while questioning the rationale for the wage freeze (see Bristol TC and Shrewsbury TC) as they highlighted restrictions imposed on building houses when the armed forces were being maintained at inflated levels (Swindon TC).[732] In 1948 these disagreements among TCs about the government's approach to wage restraint rumbled on. There followed debates and then resolutions over the wage freeze and devaluing the currency. The spectre of a return to 1930s levels of unemployment would not be tolerated. One TC succinctly placed the existing economic troubles in context:

> We are not unmindful of the years between the two Wars when the Tory Party made slashing attacks on even the limited social services, nor can we forget how advantage was taken of the millions of unemployed workers to force down wages of those still fortunate enough to be employed until many areas of the country became industrial graveyards.[733]

TCs nationally demanded price controls to ease the cost of living rises, to impose strict limitations on profits, elimination of wasteful practices in distributing consumer goods, a minimum wage, and improved conditions to attract workers into essential industries. Edinburgh TC rejected attempts by employers or government to impose restrictions on wage increases when taxation on profits in industry should be the priority. Wage increases in 1947 had been lower than any year since 1943, wholesale prices the highest since 1940. The optimism of 1945 was fading. In Coventry, the TC echoed Penrith TC, objecting to the award of enormous wealth to the Duke and Duchess of Edinburgh (an issue cropping up ever since) as hardly conducive to 'increased productive effort by workers' who had been called upon to endure enormous wartime sacrifices and hardship. 'The state cannot afford the luxury of granting such sums to people who already have ample means on which to live.'[734]

In 1948 an employment strategy emerged from TCs. Newcastle (Staffs.) TC cautioned that if the wage freeze continued while the cost of living was rising so much, industrial disturbances would result. In March, Birmingham TC argued that the government's White Paper (on Personal Incomes, Costs and Prices) would not solve this *impasse*.[735] Underlying TCs' belief a planned solution could rehabilitate the country's economy, they repeated: essential commodities' prices should be stabilised, with more taxes on profits, a capital levy, and, as much as possible, elimination of wasteful, luxury expenditure. TCs existed to maintain workers' incomes; this was embedded in resolutions from TCs in Bath, Croydon, Coventry, Bristol and Manchester & Salford. TC Conferences were held on the threats of redundancy and the TUC's acceptance of wage freezing before such a scheme had been accepted by the movement. Control of profits and prices was uppermost for TCs (see Coventry, Greenwich and Uxbridge TCs).

TCs' class-based politics can be further exemplified in three TCs. Bridgewater TC drew the attention of the Minister of Labour to time spent by individuals in Somerset hunting deer ('such individuals could be more usefully employed')! Telford TC was astonished by the anti-working-class attitude of the government in freezing wages. And Kidderminster TC was outraged by certain employers' soaring profits: 'a gross injustice to the productive and consumer elements of the population'.[736] Similar sentiments were expressed by Scunthorpe, Colchester, Keighley, Huddersfield, Plymouth and Swindon TCs. For many, the forebodings of the 1930s had returned. London TC summarised: 'It represents the end of a period when the employers even pretended a concern with the nation's interest and opens a new period of increasing resistance to the legitimate claims of the working class.'[737]

*

Banishing the memories of humiliating, wasteful unemployment and that lived experience of hopelessness in numerous 1930s communities, could the interventionary state answer the yearning for personal and social security? For insurance against unemployment, accident and old age? For free medical care, social services' state provision, expanding education opportunities? For new towns, urban recreation centres, subsidised public transport, and publicly funded arts/culture? The liberating possibilities centred upon a transfer of resources through taxation, redistribution of wealth and resultant social cohesion.

In the 1930s, specifically in the regions of the old industries, there was an economic structure that failed millions through the depressing inertia of enforced unemployment. As one TC put it:

> When the real history of our times comes to be written, the staggering, colossal ineptitude of our ruling class will be a subject of sheer amazement… it has been powerless, paralyzed, completely incapable of dealing effectively with any of our grave social problems from unemployment to housing.[738]

And today, in 2020s Britain, the problem remains:

> With its ceaseless boom and bust cycles, capitalism is itself fundamentally and irreducibly bi-polar, periodically lurching between hyped-up mania (the irrational exuberance of 'bubble thinking') and depressive come-down.[739]

It was the irrational logic of corporate capitalism that failed to solve the problem of mass unemployment. Welfare cuts and oscillations in 'levelling up' agendas have since eclipsed the undoubted achievements of the post-war Labour government (despite that wage freeze). Only a more socially-orientated society, nurtured by a more egalitarian social system, with a radical agenda, can provide the *fundamental transformations* required. The final analysis goes to and extended quote from Albert Einstein (from 1949):

The situation prevailing in an economy based on the private ownership of capital is thus characterized by two main principles: first, means of production (capital) are privately owned and the owners dispose of them as they see fit; second, the labor contract is free. Of course, there is no such thing as a pure capitalist society in this sense. In particular, it should be noted that the workers, through long and bitter political struggles, have succeeded in securing a somewhat improved form of the "free labor contract" for certain categories of workers. But taken as a whole, the present day economy does not differ much from "pure" capitalism.

Production is carried on for profit, not for use. There is no provision that all those able and willing to work will always be in a position to find employment; an "army of unemployed" almost always exists. The worker is constantly in fear of losing his job. Since unemployed and poorly paid workers do not provide a profitable market, the production of consumers' goods is restricted, and great hardship is the consequence. Technological progress frequently results in more unemployment rather than in an easing of the burden of work for all. The profit motive, in conjunction with competition among capitalists, is responsible for an instability in the accumulation and utilization of capital which leads to increasingly severe depressions. Unlimited competition leads to a huge waste of labor, and to that crippling of the social consciousness of individuals which I mentioned before.

This crippling of individuals I consider the worst evil of capitalism. Our whole educational system suffers from this evil. An exaggerated competitive attitude is inculcated into the student, who is trained to worship acquisitive success as a preparation for his future career.

I am convinced there is only one way to eliminate these grave evils, namely through the establishment of a socialist economy, accompanied by an educational system which would be oriented toward social goals. In such an economy, the means of production are owned by society itself and are utilized in a planned fashion. A planned economy, which adjusts production to the needs of the community, would distribute the work to be done among all those able to work and would guarantee a livelihood to every man, woman, and child. The education of the individual, in addition to promoting his own innate abilities, would attempt to develop in him a sense of responsibility for his fellow men, in place of the glorification of power and success in our present society.[740]

CHAPTER 9

Women in Trade Unions

> We are not women arrayed in struggle against men but workers who are in struggle against the employers.
> ~ Eleanor Marx, quoted in Judith Orr, *Marxism and Women's Liberation 2015, p199*

There have been many studies of the history of women in unions but in our original research for this book there was scant evidence of women's activities in trades councils, particularly in TCs' annual reports and conferences in the UK 1920–50. However, this does not mean women were inactive in trade union politics. Some sources, (often online), show women to have been *centrally involved in working-class organisation* during this time, before and afterwards.[741] This chapter is dedicated to an overview of women and their significant contributions in British trade unions before, during and after 1920–50. It provides a flavour of the union activism and industrial politics in which women were involved, with an arc of hope and determination directed towards a future of equal rights and inspired, emancipatory politics, where women's industrial actions fuse with political activity. (LGBT industrial and political issues, although important, are beyond the scope of this chapter. For more on this subject see Laura Miles' *Transgender Resistance: Socialism and the Fight for Trans Liberation* (2020).)

1. WOMEN IN UNIONS 1875–1914

During the Second Industrial Revolution women were perceived by most working men to be best suited to a life of domesticity. Women's opportunities, rights and responsibilities at work were minimal, for a long time considered 'dangerous', embodying a social 'otherness' not worthy of industrial empowerment.[742] Rebecca Zahn and Nicole Busby maintain: 'Once they ventured beyond work such as spinning and weaving – considered extensions of 'womanly duties' – into the factories, women workers were considered a real threat to societal order and moral values.'[743]

Paid employment would eventually provide women with the potential for independence in many spheres of their lives. But, for now, circumscribed roles for women were a boon for employers, as Lindsey German confirms: 'men and women workers have been… pitted against one another when it comes to jobs, wages and union organisation.'[744] Unfortunately the patriarchal trade union bureaucracy and local unions tended to reinforce this dichotomy. At a meeting of the TUC in 1875, TUC Parliamentary Secretary Henry Broadhurst declared a woman's place was in the home 'instead of being dragged into competition for livelihood against the great and strong men of the world'.[745] In *Women at Work*, Mary Davis suggests:

> From this kind of thinking sprang the widespread acceptance of the notion of the 'family wage' to be won by the male breadwinner. Hence, not only was unequal pay accepted as a norm, but women's work was only tolerated if not threatening to the man.[746]

Yet, after prolonged dedicated industrial and political activism and endeavours, from the late 19th century a 'period of blossoming of women's organising' commenced.[747] This process benefitted from the first wave of feminism, with campaigns for women's voting rights, a process set in motion by women's increasingly persistent campaigning in unions – at meetings, on the streets and, gradually, in places of work – and maintained until the breakthrough: gaining equal franchise in 1928. The famous 1888 Matchwomen's Strike was an essential part of what became a 'new unionism',[748] its swift success bolstered by working men including, as German acknowledges:

> widescale donations and the intervention of the London Trades Council. Wages went up, the hated fines and deductions were abolished and the women formed the Matchmakers' Union. With around 800 members, this was the biggest women's union yet.[749]

The strike triggered a series of further industrial actions that shook traditionalist structures of the old unions and the emerging TUC.[750] A generalised radicalisation took place, with new and upcoming trade union leaders inspired by socialist ideas, including Mary Macarthur, Sylvia Pankhurst and Eleanor Marx.[751] Over the next 20 years UK trade union membership grew from 750,000 to 6,500,000, and during World War I specifically female trade union membership rose from under 400,000 to over 1,000,000 (17% of members), a growth of 160%, with the largest increase in the general labour unions.[752]

New organisations seeking equal rights for women had been established and developed, including the Women's Protective and Provident League (from 1874), which was replaced by the Women's Trade Union League (WTUL) in 1889, from which came Clementina Black. Before becoming WTUL secretary, Black had proposed the first successful 'equal pay' resolution at the 1888 TUC Congress and, although the general secretary opposed this, it was a symbolic victory, even if not acted upon. (The WTUL was dissolved in 1921 as the TUC incorporated it into the Women Workers' Group.)[753]

Other all-female union groups included the Co-operative Women's Guild (from 1883), led by Alice Acland, which by 1933 had over 70,000 members in 1,500 branches; the National Union of Women's Suffrage Societies (NUWSS) (1897), founded by Millicent Fawcett; and the Women's Social and Political Union (WSPU) (1903), founded by Emmeline Pankhurst. Both the NUWSS and the WSPU campaigned for the vote, while the National Federation of Women Workers (NFWW) (from 1906), which confronted barriers for women's membership in trade unions, had a membership that rose to c.80,000.[754]

In 1920 in *Women in Trade Unions*, Barbara Drake (later of the LRD) reported that, as male unions refused to admit women, skilled women mechanics 'threw in their lot with other women, and joined general labour unions'.[755] (Drake added that between 1886 and 1896 women trade unionists had increased from around 37,000 to nearly 118,000, and by 1906 they numbered 167,000, of whom just 5,000 were in women's societies.)[756]

Women's groups sought numerous demands: equal pay for equal work, regulation of wages in low-paid trades, a 48-hour week, more women factory inspectors, protection in dangerous trades, maternity provision, co-operative homes for 'working girls', reforms in technical education and, of course, continued agitation for the vote for women[‡]. Some of these demands remain on working women's agendas, having been raised and promoted throughout the 20th century and since, similar arguments repeatedly deployed.[757]

2. LEADERS

In trade union politics some women emerged as leaders. Mary Macarthur's organising strategies were formative in the extension of women's industrial and political activism. The organisation she ran, the NFWW, grew rapidly. Its paper, *The Woman Worker*, built a circulation of 32,000 by 1909 and the NFWW embraced 20,000 members by 1914. Macarthur's activism was sharpened by the Great Unrest of 1910–14, when workers, who experienced a reduction in real wages, reacted with major industrial action. There were huge demonstrations in London's Hyde Park in 1908, 1910 and 1911, and thousands of political meetings.[758] The

---

‡ 'Working girls' was a phrase used to describe young working women.

WTUL reported 21 strikes in 1911–12, 18 culminating in victory, with 10 million strike days in 1911 alone.[759]

Macarthur was at the heart of industrial activities. She helped inspire confidence in working women who increasingly identified as being part of a collective. This was reflected in a surge of women joining trade unions. Between 1906 and 1914, union membership for women swelled from almost 167,000 to about 358,000.[760] However, in 1914, on the issue of military intervention, Macarthur supported the government. Her politics became compromised, moving away from the radical stances she had maintained during the Great Unrest. In 1915 she defended the controversial Queen Mary's Work for Women Fund, which involved sweatshop labour, which Macarthur had previously opposed. When Macarthur adopted this approach, Sylvia Pankhurst dubbed it 'Queen Mary's sweatshops.'[761] The Women War Workers' Committee, over which Macarthur presided, laid down conditions for: 'trade union membership, the same rate of pay for the same work, no sweating [sweatshop labour], training for the unemployed, and priority after the war for men whose jobs had been filled by women'.[762] According to German, the last point, (seemingly jarring,) was consistent with NFWW policy.[763]

To her credit, Macarthur dedicated her whole adult life to organising and encouraging working women, raising political consciousness and financial funds for workers, and partaking in and winning strikes. Her involvement in the Chain-Makers' Strike of 1910 was a highlight, in which she helped raise £4,000 for strikers, the Chain-Makers' Association membership reaching 1,700, a union to be reckoned with and the strike a huge success. Macarthur's attendance at the 1919 International Women's Labour Conference and the International Labour Conference in Washington were other peaks, the former for a minimum age for work by 16, a 44-hour week, maximum eight-hour day and abolition of night work (except for essential services).[764]

Historian Sarah Boston assessed Macarthur: 'No other woman in the history of women's struggle to organize made such a significant contribution.'[765] Boston insisted that Macarthur's separatist methodology was *tactical*, not ideological, 'a necessity of circumstance, not a feminist principle.'[766] Macarthur exemplifies this in August 1920 in *The Woman Worker*, in which she anticipated a time where women and men would organise together, with equal rights.[767] Despite her shortcomings over the war, Macarthur undoubtedly made a great contribution to women's social, industrial and political advancement, and was much mourned by the movement when she died on 1 January 1921 at just 40 years of age.

*

Sylvia Pankhurst famously campaigned for votes for women, as well as confronting other aspects of women's oppression. She fought for male and female workers' rights and campaigned against British imperialism in Ireland and, in 1913, spoke at a rally at the Albert Hall alongside Irish radical James Connolly (much to her mother Emmeline's and sister Christabel's annoyance).

In 1914 Pankhurst set up the East London Federation of Suffragettes (ELFS), which separated from the WSPU.

Pankhurst focused ELFS energies on working-class issues – poverty, low pay and childcare. The group was a hands-on organisation, ran a maternity clinic, a day nursery, a school, two low-cost restaurants, and a toy factory. In 1916 it became WSF, the Workers' Suffrage Federation. The group expanded and its newspaper, *The Women's Dreadnought*, soon attracted 10,000 readers. In 1917, inspired by the Russian Revolution, the paper became *The Workers' Dreadnought*, as Pankhurst, who opposed the war, was won to the cause of revolution while the other Pankhursts indulged in jingoism, renaming their newspaper *Britannia* and pledging support for the war.[768] Angry at the rising cost of living, Pankhurst wrote to the PM demanding war bonuses for working women equal to working men.[769]

She suffered for her beliefs, as her radical politics led to her imprisonment; but, when free, she dedicated herself to workers' basic rights, joining communist organisations for the liberation of working women and men. In 1928 the movement she and her family had helped to lead achieved equal voting rights. She spent later years campaigning against colonialism and died in 1960.

*

Other women leaders who stood for working women through trade union activity include, Margaret Bondfield, Gertrude Tuckwell, Mary Bell, Mary Barbour, Mary Burns Laird and Helen Crawfurd, the latter three particularly active on the Clyde in West Scotland.

As well as women organising women, there have been male trade unionists who supported women workers. In her history of women trade unionists, Boston mentioned a Mr Tate, an NUT member, who formed the Equal Pay League (EPL) in 1904 (an organisation that lasted until 1961). By 1920, the EPL had 21,000 members. Willie Gallagher, the famous communist leader, campaigned for women workers – in Parliament as an MP, and with workers on the Clyde. AEU president Jack Tanner was also notable for his support for working women in trade unions, and argued for 'lightening women's burden', although he never questioned whether work in the home should be men's work too![770]

William John Davis, General Secretary of the National Society of Amalgamated Brassworkers and Metal Mechanics, promoted legislation banning women from roles in the brass trade, then opposed sweatshop conditions in the Birmingham metal trades, and later, influenced by Mary Macarthur, sought women's equal rates for the same job.[771] Embodied in Davis's journey is a snapshot of the sometimes contradictory attitudes in male trade unionist activity – from chauvinist–conservative to socially-informed behaviour, altered through interaction with others and influenced by a process of political engagement.

3. WOMEN IN UNIONS 1914–45

The impact of World War I on women's trade unionism was dramatic and transformational, empowering working women in the UK as never before. During an appallingly destructive four years, the war had positive by-products: huge numbers of women joined the workforce and general unions' female membership increased from 23,534 in 1914 to 216,000 in 1918; 650 women in transport unions mushroomed to 54,000, in clothing unions 26,000 swelled to 119,000; and there was a leap in women's membership in distributive and clerical trade unions, as well as newly expanding industries where women often had to replace men.[772]

In many areas women's social emancipation blossomed. Workplace women's football drew crowds in the tens of thousands and some women, bolstered economically and newly socially confident, attended restaurants unaccompanied – labelled 'Dining Out Girls' by the retrogressive *Daily Mail*.[773] Writer and activist Clementina Black wrote at the time: 'I have become convinced that the moral and mental effect upon the women themselves of being wage earners is good.'[774]

Barbara Drake commented on women's increasing unionisation after World War I, observing that working women developed class consciousness as they identified with 'the power of organisation… and the value of their labour'.[775] This was reflected in women's union membership in 1920 peaking at nearly 1,500,000 (25% of the female workforce) and in new forms of women's organisation.[776] When, in 1920, the TUC voted to form its first General Council, with 17 industrial groupings, the NFWW sought women's representation, and an eighteenth group, representing women, was created, with two women's positions guaranteed; (as mentioned,) the Women Workers' Group (later known as the Women's Advisory Committee) now replaced the WTUL and in 1926 an annual women's conference was first held to assist in the General Council in matters relating to women workers.[777]

However, just as women's lives seemed to be improving, their collective advance was halted. After the war, canteens and day nurseries were closed, and, in sport and leisure, in 1921 the English Football Association banned women's football teams (a ban that remained in place until 1971)! (While many now celebrate the rise of women's football, few know of its past popularity.)

By the 1930s, with the industrial downturn after the 1929 economic slump, of 5,750,000 working women, just one-sixth remained in unions, even less in trades councils. Sue Ledwith deduces that this was because of 'exclusionary attitudes and practices of male trade unionists'[778] and the traditional values of the TUC leadership. In response to this process, Drake argued for *women's advisory councils in mainstream unions* to support women with their specific concerns and encourage participation in union activity.[779] However, during the middle to late interwar years, with an increase in patriarchal attitudes in union politics amongst both union leaders and the rank and file, women trade unionists were marginalised (not unlike the sidelining of communists recorded above in Chapters 5–7).

Undeterred, women continued to challenge male domination in workplaces and in the unions. This led to some small victories such as the 1942 engineers' union finally voting to accept women members, and new rules formulated that led to a separate Annual Conference for Women and the right to vote in all elections, with the first women's conference held in 1943. However, despite the then AEU president paying tribute to the major contribution by women *at home, at work and in the union*, some doubted the reality of such 'inclusionary gestures'.[780] The 'empowerment of women' was one step forward/two steps back during the interwar years.

As in World War I, women's economic and social roles radically changed during World War II. Women were suddenly informed that their place was not *only* in the home but also in (unequally paid) employment in key factories. This transformation did not occur due to a burst of enlightened insight from employers, government or male workers but because of wartime economic requirements. To defend Britain and her Empire required a *national* war effort. A labour shortage meant employing more women. Thus could be jettisoned two decades of mass unemployment. Soon, 75% of new workers were married women and 3 million married women and widows were in employment, doubling pre-war figures. In this endeavour, working-class women were aided by the introduction of factory canteens and inexpensive government-run restaurants, and school children attended nurseries and received free school meals and free milk.[781]

4. WORKING WOMEN AFTER THE WARS

After World War II, many women did not want to lose their new-found freedoms just because the war had ended. This included paid work: in 1939, 90% of women workers stated that they would give up their work outside the home when the war ended, but in 1945 85% preferred to continue their non-domestic paid employment.[782] However, post-war, women were forced out or resigned from jobs and between 1943 and 1947 1,150,000 women left industries.[783]

As a result, women's representation in trade unions decreased substantially. Many women left unions and were now frequently unorganised where they worked, and outnumbered in unions and trades councils, with union executives represented and controlled by men. This meant women's voices were rarely heard or acted upon. But one gain was lasting: the marriage bar (which prevented married women from gaining employment) was abolished for women in the civil service and most local government work in 1946.[784]

However, working-class women's freedoms were threatened post-war. In 1946, the government drastically reduced the day nursery grant by 50%. This resulted in many day nurseries closing with the cost of childcare placed upon familes. This decision was denounced by women trade unionists including Ms Harrison of the FBU and, although motions were passed recognising that some women had no choice but to seek work, day nurseries stayed closed.[785] Boston's devastating conclusion passed judgement on the shortcomings in trade union leadership: 'While the government was enacting legislation to establish the welfare state, the TUC was advocating private enterprise for child care.'[786]

Subsequent to brief wartime reprieve, little had changed for women since Henry Broadhurst's outburst in 1875; women were again told their proper place was at home, with motherhood and home-making.[787] The 1947 TUC annual report stated bluntly:

> There is little doubt in the minds of the General Council that the home is one of the most important spheres for a woman worker and that it would be doing a great injury to the life of the nation if women were persuaded or forced to neglect their domestic duties in order to enter industry particularly where there are young children to cater for.[788]

Prejudices about the role of women in employment were not suddenly banished by 1945 (nor by the end of our focus, in 1950). Batons would be passed onto future generations to raise questions regarding women's trade union representation, employment, social and civil rights and freedoms. Boston highlighted the huge wastage of the skills that women had acquired during the war as in the British economy, with a post-war labour *shortage*, women paid the price for government and trade union obdurate prescribing of gender roles.[789] Although referring to World War I, Lloyd George's observation remains apt for World War II: 'It is a strange irony, but no small compensation, that the making of weapons of destruction would afford the occasion to humanise industry. And yet such is the case.'[790] As working women's increased empowerment through paid work and socialised childcare was so short-lived, maintained only during two destructive global wars, this irony has also been a devastating loss.

5. STRIKING BACK FOR EQUAL PAY (1916 ONWARDS)

At the core of women's battles in unions and trades councils has been the issue of equal pay. In the early days of trade unions, despite some progressive rhetoric, unions did little that was tangible for the cause of *equal* pay. For decades the TUC remained ambivalent about the issue, urging governments to implement equal pay in the public sector while accepting it as a *fait accompli* in the private sector. A related problem was 'dilution', when women were paid considerably less than the male workers they replaced.

The striving for equal pay, as with other issues, was fought not only by women but also by some working-class men. The Clyde Workers' Agreement of 1916 had been a product of campaigning by the Clyde Workers Committee, a grouping chaired by W. Gallagher and led by left-wing activists, later to join the British CP. It was soon joined by Mary Barbour, Mary Burns Laird and Helen Crawfurd, among others, and resulted in the creation of the Shop Stewards Movement, the rank-and-file organisation that could bypass the official channels of unions – for better working conditions. The activities on the Clyde illustrated that workers could campaign against dilution through joint activity by women and men, and could be more effective than the women's NFWW union campaigning on its own.[791]

Another set piece for equal pay took place in 1918 amongst women tram workers in the South-East, about an unequal war bonus. Strike action spread to the London Underground rail network, with NFWW founder and leader Macarthur describing it as 'a landmark for the women's movement and for trade unionism'.[792] It was a success, leading to a government special enquiry into applying wage equality to all industries, and a report of the War Cabinet Committee on Women in Industry, with trade union historian Beatrice Webb falling short of demanding 'equal pay for equal work'. (Her husband Sidney Webb thought women's work inferior!)[793]

Between the wars, in a climate of rising unemployment, cost cutting and unions reverting to sectionalist approaches, 'equal pay' was seen by many men as a threat to their own livelihood. Women's employment rose slowly from 27% of the workforce in 1923 to 30% in 1939, some men blaming their own challenged circumstances on women's *cheap labour*, today encapsulated in the debate over 'cheap foreign labour', a repeated sideshow for systemic problems. In 1935, the UPOW union called for a halt to female employment altogether.[794]

The TUC sought to tackle the issue of women being underpaid by creating *committees*. In 1921 it formed the Women's Workers' Group (later the Women's Advisory Committee) and in 1926 founded the prementioned Annual Women's Conference. However, committees rarely solve such issues, as the enduring intransigence over equal pay has exhibited. Predictably, *recruitment campaigning* was seen as a solution![795]

Post-World War II, the argument for unequal pay was 'the continuing need for counter-inflationary policies', which meant that government action on equal pay 'would be inappropriate *at the present time*'.[796] This has been a hardy perennial for the TUC General Council. The time never seems to be right. Such temporal excusing has been combined with an ideology sanctioning women's subjugation and ingrained notions of a 'family wage', with men being the primary breadwinners.[797] Unions in industries with a high proportion of women have often refused to campaign for or demand equal pay, and instead pursued claims *maintaining pay differentials* between the sexes. Post-war, these differentials often *increased*. The 1949 TUC conference scrapped the issue altogether. This meant that at this time women's earnings remained, shockingly, on average 50% of men's.[798]

Ledwith deduces: 'Clearly women could not rely on class solidarity. They had to do it themselves.'[799] In the 1930s this approach resulted in women civil servants instigating and organising in a woman's union, leading campaigns for equal pay, and, together with teachers, post office workers and local government officers, continuing to apply social pressure. By the 1950s this meant confronting governments and a union leadership that perpetually claimed that they *could not afford* equal pay, that the economy would *collapse* if women received equal pay.[800]

In 1955 the government finally promised to equalise pay in the public sector *'within six years'*. Although a victory for women, the resultant bill was restricted to a minority of *skilled* and *professional* women, with nurses, women clerical, and manual workers in the public sector denied the same right. It would be a further decade, after repeated stonewalling, following the celebrated 1968 Ford Women Workers' Strike, for women to receive significant pay parity. Yet, although the Equal Pay Act has been in place since the 1970s, it has not actually resulted in equal pay. Today in the UK women are still paid 30% less than men (and own just 1% of the world's wealth)![801]

6. WOMEN TRADE UNIONISTS SINCE THE 1970S

Half a century after the first wave of feminism, a process of confronting women's oppression, which was the making of Mary Macarthur and Sylvia Pankhurst and produced votes for women, came the second wave, striving for equal pay and rights in the workplace and at home. This was inspired by activists in the US, and was in the UK linked with working-class men, who, in the late 1960s and early 1970s, sought increases in their own rights and pay through trade union activity. Workers' actions, often involving strikes, with dock workers and miners, were crucial, and in 1974 resulted in the demise of Edward Heath's Conservative government.

However, since the late 1970s and 1980s and the unleashing of neoliberal economics, male and female workers' rights have been threatened and union membership fallen dramatically. This process was accelerated by Margaret Thatcher's confrontation with unions, most notably with her 1984–85 onslaught on Britain's coal miners, until then the most powerful union in the country.

Throughout their history in trades councils and trade unions, working women have developed traditions of *organising in communities*. In strike situations, family poverty and debt have sometimes led to women pressurising their partners to return to work, while at other times realising new-found capabilities. The latter was the case with the 1920s South Wales miners' wives who tarred and feathered strike-breakers, and has echoed through time with Women Against Pit Closures in the 1984 Miners' Strike taking on new social roles, raising funds and addressing huge rallies.[802] However, through combined efforts recalling those against the miners in 1926, the government and employers ideologically and literally attacked the exhaustive efforts by miners and the many who supported them.

This has had an impact. In recent years the proportion of trade union members in workplaces of 25+ has plummeted from 65% in 1980 to 26% in 2011,[803] although today many women are in paid employment. According to a March

2023 report, 72.3% of women are in work, below the male employment rate of 79%. In total, 9.74 million women work full-time and 5.92 million work part-time.[804]

The nature of women's work is constantly changing. From being confined to the home in the late 19th century to working with textiles, manufacturing war work, involvement in the welfare state, to secretarial, teaching, bookkeeping, waitressing and nursing in the 1970s, to boosting health, social work and the 'service industry' today, the world of working women is constantly in flux. This list of occupations are generalisations but they highlight the changing nature of working women over the last century.

7. WOMEN'S UNION ORGANISING TODAY

The debate continues to this day about how women want to organise politically. Some women embrace *autonomous organising* for women, centred on women's groups, black women's groups, women's education and for constructed spaces for women.[805] It can mean confronting black women's multifaceted subjugation – in education, housing, immigration and asylum legislation, and racism with the police, the media and society in general. Others accentuate 'working class unity across the sexes', through industrial and political activity in trade unions, shop stewards' networks and trades councils. Both autonomous activism and uniting with working men require developing 'collective political strategies... to change structures and cultures' and seizing opportunities when conditions are favourable, pursuing counter-hegemonies for gender and diversity.[806] Many people see no contradiction between striving for working women's rights and men's at the same time.

In 2013 Frances O'Grady became the first female TUC general secretary. Although essentially a change of management, this was a marker of the progressive change by and for women in the trade union movement. Davis contends: 'Change for women workers will only come about through the determined efforts of our own trade unions.'[807] This can mean linking up with campaigns in and outside the workplace, engaging with issues such as challenging abuse, prejudice and oppression, and championing equality and social and economic justice. It can be built amongst women's groups and male workers, developing networks of shop stewards, capable of uniting independently of trade union officials, if needs be.

In the 2020s the social role of women in political organising is advancing in unions and workplaces, with strikes by railway workers, nurses, junior doctors, postal workers, barristers, teachers, civil servants, and university staff, alongside dynamic campaigns concerning the climate crisis, Black Lives Matter (BLM), LGBTQ+ and the #MeToo movement (against sexual abuse, sexual harassment and rape culture). The climate crisis has been led by Greta Thunberg, who has inspired and galvanised youth across the globe; BLM has been the largest protest movement in US history and has gone global; LGBTQ+ rights is a visible cause internationally; and with the #MeToo campaign, abused and harassed women and men are speaking out about their traumatic experiences.

8. CONCLUSION

Since the 1920s women's lives in the UK have been transformed through political and social advances, in which union activity has been focal. Women have won the vote and gained access to birth control, abortion has been legalised, and rape in marriage criminalised. Women have access to employment and education in ways denied to them in the past. For three decades more women than men have attended universities and they now outnumber men in trade unions.[808] Such hard-won rights are in no small part due to working women's persistence; they have helped create changes in social conditions so that women today are in many ways more liberated then their ancestors. Technological advancement (including washing machines, dishwashers, mass production of transport vehicles and clothes, mass entertainment, building and food production, vaccinations against disease, computers and the internet) has also been beneficial to working-class women (although with technological advance can come new forms of exploitation, as monitored Amazon employees know).

The challenge for trade unions and their trades councils now is to be relevant, supportive and effective, and for women to take the lead. Zahn and Busby highlight this:

> trade union renewal depends on representative membership which reflects the changing world of work. Women play a pivotal role in this regard. Today, women trade union members outnumber men and the average British trade unionist is a young, degree-educated, white, professional woman. Yet trade unions are struggling to shake off their image as the representatives of white, working-class and blue-collar men with the large proportion of women members

not always reflected in branch officers, workplace representatives and national officers.[809]

Eight years on, that analysis remains pertinent for women participating in trades councils.

For women, and increasingly men, restricted by the triple demands of work, childcare and union politics, essential reforms are necessary. State-funded childcare, extended paternity and maternity leave, free school breakfast clubs and creches at meetings and work, etc. are required. Only with such policies in place can both men and women fully contribute to trade union politics, whatever their age or family arrangement. Alongside progress in pay, rights and conditions, these requirements are fundamental for workers. Such demands may not sit well with employers or governments with economic austerity in their policy arsenal, but are crucial for people active in unions and trades councils.

CHAPTER 10

Trades Councils Yesterday and Today:
In the Movement, Of the Movement

We studied the history of how the first major unions were built. We learned from the Industrial Workers of the World, and even more from the building of the Congress of Industrial Organizations... But here's the basic thing, you have an actual worker-led project—a black and brown-led, multi-racial, multi-national, multi-gender, multi-ability organizing team. You get the communists involved, you get some socialists and anarcho-syndicalists, you bring together a broad progressive coalition. Do not be afraid to fight, to get as dirty as the bosses. Do not be afraid to agitate and to antagonize the bosses, as a union should.

~ *Justine Medina, Amazon Labour Union organizing committee at labornotes.org/2022/04/amazon-workers-staten-island-clinch-historic-victory*

1. POLITICAL INHERITANCE: THE 1984-85 MINERS' STRIKE AND AFTER[810]

How do trades councils operate today? To answer this question we need to understand developments affecting TCs and unions in recent decades, both impacting upon society and as a product of it. TCs are affected by the subjective political role of individuals in their localities and the objective social context in which they operate, the latter conditioned particularly by (among other aspects) the levels of class-consciousness and how this is manifested in the working class and trade union movement. During the timeframe that provided the basis for my co-author's original research (above), the focal point was the 1926 General Strike. Since that time, the miners' strike of 1984-85 was for many of today's older TC members a watershed.

From the 1940s, high levels of employment led to a growth in workers' bargaining power and confidence, with extensive shop-floor organisation, frequently resulting in successful industrial actions. Dubbed 'do-it-yourself reformism',[811] this approach repeatedly won material improvements often with trade union and/or Labour Party support. Such activities were restricted by the incomes policies of Harold Wilson's Labour and Edward Heath's Conservatives, who sought to curb workers' interventions and increase the role of national union officials. This precipitated *more* strikes, involving 'flying pickets', which spread action to further workplaces, giving rise to rank and file workers' organisations and the defeat of the Conservative government in 1974 (noted in chapter 9).

Following the first major economic crisis since World War II, the Labour government used a social contract to introduce wage controls, inhibiting workers' bargaining power by moving to national agreements, as the return of increased unemployment depleted workers participation. Thomas et al maintain 'that the balance of power inside the unions shifted toward the bureaucracy. In 1976-8 workers experienced the first fall in wages since the 1920s'.[812] Soon they would face an onslaught that would greatly challenge them.

The miners' strike of 1984-85 (explored in Robert Gildea's *Backbone of the Nation: Mining Communities and the Great Strike of 1984-85* (2023)) was triggered by the Conservative government's decision to close 20 collieries, which miners and the NUM leader Arthur Scargill sought to keep open. So a strike to defend the mines commenced in Yorkshire, before spreading to coalfields across the country. PM Margaret Thatcher thought any industrial action would be defeated in weeks. However, it grew into a year-long industrial convulsion, with 26 million days 'lost' to strike action, the most for any year in the UK since 1926.

In her first term in office, Thatcher subtly established herself as an ideological warrior for the ruling class, persuading many that union power needed to be challenged and that the privatisation of industry would enrich ordinary people. She was driven by a free market neoliberal ideology to impose constrictions on the welfare state, privatise state-owned industries and confront the trade union movement, which she dubbed 'the enemy within'. As such, her government applied the 'Ridley Plan' of 1977, 'The Final Report of the Nationalised Industries Policy Group', which provided a strategy to undermine the unions, one by one.

Before the strike began, in March 1984, the Government had built up coal stocks, ensured docks could handle large-scale coal imports, and that oil and nuclear power stations were capable of handling demand for extra energy. The police were trained to break strikes and Ian MacGregor, an industrialist with a track record of confronting trade unions in the UK and the US, was appointed chairman of the National Coal Board (the statutory corporation which ran the nationalised coal mining industry in the UK).

The government's operation was more extensive than when its predecessors faced the miners (and their advocates) in 1926. In the 1980s' strike, the police harassed pickets and prevented them from travelling to other coal pits; they also invaded mining villages, attacking and arresting miners and their supporters. At the Orgreave coke-plant in South Yorkshire the police assaulted striking miners and the BBC misleadingly edited the video footage so it appeared that the pickets had been the first to use violence, when the opposite was the truth.

Central to TCs' *raison d'etre* has been their capacity to organise solidarity for workers in industrial action (as this book has illuminated) and they were a significant force for this for the 1980s' striking miners. The strike was supported by their communities, especially miners' wives, who ran communal kitchens, marched, picketed and co-ordinated solidarity actions. TCs were part of this collective ethos. One former Colchester TC delegate reports 300 miners staying with delegates and others in the wider labour movement. Here, just as in the General Strike 60 years previously, the local TC was helpful in co-ordinating the billeting of strikers with local activists, as well as raising money to support their families in the coalfields. Plus there was support from black, Asian and immigrant communities and LGBT+ groups.

The strike transformed those involved. There were mass meetings (with TCs involved) where communities engaged in self-management. Activist and journalist Paul Foot commented in 1985:

> People were changing. In the strength of their collective action they felt a new confidence in themselves and the people all around them. Ideas and prejudices which had been grafted into them like barnacles were suddenly blasted away... The seeds of a new society founded on cooperation, common interest and human effort bent to human need were sown in the struggle.[813]

What was the position of the TUC leadership and the Labour Party? At its conference in September 1984, the TUC assured miners they would mobilise solidarity action, which concerned the Conservative government. This failed to materialise. Although many local Labour Party members supported the miners, Labour leader Neil Kinnock insisted the miners held a ballot. He offered lukewarm support, exemplifying a Labourist tendency for desultory encouragement for striking workers and the blunting of industrial campaigns.

As economic hardship took its toll on strikers, with many miners and their families afflicted by deprivation, increasing numbers drifted back to work, the longest mass strike in British history eventually defeated. After 362 days on strike, brass bands, parades and colourful flags proudly accompanied many of the miners back to work. Between 1980 and 1994 (following another round of government implementations) more than 200,000 miners lost their jobs. Only 7 coalmines in the UK remain. The various employment acts increasingly curtailing union activities, passed by Conservative governments since the strike, have codified this defeat.

The impact of such a gruelling strike and its failure was devastation for the trade union movement. Since the strike, many workers in unions, TCs and beyond had their political confidence shattered. This has taken decades to rebuild, and in some cases has not yet been re-built. Ken Muller, now of Islington TC, noticed how, following the strike, TCs became more engaged in individual case works and procedure, supporting workers locally, but with limited aspirations towards more radical activities, union leaders frequently insisting that large-scale industrial action could not succeed. However, this logic has been repeatedly challenged and began to transform for many thousands of workers from 2022 onwards.

2. THE 2022-23 STRIKES: SIGNS OF A RECOVERY

Across the UK, emerging out of the Covid crisis, a collective trauma that stretched across the globe, was a recognition that key workers had sustained the economy. The labour of those in health and social care, public services, local and national government, food production, processing, distribution, sales and transport deliveries, as well as those providing other essential goods, showed how dependent society is on what were now acknowledged in the media as *key workers* (last recognised as such in World War II.)

During this time, millions of workers experienced an

enforced isolation, creating high levels of insecurity and mental health problems, alongside a yearning for normal human interaction. Workers were given inconsistent instructions, the demands of the economy and public safety resulting in contradictory pressures. Then, inflation peaked at 18%, food prices soared and a 'cost of living crisis' intensified, exacerbated by rising energy costs (partly due to the impact of the war in Ukraine, but also systemic tendencies and corporate greed).

This approach has been emboldened by an *intensification of neoliberal economic orthodoxy*, which seeks to buffer the system by safeguarding big finance, while extracting ever-greater profits from workers, resulting in stagnant incomes and worsened conditions for the majority. Millions of workers have experienced reductions in pay in real terms, particularly following the 2008 economic crash, and despite (and sometimes because of) vast profiteering by wealthy shareholders, they have been denied pay rises over several years and so concluded: the time had come for a commensurate rate of pay, by strikes if necessary.

With a greater awareness of their vital function in the economy, workers gained more recognition in terms of self-worth in the economy and of their crucial role in society. Many judged that a weekly clapping routine was not enough: material improvements were required. A palpable shift took place. Few in the mainstream media promoted such an interpretation or heuristic. Nevertheless, TCs revived their task (which for some had been dormant, for others pursued in straitened circumstances) as supporters of industrial action and linking up varying campaigns.

What transpired in 2022-23 was a partial *revival of*

strike action, some of it in non-unionised workplaces. And the scale of workers' participation has been historically significant. According to Thomas et al: 'By early 2023, the number of strike days taken by workers since June 2022 was already higher than for any year since 1989.'[814] There have been nationwide strikes on the rail, post, by barristers, in universities, by civil servants, nurses and junior doctors, among others. RMT leader Mick Lynch was succinct: 'the working class is back.'[815]

The Labour Party leadership adopted a conventionally limited response. Although some local party activists supported strikers, party leader Keir Starmer stipulated that members of the Shadow Cabinet should *not* attend picket lines. So, when Sam Tarry MP appeared at a rail picket at Euston station to support striking workers he was dismissed from his post as Shadow Minister for Buses and Local Transport.

How about the TUC and the trade union leadership? Although the General Council expressed some sympathy for industrial action, the union leadership's fitful strategy of frequently confining strikes to isolated campaigns, with individual strikes dotted over long periods of time, restricted workers' socio-economic impact. And yet, what has transpired post-Covid *is* a tentative advance from atomised individualism to a more *collective ethos*.

Comparisons can be made with the subsequent political advancement for workers after both world wars. Participation in the Great Unrest of 1910-14, impacted by palpable disgust for the senselessness of trench warfare, but unified by the comradeship it engendered, World War I paved the way towards the collectivism of the 1917 Russian

Revolution and the radicalisation in industrial activities here 1918-19. A generation later, after the persistent campaigning of the 1930s and the horrors of World War II, alongside its demand for high levels of employment and general sacrifice, Keynes' economic theories and Beveridge's Plan gained an audience in TCs, trade unions and in the post-war Labour government, leading to the implementation of the British welfare state and decades of relative stability.

And after the 2020-22 Covid quarantine and the accompanying tragic loss of life, many workers have again developed a collective identification with some reactivated militancy and confidence, numerous TCs rejuvenated, women and minorities at the centre of events. In the years leading up to lockdown, strike levels were at historical lows. Now TCs were galvanised: bringing their banners and unity to numerous picket lines, sharing messages of encouragement, calling protests and endorsing public meetings (some of them huge), while maintaining their established role, facilitating a plethora of evolving campaigns.

3. COMPOSITION AND RE-ORIENTATION

For a deeper understanding of how TCs organise themselves in the changing landscape of 2020's Britain, we need to know: what are their values? Their tactics? Their politics? We devised a questionnaire, which we sent to TCs across the country, receiving responses from **Chelmsford, Harlow, Islington, Lancaster & Morecambe, Southampton** and **Wolverhampton TCs**, as well as **Edinburgh TC**'s annual report, and quoted conversations with activists in **Hackney,**

Hastings, Oxford and **Colchester**. This process has presented details about TCs' current political composition and orientation, their union representation, their functioning in local communities, their role *vis-à-vis* a range of industries and crucial local issues, the breadth of their activities, and their (sometimes wryly tragi-comic) histories.

Firstly, there is a matter of *classification*. Displaying their close relationship with the TUC, TCs are now frequently known as *trades union councils*, but for consistency and avoiding confusion with the national 'TUC', we record today's trades union councils in this chapter, as throughout the book, as 'TCs'.

Then there is the issue of *leadership*. From our small sample we note that TC executives can frequently be steered by left-wing leadership. This includes members of the Labour Party, the Co-operative Party (a centre-left faction in Labour), the Socialist Workers Party (SWP), the Socialist Party (SP) and the Communist Party of Britain (founded in 1988, a breakaway from the CP). Another left-wing group involved in TCs is Socialist Appeal, a radical group in the Labour Party – until expelled in July 2021. Despite their different allegiances and ideological orientations, all these groups work together and co-operate civilly (usually). When, at a Southampton TC meeting, after one SP delegate appealed for her party's newspaper's fund, an SWP delegate supplemented: 'other socialist newspapers are available!'

As shown above, the TC movement has for decades been used as an instrument for political debate within the left, with resolutions brought to the TC by individual branches where a particular political faction dominates. In that sense, TCs continue to serve as educational cadre schools for left-wing militants (not as some have intended) as well as providing opportunities for intervening in local workplaces. It seems that today's TC delegates can be both schoolmasters *and* mechanics (see Chapter 1).

However, TCs' political orientations have always been contested. Trade union activist Mike Dukes recalls a predominantly right-wing Southampton TC in the 1970s, with members who opposed multi-cultural education, nuclear disarmament and the banning of corporal punishment. When elected president, ostensibly as a 'respectable and responsible white-collar member' who would defy the left, Dukes disappointed his right-wing backers by siding with the emerging left.

TCs continue to be represented by executive members who are delegated by their trade union branch, as a broad composition of unions across many sectors. Currently, youth, women and BAME unionists are under-represented on ECs. And, although our sample is limited, both in surveys and personal experience, we are aware that many of today's young activists gravitate to more *direct, personally-felt* issues such as BLM, LGBT+ and direct action campaigns on climate issues, and not TCs.

TC activists can be remarkably mobile, some participating in TC ECs wherever they live. Malcolm Wallace, elected as delegate to Chelmsford TC in 1972, also represented TCs in Grimsby and Epping before becoming Chelmsford TC president. Similarly, Simon Hester has served on TCs from Haringey to Hastings.

TC activists can be *durable* and *tenacious*. Some TCs function effectively having recovered following years of inactivity. When Labour Party and trade union activist

Mick Gilgunn moved to Islington in 2000 the local TC was moribund. With fellow activist Gary Heather and former TC secretary George Martindale, Gilgunn formed a steering committee for a re-launch, approaching the TUC with the help of the GLATUC. By 2007, after years of a fairly lifeless TC, highlighted by a weak response to the FBU dispute in 2002–03, Islington TC was rebuilt. Its TC president Andy Bain notes that Jeremy Corbyn was central to the TC's revival, a decade before he became Labour leader (see Islington TC plate).

Such tenacity is evident in TCs enduring through the challenges presented by the Covid crisis. Des Loughney, Edinburgh EC secretary/treasurer, notes his TC's *growth* during this time. In its 155th annual report of 7 March 2022, from 2021 to 2022 ETC incorporated 31 branches (+1), 17,543 members (up from 16,157), with branches affiliated including UNITE City of Edinburgh Council branch and the Pharmacists' Defence Association.

While the Covid epidemic adversely affected monthly meetings' attendances, using the Zoom video conferencing application proved a useful communicative technological tool to retain productive TC functioning. In fact, meetings that are simultaneously Zoom and face-to-face (known as hybrid) have continued to facilitate TCs' attendance and those organising around numerous progressive issues ever since. This has resulted in some large political meetings, showing great potential to co-ordinate disparate campaigns.

As with their 1920-50 predecessors, TC activists' dedication as campaigners for their class can be *hereditary*. TCs' roles continue to flow through families, from one generation to the next. For Mick Patrick, Harlow TC secretary: 'Is it profit before people or people before profit?

We never won anything without a fight... I am now retired but this is a full-time job. I will fight till the day I die. Then my son will take over.'

Today's TCs are defined not just through their activism, but also what are now known as their *brand identities*. Islington TC's progress has been bolstered, as many progressive organisations have, by the work of famous banner-maker, Ed Hall. Hall's website (http://www.edhallbanners.co.uk) celebrates the many trade union campaign and exhibition banners he has created over the last three decades. His work is handmade and stitched, often with painted scenes as centre-pieces. He began as Lambeth Unison branch secretary in the 1990s and has met numerous trade unionists, negotiating and then agreeing on subjects for banners and how best to represent TCs and unions. In 2011 the RMT union sponsored an exhibition featuring his works at the People's History Museum; and he has worked for the Stop the War Coalition, the Palestine Solidarity Campaign, CND, the Anti Nazi League, Unite Against Fascism, and for families and friends of those who have died in police custody. Hall's creations often front large marches, spearheading movements, his creations an asset to numerous TCs. Other notable banner makers include the late Alice Kilroy who the author was happy to have known.

4. IN CONTEMPORARY SOCIETY: INDUSTRIAL AND POLITICAL

Continuation of a Tradition

Engaging in industrial matters in their localities, TCs continue to operate in many ways as they did in the 1920-50 time-frame examined in this book, maintaining a *pivotal role linking together workers in a range of industries.* Southampton TC is typical, representing unionists working in health, communications (post workers and communication engineers), education (primary, secondary, further and higher) and transport (rail, buses and shipping), as well as council and retired workers, and facilitates workers on a variety of local issues, such as the recent dockworkers' picket.

Despite their social role, TCs are rarely prioritised by a local media who, hollowed out by online rivals taking advertising revenue, concentrate on crime and sport. However local industrial and political contributions are highlighted in some local press outlets, such as the *Islington Tribune*, *Camden New Journal* and *Westminster Extra*. As pro-active organisations, TCs square the circle by generating their own copy and posting online, while maintaining communications with some local media.

TCs remain *rooted in local communities*. Chelmsford TC president Wallace confirms that in his TC, as in all TCs, delegates report to their union branch and encourage their colleagues to participate in TC activities. Southampton TC treasurer Glyn Oliver adds that his TC is a source of information, campaigning for union solidarity, sharing details about other activities, offering financial donations, inviting strikers to speak at the TC, attending strikes and pickets, and organising petitions. Oliver envisages TCs as forums for sharing knowledge, discussing trade union, social and political issues. Such developments are being co-ordinated in TCs across the country.

Nick Kelleher, Wolverhampton, Bilston & District TUC secretary and Midlands West TUCJCC (as the TCJCC is now known) representative, comments on his TC supporting workers on picket lines, at rallies, promoting trade union membership in the wider community, and publicising union campaigns. This is a constant. Islington TC EC member Gilgunn confirms: popularising the union movement *within the local community* is a 'crucial part' of a TC, advocating campaigns and disputes, and attaching union delegates to campaigns in their own unions and with other unions; although Southampton TC's Glyn Oliver and Lancaster & Morecambe TC's president, Eugene Doherty, both concede the need for *more affiliations and delegates in TCs*.

TCs participate in solidarity actions, often raising donations, as Islington TC president Bain reports. Harlow TC secretary Patrick reports his TC building union membership and awareness of 'our living social and actual working conditions'. The process is reciprocal, as Southampton TC president Sue Atkins explains: 'I take issues of concern and interest of my Union branch to the trades council, and report back to and involve my Union branch in the activities of the trades council.' In this way, unions make TCs aware of union concerns as union members are informed about what is happening in other unions.

'Bread and Butter' issues
TCs are engaged in a commendable *breadth of activities*, campaigning on national, local and regional issues. Firstly, there are the everyday, so-called 'bread and butter' workers' and unionists' issues. For Chelmsford TC this has included a great deal over the years: endorsing the TUC Campaign for Economic and Social Advance in 1980, representing a

Local Miners' Support Committee and collecting food and money during the 1984–85 strike, and chairing the Bus Strike Support Committee during the lengthy Chelmsford TGWU strike (receiving a commemorative plate for contributions during the dispute in 1994–95).

More recently, Southampton TC has championed the 800 P&O Ferries' workers made redundant, bolstered a local UCU strike, campaigned to reinstate a sacked Blue Star bus driver, and supported industrial actions in the public sector. Wolverhampton TC has organised strike rallies for union pensions, expressed sympathy with striking railway workers (evident for many TCs), promoted the annual Workers' Memorial Day, May Day (celebrated everywhere), and marked Heart Unions recruitment week, which highlights the good works of the trade union movement. This TC has aided industrial disputes by raising £38,000 for campaigns and shown unity with local RMT cleaners in their dispute.

Islington TC has campaigned with UCU union members in disputes at the local London Metropolitan University and opposed closures at the Post Office and Clerkenwell Fire station, protecting local jobs and services. Andy Bain (from Islington TC) recalls joining pickets, donating to strike funds, publicising among affiliates, sending delegates to the TC conference, and collecting funds for national campaigns. Harlow TC records offering workers advice, essential for many TCs, while Lancaster & Morecambe TC president Eugene Doherty applauds his TC in buttressing and aiding picket lines, most recently the UCU, marching for a pay rise for health workers, and participating in a demonstration to retain the £20 benefits uplift.

Edinburgh TC has organised meetings on the impact on workers of issues such as Covid and Long Covid, retrofitting/making housing energy efficient, and disabilities in the workplace. They have provided three online delegates to the Scottish TUC and engaged in issues related to homelessness, social care and the Erasmus scheme.§ Delegates attended three online local trade union conferences (in March, July and September 2021), as well as local online events, and were central to the continuation of the ETC Support@Work Project, extending projects on disability rights, and training events for migrant workers. On International Workers' Memorial Day (28 April 2021), Edinburgh TC and the Scottish Hazards Campaign organised an event (in remembrance of workers who were killed or injured by their work) with 25 wreaths being laid at the Memorial Tree.¶

The most important economic issue for workers in unions and TCs currently is to support those workers confronted by the cost of living crisis, an issue taken up by all TCs.

Community

TCs are embedded in the communities in which they operate. Chelmsford TC has promoted the concessionary bus fares campaign with motorcades and meetings back in 1979, and, in 1999, sought with the TUC and the Unison

---

§ Established in 1987, Erasmus is a European funding programme that enables university students to study or do an internship abroad in another country.

¶ Hazards at work is a central issue for all TCs and TUs, highlighted at the annual trade union Hazards Conference, which organises for safe and healthy work environments.

union to save 79 hospital beds closed by Mid-Essex Hospital. Here, after collecting 15,379 signatures, consultations with the local MP, a public meeting, and a march/rally through town, the beds were kept.

Southampton TC has campaigned to save St. Mary's Leisure Centre and Wolverhampton TC ran the community festival Wodenstock, while promoting a range of local events through the TC website. Islington TC helped fund and took part in a successful campaign to save the A&E section of Whittington Hospital; and TC delegates have campaigned on the housing development at the former site of Holloway Prison. In June 2001, Edinburgh TC confronted the Edinburgh Integration Joint Board when the latter decided to close four local care homes

Moreover, Mick Patrick celebrates Harlow TC's record with 'Homes For All' campaigns, defending council housing and public transport, prioritising the NHS and local education needs, petitioning, organising and attending marches, giving evidence in Parliament, and doing as all TCs must: lobbying councillors and their local MP.

Politics
TCs can broaden their perspectives through activities that are more overtly political. Chelmsford TC's Wallace recalls the successful 'Chelmsford Fair Trade Campaign'[**] of which

---

[**] According to fairtrade.net, Fairtrade is about altering the way trade works through equitable pricing; promoting improved working conditions, 'and a fairer deal for farmers and workers in developing countries'. It focuses on trading partnerships seeking greater equity in international trade and sustainable development for marginalised producers and workers, particularly in the Global South.

he was the secretary for 16 years. This is an example of united front work, where TCs join others dedicated to a single issue or limited programme. Other examples include Islington TC recently engaging with the 'People's Assembly' and 'People Before Profit' (both anti-austerity organisations) and in Lancashire TC devising the 'People Before Profit' campaign.

In the late 1980s the Poll Tax campaign was a focus for many TCs. The tax, a flat-rate tax that unfairly impacted on working class communities, was challenged by the All-Britain Anti-Poll Tax Federation united front, and the widespread opposition to such a blatantly unfair imposition led to Margaret Thatcher's removal from office in 1990. Although they may not have foreseen such an illustrious outcome, TCs were part of this development.

In recent years TCs have sought to highlight *environmental issues*. Lancaster & Morecambe TC sent two coaches to a protest at the COP26[††] event in Glasgow, endorsed school student strikes on climate issues, and have organised alongside direct action campaigners Extinction Rebellion.[816] Edinburgh TC joined the Edinburgh COP26 Coalition to mobilise support for marches and other activities to protest at the COP summit in November 2021. The TC had a stall at the Edinburgh Climate Festival the preceding August and arranged 16 coaches for 800 people from Edinburgh to Glasgow for the major march on 6 November. After COP26, the local participating groups have continued as the Edinburgh Climate Campaign

---

[††] COP (The Committee of the Parties) is a conference for global governments and corporations to discuss, so far ineffectively, solutions to the climate crisis. Campaigner Greta Thunberg famously condemned 30 years of such leaders' debates contributing nothing but 'blah, blah, blah'.

(ECC), seeking local TU funding; the ECC raised £5,500, held by the TC on its behalf.

Axiomatic for TCs today is to *challenge and confront racist ideology and practice*, which divides workers. Wallace of Chelmsford TC celebrates opposing the National Front during a peak in their influence in 1977–78, while Wolverhampton's secretary Kelleher is proud of his TC's campaigning against the British National Party (BNP) (leafleting every home in every ward they stood and thus reducing the BNP vote). In 2021, this TC distributed copies of *100 Great Black Britons* to all local schools and currently they are commissioning research into Wolverhampton's historical ties to slavery.

Meanwhile, Southampton TC president Atkins celebrates her TC's connections with BLM, working for refugee rights, and participating in other anti-racist efforts. Anti-racism is key for Harlow TC and Lancaster & Morecambe TC, the latter assisting 'Stand Up to Racism' (SUTR) events by organising a coach to London for a March 2022 SUTR march, and donating money to the local slave memorial and Global Link (a pro-refugee organisation). Edinburgh TC has shown solidarity with refugees to counteract mistreatment by the government, opposing the Nationality and Borders Bill (enacted in April 2022), helping raise funds for refugees to settle in Edinburgh, and bridging campaigns on pay erosion, pay equality, workload, and contract casualisation, particularly pertinent for minorities.

Another political tradition continued in TCs is *workers' internationalism*, engaging in sympathy with workers who live abroad. This includes opposition to wars. Many TC delegates promoted and attended the immense anti-war demonstrations 2001-03, peaking with 2 million people marching for peace in the Middle East, against the US/UK war in Iraq, a demonstration the TUC did not promote. This movement helped popularise peace campaigner-turned Labour leader Jeremy Corbyn, who in September 2023 was made honorary president of Islington TC.

In recent years such internationalism has prompted campaigns for peace in Ukraine, with anti-war protests by Southampton and Wolverhampton TCs, among others. Such an outlook manifests *sympathy with marginialised communities*, hence TC involvement with the Palestine Solidarity Movement, which Wolverhampton TC and Lancaster & Morecambe TC support, the former arranging transport for local marches. Moreover, there have been numerous 'Solidarity with Revolution in Sudan' protests, relating to the heroism of the Sudanese people as they seek a fairer, more democratic society, marked by TCs including Lancaster & Morecambe.

Edinburgh TC participates in a multitude of political activities. These include marking the anniversary of the Grenfell disaster (which occurred in West London in 2017). In 2021, 80 attended a virtual meeting with Grenfell speakers, funds raised for the campaign on June 9. ETC mobilised around the campaign, 'Another Edinburgh Is Possible' (a popular community grouping, its title inspired by an anti-capitalist slogan), with local authority unions. In summer 2022, the ETC planned to campaign in local authority elections by raising care home issues.

*

Evidently, TCs in the 2020s are fundamentally embedded in overtly 'political' as well as more traditional 'industrial' actions, in communities and workplaces. Such a *holistic* approach, which caused such bitter frictions between the CP and the TUC General Council previously, no longer appears problematic. Of course, TCs sometimes consider some campaigns or political issues *ultra vires* or contradicting workers' interests.

One example is the issue of nuclear power. While some GMB members (including in unions and TCs) endorse the construction and continuance of nuclear power plants for providing thousands of workers jobs, others (including in TUs and TCs) see nuclear power as problematic. Dealing with toxic waste, many insist, is environmentally precarious and an avoidable hazard, when there are safer, cleaner alternatives for power production such as tidal, solar and wind power, and when we need to build *a green economy*.‡‡ [817] This highlights the fact that issues in TCs that affect workers and society should not be seen in a narrowly economic, *industrial* manner (only affecting numbers of jobs, for example), but require a broader *political and ideological* aspect. Jobs matter, but so does the environment and building the green economy we and the planet desperately need.§§

---

‡‡ As upcoming generations already know, burning fossil fuels for energy production, heat and transportation releases greenhouse gases like carbon dioxide, trapping heat in the atmosphere and, as the surface temperature of the Earth rises, causing climate disruption with extreme weather, biodiversity loss, worsened health and rising sea levels.

§§ Such arguments have been played out regarding the 1980's miners' strike as to the future role of UK coal mining. However, the Government's main policy was reducing trade union power; environmental benefits of switching from coal to other forms of energy production were a convenient cloak, evident in the Government's failure to provide alternative environmentally-friendly jobs for unemployed miners.

Although some TCs today embrace a dynamic, political culture, their activities are compounded by structural tensions. TCs' relationships with TUC leaders and the trade union leadership can be challenging. One TC EC delegate described the set up as 'very clunky' and bureaucratic, with organisations such as the 'Hampshire Association of TUCs' acting as a buffer between local TCs and the national TUC. Others have noted a move away from TUC hegemony to the empowering of national unions. During summer 2023 the issue of TC representation at the TUC was in the news, the TUC leadership rejecting calls for greater TC representation at the TUC Conference, an issue raised by TCs since the 1920s (see above).) Does such intransigence mean TCs are ineffective? Socialists have sought to combat TC weaknesses through conferences including a 'Workers' Summit' and developing shop stewards' networks to co-ordinate the trade union rank and file. Future debates, events and processes will show how issues of political power, broader perspectives, direction and control endure as *contested arenas* for TCs and TUC structures, where leftists can contribute, if they want to.

5. HISTORICAL SKETCHES

The following stories elucidate ways in which TCs' politics and social relations have altered over time. Glyn Oliver recalls a story passed down the generations: In the 1920s, an issue at Southampton TC was discussed in the House of Commons. Here, first Labour PM Ramsay MacDonald mentioned that two policemen were monitoring a TC meeting while *hidden underneath a piano*, in what now would be considered a remarkably low-tech form of surveillance!

Also in Southampton, Mike Dukes remembers from the 1970s celebrations for the TC at the Guildhall in the town centre, with speeches, music, dancing and assorted beverages. The venue was packed full to capacity – 'a very enjoyable, merry event which finished with the hokey cokey!' There were popular discos and dances at what is now a Southampton University building, which coincided with one of the early Southampton-staged marathons. Music has been a regular feature at trade union occasions, bonding delegates with beverages, often after conferences.

But there could also be clashes at TC cultural events. Dukes recollects the tradition of TC representatives being invited annually to offer 'loyal addresses' to the incoming mayor. He continues:

> When it was the turn of the NUT to make the address, I was selected to do the honours before an incoming Tory mayor. The event was very formal with sherry taken in the Mayor's parlour and speeches from local worthies and business. When it was my turn to speak I changed the tone by condemning the then cuts to education and the public sector and urging the Mayor to join us in campaigning against them. You can imagine how that went down!

Similarly, Secretary Kelleher from Wolverhampton TC was removed from a TUC platform when, as a TC delegate to a TUC conference, he wore a communist T-shirt just before Tony Blair addressed the conference! Also, the annual TUC Women Chain-Makers' Festival (celebrating the 1910 strike mentioned in chapter 8) was banned from the Black Country History Museum venue after Tony Benn presented the TC treasurer with a TUC silver badge on stage. Kelleher observes: 'They referred to each other as *comrade* and the festival was banned for being too political!'

Such skirmishes are not confined to TCs and happen frequently in the trade union movement. In November 2022, the Labour Party expelled the president of the UNISON union after she shared an article by Socialist Appeal, the recently proscribed organisation deemed 'incompatible' with Labour's rules, aims or values. (see above) Since 2020 the Labour Party has expelled many left-wing activists, which has impacted on TCs.

These examples reflect ongoing tensions between TC activists and local and national 'authority figures', between and within the active rank and file and the establishment. Being 'too political' or politically radical can still be controversial territory for militant TC delegates when they encounter those with more conservative outlooks in their communities. TC membership is not, and has never been, confined to supporters of the Labour Party and has always been a site of political contest, as is the Labour Party itself. These developments exhibit continuity and reverberations from the challenges encountered by TCs in the UK analysed above. Let's conclude this chapter with prospects for TCs.

6. PROSPECTS

TC delegates, despite living through traumatic events, remain optimistic, yet rational, about what is required.

Funding is essential. Mick Gilgunn of Islington TC hopes to receive a small grant from the TUC, although he dreads the copious form-filling and being required to explain *how* the grant might be used for a specific campaign. Even though the TC has had grants previously, this is a job in progress over the coming years. Gilgunn is philosophical about TCs' role in society:

> Some trade unionists underestimate the relevance of an active TC. Its importance needs to be emphasised as it is the one local broad body that can link in with campaigns and disputes on a local level. The anti-austerity campaign was one such movement, with the trades council having a leading role as we built up the contact links, but that takes a lot of time and effort. I believe the trades council is the link with social movements and that of the workplace.

TCs must be a bedrock for workers, connecting seemingly disparate problems. Edinburgh TC representatives have connected environmental issues with the cost of living crisis. They actively support energy-efficient housing, with a retrofitting campaign, intending it is properly financed, not by rent increases for tenants and not leading to increased fuel poverty; and they support those who are 'going without'. Inflation is eating into workers' living standards as corporate profits rise due to higher prices. This means that even 'increases' in workers' pay translates as cuts in real terms and this presents challenges to TCs as to how best to represent those who want a more equitable deal. How much should union organisations demand workers get paid? When is it right to strike?

Southampton TC president Atkins puts her TC's current role in socio-historical context:

> Following a decade of austerity and the Covid pandemic, workers have no option but to organise and fight back against the employers' 'fire and rehire' tactic and their policy of making us pay for the crisis to *preserve their profits*. Trade union membership is rising and industrial disputes are on the increase, many of which have been successful, e.g. the Bart's Hospital [in Central London] outsourced workers and Glasgow councilwomen fighting for equal pay. (our italics)

The challenge for TCs is to consolidate such activities, to produce the maximum benefit for delegates and the broader working-class movement. With regard to trade union officialdom, the Clyde Workers Committee was prescient in November 1915: '*We will support the officials just so long as they rightly represent the workers, but we will act independently immediately they misrepresent them.*'[818] But how this aphorism is applied is a matter for TCs to determine.

*

From this modest investigation we see trades council delegates striving for healthier, greener, more egalitarian localities, and a *real* 'levelling-up' for all they represent and their comrades at home and overseas. Although this limited sample might provide a somewhat rose-tinted interpretation, many TCs today are striving for social, political and industrial progress with community-based delegates engaging with local, national and international issues, in notable campaigns and memorable disputes, for which they seek a positive resolution.

Yes, today's TCs have their weaknesses. They urgently require an injection of youthful dynamism, more women leaders, an increased representation of ethnic minorities, and fresh affiliations. Yet, TCs continue to engage *politically and industrially* as unsung heroes of the workers' movement. Over recent decades they have made great strides in race relations, representing women and dealing with pertinent issues such as the climate crisis. They frequently promote overtly political campaigns and can adapt to new challenges, such as representing the LGBT+ community.

As a wealthy few have made fortunes out of the Covid crisis while key workers faced a greater risk of infection and premature death; as prices have soared along with profits for a rich elite; and after decades of pay has been cut or at best stagnated; many now empathise with and are increasingly won to the cause of workers on strike for better pay and conditions and insist: why shouldn't workers' pay rise? Why don't we engage in industrial action? Questions of strategy and tactics will surface. How should TCs respond? By overcoming society's atomisation and fragmentation, and coming together to discuss politics and organise activities. By being as co-ordinated, enthused, dynamic and united as TCs can be.

In 2023 there was speculation in the press of a possible general strike. According to the latest Government statistics, 13.4 million people live in poverty.[819] TCs will be required to respond to indignities such as people lacking essentials including adequate food and affordable heating. What to do? Action plans are essential. TCs must get involved. Yes, workers have experienced many defeats, but as Southampton TC president Atkins quotes Bob Crow: '*If you fight you may not always win, but if you don't fight you will always lose*'. (our italics)

TCs will need to present cases, backed by evidence; to use existing laws to ensure fairness when many unscrupulous employers are flouting labour laws. TCs will need to challenge those in power. But, to go from the current reality, and all its unnecessary deprivations, towards a better one where everyone's basic needs are met, requires concerted political commitment and activity from TCs' current crop of activists and those yet to be recruited. For TCs this means, as Islington's Andy Bain states, 'La luta continua'.

Mike's (the co-author) communist shop steward stepfather Stan Rice held to the notion that a united working class response would ameliorate society. Today this issue begs questions about methods and forms to manifest and further this response in movements, organisations and united fronts, which need to be constructed. Although TCs are one step removed from workplaces on the front line, confronted by such demands, through debate and activity, they can be a part of the process of re-building society.

Closing Remarks

> The German Communist Party made numerous profound mistakes in the first five years of its existence. But at least, if we read the records of the congresses and debates of those years, we feel in the presence of human beings attempting, however blunderingly, to change history.
> ~ *Chris Harman, The Lost Revolution, 1982, p307*

Post-1918 TC activists presumed the future was going to be about the democratic control of industry. However, it transpired it was about investments, surpluses and savings. Class inequalities were deepened. Austerity in the 1930s and '40s divorced 'the political' from 'the economic' to hinder any alternative economic arrangements. That's the marrow of this book, which originated in Mike's steaming political and economic arguments with his shop steward stepfather Stan Rice, utilising the insights of two inspirational historians, E.P. Thompson and Raphael Samuel.

Stan was a life-long AEU trade union activist and a dedicated CP member until 1968. Where Thompson had characterised the British labour movement as a hotch-potch of capitalist ideas, humanitarian aspirations and working-class attitudes,[820] Samuel, a practitioner of *history from below*, had analysed the CP's network, specifically Sheffield engineers, Clydeside shipbuilders, and South Wales and Scottish miners, as dedicated, selfless activists, impatient of weakness and backsliding. He noted that state, police harassment and union/employers' blacklisting confirmed the CP as a persecuted organisation from the 1926 General Strike to the Popular Front of the late 1930s,[821] until the German invasion of the Soviet Union, 1941.

Included in Thompson's 'The Peculiarities of the English' in *The Poverty of Theory*[822] was his deduction that, once a climactic moment has passed, the opportunity for radical changes passes 'irrevocably'. Is this what happened after the 1926 General Strike? Certainly, what followed the 1926 endeavour were limited reformist actions from organisational bases which brought minimal returns.

Yet the most challenging events 1920 to 1950 can too easily be reduced to a choice of expediencies within a status quo. We have noted that, between 1945 and 1948, vigorous socialist reforms in Britain *were* implemented, although blunted by the politics of the Cold War. Here, anti-communism provided an apologia for paralysis on wages and an ideological cloak for union leaders' accommodations with the established order.

Orthodox 'social democracy', sometimes in active liaison with employers, the media and the state, isolated any radical voices in TCs. Restrictions upon more far-reaching reforms by the TUC after 1945 (by E. Bevin, A. Deakin, W. Citrine, V. Feather, H.V. Tewson et al) were accompanied by anti-communist propaganda and, as we have witnessed, restrictive legislative measures during the wage freeze. Communism was the 'elephant in the room' for Labour and trade union leaders. The CP, although dedicated to anti-fascism and embedded in local union politics, was hindered by its sectarianism and crude perspectives, particularly in its commitment to Stalinist state power which could frame their analyses. UK union leaders were judged shabby brokers, their function to bluster, temporise, and calculate when a settlement could be reached without industrial conflict or division among the union membership, which could challenge their position. Alternatively there was that idealised perception of the CP as an alternative organisation in which a young miner could enlarge his horizons nationally and internationally, advance his political knowledge, effect contacts with intellectuals and with workers in other industries and internationally.[823]

From 1920 to 1950, the TUC General Council wanted TCs to be restricted to union recruitment and TUC publicity campaigns. How do TC/TUC relations compare in 1950 with 1920? In 1949, Newcastle & District TC general secretary D. Edwards informed V. Feather: 'Many people feel that work in the trades council is a matter of keeping the Secretary busy, but that we have no real influence in the City... we could get some more interest in the trades council if we could get more publicity for our work.'[824]

Education mattered. TCs persuaded LEAs to sponsor training courses for shop stewards (the author's stepfather Stan Rice was on one) and industrial education had a crucial place on the agenda, and at the administrative level; 160 TC secretaries since 1945 had been to TUC summer schools. *Circular 145* insisted:

> This widespread demand for schooling and discussion is a sign of the seriousness with which most trades councils take their main job of ensuring that trade unionists in their locality are kept up-to-date in their knowledge of TUC policy.[825]

As with recent TCs, tenacity was essential. Although only 10% of TCs had cash assets of at least £100, longevity of TC service was rewarded. Seventy TC delegates had completed 21 years' service by 1950 and received the TUC silver badge, while the TCJCC endured as a clique of larger TCs' representatives. Half of all the other TCs *never* had any delegates elected during these 30 years; the TCJCC (for 22 years) was represented by only 132 delegates from only 14 TCs, and less than 50% of union membership was affiliated to TCs.[826] As for affiliation fees, TC finances, which required sweepstakes and concerts to keep afloat, were constrained. Smaller TCs found it difficult to initiate campaigns and faced a largely unsympathetic (or patently hostile) conservative local press.

By 1950, TC representatives were working with local authorities and Ministry of Labour offices, on most food control committees and hospital management committees, and advising on National Savings. TCs were not, though, invited to participate in NHS consultations,[827] and limits were made apparent when Oxford & District TC requested a TUC speaker on the WFTU and V. Feather interjected –

policy on this came solely via unions through Congress: TCs' powers narrowed again.[828] Monitoring speakers and local unions' activities, infractions by association with 'other organisations', and any non-Labour electioneering, was to make TCs 'toe the line'. Post-war, TCJCC member A. Compertz pleaded that all was about votes and electioneering:

> the greatest workers' Government in our history… If they [TC delegates] attempted to say that our Government were not doing all that was possible in the workers' interests, they were undermining the possibilities for the next election.[829]

Criticising *any* policies or actions of 'the greatest workers' Government' was a threat. Here was the loyalty theme on the grand scale, and, as a corollary to this, union leaders drew attention to TCs' 'immense value' in cementing *unity* in their localities, in fact restrictive parameters within which TCs must operate.

*

The three TUC functions for TCs – recruitment, organisation and union education – were embedded. Quoted near the beginning of this book, A.B. Swales in 1925 announced that the TUC had no intention of reverting to 'narrow limitations of trades councils as purely strike committees'. TCs did not, however, evolve into councils of labour or workers' parliaments (or soviets), but recruitment agents. The CP categorised the General Strike as a 'non-revolutionary' situation, even if, in the aftermath, it gathered within its orbit the most politically conscious group of workers' representatives. Twenty-five years after Swales, Sir Luke Fawcett was echoing Alexis de Tocqueville's axiom: '*local assemblies of citizens constitute the strength of free nations*'.[830] Very true, yet what kind of local assemblies were TCs?

Defining TUC and TCJCC leaders from the 1920s were *administrative* stipulations, burgeoning *advisory* committees, and the myriad complexities in the local state. In this scenario, TCs had to be 'improved', commencing with the reconstitution of 379 local employment committees with TCs nominated to workers' panels. By 1950, TCs were thus submerged in the complex intricacies on health services, employment questions and housing strategies.[831] T. Quelch's momentous strategic formulations (1922 to 1926) bore little resemblance to the precisely defined local activities imposed by 1950 when TCs had little or no influence on TUC collective bargaining procedures, and only 20% of industries had been transferred to public ownership.[832] In these times of austerity, which have returned, TCs were exhorted to put in *extra* effort to help Britain's export trade during the country's economic difficulties.

In 1950 the TUC *Labour* journal's 'Scope for Local Talent in the Welfare State' summarised TCs' officially circumscribed functions. Yet delegates retained visions of a socialist future, untarnished by quotidian issues, keeping their eyes on the prize:

This is the age of the dignity of Labour, but this dignity can only be preserved by the organised worker, united in our determination to establish political and economic power and the achievement of Socialism.[833]

Moreover,

Trades councils' eyes are also upon the wider horizons of the destiny of the working people, seeing that their freedom can be finally won only through the transfer of political and economic power from exploiters to the exploited.[834]

Transfer of any power would be problematic. H.L. Bullock (General Council chairman) responded to such *political* interventions with the stale formula that the 'job of Trades Councils' was to administer policy made nationally by unions and to guard against those 'disloyal',[835] that code word for 'communist infiltrators'.

From the 1920s, TCs had not only symbolised but were also the core of the local labour movement, illustrating workers' capabilities in galvanising unionists into action on local and national controversies, even as they were frequently defamed as mere debating circles and miniature talking-shops. Sir Luke Fawcett harked back and forth: '*Trades Councils should become a workshop of ideas and a centre of action to kindle the spirit, faith, self-sacrifices and passion of the pioneer.*'[836] This 'big ask' was not easy when TCs had been marginalised and trivialised over these 30 years. The Labour government (by 1950) was now associated with its radical national reforms juxtaposed with austerity, rationing, rising costs of living, a wage freeze and heavier taxation on the less wealthy. Union leaders were bargaining with unaccountable financial and industrial institutions when 'joint consultation' should have included the rank and file in decision-making processes and should not so peremptorily have excluded, dismissed or demoted TCs' resolutions as 'outside official TUC policy'. Genuine workshops of ideas and centres of action would require more leeway.

So, the undeniable Red fervour of 1945 became jaundiced. Under TUC guidance, with a regressive approach to employment issues, rent increases, price inflation and the overwhelming preponderance of media anti-union bias, TCs had portrayed significant ambivalence towards union leaders' diktats during these 30 years. A minority looked beyond wages or co-operation with local managers as the zenith. TCs' *raison d'etre* was to *resist exploitation* of any union members, their brief extending to equal pay issues and progressive ideas concerning the integration of immigrant labour.

If TCs were to be 'the guardian of the social rights of the people',[837] unionists through TCs were by 1950 certainly more appropriately represented in the machinery of local government, and with the expansion of managerial and professional trade unionism, prospered with an injection of white-collar workers in newer industries. Voluntary part-time duties of TC delegates had always been taxing and the undoubted achievements of social legislation brought extensive administrative duties. Leo Panitch observed: 'Corporatist structures require of trade unions... not that they cut their ties with their base, but rather that they use those ties to legitimate state policy and elaborate their control over their members.'[838]

The ACTC 1948 approval of H.V. Tewson's formulation that government, employers and workers had 'common problems' is indicative of Panitch's insight in the context of TCs' history. From 1920 to 1950, the TUC fundamentally required TCs co-ordinate local unions in order to promote collective action on industrial matters. Ramifications of this structuring were illustrated by no TC before 1947 having publicly articulated doubts about the emergence of a centralised state. Individual TCs might condone unofficial strikes but majorities deplored them as 'harming the national economy' and had few reservations about the TUC's administrative apparatus expanding. They concurred with General Council chairman G.W. Thomson that the economic difficulties enjoined by the Labour government depended upon TCs' *loyalty*. Reinforcing this were the 1948 *Registration Scheme for Trades Councils* and *Trades Councils' Guide* (with TCs as 'local correspondents'), which offset populist widespread critiques of the wage freeze.

*

The five themes of this book – TCs in the General Strike 1926, TC/TUC structural encounters, CP/TC/TUC relations, TC ripostes to mass unemployment, and women in the unions – are paradigms for the history of regional TCs and unions, and local and national politics. On the theme of unemployment, we have analysed confrontations over the NUWM and the UAs, and the dynamic contributions by TCs throughout the UK to protect the rights and welfare of the unemployed. In this arena, CP members played a vital role.

The CP, created from existing socialist parties in 1920, planned from its inception to diminish industrial/political separations and confront TUC manipulating compartmentalisation. It combated the TUC's pluralist and somewhat hypocritical outlook that the state must distance itself from the conflicts within civil society. As analysed, the CP perceived TCs as potential soviets, as local working-class parliaments of wage labour, aspiring towards workers' self-management, an optimistic notion based on the perception of TCs' all-embracing *comprehensive* local nature; their politics of everyday industrial struggles avowed to revitalise a working-class leadership, which provided the CP with a foothold in the broader movement.

However, when this vision faded dramatically post-1926, new questions arose. Were TCs organs of class struggle or reformist, gradualist institutions? Could they be both? Were they the training grounds of future cadres for the movement or springboards for higher office in the TUC? Or both? Were they the foundations of strike organisations, Soviet-inspired visions of a technocratic triumphalism in opposition to a moribund capitalism, or local industry experts and politically neutralised? TCs were manipulable, propaganda outlets for whoever wished to make the effort to influence or dominate them, and the CP's blanket binary use of the concept 'rank and file versus bureaucrats' was not always applicable to the nuanced representation of the many complex problems facing TCs (not all union leaders were 'reactionaries'!). Union leaders could be simultaneously pressured by employers and employees, as the CP appreciated post-'26.

CP aspirations for TCs instantly clashed with already instituted, established evolutionary union practices. Hence CP/TUC's entrenched conflict over ideology, contrasting notions of 'loyalty, and TCs' possible functions as councils of action, workers' defence corps, soviets etc. This fundamental tension has to be qualified since, in practice, most TCs professed limited objectives and eventually adumbrated the rules, regulations and TUC conference decisions.

TCs' disagreements with the TUC over these 30 years could be fragmentary and ideological. To exemplify, many TCs, as we have displayed, opposed the ban on the *Daily Worker* in 1941–42 on civil liberties' grounds. Many more defended workers' standard of living because all workers were genuinely disadvantaged under Labour's post-1945 wage freeze. After 1926, the CP *and* TUC both, from diametrically opposed positions, critiqued TCs' actions: the CP because TC delegates had responded as though the issue was an economic and not a political one; the TUC because TCs had 'overstepped' their prescribed limitations. CP reassessments of TCs exposed its own ambivalence: its fractions led to denunciation of the *reformist* nature of TCs, as the Labour Party and TUC launched exposés of political infiltration of TCs and their NMM and NUWM connections.

For the TUC, CP about-turns on policies, notoriously 1929–32 and 1939–41, were a gift. After copious demonstrative circulars, the TUC could exhibit ACTCs' two-thirds majorities in favour of its trajectories with 180 to 83 votes in 1949, 160 to 90 in January 1950 and 191 to 75 in May 1950. Anti-communism as a trope gave the TUC ideological cover for accommodations with the British establishment so yearned for from above throughout the 1940s. That isolated the *c.*50,000 CP membership: 'censoring union officials' would not be tolerated, as the CP presented its perceived unedifying commentary on the TUC's inadequacies and betrayals.

The CP message for TCs from 1927 was fluid: 'change the leaders', then opposition to Mondism, united front campaigns (NUWM and NMM, and breakaway unions) to the 'class against class' hiatus (with TCs dubbed 'reformist' or, absurdly, 'social fascist'). Via hunger marches, popular fronts, opposition to NVS schemes and industrial conscription, a strategy emerged. The 'Imperialist war' phase, the People's Convention and eventually having the temerity to label Labour leaders 'pseudo-Nazis' ended with the populism of Anglo-Soviet Committees, the Second Front, JPCs and Daily Worker Unity conferences from 1942 to 1945.

In TC/TUC relations, E. Bevin's concept of administration (governance) replacing the years of advocacy (campaigning) was a polarisation within which, as exemplified, ritualistic confrontations were triggered. Every year, TUC leaders referred to TCs' historic role as the *local TUCs*. H.N. Harrison proclaimed in 1944 the TUC's 'blueprints of the new Britain', 'social equality through public ownership' yet TCs envisaged as 'purely industrial bodies'. W. Citrine had conjured a vision for TCs that 'stand with the General Council', with Harrison ridiculing 'academic chatter and idle theories'.[839]

In practice, this would lead to the emergence of corporatist industrial politics scrupulously monitoring and vetting any TC activities. Some TCs extolled the TUC/TCJCC as 'unifying the movement' and few TC delegates precisely voiced the conviction that unions could be oppressive or officials acted as 'demagogues'. They knew their annual conferences were stage-managed, the agenda carefully structured, the duration of ACTCs decided by the TUC, meetings orchestrated, and ACTC resolutions bypassed or deemed inconsequential. Union leaders' 'pragmatic' ideology was outlined in TC/TUC relations. This ideology emanated in that 1930s TUC statement: TCs had '*a service like salesmen*'. (our italics)

The 1926 General Strike, that uniquely cataclysmic, historically underestimated watershed in British 20th-century history, exhibited TCs' regional disparities, varying historical and industrial traditions, and complex affiliations with local councils. 1926 exemplified the fundamental contradictions within economistic Labourism and resistance to theoretical abstractions. A *melange* of reformist/radical credentials was prevalent in *all* TCs, the formulation 'no industrial action for political ends' acquiring a mythology in internal tussles during these 30 years. TCs, if they had a service 'like salesmen', what were they selling? To whom? At what price? Who gained most from the transactions?

TCs were and are selling protection for union members, safeguarding, shielding, a kaleidoscope for militants, careerists, pragmatists and idealists, a stage for competing policies and ideologies, for rights for all unionists, for local and national representation, in which workers can pool their resources and maximise their potential. TCs are often ossified organisations (not always, happily); they can be fairly moribund and ignored by most workplace trade union members and generally by the right who don't see them as ideological battlegrounds. Yet, in the absence of any other official and semi-official trade union transmission belt in localities, TCs can explode into life at key moments in the labour movement, acting as focal and organisational points for the left and the local trade union movement. This had been evident in 1926.

From numerical and political heights, in the second half of the 20th century, the British CP declined following anti-Stalinist uprisings in Hungary in 1956 and Czechoslovakia in 1968, which opposed USSR authoritarianism. After the fall of the Berlin Wall in 1989 and the collapse of the USSR and the Warsaw Pact in 1991, the British CP was dissolved, although it led to new organisations.

The bruising experiences in British trade unionism 1920–50, accentuated in the General Strike, has proven that unionists cannot rely on top-down bureaucracies (like the General Council) to achieve liberation on their behalf; they will have to do this themselves. Campaigners in the Communist Party showed through the Minority Movement how radical groups of workers can relate to a broader base, engaging non-communists in political trade unionism. Alex Callinicos comments:

> The Communist Party acted as a political driving force behind the growth of the stewards movement. Its members were among the best fighters organising inside individual factories. At the same time the Communists sought to link together different workplaces in a movement capable both of supporting particular struggles and pursuing a co-ordinated strategy.[840]

However, their political mistakes – sectarianism, vacillations and entrapment within Cold War politics – led to their demise. We can learn from their mistakes by not repeating them.

*

Women's role within the British working class movement reached new heights with their economic, social and cultural empowerment through World War II. Government support through grant-funded nurseries, subsidised restaurants, free school meals and free milk were not a product of sudden, more enlightened values but wartime economic exigency. Just as they were granted during the war, some were removed post-war. Nevertheless, working women's wartime experiences proves that full employment, guaranteed leisure time, an enhanced standard of living and socialised childcare are possible. With a costly ongoing proxy war in Eastern Europe and a major cost of living crisis at home today, such reforms are still required, the exorbitant costs of childcare, social housing and low wages being vital issues.

Although women won equal voting rights in 1928, they still in 2024 do not have pay parity. Gaining such reforms and achieving gender equality at last would be life-changing. People's experience of social and economic hardships are conditioned by their social relationships, especially, whether they acknowledge it or not, as members of a *social class*. By identifying as members of the working class, an exploited class, working-class women have a shared economic interest in combining with working-class men to unite across gender (and manufactured racial barriers) to confront those that exploit them, to use their economic power (including the existing strike weapon) to put an end to their social, economic and social subjugation, which is generated by a system that daily seeks to *divide* workers.[841]

Martha Gimenez comments: 'While racism and sexism have no redeeming feature, class relations are, dialectically, a unity of opposites; both a site of exploitation and, objectively, a site where the potential agents of social change are forged.'[842] Uniting with working men can therefore prove to be advantageous over organising solely with other women.

Judith Orr's first-hand account of the 2011 radical uprising collectively known as the Arab Spring, evinces the potential for such a strategy. She quotes Sameh Naguib, a participator at the epicentre of the revolutionary situation that manifested itself in strikes and an occupation of Tahir Square, Cairo:

> The space in Tahrir was not simply occupied physically but spiritually. Harassment against women disappeared, tension between Copts and Muslims evaporated. People shared food, water, cigarettes. Songs, music, poetry and changes filled the air.[843]

Another observer added: 'They said we were divided, extreme, ignorant, fanatic – well here we are: diverse, inclusive, hospitable, generous, sophisticated, creative and witty.'

Although short-lived, the Arab Spring provides a fresh example of what is possible for humanity where previously there was misery and division, when workers come together, and with women at the helm. As co-ordinators of the working-class movement for social change, contemporary *trades union councils* can provide a vehicle for advancing the cause and socio-economic position of marginalised working women, as it was advanced in Cairo, to simultaneously elevate the lives of women and men. However, to realise such potential, TCs need to be part of a broader project. But what kind of project?

*

In the 21st century activists emphasise *thinking global and acting local*. When trades councils next fuse their local and national influences – emboldened by their achievements, but aware of the blunders and, sadly, false paths in their history – they can fashion their unique position inside society to bolster others, and unite further campaigns. Their recent role in support of myriad strikes in 2022-23 suggests that TCs could be deployed as 'councils of action', bringing activists together and improving workers' lives. Any such future developments would emerge organically and democratically, so cannot be fully envisioned in advance.

Studies of such organisations (see Immanuel Ness and Dario Azzellini's *Ours to Master And to Own*) reveal that, far from being an outmoded concept, there are 'increasing instances of workers' control in the contemporary epoch', challenging repression in workplaces and communities, participating in co-operatives and councils.[844] Recent examples of such organisation have emerged with workers' councils in Argentina, social fora in Porto Alegre in Brazil, and in neighbourhood committees in Sudan. Others will follow.

In the 1920s, those trailblazing communists – Quelch, Murphy, Campbell and the rest – with all their faults, manifested their worth through their praxis, and foresaw TCs as holistic bodies to *empower and emancipate* unionists. For them, the trajectory of a crisis-ridden economic, political and ideological system, analysed as moribund, was replaceable. Their project was mainly unsuccessful, although their efforts were courageous and inspirational, and they had some victories: in unemployment campaigns, uniting anti-fascists, ideologically preparing the paradigm for the reforms of the 1945 Labour government, and protecting the rights of workers.

Although they did not reach the peaks of their political cousins in 1920s Germany (noted above), we have shown how CP members helped broadened workers' consciousness in the first few years of the party's existence here. The lessons of the past 100 years, are that providing patient groundwork, connecting communities, and helping to build disparate local campaigns is the future for TCs. When the time is right we will see many previously inactive people gravitating towards foci of activity and TCs could then grow in influence.

Today's trades councils do continue to be affected by the cramping electoral logic of Labourism, and blunting of industrial campaign. Yet TCs combine 'pessimism of the intellect and optimism of the will',[845] with an arc of hope channelling actions towards a better future.[846] They progress dialectically, linking workers and politics, embodying environmental activist Greta Thunberg's axiomatic truth that 'Hope begins when we open our eyes and swap the impotence of words for the power of collective action.'[847]

There is a sense in which *all TC activities are political*. Deciding to raise funds and supporting local actions are political choices that have long-term political implications.[848] As such, politically engaged, inclusive, trades union councils will continue to champion local, national and international issues, facilitating and mobilising to stimulate debate and actions, to represent and cultivate a better future where workers overcome the containment imposed by the trade union bureaucracy. It may take time, but social change in trades councils can be part of a broader cultural transformation that is not only possible, but necessary.

APPENDIX 1

Conference Chronologies

1. ANNUAL CONFERENCES OF TRADES COUNCILS 1925-50

* Denison House, London, 27 February 1925.
* Denison House, London, 26 March 1926.
* Caxton Hall, London, 27 May 1927.
* Transport Hall, London, 19 May 1928.
* Transport Hall, London, 29 June 1929.
* Transport Hall, London, 24 May 1930.
* Transport Hall, London, 30 May 1931.
* Transport Hall, London, 28 May 1932.
* Birmingham YMCA, 27 May 1933.
* Dorchester Town Hall, 31 August–1 September 1934.
* Co-Op Buildings, York, 25 May 1935.
* Transport Hall, London, 23 May 1936.
* Transport Hall, London, 29 May 1937.
* Transport Hall, London, 28 May 1938.
* Bloomsbury, London, 20–21 May 1939.

* Westminster, London, 27 July 1940.
* Conway Hall, London, 28 June 1941.
* Albert Hall, Manchester, 30 May 1942.
* Nottingham, 29 May 1943.
* Leicester, 20 May 1944.
* Beaver Hall, London, 26–27 May 1945.
* Derby, 25–26 May 1946.
* London, 31 May–1 June 1947.
* Derby, 5–6 June 1948.
* Weston-super-Mare, 28–29 May 1949.
* Nottingham, 21 May 1950.

2. TUC ANNUAL CONFERENCES 1926-50
* Bournemouth, 10–11 September 1926.
* Edinburgh, 5–6 September 1927.
* Swansea, 3–8 September 1928.
* Belfast, 2–6 September 1929.
* Nottingham, 1–5 September 1930.
* Bristol, 7–11 September 1931.
* Newcastle, 5–9 September 1932.
* Brighton, 4–8 September 1933.
* Weymouth, 3–4 September 1934.
* Margate, 2–6 September 1935.
* Plymouth, 7–11 September 1936.
* Norwich, 6–10 September 1937.
* Blackpool, 5–9 September 1938.
* Bridlington, 4–5 September 1939.
* Southport, 7–9 October 1940.
* Edinburgh, 1–4 September 1941.
* Blackpool, 7–11 September 1942.
* Southport, 6–10 September 1943.

* Blackpool, 16–20 October 1944.
* Blackpool, 10–14 September 1945.
* Brighton, 21–25 October 1946.
* Southport, 1–5 September 1947.
* Margate, 6–10 September 1948.
* Bridlington, 5–9 September 1949.
* Brighton, 4–8 September 1950.

APPENDIX 2

1923 and 2023 Comparisons

1. Learning to live with a virus (influenza, Covid), juggling or maintaining the economy and removing people's freedoms.
2. So-called 'levelling up' agenda for reducing regional inequalities, boosting the economy of left-behind regions, spreading opportunity beyond the South-East, via a new system of local government with directly elected leaders taking responsibility for their own areas. Would this narrow the economic and social gap between regions?
3. Overhauling the house-building system, building in designated areas or focusing on social housing or expanding access to credit, or homeowners voting on whether their neighbourhood should be allowed to build more.
4. Controlling the media output, protecting citizens from 'harmful content'.

5. Dealing with import complications from Britain to Northern Ireland. Growing trade friction with the rest of Europe as trade with the Continent has slumped. Northern Ireland Protocol row threatens existence of the Union; growth in support for Sinn Fein as most popular party (plus possible Scottish independence).
6. Can there be a future Labour government, after local government elections as the first test of whether they translate into national results?
7. Baldwin v MacDonald; Conservatives v Starmer. All depends on backbenchers and what the Labour Party 'stands for', via a manifesto removing left-wing policies or risking a backlash from Labour activists.
8. Liberals 1923/Lib Dems 2023 – desperate to keep in the spotlight with few MPs.
9. Anti-democratic populists exploiting patriotism. Authoritarians v moderates in Russia, China, the USA etc…
10. Immigration and border security issues for the UK.
11. Threats to freedom as laws challenge protest as a fundamental right.
12. The nation state as the primary focus of communal loyalty; demands for self-determination or British exceptionalism?
13. Exposés of government incompetence and inability to fulfil economic promises.
14. Politicians seeking to escape follies by demonising minorities and cooking up 'culture wars'.
15. Rising energy and fuel prices and the cost of living, and worries about pensions.

BIBLIOGRAPHY

Texts and Events Referred to in the Book

NEWSPAPERS, JOURNALS, MAGAZINES, PROGRAMMES, HANDBOOKS, MANIFESTOS, MANUALS, ONLINE SOURCES AND BOOKS

V.L. Allen, 'Militant Trade Unionism', 1966.

V.L. Allen, 'The Re-organisation of the TUC 1918–27', *British Journal of Sociology*, Volume 11, March 1960.

G. Allison, 'The General Strike', *Communist Review*, May 1946.

P. Allott, *Labour Monthly*, September 1936.

P. Anderson, 'The Limits and Possibilities of Trade Union Action', in R. Blackburn and A. Cockburn (editors) *The Incompatibles: Trade Union Militancy and the Consensus*, 1967.

R.P. Arnot, *Twenty Years: The Policy of the CPGB*, 1940.

M. Ashraf, *Bradford Trades Council 1872–1972*, 1972.

David Austin, *Philosophy Now*, February/March 2022.

Baths and Wilts Chronicle, 14 March 1935.

L. Bather *A History of Manchester and Salford Trades Council*, PhD, 1956.

A. Beevor, *The Second World War*, 2012.
Rafael Behr, *Politics: A Survivor's Guide*, 2023.
T. Bell, *The Communist Party*, 1937.
John Berger, *Ways of Seeing*, 1972.
Martin R Beveridge *The Socialist Ideal and the Labour Party: From Attlee to Corbyn 2022*
W. Beveridge, *Unemployment: A Problem of Industry*, 1931.
E. Bevin, 'The Election and the Trade Union Movement', *Labour Magazine*, December 1931.
E. Bevin, Preface, W. Hamling, *A Short History of Liverpool TC*, 1948.
R. Birch, 'A Wage Based on Human Needs' (CP), 1946.
Birmingham Gazette, 1 and 4 November 1949.
Birmingham Public Libraries, Social Sciences Department, WEA, *Nine Days in Birmingham, The General Strike 1926-1976*
R. Black, *Stalinism in Britain. A Trotskyist Analysis*, 1970.
Blackpool Trades Council Seventy-Fifth Anniversary, 1966
'Blueprints of the New Britain', *Labour* Journal, July 1946.
Blyth News, 6 June 1935.
Sarah Boston, *Women Workers in Trade Unions*, 1980.
A.W. Brady, 'Trade Unions and National Service', *Labour Monthly*, May 1939.
A. Briggs and J. Saville (editors), *Essays in Labour History,* 1960 (1971 Volume).
Brighton Argus, March 1950.
Brighton & Hove Gazette, 18 and 25 March 1950.
I. Buchanan, Alison Pratt and Brigid Francis-Devine, *Women and the UK Economy* at researchbriefings.files.parliament.uk/documents/SN06838/SN06838.pdf
A. Bullock, *The Life and Times of Ernest B Bevin*, Volume 1, 1960.
B. Burke, *Rebels With a Cause – History of Hackney Trades Council, 1900–1975*, 1975.
E. Burns, *Communist Affiliation*, 1936.

E. Burns, *The General Strike, May 1926 – Trades Councils in Action*, 1975.

E. Burns, *Labour Party and Communist Party: The Case for Affiliation* (CP), February 1943.

Alex Callinicos, *Socialists in the Trade Unions*, 1995.

J.R. Campbell, A.R. Stewart, *Communist Review*, December 1926.

J.R. Campbell, 'Blackpool and After', *Labour Monthly*, October 1942.

J.R. Campbell, 'Chamberlain over the TUC', *Labour Monthly*, October 1938.

J.R. Campbell, *Communist Review*, October 1924.

J.R. Campbell, 'The Scaffolding of Servitude: The Meaning of Essential Work Orders', *Labour Monthly*, July 1941.

J.R. Campbell, 'Some Aspects of Our Industrial Work', *Communist Review*, January 1935.

J.R. Campbell, 'Trade Unions and the General Election' (CP), 1945.

J.R. Campbell, 'Workers and the British Totalitarians', *Labour Monthly*, March 1941.

L. Cannon, *The Road from Wigan Pier*, 1973.

Dan Carrier, *Westminster Extra*, 21 January 2022, 'Heightened Census'.

M. Carritt, *Brighton Trades Council: The History of Sixty Years*, 1950.

G.E. Cheshire, *Twenty-Five Years of Progress: History of Aylesbury & District Trades Council 1911–1936*, 1936.

W.L.S. Churchill, *The Second World War*, Volume 2, 1949.

CI EC, Resolution, March 1926.

CI EC, 'Theses on the Lessons of the British General Strike', *Communist Review*, July 1926.

Lord Citrine, *Men and Work*, 1964.

Lord Citrine *Two Careers*, 1967.

W. Citrine, 'Democracy or Disruption', *Labour Magazine*, December 1927.

W. Citrine, Diary Entry, 4 May 1926.

W. Citrine, 'In Defence of Freedom: Fascism at Home and Abroad', *Labour Magazine*, June 1933.
W. Citrine, *Industrial Review*, Supplement, March 1928.
W. Citrine, *Labour* Journal, May 1943.
W. Citrine, *Labour Magazine*, March 1928.
W. Citrine, *Labour Magazine*, June 1928.
W. Citrine, *New Clarion*, 24 June 1933.
W. Citrine, *The TUC in Wartime*, June 1940.
W. Citrine, *The TUC in Wartime*, June 1944.
W. Citrine, *The TUC in Wartime*, April 1945.
W. Citrine, 'What the TUC Is Doing', 1 March 1937.
J.F. Clarke and T.P. McDermott, *Newcastle & District Trades Council: 1873–1973*, 1973.
T. Clarke and L. Clements, *Trade Unions under Capitalism*, 1977.
F. Clay, 'Trade Union Work in Portsmouth', *Discussion*, Number 12, February 1937, (CP).
H. Clay, 'Tolpuddle and Today', *Socialist Leaguer*, July 1934.
H.A. Clegg, *General Union: A Study of the NUGMW*, 1954.
H.A. Clegg, 'Some Consequences of the General Strike', *Manchester Statistical Society*, 1954.
J.C. Clews, *Communist Propaganda Techniques*, 1964.
Tony Cliff and Donny Gluckstein, *Marxism and Trade Union Struggle: The General Strike of 1925*, 1986 (2015 edition)
A. Clinton, *The Trade Union Rank and File: Trades Councils in Britain 1900–40*, 1977.
Clyde Workers' Commitee leaflet in The Beveridge Collection, the British Library of Political and Economic Science, section 3, item 5.
J.R. Clynes, *Memoirs: 1924–37*, 1937.
Ken Coates, *Essays in Industrial Democracy*, 1971.
J. Cohen, 'Marxism and Reformism in the General Strike', *Marxism Today*, May 1976.
G.D.H. Cole, *An Introduction to Trade Unionism*, 1953.

G.D.H. Cole, *Socialist Leaguer* pamphlet, 1934.
G.D.H. Cole, *A Study Guide on Socialist Policy* 1933.
G.D.H. Cole, *Trade Unionism Today*, 1939.
C. Cockburn, *The Local State*, 1977.
The Communist, 27 July, 12 August and 28 October 1922.
The Communist, December 1927, Editor, p250.
Communist Industrial Policy, 1922.
Communist Review, Editorials, February and June 1926.
Communist Review, 'Problems of Party Organisation', December 1934.
A. Conley, 'The Trades Council Movement', *Industrial Review*, March 1928.
A. Conley, 'Trades Councils and the TUC', *London Trade Union Handbook*, 1929.
J. Corbett, *The Birmingham Trades Council*, 1966.
Idris Cox, *Communist Review*, July 1935, p127.
CP, *An Urgent Memo on Production*, March 1942.
CP, *Brief Summary of District Organisation Reports*, 1926.
CP, *The Communist Party and the National Front*, April 1942.
CP, *Congress Report*, February 1935.
CP, *Congress 1935, 'A Call to All Workers'*.
CP, *The CP in War-Time*, April 1940.
CP, *Defend Trade Union Rights*, May 1949.
CP, *Draft Programme*, August 1939.
CP EC, *Statement*, January 1949.
CP, *Handbook for CP Members*, 'Organisation', July 1923.
CP, *Handbook*, 'Local Organisation', January 1927.
CP, *Looking Ahead*, 1946.
CP, *May Day Manifesto*, 1925.
CP, *Manifesto*, 2 September 1939.
CP, *Manual of Party Training – Principles and Organisation*, 1924.
CP, *Marxism and the Industrial Workers*, November 1941.
CP, *Memorandum*, 13 November 1942.

CP, *Statement*, 9 May 1940.
CP, *The Party Voice*, October 1939.
CP, *Trade Unions Forward*, October 1938.
CP, *War! Communist Policy*, 1939 (Marx Memorial Library).
J. Cunnison, *Labour Organisation*, 1930.
H.E. Cushnie, Brighton TC, 'When Will the Workers Wake Up?', *Unity News*, March 1926.
R.A. Dahl, 'Workers' Control of Industry and the British Labour Party', *American Political Science Review*, Volume XLI, 1947.
Daily Herald, 1 November 1927, 'The Miners' March: Mr Citrine Answers the "Sunday Worker", NAILING A LIE, Facts of the General Council's Decision'.
Daily Worker, 7 February 1930.
Daily Worker, 6 January 1931.
Daily Worker, 23 January 1931.
Daily Worker 11 April 1931.
Daily Worker, 6 January 1934.
Daily Worker, 5 July 1935.
Daily Worker, 21 January 1938.
Daily Worker, 30 September 1939.
Daily Worker, 3 April 1940.
Daily Worker, 7 April 1940.
Daily Worker, 2 May 1940.
Daily Worker, 5 May 1940.
Daily Worker, 29 June 1940.
Daily Worker, 3 July 1940.
Daily Worker, 11 September 1940.
Daily Worker, 28 September 1940.
Daily Worker, 23 December 1940.
Daily Worker, 21 January 1941.
Daily Worker, 9 July 1941.
Bob Darke, *The Communist Technique in Britain*, 1952.

Trevor Davies, *Bolton, May 1926: A Review of the General Strike as it Affected Bolton & District*, 1976.

Mary Davis, 'Women at Work' from *Britain at Work: Voice from the Workplace 1945-1995*, available at unionhistory.info/britainatwork/narrativedisplay.php?type=womenatwork, 2012.

H. Dewar, *Communist Politics in Britain*, 1976.

T. Dickson, *Scottish Capitalism*, 1980.

Dictionary of Labour Biography, Volumes 1-4, 1972-7.

Dover TC, 'In the Front Line', *Labour*, December 1941, p117.

J. Dowding, *Castleford & District Trades Council, 1890-1965*, 1965.

Barbara Drake, *Women in Trade Unions*, 1920.

A. Durr, *Who were the Guilty? The General Strike in Brighton*, 1976.

R.P. Dutt, 'The Class Fight in Britain', *Labour Monthly*, October 1948.

R.P. Dutt, 'The Future of the Trades Councils Conference', *Labour Monthly*, February 1924.

R.P. Dutt, *Labour Monthly*, October 1934.

R.P. Dutt, *Labour Monthly*, December 1939.

R.P. Dutt, *Labour Monthly*, June 1941.

R.P. Dutt, *Labour Monthly*, July 1941.

R.P. Dutt, 'Marxism and the War', *Labour Monthly*, October 1939.

R.P. Dutt, 'We Fight for LIFE' (CP Policy Series Number 1), November 1940.

R.P. Dutt, *World News & Views*, 19 July 1941.

Terry Eagleton, *Hope Without Optimism* (2017 edition).

Albert Einstein, *Monthly Review*, May 1949 available at monthlyreview.org.2009/05/01/whysocialism/

H.H. Elvin, 'Draft Memorandum on "Trade Union Recruitment"', March 1935.

H.H. Elvin, General Council Minutes, Motion on 'Unemployed Marchers', 25 November 1936.

Texts and Events Referred to in the Book

See eu.usatoday.com/story/news/2023/02/23/why-are-fossil-fuels-bad-environment-impact/10454327002/

fairtrade.net

Lord Feather, *The Nine Days in Birmingham, The General Strike 4–12 May, 1926*, from the WEA Birmingham Public Libraries, 1976.

M. Ferguson, 'Breaking Through: Mass Work in Bradford', *Communist Review*, October 1933.

L. Fischer, *The God That Failed*, 1950.

Mark Fisher, *Capitalist Realism: Is There No Alternative?*, 2009.

Reverend T.J. Fitzgerald, 'The Decline of Communism in Great Britain,' *Clergy Review* January 1935.

A. Flanders, *Trade Unions*, 1952 (1968 edition).

A. Flanders, *Trade Unions and Politics*, 1961.

A. Fleming, Manchester Committee for Defence of Canadian Seamen's Union, 1 July 1949.

P. Foot, *Paul Foot: A Tribute*, 2004.

J. Foster 'British Imperialism and the Labour Aristocracy' in J. Skelley (editor) *Strikes – A Study in Industrial Conflict. With Special Reference to British Experience Between 1911 and 1947*, 1976.

E. Friend, *London Trades Council History*, 1935.

W. Gallacher, 'The Beveridge Report', *Labour Monthly*, January 1943.

W. Gallacher, *The Last Memoirs of Willie Gallacher*, 1966.

Steven Gauge, *Political Wit*, 2011.

Lindsey German, *Sex, Class and Socialism*, 1994 (2nd edition).

Glossop Chronicle, 9 September 1949.

Robert Gildea, *Backbone of the Nation: Mining Communities and the Great Strike of 1984-85*, 2023

D. Gluckstein, *The Nazis, Capitalism and the Working Class*, 1999 (2012 edition).

D. Gluckstein *A People's History of the Second World War*, 2012.

G.M. Godden, *The Communist Attack on Great Britain*, 1935.
V. Gollancz, *The Betrayal of the Left*, 1941.
H. Gorter, *The Organisation of the Proletariat's Class Struggle*, 1921.
A. Gramsci, *Selections from Prison Notebooks*, 1971.
A.C. Grayling, *The Heart of Things. Applying Philosophy to the 21st Century* (2006 edition).
A.C. Grayling, *The Reason of Things: Living with Philosophy* (2004 edition).
Vasily Grossman, *Life and Fate*, 1959 (2020 edition).
R. Groves, *The Balham Group*, 1974.
R. Groves, 'The Menace to Unions', *The Socialist*, Number 11, October 1936.
R. Groves, *Trades Councils in the Fight for Socialism*, 1935.
Greta Thunberg quoted in theguardian.com/environment/2021/sep/28/blah-greta-thunberg-leaders-climate-crisis-co2-emissions
Ed Hall banners at edhallbanners.co.uk
P. Hall, *Blackpool Trades Council, 1891–1966*, 1966.
S. Hannah, *A Party with Socialists In It*, 2018.
W. Hannington, *Never on Our Knees* 1967.
W. Hannington, *Unemployed Struggles*, 1936.
G. Hardy, *Communist Work in the Trade Unions*, March 1926.
G. Hardy, 'The Fight for a Militant Trade Union Movement', *Communist Review*, September 1926.
Chris Harman, 'The General Strike', *International Socialism Journal*, Series 1, Number 48, June/July 1971.
Chris Harman, *The Lost Revolution*, 1982.
E.P. Harries, 'Helping the Unemployed', *Labour Magazine*, December 1932.
E.P. Harries, 'New Services for Unemployed Associations', *Industrial Review*, November 1932.
E.P. Harries, 'Social and Occupational Service for Unemployed', 23 March 1933.

E.P. Harries, 'Trades Councils in Conference', *Labour Magazine*, June 1932.

E.P. Harries, 'Unemployed Associations', *Industrial Review*, June 1932.

E.P. Harries, TCJCC On 'Unemployed Associations', 12 October 1932.

R. Hayburn, 'The Police and the Hunger Marchers', *International Review of Social History*, 1972, pp625–44.

B. Hennessy, 'Trade Unions and the British Labour Party', *American Political Science Review*, December 1955.

G. Hicks, 'Introduction' in G.E. Cheshire, *Twenty-Five Years of Progress: History of Aylesbury & District Trades Council 1911–1936*, 1936.

J. Hinton, *History Workshop Journal*, Number 10, Autumn 1980.

Christopher Hitchens, *New Statesman*, 6 October 1972.

E. Hobsbawm, *Age of Extremes: The Short Twentieth Century 1914–1991*, 1995 (2002 edition).

G. Hodgson, *The CP and Parliamentary Democracy*, 1977.

John Holloway, *Crack Capitalism*, 2010.

A.L. Horner, *Labour Monthly*, October 1928.

A.L. Horner, 'Trade Unions and Communism', *Labour Monthly*, February 1948.

A.L. Horner, 'Trade Unions and Unity' (CP), April 1937.

A.L. Horner, 'TUC 1942', *Labour Monthly*, September 1942.

Huddersfield Trades And Industrial Council 75th Anniversary (1885–1960), 1960.

A.W. Humphrey, 'Trades Councils and the TUC', *The Post*, 28 June 1924.

A. Hutt, *British Trade Unionism*, 1962.

D.A. Hyde, *I Believed: The Autobiography of a Former British Communist*, 1951.

R. Hyman, *Industrial Relations, A Marxist Introduction* 1975 (1979 edition).

Michael Ignatieff, *On Consolation: Finding Solace in Dark Times*, 2022.
Industrial News, 16 April 1940.
Industrial Relations Handbook, Number 3, 1949.
Industrial Review, January 1927.
Industrial Review, July 1927.
Industrial Review, August 1927.
Industrial Review, September 1927.
Industrial Review, November 1927.
Industrial Review, January 1928.
Industrial Review, 'Organising the Workless', March 1928.
Industrial Review, 'Trades Councils' Activities', November 1928.
Industrial Review, January 1929.
Industrial Review, April 1929.
Industrial Review, August 1929.
Industrial Review, October 1929.
Industrial Review, November 1929.
Industrial Review, December 1929.
Industrial Review, February 1930.
Industrial Review, October 1930.
Industrial Review, November 1930.
Industrial Review, February 1932.
Industrial Review, Organisation of the Unemployed', April 1932.
Industrial Review, August 1932.
Industrial Review, December 1932.
Industrial Review, August 1933.
'James Burnham and the Managerial Revolution', *Polemic*, Number 3, May 1946.
S. Jeffreys, 'The CP and the Rank and File', *International Socialism Journal*, Series 1, Winter 1980-81.
jrf.org.uk/report/uk-poverty-2023
'Judex', *The Socialist Leaguer*, Number 6, December 1934.
T. Judt, *Thinking the Twentieth Century*, 2012.

W. Kendall, *The Communist Party of Great Britain*, 1974.

P. Kerrigan, 'From Glasgow' in J. Skelley (editor) *Strikes – A Study in industrial conflict. With special reference to British experience between 1911 and 1947*, 1976.

P. Kerrigan, 'The Trade Unions: What Now?', *Labour Monthly*, November 1940.

F. Keyworth, *History Workshop Journal*, 8, 1979.

K. Knowles, *Strikes: A Study in Industrial Conflict with Special reference to the British experience between 1911 and 1947– 1911–1947*, 1952.

Labour Journal, September 1930.

Labour Journal June 1943.

Labour Journal, 'TUCs in Miniature', June 1949.

Labour Journal, August 1949.

Labour Journal, November 1949.

Labour Journal, July 1951.

Labour Journal, May 1952.

Labour Magazine, December 1926.

Labour Magazine, July 1927.

Labour Magazine, October 1930.

Labour Magazine, June 1932.

Labour Monthly, 'A Discussion on Trade Union Problems and Policy', April 1935.

Labour Monthly, 'Trade Union Problems and Policy', July 1935.

Labour Monthly, 'Why We Want Peace with the Soviet Union', November 1948.

Labour Research, 'Trades Councils Today', October 1948.

Labour's Northern Voice, January 1938.

W.J. Lane, *A Short History of Luton, Dunstable & District Trades Council*, 1941.

Lansbury's Labour Weekly, 26 March 1927.

D. Large and R. Whitfield, *The Bristol Trades Council 1873–1973*, 1973.

Sue Ledwith, 'Vive la différence? Women and Trade Unions in Britain' at https://journals.openedition.org/rfcb/1141, 2009.

A. Lees, *Birmingham Mail*, 'Too Political: Union Threat to Trades Council: Communist Caucus Alleged', 8 November 1944.

Leeds Weekly Citizen, June 1926.

Leicester Pioneer, 19 August 1921.

Leicester Trades Council, 1872–1972: Hats Off to the People, 1974.

S.W. Lerner, *Breakaway Unions and the Small Trade Union*, 1961.

Alison Light, *A Radical Romance: A Memoir of Love, Grief and Consolation*, 2019, (2020 edition).

Jack London, *The Iron Heel*, 1907.

lordslibrary.parliament.uk/trade-unions-members-and-relatuions-with-the-government

LRD Fact Service, 2 August 1940.

LRD Fact Service, January 1941.

LRD Fact Service, July 1941.

LRD Fact Service, 'Trades Councils and Production', 16 January 1942.

LRD Fact Service, 22 October 1942.

LRD Fact Service, 18 November 1943, W. Citrine on Circular 31.

LRD Fact Service, 19 November 1943.

LRD Fact Service, 31 March 1944 to 21 April 1944.

LRD Fact Service, 12 May 1944.

LRD Fact Service, 2 June 1944 to 30 June 1944.

LRD Fact Service, June 1944, Hatfield TC.

LRD Fact Service, 'Trades Councils and the Future', 10 May 1945.

LRD Fact Service, 19 October 1945.

LRD Fact Service, 4 January 1946.

LRD Fact Service, 22 March 1946 to 26 April 1946.

LRD Fact Service, 31 May 1946.

LRD Fact Service, 30 August 1946.

LRD Fact Service, 27 September 1946.

LRD Fact Service, 25 October 1946.

LRD Fact Service, 10 October 1947.
LRD Fact Service, 2 April 1948.
LRD Fact Service, 11 June 1948.
LRD Fact Service, 17 September 1948.
LRD Fact Service, 24 September 1948.
LRD Fact Service, 15 October 1948.
LRD Fact Service, 18 February 1949.
LRD Fact Service, June–September 1949.
LRD Fact Service, 24 February 1950.
LRD Monthly Circular, December 1925.
LRD Monthly Circular, May 1926.
LRD Monthly Circular, June 1926.
S. MacIntyre, 'British Labour, Marxism and Working Class Apathy in the 1920s', *History Journal*, Volume 20, Number 2, 1977.
S. MacIntyre, *Our History*, 73, 1979.
S. MacIntyre, *A Proletarian Science: Marxism in Britain 1917–1933*, 1980.
D.I. Mackay et al, 'The Discussion of Public Works Programmes, 1917-1935' *International Review of Social History* 11, 1966.
H. Mackinven, *Edinburgh & District Trades Council Centenary 1859–1959*, 1959.
J.A. Mahon, *Harry Pollitt*, 1976.
J.A. Mahon, 'Mr Citrine and Trade Union Democracy', *Labour Monthly*, May 1928.
J.A. Mahon, 'Trade Unionism and Communism – An Open Letter', 1935.
J.A. Mahon, 'Unity Versus the Manoeuvres of Citrine and Co', *Labour Monthly* August 1933.
Manchester & Salford TC, 'The People's Congress', 18 March 1931.
Manchester & Salford TC, 'Local Survey and Record' Circular, November 1933.

Manchester & Salford TC EC, 'Working Class Unity', 10 October 1933.

Manchester Guardian, 25 August 1930.

T. Mann, 'The Future of Trades Councils', *Trade Union Unity*, February 1926.

Mansfield Trades Council Diamond Jubilee, 1965.

A. Mason, *The General Strike in the North–East*, 1970.

J. McDonald, *Trades Councils*, 1930.

B. McIntosh, 'A Revolutionary Municipal Policy', *Labour Monthly*, September 1930.

J. McLean, 'The General Strike in North Lanarkshire', 1976, *Our History*.

H. McShane, *Daily Worker*, 18 November 1930.

H. McShane, *Glasgow and District Trades Council Centenary 1858–1958*, 1958.

Justine Medina quoted in labornotes.org/2022/04/amazon-workers-staten-island-clinch-historic-victory

W. Mellor, 'Towards a General Staff', *Direct Action*, 1920.

D. Melville, in *Discussion*, Number 12, February 1937 (CP).

Merseyside Council of Action, Strike Bulletins 5, 6, 9 and 10 May 1926.

Laura Miles, *Transgender Resistance: Socialism and the Fight for Trans Liberation*, 2020

R. Miliband, *Parliamentary Socialism*, 1961.

Kenneth O. Morgan, *Britain Since 1945: The People's Peace*, 2001 (2021 edition).

H. Morrison, London Labour Party, 11 March 1927.

J.T. Murphy, 'Anti-Communist Propaganda and the Task of the English Proletariat', *Pravda*, March 1927.

J.T. Murphy, *The Communist*, March 1928.

J.T. Murphy, *Communist Review*, January 1924.

J.T. Murphy, *Modern Trade Unionism*, 1935.

J.T. Murphy, *Preparing for Power*, 1932 (1972 edition).

J.T. Murphy, *A Revolutionary Workers' Government*, 1929.

J.T. Murphy, *Stop the Retreat! An Appeal to Trade Unionist*, 1922.

J.T. Murphy, *Trade Unions and Socialism*, June 1936.

National Council of Labour, 'British Labour and Communism' 1936.

National Council of Labour, Circular, 7 December 1939.

National Council of Labour, Circular 49, 'The People's Convention', February 1941.

Immanuel Ness and Dario Azzellini, *Ours to Master and to Own: Workers' Control From the Commune to the Present*, 2011

New Clarion, 16 March 1933.

News Chronicle, 19 October 1933.

T.H. Nimmo, *Birmingham Town Crier*, 14 January 1950.

National Joint Council, Circular 57 'National Demonstration on Unemployment', 15 December 1932.

NMM, *The Militant Trades Council – A Model Constitution for Trades Councils*, March 1926.

NMM, *What the Minority Movement Stands For*, 1925.

NUWM Declaration, 'United Action Against Unemployment', 19 April 1932.

Judith Orr, *Marxism & Women's Liberation*, 2015.

G. Orwell, *Tribune*, 17 March 1944.

J. Owen, 'War in the Workshops', 1942 (CP pamphlet).

Leo Panitch, 'Trade Unions and the Capitalist State', *New Left Review*, Number 125, January–February 1981.

A. Paterson, *The Weapon of the Strike*, 1922.

B. Pearce, 'Some Past Rank and File Movements', *Labour Review*, 1959.

Peterborough & District Trades Council Diamond Jubilee, 1899–1959, 1959.

F.H. Peet, 'Our Tasks in the Trades Councils', *Communist Review*, May 1926.

P. Piratin, *Our Flag Stays Red*, 1948 (1978 edition).

S. Pollard, 'Trade Union Reactions to the Economic Crisis', *Journal of Contemporary History*, Volume 4, Number 4, October 1969.

H. Pollitt, 'Can Conscription Save Peace?' (CP) May 1939.

H. Pollitt, 'The Conference of Executives', *Labour Monthly*, February 1927.

H. Pollitt, 'Defence of the People' (CP), February 1939.

H. Pollitt, 'The Future of Revolutionary Trade Unionism', *Labour Monthly*, August 1929.

H. Pollitt, 'The Manoeuvres of the TUC', *Labour Monthly*, January 1933.

H. Pollitt, 'The People's Parliament', *Labour Monthly*, December 1940.

H. Pollitt 'The Trades Councils Conference', *Labour Monthly*, November 1923.

H. Pollitt, 'Trade Unionists – What Next?' (CP), November 1948.

H. Pollitt, 'WAGES, a Policy' (CP Policy Series Number 4), December 1940.

R. Pope and F.W.A. Skerritt, *Ipswich & District Trades Council – A Short History, 1885–1967*, 1969.

L. Powell, 'JPCs', *Labour Monthly*, December 1941.

B. Pribecevic, *The Shop Stewards Movement and Workers' Control, 1910–22*, 1959.

A.A. Purcell, *The Economics of a Madhouse* 1931.

A.A. Purcell, *The Trades Councils and Local Working Class Movement*, 13 December 1930.

T. Quelch, 'Anti-Political Tomfoolery on the London TC', 12 July 1940.

T. Quelch, 'Building the Party', *Communist Review*, August 1926.

T. Quelch, *Communist Review*, January 1926.

T. Quelch, *Communist Review*, Editorial, February 1926.

T. Quelch, 'The Importance of the Trades Councils'; *Labour Monthly*, May 1926.

T. Quelch, 'Industrial London', *London Trade Union Handbook*, 1929–30.

T. Quelch, *The Trades Councils: The Need for the Extension of Their Scope and Work*, March 1922.

B. Reid, 'Why Britain Needs a Strong Labour Movement' (CP), September 1943.

G. Renshaw, *Communist Review*, December 1933.

B.C. Roberts, *TU Government and Administration in Great Britain*, 1956.

R. Robertson, *The General Strike in Southwark*, 1976.

R.W. Robson, *The Communist Party*, 1936.

John Roger and Peter McWilliams, *Wealth 101: Wealth Is Much More Than Money* (1992 edition).

R. Rosenstone, *Romantic Revolutionary*, 1975.

Sheila Rowbotham, *Hidden from History*, 1977 (3rd edition).

Arundhati Roy, *Capitalism: A Ghost Story*, 2014.

D. Rubinstein, *The Labour Left and Domestic Policy, 1945–50*, 1980.

G. Rude, 'The Trade Unions and the People's Movement', *Labour Monthly*, December 1938.

Bertrand Russell, *History of Western Philosophy*, 1946 (1947 edition).

W. Rust, 'The Issues before the TUC', *Labour Monthly*, September 1935.

Raphael Samuel, 'British Marxist Historians', *New Left Review*, Number 120, March 1980.

Raphael Samuel *The Lost World of British Communism*, published posthumously in 2006 (2017 edition).

John Saville, 'Trades Councils and the Labour Movement', *Society for the Study of Labour History*, Number 14, 1967.

Lynne Segal, Sheila Rowbotham and Hilary Wainwright, *Beyond the Fragments*, 1979.

Simon Sebag Montefiore, *Stalin: The Court of The Red Tsar*, 2003 (2014 edition).

R. Sewell, 'South Wales' in *Militant*, 9 April 1976.
J. Sheffield, 'Damping Down? A Word to Trade Unionists', *The Socialist Leaguer*, Number 12, June 1935.
I. Silone, *The God That Failed: Six studies in Communism*, 1950.
E. Silver, *Vic Feather T.U.C.*, 1973.
J. Skelley (editor) *The General Strike: A Study in Industrial Conflict. With Special Reference to British Experience Between 1911 and 1947*, 1976.
R. Skidelsky, *Politicians and the Slump*, 1967.
Pat Sloan, 'The Revolution for Socialism: 23 Years of Soviet Power' in *Russia Today Society*, 1940.
'Socialists and the Trade Unions', *Socialist Leaguer*, Number 11, May 1935.
socialistworker.co.uk
socialistparty.org.uk
Southampton Daily Echo, 20 July 1934.
Southern Daily Echo, 21 June 1934.
Southern Daily Echo, 'Trades Councils Ban on Communist Party', 29 June 1942.
Southern Daily Echo, 'Barriers to Unity with Communists', 25 July 1942.
Southern Daily Echo, February 1943.
Southern Daily Echo, 9 December 1944.
D.F. Springhall, J.R. Campbell, T.H James articles, *Communist Review*, August 1935.
C.G. Spragg, *Labour*, November 1941.
C.G. Spragg, 'Trades Councils as Watch-Dogs', *Labour*, November 1941.
J. Stanley, *History Workshop Journal*, Number 9, 1980.
A. Steel-Maitland Memorandum, 22 November 1926.
A.R. Stewart, 'The CP', *Communist Review*, July 1950.
Dan Stone, *Goodbye to All That? The Story of Europe since 1945*, 2014.

'General Strike in Middlesbrough', Bulletin 4, *Study of Labour History*, 1970.

G. Tate, *London Trades Council – A History*, 1950.

Tim Tate *Hitler's British Traitors: The Secret History of Spies, Saboteurs, and Fifth Columnists*, 2018 (2019 edition).

H.V. Tewson, Report on 'Unemployed Associations', 9 January 1932.

H.V. Tewson, 'Constitution for an Unemployed Association', 23 July 1929.

H.V. Tewson, 'Unemployed Associations', 26 August 1932.

Hugh Thomas, *An Unfinished History of the World*, 1979 (1981 edition).

Mark L Thomas, Jessica Walsh and Charlie Kimber, *The Revival of Resistance*, 2023

E.P. Thompson, 'The Peculiarities of the English', *The Poverty of Theory*, 1978.

E.P. Thompson, 'Socialist Humanism', *The New Reasoner*, 1957.

E.P. Thompson, *Writing by Candlelight*, 1980.

Greta Thunberg, *The New Statesman*, 21–27 October 2022.

The Times, 9 October 1924.

The Times, 5 October 1925, On Guerrilla Tactics' in TUs.

The Times, 25 June 1945.

Adam Tooze, *The New Statesman*, 21 April 2022.

Adam Tooze website at https://adamtooze.com/2020/08/28/pessimism-of-the-intellect-optimism-of-the-will-the-line-so-often-attributed-to-gramsci-was-taken-from-romain-rolland/

H. Tracey, *Labour* Magazine, May 1924.

'Trades Councils and the War Effort', *Labour* Journal, July 1942.

'Trades Councils Register', *Labour* Journal, February 1948.

'Trade Unionists in the Forces', *Labour* Journal, March 1943.

Trades Councils Report, July 1925.

Trade Union Membership at assets.publishing.service.gov.uk/government/uploads/system/

uploads/attachment_data/file/1158789/Trade_Union_Membership_UK_1995-2022_Statistical_Bulletin.pdf

E. Trory, *Between the Wars*, 1974.

E. Trory, *Imperialist War*, 1977.

E. Trory, *Soviet Trade Unions and the General Strike*, 1975.

A. Tuckett, *The Blacksmiths' History*, 1974.

A. Tuckett, *A History of Swindon Trades Council 1891–1971*, 1971.

M. Turnbull, 'The Attitude of Government and Administration Towards the Hunger Marches of the 1920s and 1930s', *Journal of Social Policy*, Volume 2, Part 1, January 1973.

H.A. Turner, *Trade Union Growth, Structure and Policy*, 1962.

M. Turner-Samuels, *British Trade Unions*, 1949.

UA President, 'Front Line Activities', *Labour* Journal, February 1934.

Unemployment figures at https://www.ons.gov.uk/economy/nationalaccounts/uksectoraccounts/compendium/economicreview/april2019/longtermtrendsinukemployment1861to2018, 28 April 2019.

J. Vincent, 'The General Strike of 1926', *The Listener*, Volume 91, 25 April 1974.

T. Wakley, *Communist Circus* (LP), 1946.

A.M. Wall, 'Lessons of the National March of the Unemployed', *Labour Monthly*, December 1936.

A.M. Wall, 'The London TC – Some Difficulties and the Remedy', *Industrial Review*, February 1928.

A.M. Wall, 'Memorandum on Services for Unemployed Workers', 26 July 1934.

G. Walpole, *Management and Men*, 1944.

Beatrice Webb Diaries, 1912–23, Volume 1, M. Cole (editor), 1952.

S. & B. Webb, *The History of Trade Unionism*, (1894 edition).

S. & B. Webb, *Industrial Democracy*, 1897.

Western Daily Press, 1 August 1933.

E.L. Wigham, *Strikes and the Government 1893–1974*, 1976.
E.L. Wigham, *Trade Unions*, 1956.
B. Williams, *Communist Review*, December 1925.
G.M. Williams, *London Trades Council 1860–1960*, 1960.
R. Willis, 'Trades Councils in War-Time', *Labour* Journal, October 1941.
The Worker, 18 November 1922.
The Worker, 19 July 1929.
The Workers' Chronicle, 14 May 1926.
Workers' Life, 3 June 1927.
World News & Views, 5 July 1941.
World News & Views, 19 July 1941.
World News & Views, 5 September 1942.
World News & Views XX111.
Workers' Weekly, CP Programme, 30 November 1923.
Workers' Weekly, 21 November 1923.
Workers' Weekly 21 December 1923.
Workers' Weekly, 21 January 1927.
Workers' Weekly, 11 November 1927.
Rebecca Zahn and Nicole Busby, 'Women's Labour and Trade Unionism – A Dangerous Combination?' in *Institute of Employment Rights*, 6 July 2016, available at https://www.ier.org.uk/comments/womens-labour-and-trade-unionism-dangerous-combination/.
Slavoj Zizek, *In Defence of Lost Causes* (2008 edition).

2. ACTCs, CP, LP, MM, TCs, UAs AND OTHER ANNUAL REPORTS, CONFERENCES AND COMMITTEES

ACTC Report, 27 February 1925, Resolutions 5 & 7, A.B. Swales' Chairman's Address, and R. Pennifold, Brighton TC, Resolution 2.

ACTC Report, TCs Report June 1925 and July 1925.

ACTC Report, 26 March 1926, A. Pugh's Chairman's Address.
ACTC Report, 31 February 1927, NMM Circular by H. Pollitt.
ACTC Report, May 1927, Final Agenda.
ACTC Report, 27 May 1927, G. Hicks.
ACTC Report, 19 May 1928, G. Hicks.
ACTC Report, 29 June 1929, Ben Tillett, Chairman's Address.
ACTC Report, 24 May 1930, Chairman's Address.
ACTC Report, 30 May 1931, A. Conley.
ACTC Report, 28 May 1932, TCJCC Report.
ACTC Report, 27 May 1933, Birmingham District Committee of NUWM.
ACTC Report, 31 August 1934.
ACTC Report, 25 May 1935, W. Kean and TCJCC Report by C. Dukes.
ACTC, 1935, Draft Memorandum.
ACTC, 23 May 1936, C. Dukes.
ACTC Report, 29 May 1937, TUC Memorandum, E. Bevin.
ACTC Report, 25 May 1938, W. Citrine.
ACTC Report, 28 May 1938.
ACTC 1939, T. Hallett on 'Trades Councils and Breakaway Unions' and TCJCC Report by E.P. Harries.
ACTC On 'National Voluntary Service', 20 May 1939, TCJCC.
ACTC Report, 20 May 1939, Camberwell TC delegate.
ACTC Report, May 1939, TCJCC Report by E.P. Harries.
ACTC Report, 27 July 1940, W. Citrine.
ACTC Report, 28 June 1941, J. Marchbank.
ACTC Report, 29 March 1942.
ACTC Report, 30 May 1942, J. Marchbank and G. Woodcock.
ACTC, 29 May 1943, On 'Beveridge Report' with W. Citrine On 'The Trade Disputes Act'; J. Marchbank, 'On Post-War Reconstruction', and R. Willis.
ACTC Report, 20 May 1944, with H.N. Harrison for the TCJCC Council.

Texts and Events Referred to in the Book

ACTC Report, 27 May 1945.

ACTC Report, July 1945, Debate on 'Post-war Reconstruction', J. Benstead, H.N. Harrison, E.P. Harries and L. Fawcett.

ACTC Report, from Derby, May 1946.

ACTC 25 May 1946, quote from H.N. Harrison and L. Fawcett from TCJCC's Report.

ACTC, 31 May 1947, Speeches from G.W. Thomson and H.N. Harrison.

ACTC Report, 1947, quote from Portsmouth TC and Luton TC delegate.

ACTC, 5 June 1948, TCJCC Report, quote from H.V. Tewson, plus opening speeches.

ACTC, 28 May 1949, TCJCC Report.

ACTC, 29 May 1949 Report, 'Trade Unions and Disruptive Bodies' Report.

ACTC, 1949, On 'JCC Election'.

ACTC Report, May 1949, with A. Compertz and Sir Luke Fawcett.

ACTC Nottingham Report, May 1950.

ACTC AR, May 1950, with F.R. Fermor and TCJCC Report.

Birmingham TC AR, 1924.

Birmingham TC AR, 1925, J.E. Corrin and F.W. Rudland.

Birmingham TC AR, 1927, J.E. Corrin and F.W. Rudland.

Birmingham TC AR, 1929.

Birmingham TC Minutes, 20 February, 17 April and 17 July 1929, J.E. Corrin.

Birmingham TC AR, 1930.

Birmingham TC AR, 1931.

Birmingham TC AR, 1932.

Birmingham TC Statement, 1934.

Birmingham TC AR, 1935.

Birmingham TC AR, 1936.

Birmingham TC AR, 1939.

Birmingham TC AR, 1940.
Birmingham TC AR, 1941.
Birmingham TC AR, 1942.
Birmingham TC 16 June 1942, CP Midlands District Committee.
Birmingham TC AR, 1943.
Birmingham TC Statement, 4 December 1944.
Birmingham TC AR, 15 September 1944.
Birmingham TC AR, 1946.
Birmingham TC Secretary, 1947.
Birmingham TC AR, 1947.
Birmingham TC AR, 1948, H. Baker.
Bournemouth TUC Report, 1926.
Brighton Conference, 'Labour and the War Economy', 3 December 1939.
Brighton TC, 3 March 1926.
Brighton TC, 5 May 1926.
Brighton TC Minutes, 15 June 1927.
Brighton TC AR, 1927.
Brighton TC AR, 1928.
Brighton TC AR, 1928.
Brighton TC, 20 February 1929.
Brighton TC Minutes, 15 January 1930.
Brighton TC Minutes, 16 April 1930.
Brighton TC Minutes, 15 April 1931.
Brighton TC Minutes, 16 August 1931.
Brighton TC Minutes, 19 July 1933.
Brighton TC Minutes, 20 June 1934.
Brighton TC Minutes, 21 November 1934.
Brighton TC Minutes, 19 December 1934.
Brighton TC Minutes, 18 March 1936.
Brighton TC, 20 October 1937.
Brighton TC Minutes, 16 February 1938.
Brighton TC Minutes, 20 September 1939.

Brighton TC Minutes, 20 March 1940.
Brighton TC Minutes, 17 April 1940.
Brighton TC Minutes, 26 October 1941.
Brighton TC Minutes, 21 February 1943.
Brighton TC Minutes, 21 March 1943.
Brighton TC Minutes, 16 June 1943.
Brighton TC AR, 1949.
Bristol TC AR, 1928, E.H. Parker.
Bristol TC AR, 1930.
Bristol TC AR, 1936, W.H. Hennessy.
Bristol TC AR, 1937.
Bristol TC AR, 1947.
Bristol UA Constitution, 14 November 1927.
Bristol UA, 13 February 1932, A. Conley and H.V. Tewson, 'Report of Conference of UAs'.
Camborne-Redruth TC, March 1944.
Conference of UA Representatives and the TCJCC, 27 July 1933.
First CP Congress, W. Paul on a code of tactics.
CP Congress Report, March 1922.
CP Congress Report, October 1922.
CP Congress Report, 1927.
CP Congress Report, February 1935.
CP Congress Report, Sussex County, 17 March 1940.
CP Industrial Bureau Report, 5 November 1939.
Coventry TC AR, September 1945.
Coventry TC AR, 1948 (Warwick University Archives).
Darlington, Leeds, Cardiff Resolution 2, April 1925.
Edinburgh T&LC Executive Report, 1920.
Edinburgh T&LC Executive Report, 1927.
Edinburgh T&LC AR 1939.
Edinburgh T&LC AR 1948.
Edmonton TC, March 1944.
Essential Work (General Provisions) Order, 24 July 1944.

Glasgow TC AR, January 1945.
Glasgow TC AR, 1946.
Hackney TC AR, July 1946.
Hampshire & Isle of Wight & Dorset Federation of TCs, Mr Gardiner, 6 January 1934.
Ipswich TC AR, 1932.
LP ACR, by the NEC, 1918.
LP ACR, EC September 1921.
LP ACR, 1925.
LP ACR, 1934.
LP ACR, 1934, E. Bevin.
LP ACR, 1935, E. Bevin.
Lancashire, Cheshire & North Wales Federation of TCs, June 1944.
Leeds TC, 'Unemployed Association' Report, 7 July 1944.
London TC AR, 1925.
London TC, 11 August 1927, A.M. Wall.
London TC, November 1931, A.M. Wall 'Memorandum on The Political Situation'.
London TC Memorandum, December 1931.
London TC Memorandum, 24 May 1934, quote from A.M. Wall.
London TC Conference, February 1936 'The Trade Unions and the War Menace'.
London TC AR, 1940, Editorial, 'How to Deal with Disruption'.
London TC AR, 1941.
London TC Minutes, 10 October 1942.
London TC AR, 1943.
London TC AR, 1946.
London TC AR, 1948.
Manchester & Salford TC, 21 December 1923.
Manchester & Salford TC AR, 1924.
Manchester & Salford TC AR, 1927.
Manchester & Salford TC AR, 1929, A.A. Purcell.

Manchester & Salford TC, 'Memorandum on Municipal Rationalisation', June 1930.
Manchester & Salford TC, 'Unemployment and the Coming Winter', August 1930.
Manchester & Salford TC, 'Economy!' 1931.
Manchester & Salford TC AR, 1931, A.A. Purcell.
Manchester & Salford TC AR, 1932, A.A. Purcell.
Manchester & Salford TC AR, 1933.
Manchester & Salford TC AR, 1934.
Manchester & Salford TC AR, 1935, Foreword by W. Citrine and W.J. Munro.
Manchester & Salford TC AR, 1935–36.
Manchester & Salford TC AR, 1937.
Manchester & Salford TC AR, 1940, W.J. Munro.
Manchester & Salford TC AR, 16 October 1941.
Manchester & Salford TC, 27 May 1942.
Manchester & Salford TC AR, 1943, W.J. Munro.
Manchester & Salford TC AR, 1944.
Manchester & Salford TC AR, 1945.
Manchester & Salford TC AR, 1946, H.E. Newbold.
Manchester & Salford TC AR, 1947.
Manchester & Salford TC, 1948.
Manchester & Salford TC AR, 1948, H.E. Newbold.
Manchester & Salford TC AR, 1949, H.E. Newbold.
Manchester & Salford TC AR, 1950.
Mansfield TC AR, 1945.
Marx Memorial House CP Historians' Group Statement, January 1952.
'Memorandum from the Unemployed Services Committee of the TUC', 21 September 1934, from Mrs Rackham.
Middlesbrough TC's Secretary Report, May 1926.
Midland Federation of Trades Councils Report, 17 October 1942.
Midland Federation of Trades Councils Report, October 1947.

MM EC, 4 April 1927.
National Strike Special Conference, 20 January 1927.
Newcastle & District TC AR, 1932.
NFTC Report, 17 November 1923.
NMM Circular to ACTC, 31 March 1927, by H. Pollitt.
NMM Conference 30 August 1925.
NMM EC Circular, *The Future of the Trades Councils*, May 1928.
Oxford T&LC AR, 1929, C. Bowles and E. Loynd.
Oxford T&LC AR, 1930.
Oxford T&LC AR, 1931.
Oxford T&LC AR, February 1933, C. Bowles.
Oxford T&LC AR, 1934.
Oxford T&LC AR, 1935.
'The People's Congress', 9 May 1931.
'The People's Convention', 12–13 January 1941.
'The People's Convention', February 1941.
Sheffield T&LC AR, 1923.
Sheffield T&LC AR, 1923, President E.G. Rowlinson.
Sheffield T&LC AR, 1926, President Rowlinson.
Sheffield T&LC AR, 1927.
Sheffield T&LC AR, 1928.
Sheffield T&LC AR, 1929.
Sheffield T&LC AR, 1930.
Sheffield T&LC AR, 1931.
Sheffield T&LC AR, 1932.
Sheffield T&LC 1933, F. Thraves.
Sheffield T&LC AR, 1937.
Sheffield T&LC, 1 June 1938.
Sheffield T&LC EC Report, 1938.
Sheffield T&LC, 1938.
Sheffield T&LC AR, 1939, C.S. Darvill.
Sheffield T&LC AR, 1940.
Sheffield T&LC AR, 16 March 1942.

Sheffield T&LC AR, 1943, A.E. Hobson.
Sheffield T&LC AR, 1944, J. Madin.
Sheffield T & LC AR, 1945.
Sheffield T&LC AR, 1946.
Sheffield T&LC AR, 1947.
Sheffield T&LC AR, 1948.
Southampton TC AR, 1933.
Southampton TC AR, 1934, R. Morley.
Southampton TC AR, 1935.
Southampton TC AR, 1937.
Southampton TC AR, 1948, J.H. Bingham.
Southampton TC, R. Morley.
Southampton TC, 'To the Unemployed Workers of Southampton', 1931.
Swindon TC, 27 September 1946.
Unemployed Services Committee Report, 17 January 1935.
Westminster TC, 28 June 1942.
Willesden Borough LP&TC, September 1944.
Wolverhampton TC AR, 1944.

3. TUC AND TCJCC

W. Milne-Bailey (editor), *Trade Union Documents*, 1929.
W.H. Barton, Report on Merseyside Council of Action, to TUC, May 1926.
Circular 2, to Trades Councils, 'Financial Assistance for Miners', 26 October 1926.
Circular 2a, to Trades Councils 27 October 1927.
Circular 4 'Food Control Committees' Order', 23 September 1943.
Circular 5, 'Local Committees in War-Time', 13 September 1939.
Circular 5, 'Organisation of Unemployed', 14 September 1933.
Circular 6, 'Works Production Committees', 2 October 1942.
Circular 7, 'Communist Delegates to Trades Councils', 28 October 1943.

Circular 9 'Organisation of Women and Young Workers', 11 November 1927.
Circular 9a, 'Area Conferences Regarding Social Insurance', 29 October 1928.
Circular 10, 'Talks by Civil Service Officials', 30 September 1937.
Circular 11, 'Affiliation of Branches to Trades Councils' 9 October 1930.
Circular 11, 'Trades Councils and War-Time Committees', 29 October 1942.
Circular 12 'Affiliation of Branches of Breakaway Unions', 12 May 1938.
Circular 12, 'Unemployment Insurance: Transitional Benefit Through Public Assistance Committees', 21 October 1931.
Circular 13, 'Recruiting Assistance to Trades Councils', 24 October 1935.
Circular 13,'Labour Problems in War-Time', 13 October 1939.
Circular 13, 'Labour Supply', 26 November 1940 by H.V. Tewson.
Circular 15, 'Organisation Activities', 25 October 1934.
Circular 16, to Trades Councils, 'Communist and Other Bodies', 26 October 1934.
Circular 18, 'Second World Peace Congress, Sheffield', 27 October 1950.
Circular 18 'Trade Unions and Communism', 27 September 1948, by H.V. Tewson.
Circular 19, 'Industrial Review', 18 January 1927.
Circular 19, 'Unemployment Insurance', November 19, 1931.
Circular 24, 'Unemployed Associations: Swansea Congress Report', 6 December 1928.
Circular 27, 'Appeals to Trades Councils', 3 December 1943.
Circular 27, 'NUWCM', 1 March 1928.
Circular 27, 'Trade Unionism During War', 23 November 1939.
Circular 28 'New Daily Herald Circulation Campaign', 10 January 1930.

Circular 28, 'Hospital Management Committees – Annual Filling of Vacancies", 2 December 1949.
Circular 29, 'The Witchcraft Trial in Moscow', 3 December 1936.
Circular 30, 'Unemployment Assistance Allowances & the Cost of Living', 25 November 1937.
Circular 31 'Trade Union Recruitment Effort', 13 April 1928.
Circular 31, 'Transfer from Distressed Areas', 31 January 1929.
Circular 32, 'Registration of Trades Councils' 8 December 1947.
Circular 32, 'Organisation of the Unemployed', 3 November 1932.
Circular 33, 'Unofficial Marches' 9 December 1937.
Circular 34, 'Trade Union Organisation', 4 December 1930.
Circular 35, 'People's Press Printing Society Limited', 28 December 1945.
Circular 36 'Government anti-Trade Union Legislation – National Campaign', 8 April 1927.
Circular 42, 'Administering Unemployment Insurance', 25 January 1929.
Circular 46, 'Trades Councils and Proscribed Organisations', 26 January 1950.
Circular 47, 'Trades Councils and Industrial Disputes', 28 January 1937.
Circular 48, 'Affiliated Membership' June 1926.
Circular 54, 'Trade Disputes and Trade Unions (Amendment) Bill 1931', 3 February 1931.
Circular 52, 'Citizens' Advice Bureaux', 8 February 1940.
Circular 55, 'Unemployed Marches', 4 February 1937.
Circular 59, 'Local Trade Union Recruitment Campaigns' 25 February 1937.
Circular 59, 'National Voluntary Service' 18 January 1939.
Circular 59 'Trade Councils' Organisation' 26 February 1942.
Circular 61, 'Industrial and Political Funds' 27 March 1947.
Circular 61, 'The Means Test', 18 February 1932.

Circular 63, 'Proscribed Bodies and Electoral Machinery', 15 March 1945.

Circular 63, 'National Unemployed Workers Committee Movement and Courts of Referees', 9 August 1928.

Circular 63, 'Trade Union Publicity Campaigns', 12 January 1949.

Circular 64, 'National Voluntary Service: Local Committees', 31 January 1939.

Circular 64, 'Ministry of Labour LECs' 14 March 1946.

Circular 67, 'Trades Councils and Policy', 2 March 1944.

Circular 68, to Trades Councils, 'The Mining Situation', 21 August 1926.

Circular 69, 'Organisation of Unemployed Persons', 5 February 1932.

Circular 69, 'Unemployment Assistance Boards Regulations', 21 February 1935.

Circular 70 'Conferences on National Insurance Scheme and the NHS', 28 February 1948.

Circular 72, 'Textile Dispute', 30 May 1930.

Circular 73, 'Unemployed Bill, 1933', 1 February 1934.

Circular 74 'Financial Assistance for Miners', 31 August 1926.

Circular 75, 'Allotments for the Unemployed', 26 March 1931.

Circular 79, 'Refugee Organisations, Communists Activities', 1 May 1941.

Circular 80, 'Trade Union Propaganda Campaigns', 9 March 1939.

Circular 81, 'Representation upon Food Control Committees', 30 May 1940.

Circular 83, 'Propaganda Weeks', 2 March 1933.

Circular 84, 'Unemployment Research and Advice Bureau', 17 March 1938.

Circular 85, 'National Unemployed Workers Movement', 21 April 1932.

Circular 88, 'Trade Union Recruitment Weeks', 8 March 1934.

Circular 94, 'Review of Unemployed Workers', 18 July 1940.
Circular 95, 'WFTU (World Federation of Trade Unions) Disruptive Activity', 2 June 1950.
Circular 97, 'Trade Union Recruitment' 11 April 1935.
Circular 99, 'Fuel Advisory Committees', 29 July 1940.
Circular 100, 'Organisation of Women' 11 April 1935.
Circular 101, 'Representation on Food Control Committees', 8 August 1940.
Circular 103, 'ACTC 1934: Report from Unemployed Associations', 19 April 1934.
Circular 104 'Trades Councils' Propaganda Campaigns', 27 June 1946.
Circular 107, 'Demonstrations Re Commissions Report on Unemployment Insurance', 6 June 1931.
Circular 116, 'National Voluntary Service Representatives on Local Committees', 25 May 1939.
Circular 120, 'Communist and Other Bodies', 5 June 1934.
Circular 127, 'Allotment Gardens for Unemployed Persons', 18 August 1932.
Circular 131 to Trades Councils, 'Help the Spanish Workers!' 27 July 1936.
Circular 135, 'Trades Councils and Political Activities', by W. Citrine.
Circular 138, 'Unemployed Assistance Regulations', 13 August 1936.
Circular 139a, 'Public Assistance Committees and National Health Insurance Arrears', 3 August 1933.
Circular 145 'TUC Weekend Schools', 7 September 1949.
TCJCC Minutes, 10 July 1924.
TCJCC (General Council only) Minutes, 8 December 1924.
TCJCC Minutes, 8 December 1924, pp1–3.
TCJCC Minutes, 13 July 1925 On Organisation, Bolton TC.
TCJCC Minutes, 6 November 1925.

TCJCC Minutes, 20 November 1925 to 20 April 1926.
TCJCC on 'Workers' Sports Organisation', 4 June 1926.
TCJCC Minutes, 15 June 1926.
TCJCC Minutes, 5 August 1926.
TCJCC Minutes, 17 November 1926.
TCJCC Minutes, 18 January 1927.
TCJCC Minutes, 19 February 1927.
TCJCC Minutes, 22 February 1927.
TCJCC Minutes, 26 April 1927.
TCJCC Minutes, 28 July 1927.
TCJCC Minutes, 25 October 1927.
TCJCC Minutes, 19 December 1927, Bristol UA.
TCJCC Minutes, 21 February 1928.
TCJCC Minutes, 23 October 1928.
TCJCC Minutes, 22 November 1928.
TCJCC Minutes, 18 January 1929.
TCJCC Minutes, 22 January 1929.
TCJCC Minutes, 28 June 1929.
TCJCC Minutes, 21 August 1929.
TCJCC Minutes, 11 December 1930.
TCJCC Minutes, 23 September 1931.
TCJCC Minutes, 18 December 1931.
TCJCC Minutes, 12 July 1932.
TCJCC Minutes, 8 September 1932.
TCJCC Minutes, 18 November 1932.
TCJCC Minutes, 19 January 1933.
TCJCC Minutes, 17 March 1933.
TCJCC Minutes, 22 November 1934.
TCJCC Minutes, 19 October 1934.
TCJCC Minutes, 22 November 1934, A.E. Hobson.
TCJCC Minutes, 10 January 1935.
TCJCC Minutes, 19 March 1935.
TCJCC Minutes, 30 June 1936.

Texts and Events Referred to in the Book

TCJCC Minutes, 17 November 1936.
TCJCC Memorandum, 'Trades Councils – Their Industrial Functions and Activities', 17 November 1936.
TCJCC Minutes, 19 January 1937.
TCJCC Minutes, 20 July 1937.
TCJCC Minutes, 15 December 1937.
TCJCC Minutes, 19 July 1938.
TCJCC Minutes, 14 February 1939.
TCJCC Minutes, 18 April 1939.
TCJCC Minutes, 16 May 1939.
TCJCC Minutes, 12 September 1939 to 8 January 1940.
TCJCC Minutes, 4 March 1940.
TCJCC Minutes, 15 April 1940.
TCJCC Minutes, 13 June 1940.
TCJCC Minute 9a, 15 December 1940.
TCJCC Minutes, 8 August 1941.
TCJCC Minutes, 16 March 1942.
TCJCC Minutes, 25 June 1942.
TCJCC Minutes, 12 January 1943.
TCJCC Minutes, 16 March 1943.
TCJCC Minutes, 20 August 1943.
TCJCC Minutes, 8 December 1943.
TCJCC Minutes, 18 April 1944.
TCJCC Minutes, 19 May 1944.
TCJCC Minutes, 6 June 1944.
TCJCC Minutes, 6 October 1944.
TCJCC Minutes, 28 November 1944.
TCJCC Minutes, 27 May 1945.
TCJCC Minutes, 23 July 1945.
TCJCC Minutes, 17 December 1945.
TCJCC Minutes, 1 April 1946.
TCJCC Minutes, 24 May 1946.
TCJCC Minutes, 12 August 1946.

TCJCC Minutes, 2 December 1946.
TCJCC Minutes, 10 November 1947.
TCJCC Minutes, 5 January 1948.
TCJCC Minutes, 16 August 1948.
TCJCC Minutes, 15 March 1949.
TCJCC Minutes, 4 April 1949.
TCJCC Minutes, 28 June 1949.
TCJCC Minutes, 22 August 1949.
TCJCC to TCs, 'Unemployed Associations', 3 March 1928.
TCJCC, 'Organisation of Unemployed Associations', 25 January 1932.
TCJCC, 'Suggested Activities for Unemployed Associations', 19 March 1935.
TCJCC, Summary of Replies from TCs regarding Circular 16, 19 March 1935.
TCJCC Report, 'Unemployed Marches', May 1937.
TCJCC on 'Unemployed Associations', 15 February 1938.
TUC Bournemouth ACR, Autumn 1926, A. Conley.
TUC Edinburgh ACR, Autumn 1927, General Council Report.
TUC Swansea ACR, Autumn 1928.
TUC Belfast ACR, Autumn 1929, F. Rowland.
TUC Nottingham ACR, Autumn 1930.
TUC Newcastle ACR, Autumn 1932.
TUC Brighton ACR, Autumn 1933, W. Citrine.
TUC Weymouth ACR, Autumn 1934.
TUC Scotland ACR, 15 February 1935.
TUC Margate ACR, Autumn 1935, G. Hicks and General Council Report from E. Bevin.
TUC Plymouth ACR, Autumn 1936.
TUC Norwich ACR, Autumn 1937.
TUC Blackpool ACR, Autumn 1938.
TUC Bridlington ACR, Autumn 1939.
TUC Southport ACR, Autumn 1940.

TUC Edinburgh ACR, Autumn 1941, J. Marchbank.
TUC Blackpool ACR, Autumn 1942.
TUC Southport ACR, Autumn 1943.
TUC Blackpool ACR, Autumn 1945, 'Political Activities' section, J. Porter.
TUC Brighton ACR, Autumn 1946.
TUC Southport ACR, 1947.
TUC Margate ACR, Autumn 1948.
TUC Bridlington ACR, Autumn 1949.
TUC Brighton ACR, Autumn 1950.
TUC/TCs Preliminary Conference, 7 May 1924, D. Carmichael.
TUC, *Model Rules for Trades Councils*, 1925.
TUC, *Hunger March, A Communist Stunt*, 1 November 1927.
TUC, *Industrial News*, Number 60, 1 November 1927.
TUC Industrial Conference Report, 1928.
TUC Organisation Committee Report, 24 July 1929.
TUC General Council, *Facilities for the Unemployed*, 11 December 1931.
TUC, *Organisation of the Unemployed*, 14 December 1931.
TUC General Council *Explanatory Notes on Formation of Unemployed Associations*, 2 February 1932.
TUC Report, 1932.
TUC General Council, On *Disruptive Bodies*, 24 October 1934.
TUC General Council, *Action Against Disruptive Bodies*, by E.P. Harries, 21 May 1935. TUC, *Trades Councils and War-Time Committees*, 1942.
TUC, *Model Rules, Constitution and Standing Orders for Trades Councils or Industrial Sections of a Trades & Labour Council*, 1943.
TUC, *The TUC in War-Time*, February 1943.
TUC General Council, to Leeds T&LC, 22 April 1944.
TUC, *Details of the Method of the Election for the TCJCC*, 1946.
TUC, *Trade Union Structure and Closer Unity*, March 1947.

TUC, *What the TUC is Doing*, May 1947.

TUC General Council, *Defend Democracy – Communist Activities Examined*, 24 November 1948 (pamphlet).

TUC, *Trades Councils' Guide*, 1948.

TUC, *Labour* Journal, February 1949.

TUC, *The Tactics of Disruption – Communist Methods Exposed*, March 1949.

TUC Journal, 'The Growth of Local TUCs', August 1949.

TUC, 'Trades Councils Move to Safeguard Democracy', *Labour* Journal May 1950.

4. LETTERS, TUC FILES AND ARCHIVES, AND LSE LIBRARY

H. Baker/V. Feather letters, 22 and 28 December 1943.

H. Baker to V. Feather, 16 September 1947.

E. Bevin to G.D.H. Cole, 25 January 1937.

R. Boyfield/H.E. Newbold letters, 4 and 22 July 1950.

Bristol Electrical Trades Union Number 1 to V. Feather, 20 March 1948.

R. Chick to W. Citrine, 21 June 1934 (TUC Files).

R. Chick/W. Citrine/E.P. Harries letters, 22 and 23 June 1934.

R. Chick/E.P. Harries letters, 17 and 18 January 1932.

Citrine to Trades Council Federations, 5 March 1928.

Citrine to Trades Councils, 15 November 1928.

CP letter, 'The Communist Party and the Trade Unions', H. Tracey Papers (TUC), 12 September 1935.

Dartford TC letter to the TUC, July 1948.

F. Day/W. Citrine letters, 20 December 1931 and 4 April 1932.

F. Day to W. Citrine, 24 May 1942.

T. E. Eaton to E.P. Harries, 21 July 1933 (TUC Files).

T. E. Eaton to E.P. Harries 15 September 1933 (TUC Files).

D. Edwards to V. Feather, 26 February 1949.

V. Feather to H. Baker, 2 November 1944.

Texts and Events Referred to in the Book

V. Feather to H. Baker, 14 November 1944.
V. Feather/H.E. Child letters, 15 and 29 December 1944.
V. Feather to W. Citrine, 5 March 1941.
V. Feather to J.A. Evison, 25 and 30 November 1948.
V. Feather to E. Haynes, 2 November 1944.
V. Feather to R.T. Jenner (Oxford T&LC Secretary), 3 February 1949.
V. Feather to E. Kavanagh (Leeds TC), 24 October 1949.
V. Feather to W.J. Munro, 18 October 1940.
V. Feather to C.G. Spragg, 11 June 1942.
V. Feather to C.G. Spragg 4 January 1943.
V. Feather to C.G. Spragg, 5 January 1943.
V. Feather to C.G. Spragg, 16 April 1943.
V. Feather to C.G. Spragg, 30 March 1944.
V. Feather/G.F. Tutt letters, 26 April and 27 June 1942.
V. Feather to Tutt, 27 October 1942.
V. Feather/R. Willis letters, 28 October and 27 November 1942.
H. Gilman and A.L. Ward to V. Feather, February 1949.
W. Hannington, 'Crimes Against the Unemployed' pamphlet, 1932 (LSE Library).
W. Hannington, letters on UAs, 13 September and 25 May 1935 (TUC Files).
J.T. Hargreaves to A.J. Heal, Area Secretary, T&GWU, 30 August 8 1941 (TUC Files).
E.P. Harries to Day, 23 December 1931.
E.P. Harries to A.E. Hobson.
E.P. Harries to F.M. Lees, 23 October 1934.
E.P. Harries to Milne-Bailey, 18 April 1932 (TUC Files).
E.P. Harries to NUR Sheffield Number 7 Branch, 18 October 1940.
E.P. Harries to G.R. Shepherd, 25 July 1934.
W.F. Harrison to H.V. Tewson, 28 September 1948.
E. Haynes to V. Feather, 1 November 1944.

F.C. Henry/H.V. Tewson/R. Boyfield/H.E. Newbold letters, 27 July 1949 to 12 September 1949.

E.J. Hibberd to W. Citrine, 25 July 1946.

A.E. Hobson to R. Boyfield, 5 February 1951.

A.E. Hobson to W. Citrine, 30 November 1942.

A.E. Hobson, Sheffield T&LC letter to the TUC, 30 December 1947.

A.E. Hobson/H.V. Tewson/V. Feather letters, 26 to 30 November 1948.

B. Kilgarriff/R. Boyfield letters, 12, 14, and 20 November, and 21 December 1950, and 12, 16, 28 January, and 8 and 10 August 1951.

London TC Fraction, 'Instructions', 10 March 1927 (in TUC files on London TC).

A.C. Lowcock to H.V. Tewson, 18 February 1947.

F. Meade/V. Feather letters, 21 September and 28 October 1948.

J.S. Middleton to E.P. Harries, 2 December 1937.

R. Miller/R. Boyfield letters, 12 September 1949 to 24 February 1950.

Miners' March, History of Case, File Number 21 (TUC Files).

H. Morrison, Labour Party/TUC letter, 16 February 1927.

W.J. Munro to E.P. Harries, 15 October 1940.

W.J. Munro to C.R. Shepherd (LP National Agent), 14 January 1936 (TUC Files).

National Union of General and Municipal Workers Head Office to E.P. Harries, 6 June 1940.

Newcastle TC Secretary to W. Citrine.

Oxford T&LC Secretary to TUC General Council, 16 February 1937.

Oxford T&LC to TUC, 20 December 1948.

E.H. Parker to V. Feather, 29 May 1941 (TUC Files).

E.H. Parker to H.V. Tewson, 18 November 1931.

E.H. Parker letter to TUC, 30 August 1937.

Texts and Events Referred to in the Book

A.A. Purcell to E.P. Harries, 25 October 1933.

A.A. Purcell to W. Citrine, 3 November 1933.

R.W. Robson in H. Tracey Papers (TUC) 30 August 1926.

R.W. Robson to local CPs, 18 February 1927.

F.W. Rudland, Birmingham TC letters, 15 March and 22 June 1937.

F.W. Rudland/W. Citrine letters, 17 and 18 November 1931.

Sheffield T&LC Secretary to E.P. Harries, 15 October 1940.

G.R. Shepherd to V. Feather, 1 February 1945.

W. Short to W. Citrine, for Newcastle & District TC, 29 March 1937.

Southampton TC Chairman to R. Boyfield, 20 February 1951.

C.G. Spragg to V. Feather, 3 January 1943.

C.G. Spragg to V. Feather, 15 April 1943.

C.G. Spragg to V. Feather, 9 November 1944.

C.G. Spragg to H.V. Tewson, 11 November 1942.

TCJCC Secretary to W.E. Harrison (CSCA, Liverpool), 8 October 1948 (TUC Files).

TUC General Council, *March of Unemployed*, 10 December 1928 (TUC File No.135, 'NUWM: History of Case').

H.V. Tewson to C.G. Spragg, 17 November 1942.

G.F. Tutt/V. Feather letters, 12 September 1942 and 24 October 1942.

T. Williamson (NUG&MW)/R. Boyfield letters, 22 March 1949 and 23 March 1949.

Willis/P. Allott, letters, 7 January 1943 and 8 January 1943.

Willis/V. Feather letters, 13 January 1942, 28 January 1942 and 30 January 1942.

J. Yarwood/H.V. Tewson letters, 29 September 1926 and 29 October 1926 (TUC Files).

J.P. Young, Chelmsford TC to V. Feather, January 1944 (TUC Files).

Endnotes

1. Christopher Hitchens, *New Statesman*, 6 October 1972.
2. S. & B. Webb, *The History of Trade Unionism* (1894 edition), pp224, 440.
3. S. & B. Webb, *Industrial Democracy*, 1897 pp269, 274–5.
4. A. Clinton, *The Trade Union Rank and File: Trades Councils in Britain 1900–40*, 1977.
5. A. Gramsci, *Selections from Prison Notebooks*, 1971, Chapter 1.
6. G.D.H. Cole, *An Introduction to Trade Unionism*, 1953, p134.
7. Ibid, pp138–9.
8. M. Turner-Samuels, *British Trade Unions*, 1949, pp80–86.
9. A. Flanders, *Trade Unions*, 1952 (1968 edition), pp66–9.
10. H.A. Clegg, *General Union: A Study of the NUGMW*, 1954, pp287, 296–7.
11. L. Bather, *A History of Manchester and Salford Trades Council*, PhD, 1956, p224.
12. E.L. Wigham, *Trade Unions*, 1956, pp68, 78–80.
13. B.C. Roberts, *TU Government and Administration in Great Britain*, 1956, pp451–2.
14. A. Flanders, *Trade Unions and Politics*, 1961, pp1–3.
15. H.A. Turner, *Trade Union Growth, Structure and Policy*, 1962, pp270–71, 316–17.

16 A. Clinton, op cit 1977, pp1-7, 137, 142-3, 181-4.
17 Cf. R. Hyman, *Industrial Relations, A Marxist Introduction*, 1975 (1979 edition), Chapter 6.
18 *Dictionary of Labour Biography*, Volume 1, 1972, pp275-8.
19 W.J. Munro, Manchester & Salford TC annual report (AR), 1935-36, p11.
20 Frank Jackson, see J. Stanley, *History Workshop Journal*, Number 9, 1980 pp212-3.
21 A. Tuckett, *The Blacksmiths' History*, 1974, p385.
22 J. Dowding, *Castleford Trades Council 1890-1965*, pp11-13.
23 *Dictionary of Labour Biography*, Volumes 1-4, 1972-77; B. Harrison in F. Keyworth, *History Workshop Journal*, 8, 1979, pp220-22.
24 *Dictionary of Labour Biography*, Volume 4, 1977.
25 Raphael Samuel, *The Lost World of British Communism*, 2006 (2017 edition).
26 S. MacIntyre, *Our History*, Number 73, 1979, p22.
27 C. Cockburn, *The Local State*, 1977, pp48-9.
28 B. Hennessy, 'Trade Unions and the British Labour Party', *American Political Science Review*, December 1955, pp1050-66.
29 T. Clarke and L. Clements, *Trade Unions under Capitalism*, 1977, pp133, 310-24.
30 P. Anderson, 'The Limits and Possibilities of Trade Union Action', in R. Blackburn and A. Cockburn (editors), *The Incompatibles: Trade Union Militancy and the Consensus*, 1967, pp263-80.
31 John Saville, 'Trades Councils and the Labour Movement', *Society for the Study of Labour History*, Number 14, 1967, pp29-34.
32 H. Gorter, *The Organisation of the Proletariat's Class Struggle*, 1921.
33 Jack London, *The Iron Heel*, 1907, p70.

34 TUC, *Model Rules for Trades Councils*, 1925, p1.
35 Ken Coates, *Essays in Industrial Democracy*, 1971, pp17, 37.
36 TUC, *Trades Councils Guide*, 1948, 'What Are Trades Councils?', p1.
37 M. Carritt, *Brighton Trades Council: The History of Sixty Years*, 1950, p18.
38 D. Large and R. Whitfield, *The Bristol Trades Council 1873-1973*, p18.
39 C. Bowles, Oxford T&LC AR, 1933, p1.
40 Oxford T&LC AR, 1934, p5.
41 J. Jacobs, 'Foreword' in G. Tate, *London Trades Council - A History*, 1950, p viii.
42 T. Quelch, 'Industrial London', *London Trade Union Handbook*, 1929-30, pp18-19.
43 T. Quelch, 'Anti-Political Tomfoolery on the London TC', 12 July 1940. See J.F. Clarke and T.P. McDermott, *The Newcastle and District Trades Council 1873-1973*, pp26, 41.
44 Edinburgh TC Executive Report, 1920 in H. Mackinven, *Edinburgh and District TC Centenary, 1859-1959*, p56.
45 TCJCC Secretary to W.E. Harrison (CSCA, Liverpool) 8 October 1948 (TUC Files).
46 R. Pope and F.W.A. Skerritt, *Ipswich & District Trades Council - A Short History, 1885-1967*, 1969, pp24, 28-9.
47 A. Tuckett, *A History of Swindon Trades Council 1891-1971*, pp70-71, 91-2.
48 W.J. Lane, *Thirty Years of Progress. A Short History of Luton, Dunstable & District Trades Council*, 1941, pp10-11.
49 P. Hall, *Blackpool Trades Council, 1891-1966*, 1966, p53.
50 B. Burke, *Rebels With a Cause - The History of Hackney Trades Council, 1900-1975*, 1975, p10.
51 G. Hicks, 'Introduction' in G.E. Cheshire, *Twenty-Five Years of Progress: History of Aylesbury & District Trades Council 1911-1936*, 1936, p11.

52 *Leicester Trades Council,1872–1972: Hats Off to the People*, 1974, p17.
53 *Peterborough & District Trades Council Diamond Jubilee, 1899–1959*, 1959, pp1–3.
54 *Huddersfield Trades Council 75th Anniversary 1885–1960*, 1960, p23.
55 W. Milne-Bailey (editor), *Trade Union Documents*, 1929, p27.
56 B. Pearce, 'Some Past Rank and File Movements', *Labour Review*, 1959, pp3–4.
57 B. Pribecevic, *The Shop Stewards Movement and Workers' Control, 1910–22*, 1959, p20.
58 J. Hinton, 'The Clyde Workers' Committee and The Dilution Struggle', in A. Briggs and J. Saville (editors) *Essays in Labour History*, 1960 (1971), pp152–84.
59 T. Quelch, *The Trades Councils: The Need for the Extension of Their Scope and Work*, 1922.
60 Labour Party Annual Conference Report (ACR) by the NEC, 1918, p23.
61 J. Cunnison, *Labour Organisation* 1930, p8, pp212–13.
62 H. Tracey, *Labour* Magazine, May 1924, pp39–40.
63 A. Conley, 'Trades Councils and the TUC', *London Trade Union Handbook* 1929; see also A.W. Humphrey, 'Trades Councils and the TUC', *The Post*, 28 June 1924; TCJCC Minutes, 10 July 1924.
64 TUC Report, September 1924 pp324–27.
65 TCJCC Minutes, 8 December 1924 pp1–3.
66 ACTC Report, 27 February 1925, A.B. Swales' Chairman's Address.
67 A. Clinton, op cit, 1977, pp111–13.
68 ACTC, 27 February 1925, R. Pennifold, Brighton TC; Resolution 2 from Darlington, Leeds and Cardiff, April 1925.
69 Trades Councils Report, July 1925; Bolton TC in TCJCC Minutes, 13 July 1925.

70 Lord Citrine, *Men and Work*, 1964, pp227-8. See also TCJCC Minutes, 20 November 1925 to 20 April 1926.
71 T. Mann, 'The Future of Trades Councils', *Trade Union Unity*, February 1926.
72 ACTC Report, 26 March 1926, A. Pugh's Chairman's Address.
73 W. Paul on a code of tactics, First CP Congress. See also EC to LP ACR September 1921.
74 T. Quelch, op cit, *Labour Monthly*, Volume 2, Number 3, March 1922 pp238-45.
75 J.T. Murphy, *Stop the Retreat! An Appeal to Trade Unionists*, 1922.
76 T. Quelch, op cit, and CP, *Congress Reports*, March and October 1922; also in *The Communist*, 27 July, 12 August, 28 October 1922, our italics.
77 *The Worker*, 18 November 1922.
78 Communist Industrial Policy 1922 p3; H. Dewar, *Communist Politics in Britain* 1976 pp28-34.
79 Communist Industrial Policy, 1922 pp9-12; J.T. Murphy, op cit, 1922, pp6-8.
80 NFTC Report 1923, 17 November 1923, pp1-9.
81 CP, *Handbook for CP Members*, 'Organisation', July 1923, pp9-10; H. Pollitt, 'The Trades Councils Conference', *Labour Monthly*, November 1923, pp280-81; J.A. Mahon, *Harry Pollitt*, 1976, p110.
82 CP Programme, *Workers' Weekly*, 30 November and 21 December 1923.
83 R.P. Dutt, 'The Future of the Trades Councils Conference', *Labour Monthly*, February 1924, Volume 6, Number 2, pp87-96.
84 Ibid. R.P. Dutt; see J.T. Murphy, *Communist Review*, January 1924.
85 Ibid. R.P. Dutt, see CP, *Manual of Party Training – Principles and Organisation*, 1924, pp28, pp47-8.

86 G. Hodgson, 'The CP and Parliamentary Democracy', in *Socialism and Parliamentary Democracy* 1977, pp138–79.
87 J.R. Campbell, *Communist Review*, October 1924; D. Carmichael and E.G. Rowlinson, TUC/TCs Preliminary Conference, 7 May 1924.
88 *Workers' Weekly*, 21 November 1923 on CP members in T&LCs.
89 *The Times*, 9 October 1924, on 'loyal TU members'; CP, *May Day Manifesto*, 1925.
90 NMM, *What the Minority Movement Stands For*, 1925.
91 ACTC 27 February 1925 Report, Resolutions 5 & 7; TCJCC Minutes on 'Organisation', 13 July 1925.
92 E.L. Wigham, *Trade Unions*, 1956 p67; NMM Conference, 30 August 1925; G.M. Godden, *The Communist Attack on Great Britain*, 1935, p34.
93 LP ACR, 1925, pp183–4 for E. Bevin on the CP; *The Times*, 5 October 1925, on CP 'Guerrilla Tactics' in TUs 'as a menace to the working class'.
94 TCJCC Minutes, 6 November 1925; B. Williams, *Communist Review*, December 1925; T. Quelch, *Communist Review*, January 1926 and *Communist Review*, Editorial, February 1926.
95 CP, *Brief Summary of District Organisation Reports*, 1926, pp1–6; G. Hardy, *Communist Work in the Trade Unions*, March 1926; and CI EC Resolution, March 1926.
96 NMM, *The Militant Trades Council – A Model Constitution for Trades Councils*, March 1926.
97 E. Burns, *The General Strike, May 1926 – Trades Councils in Action*, 1975 edition; LRD Monthly Circulars, December 1925, p276; May 1926 p107; June 1926 p123; Brighton TC, 5 May 1926.
98 Quote from A. Durr, *Who Were the Guilty? The General Strike in Brighton*, 1976, pp8–11, 16, 23.

99 Jack Dash, quoted in R. Robertson, *The General Strike in Southwark*, 1976, p29.
100 Julie Jacobs quote from Hackney in J. Skelley (editor), *The General Strike*, 1976, pp362-3.
101 J. Attfield and J. Lee, 'Deptford & Lewisham', in ibid, pp262-79.
102 G. Tate, *The London Trades Council, 1860-1950*, 1950, pp ii, 120-22.
103 J. Corbett, *The Birmingham Trades Council*, 1966, pp104, 122-3; Birmingham Public Libraries Social Sciences Dept/ WEA, *The Nine Days in Birmingham, The General Strike 4-12 May 1926*, 1976, pp3-4, 10.
104 Birmingham TC AR, 1927 pp5-6, J.E. Corrin, F.W. Rudland.
105 D. Large and R. Whitfield, *The Bristol Trades Council 1873-1973*, 1973, pp17-21.
106 R. Sewell, 'South Wales' in *Militant*, 9 April 1976.
107 A. Tuckett, *'Up With All's That Down'. A History of Swindon Trades Council, 1891-1971*, 1971, p63.
108 Quote from Manchester & Salford TC, 21 December 1923.
109 W.H. Barton, Report on Merseyside Council of Action, to TUC, May 1926.
110 Merseyside Council of Action, Strike Bulletins 5 and 6, 9 and 10 May 1926.
111 *Blackpool Trades Council 75th Anniversary*, 1966, pp29-31.
112 Trevor Davies, *Bolton, May 1926: A Review of the General Strike as it Affected Bolton & District*, 1976 pp1-2.
113 Quote from E.G. Rowlinson, Sheffield T&LC AR, 1926, pp8-13.
114 M. Ashraf, *Bradford Trades Council 1872-1972*, 1972, pp114-6; see also E. Silver, *Vic Feather T.U.C.*, 1973, pp55-6.
115 J. Dowding, *op cit*, 1965, p23; see also *Leeds Weekly Citizen*, June 1926.
116 Quote from *The Workers' Chronicle*, 14 May 1926; see also A. Mason, *The General Strike in the North-East*, 1970.

117 J. Yarwood/H.V. Tewson letters, 29 September and 29 October 1926 (TUC Files); J. Yarwood 1932 quoted in J.F. Clarke and T.P. McDermott, *Newcastle & District Trades Council: 1873–1973*, 1973, p27.
118 'General Strike in Middlesbrough', Bulletin 4, *Study of Labour History*, 1970.
119 Middlesbrough TC's Secretary Report, May 1926.
120 J. McLean, 'The General Strike in North Lanarkshire', in *Our History*, 1976, pp3–5, 9–12.
121 P. Kerrigan, 'From Glasgow' in J. Skelley (editor), op cit, 1976, pp315–21; H. McShane, *Glasgow and District Trades Council Centenary 1858–1958*, 1958, pp35–6. The TC had raised £3,216 for the miners by October 1926.
122 Leicester Trades Council, *Hats Off to the People 1872–1972*, 1974, p17.
123 J. Foster 'British Imperialism and the Labour Aristocracy', in J. Skelley, op cit, 1976, pp27–52.
124 J. Vincent, 'The General Strike of 1926', *The Listener*, Volume 91, 25 April 1974.
125 W. Citrine, Diary Entry, 4 May 1926, Lord Citrine, op cit, 1964, see pp177–80.
126 H.A. Clegg, 'Some Consequences of the General Strike', *Manchester Statistical Society*, 1954 p10: 'The path from revolutionary idealist to responsible administrator is well-worn.'
127 TCJCC Minutes, 15 June 1926; TUC Bournemouth ACR, Autumn 1926, p166, pp345, p465.
128 ACTC Final Agenda, May 1927.
129 J.T. Murphy, *A Revolutionary Workers' Government*, 1929 pp10–16.
130 A.A. Purcell, *The Trades Councils and Local Working Class Movement*, 13 December 1930 p14.
131 J.T. Murphy, *Modern Trade Unionism*, 1935, pp102, 149.

132 G.D.H. Cole, *Trade Unionism Today*, 1939, pp187-8; see also G. Allison, 'The General Strike', *Communist Review*, May 1946; K. Knowles, *Strikes: A study in industrial conflict with special reference to the British experience between 1911-1947*, 1952, p112 on the TUC in 1926.
133 A. Hutt, *British Trade Unionism* 1962 edition, p113.
134 Chris Harman, 'The General Strike', *International Socialism Journal, Series 1, Number 48*, June/July 1971, p26.
135 J. Cohen, 'Marxism and Reformism in the General Strike', *Marxism Today*, May 1976.
136 TCJCC Minutes, 5 August 1926.
137 E. Trory, *Soviet Trade Unions and the General Strike*, 1975 p4 and p47.
138 National Strike Special Conference, 20 January 1927; see also Lord Citrine, op cit, 1964, pp316-8.
139 T. Quelch, 'The Importance of the Trades Councils'; *Labour Monthly*, May 1926; F.H. Peet, 'Our Tasks in the Trades Councils', *Communist Review*, May 1926.
140 Ibid, F.H. Peet, pp34-38; Editorial, *Communist Review*, June 1926, pp53-6; and CI EC, 'Theses on the Lessons of the British General Strike', *Communist Review*, July 1926.
141 W. Mellor, 'Towards a General Staff', *Direct Action*, 1920, pp111-22.
142 A. Paterson, *The Weapon of the Strike*, 1922, pp259-79.
143 V.L. Allen, 'The Re-organisation of the TUC 1918-27', *British Journal of Sociology*, Volume XI, March 1960.
144 A. Flanders, *Trade Unions and Politics*, 1961, p12.
145 Sheffield T&LC AR, 1923, President E.G. Rowlinson.
146 J.E. Corrin, F.W. Rudland, Birmingham TC AR, 1924-5, p8.
147 Manchester & Salford TC AR, 1924, pp3-4.
148 W. Citrine, *Labour* Journal, May 1943, quote p258.
149 ACTC Report, February 1925, A.B. Swales; *Labour Magazine*, December 1926, p378 on TCs.

150 ACTC Report, 28 May 1938.
151 Edited by M. Cole, Volume 1, *Beatrice Webb Diaries, 1912–23*, 1952, p19.
152 TUC Circular 48 'Affiliated Membership', June 1926.
153 TCJCC on 'Workers' Sports Organisation', 4 June 1926; TCJCC Minutes, 15 June 1926.
154 Circular 68 to TCs 'The Mining Situation', 21 August 1926; Circular 74 'Financial Assistance for Miners', 31 August 1926.
155 TUC Bournemouth Report September 1926, pp163-7.
156 Circular 2 to TCs, 'Financial Assistance for Miners', 26 October 1926; TCJCC Minutes, 17 November 1926.
157 See A. Steel-Maitland Memorandum, 22 November 1926. In 1913, there were 329 TCs, by 1925 480 TCs, *Labour Magazine*, December 1926, p378.
158 Sheffield T&LC AR, 1927, President E.G. Rowlinson, pp8-9.
159 *Industrial Review*, January 1927; TCJCC Minutes, 18 January and 22 February 1927.
160 Circular 19, 'Industrial Review', 18 January 1927; quote from Brighton TC AR, 1927, p6.
161 TCJCC Minutes, 26 April 1927; Circular 36 'Government anti-Trade Union Legislation – National Campaign', 8 April 1927.
162 ACTC TCJCC Report by G. Hicks, 27 May 1927.
163 *Labour Magazine*, July 1927, pp122-3; Brighton TC Minutes, 15 June 1927.
164 *Industrial Review*, July 1927, p1; TCJCC Minutes, 28 July 1927.
165 Manchester & Salford TC AR, 1927.
166 Birmingham TC AR, 1927, pp6-7.
167 Edinburgh T&LC Executive Report, 1927.
168 G.E. Cheshire, op cit, 1936, p30; P. Hall, op cit, 1966 p32; *Huddersfield Trades And Industrial Council 75th Anniversary* (1885–1960), 1960, op cit, p11.

169 TUC Industrial Conference Report, 1928, pp45–50.
170 TUC Edinburgh ACR, Autumn 1927, General Council Report, p112.
171 *Industrial Review*, August 1927, p1, and September 1927, p2; Circular 9 'Organisation of Women and Young Workers', 11 November 1927.
172 *Industrial Review*, November 1927 p7; TCJCC Minutes, 19 December 1927.
173 A. Conley, 'The Trades Council Movement', *Industrial Review*, March 1928.
174 Brighton TC AR, 1928 p15; Circular 31 'Trade Union Recruitment Effort', 13 April 1928.
175 ACTC Report with G. Hicks, 19 May 1928; E.L. Wigham, *Strikes and the Government 1893–1974*, 1976, Chapter 5 'The Challenge Abandoned 1926–1939', pp65–82.
176 *Industrial Review*, 'Trades Councils' Activities', November 1928.
177 Quote by T. Quelch, op. cit., 1929–30, pp17–21.
178 Sheffield T&LC AR, 1929, p7.
179 ACTC, Ben Tillett, Chairman's Address, 29 June 1929.
180 TCJCC Minutes, 21 August 1929; TUC Belfast ACR, Autumn 1929, pp114–20.
181 A.A. Purcell, Manchester & Salford TC AR, 1929, p5.
182 Brighton TC Minutes, 15 January 1930; Circular 28 'New Daily Herald Circulation Campaign', 10 January 1930; and J. Cunnison, op. cit., 1930, p214.
183 Sheffield T&LC AR, 1930, p7.
184 Birmingham TC AR, 1930, p7 and Brighton TC Minutes, 16 April 1930.
185 ACTC Report 1930, Chairman's Address; Circular 72, 'Textile Dispute', 30 May 1930.
186 Quote from TUC Nottingham ACR, Autumn 1930 p107; see also Bristol TC AR, 1930, p1.

187 *Labour Magazine*, October 1930, p257; and *Manchester Guardian*, 25 August 1930.
188 Circular 11, 'Affiliation of Branches to Trades Councils' 9 October 1930.
189 Quote in Circular 34,' Trade Union Organisation', 4 December 1930; TCJCC Minutes, 11 December 1930.
190 Oxford T&LC AR 1931, p4.
191 Quote in Sheffield T&LC AR, 1931 p6.
192 Circular 54, 'Trade Disputes and Trade Unions (Amendment) Bill 1931', 3 February 1931.
193 Quote from the 'People's Congress' by Manchester & Salford TC, 18 March 1931; see also A.A. Purcell, *The Economics of a Madhouse*, 1931.
194 ACTC Report, 30 May 1931, A. Conley speech.
195 A.M. Wall, 'Memorandum on The Political Situation' to London TC, November 1931.
196 Manchester & Salford TC AR, 1931 p5: see also E.H. Parker to H.V. Tewson, 18 November 1931.
197 E. Bevin, 'The Election and the Trade Union Movement', *Labour Magazine*, December 1931.
198 Quote from E.P. Harries, 'Trades Councils in Conference', *Labour Magazine*, June 1932, p69.
199 ACTC Report, TCJCC Report, 28 May 1932.
200 TCJCC Minutes, 8 September 1932.
201 Quote from Oxford T&LC AR, February 1933, p1.
202 Circular 83, 'Propaganda Weeks', 2 March 1933.
203 W. Citrine, *New Clarion*, 24 June 1933.
204 J.R. Clynes, *Memoirs: 1924–37*, 1937, p280; G.D.H. Cole, *A Study Guide on Socialist Policy*, 1933, pp9–10.
205 Quotes from TUC Brighton Report September 1933, pp64–5, 370–79; *New Clarion*, 16 March 1933.
206 Manchester & Salford TC EC, 'Working Class Unity', 10 October 1933; A.A. Purcell to E.P. Harries, 25 October 1933 and to W. Citrine, 3 November 1933.

207 Manchester & Salford TC, 'Local Survey and Record' Circular, November 1933.
208 Quote from Manchester & Salford TC AR, 1933, pp4-5.
209 Mr Gardiner, Hampshire & Isle of Wight & Dorset Federation of TCs, 6 January 1934.
210 Circular 88, 'Trade Union Recruitment Weeks', 8 March 1934.
211 Manchester & Salford TC AR, 1934, pp2, 8-9; ACTC Report 31 August 1934.
212 London TC Memorandum, 24 May 1934, quote from A.M. Wall; H. Clay, 'Tolpuddle and Today' in *Socialist Leaguer*, July 1934.
213 TUC Weymouth ACR, Autumn 1934, pp96, 102, 142; W.J. Lane, op cit 1941, pp18-19.
214 E. Friend, *London Trades Council History* 1935, pp101-5; see also W. Citrine, 'In Defence of Freedom: Fascism at Home and Abroad', *Labour Magazine*, June 1933.
215 TUC Weymouth ACR, Autumn 1934, pp203-5, 371-3; see also LP ACR, 1934, pp183-4 and pp201-2.
216 Circular 15, 'Organisational Activities', 25 October 1934; see also R.A. Dahl, 'Workers' Control of Industry and the British Labour Party', *American Political Science Review*, Volume XLI 1947, pp875-900.
217 'Judex', *The Socialist Leaguer*, Number 6, December 1934.
218 R. Groves, *Trades Councils in the Fight for Socialism*, 1935, pp6-9.
219 Oxford T&LC AR, 1935, p1.
220 J.T. Murphy, *Trade Unions and Socialism*, June 1936.
221 Birmingham TC AR 1935; Southampton TC AR 1935; see also A. Bullock, *The Life and Times of Ernest B Bevin*, Volume 1, 1960, p589; and R. Miliband, *Parliamentary Socialism*, 1961 p206.
222 Circular 97, 'Trade Union Recruitment', 11 April 1935, ACTC Draft Memorandum, 1935, pp1-2; TCJCC Minutes,

19 March 1935; and Circular 100, 'Organisation of Women', 11 April 1935, our italics.
223 ACTC Report, W. Kean, 25 May 1935.
224 'Socialists and the Trade Unions', *Socialist Leaguer* Number 11, May 1935.
225 W. Citrine, Foreword to Manchester & Salford TC AR, 1935, p1.
226 Quote from Lord W. Citrine, op cit, 1964, p274 and p315.
227 E. Bevin, LP ACR, 1935, p243; Circular 13, 'Recruiting Assistance to Trades Councils', 24 October 1935; W. Rust, 'The Issues before the TUC', *Labour Monthly*, September 1935, pp526-9.
228 Manchester & Salford TC AR, 1935, pp3, p9.
229 Quote by W.J. Munro in ibid, p4; W.J. Munro to C.R. Shepherd (LP National Agent), 14 January 1936 (TUC Files).
230 Brighton TC Minutes, 18 March 1936.
231 London TC Conference 'The Trade Unions and the War Menace', February 1936.
232 Circular 131 to TCs, 'Help the Spanish Workers!', 27 July 1936; Sheffield T&LC AR, 1937, p8.
233 TCJCC Minutes, 30 June 1936; Circular 47, 'Trades Councils and Industrial Disputes', 28 January 1937.
234 Circular 135, 'TCs and Political Activities', by W. Citrine, pp6-8; see also R. Groves, 'The Menace to Unions', *The Socialist*, Number 11, October 1936; and Birmingham TC AR, 1936 p7.
235 E. Bevin, December 1936, qu. A. Bullock, op cit, 1960, p600.
236 TCJCC Minutes,17 November 1936; ACTC Report, 29 May 1937, TUC Memorandum.
237 Circular 59, 'Local Trade Union Recruitment Campaigns', 25 February 1937; Southampton TC AR, 1937 p2.
238 ACTC 29 May 1937, E. Bevin.

239 Circular 10, 'Talks by Civil Service Officials', 30 September 1937; TCJCC Minutes, 15 December 1937.
240 Manchester & Salford TC AR 1937, quote p8.
241 Sheffield T&LC 1 June 1938; E.P. Harries to A.E. Hobson; see also Circular 12 'Affiliation of Branches of Breakaway Unions', 12 May 1938.
242 ACTC 25 May 1938, W. Citrine.
243 Sheffield T&LC 1938, p7; Sheffield EC Report, 1938, pp11–13.
244 Circular 59, 'National Voluntary Service' 18 January 1939; Circular 64, 'NVS Local Committees', 31 January 1939.
245 ACTC On 'National Voluntary Service', 20 May 1939, TCJCC.
246 Birmingham TC AR, 1939, p8.
247 ACTC Report 20 May 1939; H. Pollitt, 'Defence of the People' (CP), February 1939.
248 Circular 80, 'Trade Union Propaganda Campaigns', 9 March 1939; Lord Citrine, op cit, 1964, p372.
249 ACTC Report, 20 May 1939, Camberwell TC delegate.
250 Circular 116, 'National Voluntary Service Representatives on Local Committees', 25 May 1939.
251 Kenneth O. Morgan, *Britain Since 1945: The People's Peace*, 2001 (2021 edition), p20.
252 C.G. Spragg, 'Trades Councils as Watch-Dogs', *Labour*, November 1941, pp91–3; TUC Bridlington ACR, Autumn 1939, pp121–2, p136.
253 Sheffield T&LC AR, 1939, C.S. Darvill.
254 Circular 5, 'Local Committees in War-Time', 13 September 1939.
255 W.J. Lane, op cit, 1941, p26; Edinburgh T&LC AR, 1939.
256 Sheffield T&LC AR, 1939, p10.
257 Circular 13 'Labour Problems in War-Time', 13 October

1939; Circular 27, 'Trade Unionism During War', 23 November 1939.
258 Birmingham TC AR, 1939, p6.
259 Circular 81, 'Representation upon Food Control Committees', 30 May 1940.
260 Circular 52, 'Citizens' Advice Bureaux', 8 February 1940.
261 J. Corbett, op cit, 1966, p149.
262 TCJCC Minutes, 26 July 1940; W. Citrine, *The TUC in Wartime* (on 'Disruptive Trades Councils'), June 1940, p13.
263 ACTC Report 27 July 1940, quote Darlington TC delegate. (our italics).
264 Ibid. quote by C.G. Spragg. Only 27 TC delegates attended 'The People's Convention', 12 January 1941 (of 2,234 delegates); see S. Jeffreys, 'The CP and the Rank and File', *International Socialism* Journal, Series one Winter 1980–81, p15.
265 Manchester & Salford TC 1940, quote p7; Circular 13, 'Labour Supply', 26 November 1940, by H.V. Tewson, versus R.P. Dutt, 'We Fight for LIFE' (CP Policy Series Number 1), November 1940.
266 London TC AR 1941, quote; see also CP, 'The CP in War-Time', April 1940.
267 E.H. Parker to V. Feather, 29 May 1941 (TUC Files).
268 Birmingham TC AR 1941; Pat Sloan, 'The Revolution for Socialism: 23 Years of Soviet Power!' in *Russia Today Society*, 1940.
269 Manchester & Salford TC AR, 16 October 1941, quote pp5–7; LRD Fact Service July 1941, p111.
270 C.G. Spragg, op cit, November 1941, quote pp91–2; see R. Willis, 'Trades Councils in War-Time', *Labour* Journal, October 1941, pp62–3; L. Powell, 'JPCs', *Labour Monthly*, December 1941.

271 Dover TC, 'In the Front Line', *Labour*, December 1941, quote p117.
272 LRD Fact Service, 'Trades Councils and Production', 16 January 1942.
273 Sheffield T&LC AR, 1942, p3.
274 TCJCC Minutes, 16 March 1942.
275 F. Day to W. Citrine, 24 May 1942; Circular 59 'Trade Councils' Organisation' 26 February 1942 and 'Trades Councils and the War Effort', *Labour* Journal, July 1942, pp343–4.
276 TCJCC Minutes, 25 June 1942.
277 For example Sheffield T&LC AR, 1942 pp8–9.
278 London TC Minutes, 10 October 1942, quote; note also J. Owen, 'War in the Workshops', 1942 (CP pamphlet); and Circular 6, 'Works Production Committees', 2 October 1942.
279 Midland Federation of Trades Councils Report, 17 October 1942; Circular 11, 'Trades Councils and War-Time Committees', 29 October 1942.
280 Birmingham TC AR 1942, p7; Circular 27, 'Appeals to Trades Councils', 3 December 1943.
281 Sheffield T&LC AR 1942, p1.
282 ACTC On 'Beveridge Report', 29 May 1943; W. Gallacher, 'The Beveridge Report', *Labour Monthly*, January 1943.
283 ACTC 'On Post-War Reconstruction' 29 May 1943; Birmingham TC AR, 1943, pp3–6.
284 Bertrand Russell, *History of Western Philosophy*, 1946 (1947 edition), p818.
285 *Southern Daily Echo*, February 1943; 'Trade Unionists in the Forces', *Labour* Journal, March 1943, p218.
286 ACTC, 29 May 1943, J. Marchbank; Circular 4 'Food Control Committees' Order', 23 September 1943.
287 ACTC, ibid, R. Willis; *Labour* Journal June 1943, p300.
288 ACTC ibid, W. Citrine on 'The Trade Disputes Act'.

289 London TC AR, 1943.
290 TCJCC Minutes, 20 August 1943; LRD Fact Service, 22 October 1942 and 19 November 1943.
291 T. Judt, *Thinking the Twentieth Century* 2012, p340.
292 Sheffield T&LC AR, 1943, p4.
293 Birmingham TC AR, 1943 p3, 8; G. Walpole, *Management and Men*, 1944, p43.
294 Circular 67, 'Trades Councils and Policy', 2 March 1944.
295 LRD Fact Service, 31 March to 21 April 1944; TCJCC Minutes, 18 April 1944.
296 ACTC Report, 20 May 1944; TCJCC Minutes, 28 November 1944.
297 ACTC, 20 May 1944, H.N. Harrison.
298 LRD Fact Service, June 1944, Hatfield TC quote; TCJCC Minutes, 6 June 1944; W. Citrine, *The TUC in Wartime*, June 1944, pp29–30.
299 Birmingham TC Statement, 4 December 1944, p2; Manchester & Salford TC AR, 1944, p3.
300 ACTC Report, July 1945, on 'Post-war Reconstruction'.
301 W. Citrine, *The TUC in Wartime*, April 1945, quote p32.
302 Discussed in TCJCC Minutes, 27 May 1945.
303 ACTC Report July 1945, J. Benstead and E.P. Harries.
304 TCJCC Minutes, 6 June 1944.
305 Manchester & Salford TC AR, 1945, quote p18.
306 F. Thraves, Sheffield T & LC AR, 1945, pp6–7.
307 Blackpool TUC Report, September 1945, p89.
308 S. Hannah: *A Party with Socialists In It: A History of the Labour Left*, 2018, p80.
309 Sheffield T&LC AR, 1946, quote pp5–6.
310 Manchester & Salford TC AR 1946, H.E. Newbold, p5, our italics.
311 Circular 64, 'Ministry of Labour LECs' 14 March 1946, Brighton September 1946, p45.

312 TUC, *Details of the Method of the Election for the TCJCC*, 1946; TCJCC Minutes, 12 August 1946.
313 ACTC 1946 H.N. Harrison Report; 'Blueprints of the New Britain', *Labour* Journal, July 1946, p342; Circular 104 'TCs' Propaganda Campaigns', 27 June 1946.
314 Kenneth O. Morgan, op cit, 2021, p34.
315 Birmingham TC 1946 AR, quote p7; TUC, *Trade Union Structure and Closer Unity*, March 1947.
316 Manchester & Salford TC AR, 1946, quote from H.E. Newbold, pp19–20.
317 Kenneth O. Morgan, op cit, 2021, p39.
318 ACTC Report 1947, quote from Portsmouth TC; *Industrial Relations Handbook* Number 3, 1949.
319 Kenneth O. Morgan, op cit, 2021, p40.
320 Circular 61, 'Industrial and Political Funds' 27 March 1947; Manchester & Salford TC AR, 1946: 'The Man Who Throws the Spanner' depicting the unofficial striker throwing the spanner into 'TU administration'.
321 ACTC, 31 May 1947, G.W. Thomson, H.N. Harrison, speeches.
322 Midland Federation of Trades Councils Report, October 1947.
323 Circular 32, 'Registration of Trades Councils' 8 December 1947; Bristol TC AR 1947, p4.
324 'Trades Councils Register', *Labour* Journal, February 1948, p187; TUC Margate Report, September 1948 p105; ACTC, 5 June 1948, TCJCC Report.
325 TUC 'Trades Councils' Guide' 1948; quote from TCJCC Minutes, 5 January 1948.
326 Circular 70 'Conferences on the National Insurance Scheme and the NHS', 28 February 1948, H. V. Tewson at ACTC, 5 June 1948.
327 Kenneth O. Morgan, op cit, 2021, p72 and p42. (our italics).

328 ACTC Report, 5 June 1948, H.V. Tewson.
329 ACTC ibid, opening speeches.
330 Birmingham TC AR, 1948, p8.
331 LRD Fact Service, 11 June 1948, quote from Deptford TC.
332 S. Hannah, op cit, 2018, pp83–4.
333 TUC Margate Report, September 1948, pp103–4,330–31; TCJCC Minutes, 16 August 1948.
334 Manchester & Salford TC, 1948, H.E. Newbold p19; J.H. Bingham, Sheffield T&LC AR, 1948, p5; *Labour Research* 'Trades Councils Today', October 1948.
335 Quote from TCJCC Report, ACTC 28 May 1949; see also Bridlington TUC ACR, Autumn 1949, pp102–3.
336 Hugh Thomas, *An Unfinished History of the World*, 1979 (1981 edition), pp519–29.
337 R.W. Robson, in H. Tracey Papers (TUC), 30 August 1926.
338 Lord Citrine, *Two Careers*, 1967, p27; see Raphael Samuel, 'British Marxist Historians', *New Left Review*, Number 120, March 1980, pp49–50.
339 T. Quelch, 'Building the Party', *Communist Review*, August 1926.
340 S. Sebag Montefiore, *Stalin: The Court of the Red Tsar,* 2003 (2014 edition), pp88–9.
341 TUC Bournemouth ACR, Autumn 1926, A. Conley, pp341–2; G. Hardy, 'The Fight for a Militant Trade Union Movement', *Communist Review*, September 1926.
342 J.R. Campbell, A.R. Stewart, *Communist Review*, December 1926, pp362–3, p381.
343 *Workers' Weekly*, 21 January 1927; J.T. Murphy op. cit. 1935, pp28–9.
344 H. Pollitt, 'The Conference of Executives', *Labour Monthly*, February 1927, pp100–4.
345 CP, *Handbook*, 'Local Organisation', January 1927 pp10, 28–9; see S. MacIntyre, 'British Labour, Marxism and

Working Class Apathy in the 1920s', *History Journal*, Volume 20, Number 2, 1977.
346 H. Morrison, LP/TUC letter, 16 February 1927; R.W. Robson to local CPs, 18 February 1927.
347 History of NMM, TUC files; see also *Industrial Review*, August 1927.
348 TCJCC Minutes, 22 February 1927, GC members; TUC Edinburgh Conference Report, September 1927, pp151-2.
349 ACTC, 31 March 1927, NMM Circular by H. Pollitt.
350 J.T. Murphy, 'Anti-Communist Propaganda and the Task of the English Proletariat', *Pravda*, March 1927; I. Silone, *The God That Failed: Six Studies in Communism* 1950, p104 on J.T. Murphy.
351 R.P. Arnot, *Twenty Years: The Policy of the CPGB*, 1940, p27; T. Dickson, *Scottish Capitalism*, 1980, p281.
352 H. Morrison, London Labour Party, 11 March 1927; *Lansbury's Labour Weekly*, 26 March 1927.
353 London TC Fraction, 'Instructions', 10 March 1927 (in TUC files on London TC).
354 *Workers' Life*, 3 June 1927; London TC, 11 August 1927, A.M. Wall.
355 A.M. Wall, 'The London Trades Council – Some Difficulties and the Remedy', *Industrial Review*, February 1928; MM EC, 4 April 1927; TCJCC Minutes, 26 April 1927.
356 TCJCC, 28 July 1927; TUC Edinburgh CR, September 1927, pp151-2.
357 S.W. Lerner, *Breakaway Unions and the Small Trade Union*, 1961, p106; TCJCC Minutes, 21 February 1928.
358 W. Citrine, 'Democracy or Disruption', *Labour Magazine*, December 1927, pp342-5; CP Congress Report, 1927.
359 W. Citrine *Labour Magazine*, March 1928, pp487-91.
360 W. Citrine, *Labour Magazine*, June 1928, pp55-9.

361 J.A. Mahon, 'Mr Citrine and Trade Union Democracy', *Labour Monthly*, May 1928, pp295-302; S. Hannah, op cit, 2018, p92.

362 NMM EC Circular, 'The Future of the Trades Councils ~ An issue that must be faced', May 1928.

363 R. Groves, *The Balham Group*, 1974 p16; J.T. Murphy, *The Communist*, March 1928, p161.

364 J.C. Clews, *Communist Propaganda Techniques*, 1964, pp283-4 on 31 CP 'front' organisations 1920-50.

365 Birmingham TC Minutes, 20 February, 17 April and 17 July 1929.

366 *Industrial Review*, April 1929, pp6-7; TCJCC Minutes, 28 June 1929.

367 *The Worker* 19 July 1929; see H. Pollitt, 'The Future of Revolutionary Trade Unionism', in *Labour Monthly*, August 1929.

368 TUC Belfast CR, September 1929 pp169-78.

369 J. McDonald, *Trades Councils*, 1930, pp6, 10-14.

370 A.A. Purcell, *The Trades Councils and the Local Working Class Movement* December op. cit. 1930, p7.

371 Birmingham TC AR, 1931, p8.

372 Brighton TC Minutes, 16 August 1931; E. Trory, '*Between the Wars*', 1974, pp25-7. See Bob Darke, *The Communist Technique in Britain*,1952, p32.

373 Sheffield T&LC AR, 1932, pp6-9, F. Thraves; S. Hannah, op cit, 2018, p53.

374 T. E. Eaton to E.P. Harries, 21 July 1933 and 15 September 1933 (TUC Files).

375 Manchester & Salford TC AR, 1932, A.A. Purcell, pp6-10; Quote from J.A. Mahon, 'Unity Versus the Manoeuvres of Citrine and Co', *Labour Monthly*, August 1933.

376 TUC Brighton ACR, Autumn 1933, pp327-9 for delegates' comments on this debate.

377　*News Chronicle*, 19 October 1933.
378　M. Ferguson, 'Breaking Through: Mass Work in Bradford', *Communist Review*, October 1933, pp393–5.
379　G. Renshaw, *Communist Review*, December 1933; P. Piratin, *Our Flag Stays Red*, 1948 (1978 edition), p14.
380　G.M. Godden, op. cit. 1935.
381　*Southampton Daily Echo, 20 July 1934*.
382　Circular 120, 'Communist and Other Bodies', 5 June 1934.
383　*Southern Daily Echo*, 21 June 1934; R. Chick to W. Citrine, 21 June 1934 (TUC Files).
384　R. Chick/W. Citrine/E.P. Harries letters, 22 June 1934, 23 June 1934; Southampton TC AR, 1934, pp1–2.
385　E.P. Harries to F.M. Lees, 23 October 1934; Oxford T&LC AR February 1934; on BUF, Tim Tate, *Hitler's British Traitors: The Secret History of Spies, Saboteurs, and Fifth Columnists*, 2018 (2019 edition), p91.
386　Brighton TC Minutes, 20 June 1934, 21 November 1934, 19 December 1934; *Daily Worker*, 6 January 1934.
387　ACTC Report, 31 August 1934.
388　TUC Weymouth ACR, Autumn 1934, pp211, 232–4, pp348–51 for the debates.
389　E. Bevin, LP ACR, 1934, pp140–41.
390　R.P. Dutt, *Labour Monthly*, October 1934.
391　TCJCC Minutes, 19 October 1934.
392　TUC General Council, *On Disruptive Bodies*, 24 October 1934.
393　Reverend T.J. Fitzgerald, 'The Decline of Communism in Great Britain', *Clergy Review*, January 1935, pp103–5.
394　TUC Scotland ACR, 15 February 1935; CP Congress Report, February 1935.
395　TCJCC Minutes, 22 November 1934.
396　Ibid, with A.E. Hobson for Sheffield T&LC.
397　*Communist Review*, 'Problems of Party Organisation', December 1934, p220.

398 TCJCC Minutes, 10 January 1935; R. Black, *Stalinism in Britain. A Trotskyist Analysis*, 1970, p61.
399 J.R. Campbell, 'Some Aspects of Our Industrial Work', *Communist Review*, January 1935.
400 TCJCC, 'Summary of Replies from TCs regarding Circular 16', 19 March 1935.
401 *Labour Monthly*, 'A Discussion on Trade Union Problems and Policy', April 1935, pp243-8.
402 E.P. Harries, TUC General Council, *Action Against Disruptive Bodies*, 21 May 1935, pp1-3.
403 L. Cannon, *The Road from Wigan Pier*, 1973, p61 on then CP member Les Cannon.
404 C. Dukes, ACTC AR 25 March 1935.
405 J. Sheffield, 'Damping Down? A Word to Trade Unionists', *The Socialist Leaguer*, Number 12, June 1935.
406 Idris Cox, *Communist Review*, July 1935, p127.
407 *Labour Monthly*, 'Trade Union Problems and Policy', July 1935, pp431-7.
408 CP Congress 1935 'A Call to All Workers'; *Daily Worker*, 5 July 1935.
409 D.F. Springhall, J.R. Campbell articles, *Communist Review*, August 1935, pp143, p152. See T.H. James, 'Some Mistakes in United Front Work', in the same, pp153-4.
410 TUC Margate ACR, Autumn 1935, General Council Report from E. Bevin, pp110-2 and also G. Hicks, p262.
411 The General Council claimed 'acceptance' from 353 TCs.
412 CP letter, 'The Communist Party and the Trade Unions', 12 September 1935, H. Tracey Papers.
413 J.A. Mahon, 'Trade Unionism and Communism – An Open Letter', 1935, p16.
414 ACTC, 23 June 1936, C. Dukes; see also E. Burns, *Communist Affiliation*, 1936.

415 P. Allott, *Labour Monthly*, September 1936 p555; TUC Plymouth ACR, Autumn 1936, p270.
416 National Council of Labour, 'British Labour and Communism' 1936, pp6-7, 12.
417 TUC Plymouth ACR, Autumn 1936, pp423-37.
418 TCJCC Memorandum, 'Trades Councils – Their Industrial Functions and Activities', 17 November 1936.
419 Circular 29, 'The Witchcraft Trial in Moscow', 3 December 1936; E. Bevin to G.D.H. Cole, 25 January 1937.
420 D. Melville, in *Discussion*, Number 12, February 1937 (CP) and F. Clay, 'Trade Union Work in Portsmouth' in the same issue.
421 F.W. Rudland, Birmingham TC letters, 15 March and 22 June 1937; W. Citrine, 'What the TUC Is Doing', 1 March 1937; A.L. Horner, 'Trade Unions and Unity' (CP), April 1937, p8.
422 *Labour's Northern Voice*, January 1938 p3; TCJCC Minutes, 20 July 1937; *Daily Worker*, 21 January 1938.
423 Brighton TC Minutes, 16 February 1938, but see D. Hyde, *I Believed: The Autobiography of a Former British Communist*, 1951, pp65-6.
424 J.R. Campbell, 'Chamberlain over the TUC', *Labour Monthly*, October 1938, pp618-9; CP, *Trade Unions Forward*, October 1938, pp13-5.
425 TUC Blackpool ACR, Autumn 1938, p119; TCJCC Minutes, 19 July 1938.
426 TCJCC Minutes, 14 February 1939, 18 April 1939 and 16 May 1939; ACTC 1939, T. Hallett on 'Trades Councils and Breakaway Unions'.
427 See G. Rude, 'The Trade Unions and the People's Movement', *Labour Monthly*, December 1938, p748; A.W. Brady, 'Trade Unions and National Service', *Labour Monthly*, May 1939, pp288-289; H. Pollitt, 'Can Conscription Save Peace?', May 1939 (CP).

428 D. Gluckstein, *A People's History of the Second World War*, 2012, pp8–9.
429 L. Fischer, *The God That Failed*, 1950, p225; W. Kendall, *The Communist Party of Great Britain*, 1974, p121.
430 CP Draft Programme, August 1939; E. Trory, *Imperialist War*, 1977, p27, pp138, 200.
431 Sheffield T&LC AR, 1940; Churchill wanted communists interned, see W L S Churchill, *The Second World War*, Volume 2, 1949, pp39, 60.
432 London TC AR, 1941.
433 TCJCC Minutes, September 1939. See also CP, *Manifesto*, 2 September 1939.
434 Brighton TC Minutes, 20 September 1939.
435 TCJCC Minutes, 12 September 1939 to 8 January 1940; CP, *The Party Voice*, October 1939, p3.
436 *Daily Worker*, 30 September 1939; CP, *War! Communist Policy*, 1939 (Marx Memorial Library).
437 R.P. Dutt, 'Marxism and the War', *Labour Monthly*, October 1939.
438 CP Industrial Bureau Report, 5 November 1939.
439 Brighton Conference, 'Labour and the War Economy', 3 December 1939.
440 National Council of Labour Circular, 7 December 1939; R.P. Dutt, *Labour Monthly*, December 1939.
441 CP Congress, Sussex County, 17 March 1940; Brighton TC Minutes, 20 March and 17 April 1940.
442 TCJCC Minutes, 4 March, 15 April, and 13 June 1940.
443 *Daily Worker*, 3 and 7 April 1940.
444 *Industrial News*, 16 April 1940.
445 London TC AR, 1940 Editorial, 'How to Deal with Disruption'.
446 *Daily Worker*, 2 and 5 May 1940.
447 CP, *Statement*, 9 May 1940.

448 National Union of General and Municipal Workers Head Office to E.P. Harries, 6 June 1940; see also Sheffield T&LC Secretary to E.P. Harries, 15 October 1940 and E.P. Harries to NUR Sheffield Number 7 Branch, 18 October 1940.
449 V. Gollancz, *The Betrayal of the Left*, 1941, pp65–70; *Daily Worker*, 29 June and 3 July 1940.
450 T. Quelch, 12 July 1940.
451 ACTC Report, 27 July 1940, W. Citrine.
452 LRD Fact Service, 2 August 1940.
453 TUC Southport ACR, Autumn 1940, pp108, 320–22, our italics.
454 *Daily Worker*, 11 September 1940, 28 September 1940.
455 P. Kerrigan, 'The Trade Unions: What Now?', *Labour Monthly*, November 1940, pp592–5.
456 W.J. Munro to E.P. Harries, 15 October 1940 (TUV Archives).
457 V. Feather to W.J. Munro, 18 October 1940; Manchester & Salford TC AR, 1940, W.J. Munro, p3.
458 W.J. Munro, Manchester & Salford TC meeting. TCJCC Minute 9a, 15 December 1940.
459 *Daily Worker*, 23 December 1940.
460 Manchester & Salford TC AR, 1940 p5; LRD, January 1941, p15 on Cardiff TC.
461 H. Pollitt, 'The People's Parliament', *Labour Monthly*, December 1940, pp622–3, our italics.
462 The People's Convention', 13 January 1941, pp1–2; W. Gallacher, *The Last Memoirs of Willie Gallacher*, 1966, p278.
463 *Daily Worker*, 21 January 1941.
464 V. Feather to W. Citrine, 5 March 1941, TUC Blackpool ACR, 1942, p30; National Council of Labour Circular 49, 'The People's Convention', February 1941; Circular 79,

'Refugee Organisations, Communists' Activities', 1 May 1941.
465 J.R. Campbell, 'Workers and the British Totalitarians', *Labour Monthly*, March 1941, pp134–5.
466 Circular 79, op cit, 1941.
467 R.P. Dutt, *Labour Monthly*, June and July 1941.
468 *World News & Views*, 5 July 1941 on the CP, government measures and 'effective defence'.
469 ACTC 1941, J. Marchbank.
470 London TC AR, 1941.
471 *World News & Views*, 19 July 1941. *Daily Worker*, 9 July 1941.
472 Ibid. R.P. Dutt, on 'fullest mobilization and unity' and 'a completely different approach to people and organisations.' WN&V, p449.
473 Birmingham TC AR, 1941, pp12–3; CP, *An Urgent Memo on Production*, March 1942.
474 J.R. Campbell, 'The Scaffolding of Servitude: The Meaning of Essential Work Orders', *Labour Monthly*, July 1941, pp319–26.
475 TCJCC Minutes, 8 August 1941.
476 J.T. Hargreaves to A.J. Heal, Area Secretary, T&GWU, 30 August 1941 (TUC Files).
477 TUC Edinburgh ACR, Autumn 1941, pp230–31.
478 Ibid. J. Marchbank, p104.
479 Brighton TC Minutes, 26 October 1941; CP, *Marxism and the Industrial Workers*, November 1941.
480 R. Willis/V. Feather letters, 13, 28, and 30 January 1942.
481 V. Feather/R. Willis letters, 28 October and 27 November 1942; R. Willis/P. Allott, letters, 7 and 8 January 1943.
482 CP, *The Communist Party and the National Front*, April 1942.
483 G Woodcock, ACTC Report, 30 May 1942.
484 CP Midlands District Committee to Birmingham TC, 16 June 1942.

485 V. Feather to C.G. Spragg, 11 June 1942; V. Feather/G.F. Tutt letters, 26 April 1942 and 27 June 1942.
486 R. Chick, see *Southern Daily Echo*, 'Trades Councils Ban on Communist Party', 29 June 1942.
487 H. Child, *Southern Daily Echo*, 'Barriers to Unity with Communists', 25 July 1942.
488 A.L. Horner, 'TUC 1942', *Labour Monthly*, September 1942, pp276-7; WNV, 5 September 1942, pp361-2.
489 P. Allott, TUC Blackpool ACR, Autumn 1942. Full debate pp153-60.
490 J.R. Campbell, 'Blackpool and After', *Labour Monthly*, October 1942, p311.
491 G.F. Tutt/V. Feather letters, 12 September 1942 and 24 October 1942.
492 V. Feather to G.F. Tutt, 27 October 1942.
493 See CP, *Memorandum* Trade Union Policy in the War Against Fascism, 13 November 1942.
494 C.G. Spragg to H.V. Tewson, 11 November 1942.
495 H.V. Tewson to C.G. Spragg, 17 November 1942.
496 A.E. Hobson to W. Citrine, 30 November 1942.
497 Op cit, CP *Memorandum*, 13 November 1942.
498 TCJCC Minutes, 12 January 1943.
499 Ibid.
500 J. Hinton, op. cit. 1980, p112.
501 A.E. Hobson, Sheffield T&LC, 1943 pp3-7.
502 V. Feather to C.G. Spragg, 4 January 1943.
503 C.G. Spragg to V. Feather, 3 January 1943 and V. Feather to C.G. Spragg, 5 January 1943.
504 C.G. Spragg to V. Feather, 15 April 1943.
505 V. Feather to C.G. Spragg, 16 April 1943.
506 E. Burns, *Labour Party and Communist Party: The Case for Affiliation* (CP), February 1943, p8.
507 Brighton TC Minutes, 21 February 1943, 21 March 1943 and 16 June 1943; TCJCC Minutes, 16 March 1943.

508 ACTC Report, 29 May 1943, J. Marchbank.
509 W.J. Munro, Manchester & Salford TC AR, 1943 p5.
510 P. Allott, TUC Southport ACR, Autumn 1943, pp337–9.
511 D. Gluckstein, *The Nazis, Capitalism and the Working Class*, 1999 (2012 edition), pp187–9.
512 Vasily Grossman, *Life and Fate* [1959] (2020 edition).
513 TUC, *Model Rules, Constitution and Standing Orders for Trades Councils or Industrial Sections of a Trades & Labour Council*, 1943; B. Reid, 'Why Britain Needs a Strong Labour Movement' (CP), September 1943, pp7–9
514 Circular 7, 'Communist Delegates to Trades Councils', 28 October 1943; LRD Fact Service, 18 November 1943.
515 Sheffield T&LC AR, 1944, J Madin, p7.
516 J.P. Young, Chelmsford TC to V. Feather, January 1944 (TUC Files).
517 V. Feather to C.G. Spragg, regarding Hannington, 30 March 1944.
518 LRD Fact Service, 12 May 1944, see also 2 June 1944 to 30 June 1944; TCJCC Minutes, 19 May 1944.
519 ACTC Report, 20 May 1944; see G. Orwell, *Tribune*, 17 March 1944 on 'dead metaphors of the CP'.
520 Birmingham TC AR, 15 September 1944; Manchester TC AR, 1944.
521 E. Haynes to V. Feather, 1 November 1944; A. Beevor, *The Second World War* 2012, p522.
522 E. Haynes/V. Feather 1–2 November 1944.
523 A Lees, *Birmingham Mail*, 'Too Political: Union Threat to Trades Council: Communist Caucus Alleged', 8 November 1944.
524 C.G. Spragg to V. Feather, 9 November 1944; V. Feather to H. Baker, 14 November 1944.
525 Ruislip-Northwood TC meeting, 9 October 1944 in TCJCC Minutes, 28 November 1944.

526 *Southern Daily Echo*, 9 December 1944.
527 V. Feather/H. Child letters, 15 and 29 December 1944.
528 G.R. Shepherd to V. Feather, 1 February 1945; see J.R. Campbell, 'Trade Unions and the General Election' (CP).
529 LRD Fact Service, 'Trades Councils and the Future', 10 May 1945, quote.
530 Huddersfield TC (1885-1960), op cit. p15; Manchester & Salford TC AR, 1945, pp14-6.
531 D.A. Hyde, op. cit. 1951, pp86-92, in which this quote appears.
532 Coventry TC, September 1945; see also TCJCC Minutes, 17 December 1945. TUC Blackpool ACR, Autumn 1945, 'Political Activities' section.
533 Circular 35, 'People's Press Printing Society Limited', 28 December 1945.
534 London TC AR, 1946; CP, *Looking Ahead*, 1946.
535 T. Wakley, *Communist Circus* (LP), 1946.
536 R. Birch, 'A Wage Based on Human Needs' (CP), 1946, pp6-12; LRD Fact Service, 4 January 1946.
537 LRD Fact Service, 22 March 1946 to 26 April 1946.
538 ACTC Report, from Derby, May 1946; TCJCC Minutes, 24 May 1946.
539 See 'James Burnham and the Managerial Revolution', *Polemic*, Number 3, May 1946.
540 E.J. Hibberd to W. Citrine on 'Southampton TC's CP members', 25 July 1946.
541 Hackney TC AR, July 1946; see also Swindon TC, 27 September 1946.
542 *World News & Views XX111*, p99.
543 E. Silver, op cit 1973, quote p91.
544 Dan Stone, *Goodbye to All That? The Story of Europe since 1945*, 2014, p59.
545 A.C. Lowcock to Tewson, 18 February 1947.

546 A.L. Horner, 'Trade Unions and Communism', *Labour Monthly*, February 1948.
547 Adam Tooze, *The New Statesmen,* 21 April 2022.
548 ACTC AR, 1947.
549 Birmingham TC Secretary, 1947.
550 A.E. Hobson, Sheffield T&LC letter to the TUC, 30 December 1947.
551 Sheffield T&LC AR, 1947 p6.
552 Manchester & Salford TC AR, 1947.
553 LRD Fact Service, 2 April 1948.
554 TCJCC Minutes, 16 August 1948.
555 E. Bevin, Preface, W. Hamling, *A Short History of Liverpool TC,* 1948 p3; W.F. Harrison to H.V. Tewson, 28 September 1948.
556 TUC Margate ACR, Autumn 1948, pp305–6 and pp532–8.
557 LRD Fact Service, 17 and 24 September, and 15 October 1948.
558 Circular 18 'Trade Unions and Communism', 27 September 1948, by H.V. Tewson.
559 Ibid.
560 R.P. Dutt, 'The Class Fight in Britain', *Labour Monthly*, October 1948, pp289–91.
561 F. Meade/V. Feather letters, 21 September, and 28 October 1948.
562 H. Pollitt, 'Trade Unionists – What Next?' (CP), November 1948, p14; quote from *Labour Monthly*, 'Why we want Peace with the Soviet Union', November 1948; TUC General Council, *Defend Democracy - Communist Activities Examined*, 24 November 1948, pp6–10.
563 H. Baker, Birmingham TC AR, 1948.
564 TUC General Council, op cit, 1948.
565 V. Feather to J.A. Evison, letters 25 and 30 November 1948.
566 V. Feather/A.E. Hobson/H.V. Tewson letters, 26 to 30 November 1948.

567 TUC, *Labour* Journal, February 1949, pp184–6 reports on CP members in TCs.
568 H. Gilman and A.L. Ward to V. Feather, February 1949.
569 T. Williamson (NUG&MW)/R. Boyfield letters, 22 and 23 March 1949.
570 TUC, *The Tactics of Disruption – Communist Methods Exposed*, March 1949.
571 CP EC, *Statement*, January 1949; TCJCC Minutes, 4 April 1949.
572 ACTC Report, 29 May 1949, 'Trade Unions and Disruptive Bodies'; *Labour* Journal, August 1949; TUC Journal 'The Growth of Local TUCs', August 1949.
573 CP, *Defend Trade Union Rights*, May 1949, pp3–11, 16, 25–27.
574 A. Fleming, Manchester Committee for Defence of Canadian Seamen's Union, 1 July 1949; F.C. Henry/H.V. Tewson/R. Boyfield/H.E. Newbold letters, 27 July to 12 September 1949.
575 *Glossop Chronicle*, 9 September 1949, quote.
576 *Brighton & Hove Gazette*, 18 and 25 March 1950.
577 TUC Bridlington ACR, Autumn 1949, pp350–60.
578 R. Miller/R. Boyfield letters, 12 September 1949 to 24 February 1950.
579 T.H. Nimmo, *Birmingham Town Crier*, 14 January 1950; *Birmingham Gazette*, 1 and 4 November 1949.
580 V. Feather to E. Kavanagh (Leeds TC), 24 October 1949, our italics; *Labour* Journal, November 1949 p517.
581 Circular 46, 'Trades Councils and Proscribed Organisations', 26 January 1950.
582 *Brighton Argus*, March 1950.
583 ACTC Nottingham Report, May 1950.
584 V. Feather/E. Kavanagh, op cit, 1949.
585 ACTC AR, May 1950, F.R. Fermor.

586 E. Silver, op cit, 1973, pp100-2 ignores V. Feather's TC correspondence.
587 TUC, *Trades Councils Move to Safeguard Democracy*, Labour Journal May 1950, p729; Circular 95, 'WFTU (World Federation of Trade Unions) Disruptive Activity', 2 June 1950; R. Boyfield/H.E. Newbold letters, 4 and 22 July 1950.
588 A.R. Stewart, 'The CP', *Communist Review*, July 1950, pp230-1.
589 TUC Brighton ACR, 1950.
590 G.M. Williams, *London Trades Council 1860-1960*, 1960, p27.
591 TUC Brighton ACR, op cit, 1950.
592 Circular 18, 'Second World Peace Congress, Sheffield', 27 October 1950.
593 B. Kilgarriff/R. Boyfield letters, 12, 14 and 20 November, 21 December 1950, and 12 January 1951.
594 Ibid, 16 and 28 January 1951, and later 8 and 10 August letters 1951.
595 Letter to R. Boyfield, 20 February 1951.
596 A.E. Hobson to R. Boyfield, 5 February 1951.
597 Lynne Segal, Sheila Rowbotham and Hilary Wainwright, *Beyond the Fragments*, 1979, our italics.
598 Tony Cliff and Donny Gluckstein, *Marxism and Trade Union Struggle: The General Strike of 1926*, 1986 (2015 edition), chapter 1.
599 Lord Citrine, op cit, 1964, pp256-7.
600 See J.T. Murphy, *Preparing for Power*, 1932 (1972 edition), pp66, 151.
601 Alison Light, *A Radical Romance: A Memoir of Love, Grief and Consolation*, 2019 (2020 edition), p190.
602 Rafael Behr, *Politics: A Survivor's Guide*, 2023, p189.
603 Dan Carrier, *Westminster Extra*, 21 January 2022, 'Heightened Census'.

604 *Mansfield Trades Council Diamond Jubilee*, 1965, p14; D.I. Mackay et al, 'The Discussion of Public Works Programmes, 1917-1935' *International Review of Social History* 11, 1966, pp8-17. The NUWCM was formed on 15 April 1921.
605 H. Mackinven, *Edinburgh &* op. cit, 1959, p56; see also *Leicester Pioneer*, 19 August 1921.
606 Sheffield T&LC AR 1923, pp3-10.
607 M. Turnbull, 'The Attitude of Government and Administration towards the Hunger Marches of the 1920s and 1930s', *Journal of Social Policy*, Volume 2, Part 1, January 1973; NFTC Report, 17 November 1923, pp11-14; TUC Organisation Committee Report, 24 July 1929.
608 W. Hannington, *Never on Our Knees*, 1967, pp78-102; ACTC Report, 27 February 1925.
609 TCs' reports to ACTC, June 1925 p6, and July 1925, p10.
610 London TC AR, 1925.
611 TUC Bournemouth ACR, September 1926 referenced this.
612 Ibid, pp130, 166; see R. Skidelsky, *Politicians and the Slump*, 1967, p433; and V.L. Allen, 'Militant Trade Unionism', 1966, pp39-42.
613 S. Pollard, 'Trade Union Reactions to the Economic Crisis', *Journal of Contemporary History*, Volume 4, Number 4, October 1969.
614 ACTC Report, 27 May 1927, G. Hicks; TCJCC Minutes, 25 October 1927.
615 Bristol UA Constitution, 14 November 1927; see also Bristol TC AR 1928, E.H. Parker.
616 TCJCC Minutes, 19 December 1927; Miners' March to London, History of Case, File Number 21.1.19 (TUC Files).
617 *Daily Herald*, 1 November 1927 'The Miners' March: Mr Citrine Answers the "Sunday Worker"; NAILING A LIE;

Facts of the General Council's Decision'; see Circular 2a to Trades Councils, 27 October 1927.
618 TUC, *Hunger March, A Communist Stunt. No Support from the Miners' Federation*, November 1927.
619 A. Lockwood in TUC *Industrial News*, Number 60, 1 November 1927; *Workers' Weekly*, 11 November 1927.
620 The Editor, 'The Outlook', *The Communist*, December 1927, p250.
621 TUC Swansea ACR, Autumn 1928, pp149–50, pp363–5.
622 *Industrial Review*, January 1928, pp12–13; TCJCC Minutes, 19 December 1927, Bristol UA.
623 Circular 27, 'NUWCM', 1 March 1928; W. Citrine, *Industrial Review*, Supplement, March 1928.
624 TCJCC to TCs 'Unemployed Associations', 3 March 1928; W. Citrine to Trades Council Federations, 5 March 1928.
625 *Industrial Review*, 'Organising the Workless', March 1928; Sheffield T&LC AR, 1928, p10.
626 Circular 63, 'NUWCM and Courts of Referees', 9 August 1928.
627 Edinburgh T&LC AR (1928); Circular 9a, 'Area Conferences Regarding Social Insurance', 29 October 1928; TCJCC Minutes, 23 October 1928; A.L. Horner, *Labour Monthly*, October 1928, pp598–9.
628 TCJCC Minutes, 22 November 1928; see also Circular 24, 'Unemployed Associations': Swansea Congress Report, 6 December 1928 and W. Citrine letter to Trades Councils, 15 November 1928.
629 TUC General Council, *March of Unemployed*, 10 December 1928 (TUC File No.135, 'NUWM: History of Case').
630 Willie Gallacher, op cit, 1966, pp234–5.
631 F. Rowland, TUC Belfast ACR, Autumn 1929, pp329–30.
632 Circular 31, 'Transfer from Distressed Areas', 3 January 1929; Circular 42, 'Administering Unemployment

Insurance', 25 January 1929; *Industrial Review*, January 1929, p9; Brighton TC, 20 February 1929.
633   ACTC Report 29 June 1929; W. Beveridge, *Unemployment: A Problem of Industry*, 1931, p280.
634   TUC Belfast ACR, Autumn 1929, pp299–300; *Industrial Review*, October-December 1929.
635   *Industrial Review*, February 1930.
636   *Daily Worker*, 7 February 1930.
637   Newcastle TC Secretary to Citrine, 10 May 1931; see Birmingham TC AR, 1930.
638   ACTC Report, 24 May 1930.
639   Manchester & Salford TC 'Memorandum on Municipal Rationalisation', June 1930.
640   Manchester & Salford TC 'Unemployment and the Coming Winter', August 1930; *Labour* Journal, September 1930.
641   B. McIntosh, 'A Revolutionary Municipal Policy', *Labour Monthly*, September 1930, pp562–3.
642   *Industrial Review*, October and November 1930; H. McShane, *Daily Worker*, 18 November 1930.
643   Oxford TC AR, 1930.
644   *Daily Worker*, 6 and 23 January 1931.
645   Quote in H. Mackinven, op cit, 1958, p60; Circular 75, 'Allotments for the Unemployed', 26 March 1931.
646   *Daily Worker*, 11 April 1931; Brighton TC Minutes, 15 April 1931.
647   'The People's Congress', 9 May 1931; see Manchester & Salford TC, 'Economy!' 1931, pp1–4.
648   Circular 107, 'Demonstrations re. Commissions Report on Unemployment Insurance', 6 June 1931; ACTC Report, 30 May 1931.
649   Manchester & Salford TC AR, 1931, pp5–7. What would have been made of the recent pandemics or climate crisis?
650   TCJCC Minutes, 23 September 1931.

651 Birmingham TC AR, 1931, pp6–11.
652 Brighton TC Minutes, 16 December 1931; see T. Bell, *The Communist Party*, 1937, pp145–6.
653 London TC Memorandum, December 1931.
654 Manchester & Salford TC AR, 1931, p7, A.A. Purcell.
655 E.g. Southampton TC, 'To the Unemployed Workers of Southampton', 1931.
656 Circular 12, 'Unemployment Insurance: Transitional Benefit Through Public Assistance Committees", 21 October 1931. F.W. Rudland/Citrine letters 17 November 1931 and 18 November 1931; Circular 19, 'Unemployment Insurance', November 19, 1931.
657 TUC, *Educational and Creative Facilities for the Unemployed*, 11 December 1931, H.V. Tewson; TUC, *Organisation of the Unemployed*, 14 December 1931.
658 H.V. Tewson, Report on 'Unemployed Associations', 9 January 1932.
659 F. Day/Citrine letters, 20 December 1931 and 4 April 1932; E.P. Harries to F. Day, 23 December 1931.
660 R. Chick/E.P. Harries letters, 17 and 18 January 1932.
661 H.V. Tewson, op cit 'Unemployed Associations', 9 January 1932; TCJCC, 'Organisation of Unemployed Associations', 25 January 1932.
662 TUC Report, 1932, p232; see W. Hannington, 'Crimes Against the Unemployed' pamphlet, 1932, p3 (LSE Library).
663 Quote from Manchester & Salford TC AR, 1932.
664 Newcastle & District TC AR, 1932.
665 TUC General Council, *Explanatory Notes on Formation of Unemployed Associations*, 2 February 1932; Circular 69, 'Organisation of Unemployed Persons", 5 February 1932.
666 Bristol UA, 13 February 1932 A. Conley, H.V. Tewson, 'Report of Conference of UAs', February 1932.

667 Circular 61, 'The Means Test', 18 February 1932; *Industrial Review*, February 1932.
668 *Industrial Review*, Organisation of the Unemployed', April 1932, p10.
669 NUWM Declaration, 'United Action Against Unemployment', 19 April 1932.
670 E.P. Harries to W. Milne-Bailey, 18 April 1932 (TUC Files).
671 H.V. Tewson, ACTC Report, 28 May 1932; Circular 85, 'NUWM', 21 April 1932; Cf. TUC File Number 135, 'NUWM: History of Case'.
672 https://www.ons.gov.uk/economy/nationalaccounts/uksectoraccounts/compendium/economicreview/april2019/longtermtrendsinukemployment1861to2018, 28 April 2019.
673 Unemployed figures at E.P. Harries, *Industrial Review*, August 1932.
674 H.V. Tewson, 'Unemployed Associations Report', 26 August 1932; see E.P. Harries, 'Unemployed Associations', *Industrial Review*, June 1932, p14; TCJCC Minutes, 12 July 1932.
675 E.P. Harries, TCJCC Progress Report on Unemployed Associations, 12 October 1932; Circular 127, 'Allotment Gardens for Unemployed Persons', 18 August 1932; *Industrial Review*, August 1932.
TUC Newcastle ACR, 1932, pp121–3 and pp277–9.
676 Birmingham TC AR 1932 p8; R. Hayburn, 'The Police and the Hunger Marchers', *International Review of Social History* 1972, pp625–44. E.P. Harries, 'New Services for Unemployed Associations', *Industrial Review*, November 1932. Circular 32, 'Organisation of the Unemployed', 3 November 1932.
677 TCJCC Minutes, 18 November 1932.
678 E.P. Harries, 'Helping the Unemployed', *Labour Magazine*, December 1932; E.P Harries *Industrial Review*, November 1932.

679 TCJCC Minutes, 19 January 1933, 17 March 1933; NJC, Circular 57 'National Demonstration on Unemployment', 15 December 1932; s H. Pollitt, 'The Manoeuvres of the TUC', *Labour Monthly*, January 1933, p26; E.P. Harries, 'Social and Occupational Service for Unemployed', 23 March 1933.
680 Sheffield T&LC 1933, F. Thraves, p6.
681 ACTC Report, 27 May 1933, quote from Birmingham District Committee of NUWM.
682 *Industrial Review*, August 1933, p13; ACTC, ibid.
683 Conference of UA Representatives and the TCJCC, 27 July 1933.
684 Brighton TC Minutes, 19 July 1933.
685 *Western Daily Press*, 1 August 1933; Southampton TC AR 1933, pp1–2; Oxford T&LC AR 1933, p1.
686 TUC Brighton ACR, Autumn 1933 pp273, 280–83; Circular 139a, 'Public Assistance Committees and National Health Insurance Arrears', 3 August 1933.
687 UA President quoted, 'Front Line Activities', *Labour Journal*, February 1934, p131; Circular 73, 'Unemployed Bill, 1933', 1 February 1934; G.D.H. Cole, *Socialist Leaguer* pamphlet, 1934.
688 Circular 103, 'ACTC 1934: Report from Unemployed Associations', 19 April 1934; For the TCJCC, E.P. Harries to G.R. Shepherd, 25 July 1934.
689 A.M. Wall, 'Memorandum on Services for Unemployed Workers', 26 July 1934; TUC Weymouth ACR, Autumn 1934, pp123–5.
690 Southampton TC AR, 1934, R. Morley, pp1–2.
691 'Memorandum from the Unemployed Services Committee of the TUC', 21 September 1934, quote from Mrs Rackham.
692 Birmingham TC Statement, 1934.

693 Manchester & Salford TC AR, 1935 p7. Unemployed Services Committee Report, 17 January 1935; W. Hannington, *Unemployed Struggles*, 1936, p311; TCJCC Minutes, 10 January 1935.

694 H.H. Elvin, 'Draft Memorandum on "Trade Union Recruitment"', March 1935; response from *Baths and Wilts Chronicle*, 14 March 1935. See Circular 69 'UAB Regulations', 21 February 1935.

695 TCJCC, 'Suggested Activities for Unemployed Associations', 19 March 1935.

696 N. McGretton, *Blyth News*, 6 June 1935; ACTC Report, 25 May 1935, TCJCC Report.

697 W. Hannington, letters on UAs, 13 September 1935 and 25 May 1935 (TUC Files).

698 TUC Margate ACR, 1935, quote pp112–24; see Bristol TC AR, 1936, W.H. Hennessy.

699 General Council Minutes, Motion on 'Unemployed Marchers', 25 November 1936.

700 A.M. Wall, 'Lessons of the National March of the Unemployed', *Labour Monthly*, December 1936, p744.

701 Circular 55, 'Unemployed Marches', 4 February 1937; TCJCC Minutes, 19 January 1937. Oxford T&LC secretary to TUC General Council, 16 February 1937, and W. Short, Newcastle & District TC, to Citrine, 29 March 1937.

702 TCJCC Report, 'Unemployed Marches', May 1937.

703 ACTC Report, 29 May 1937, quote, Bethnal Green TC delegate.

704 Quote from Ipswich TC AR, 1932, p2.

705 Manchester & Salford TC AR, 1937, quote pp7–8.

706 Circular 33, Trades Councils in 'Unofficial Marches'.

707 TUC Norwich ACR, Autumn 1937, pp107–8 and pp254–6; See also E.H. Parker letter to TUC, 30 August 1937. J.S. Middleton to E.P. Harries, 2 December 1937; Circular

33, 'Unofficial Marches' 9 December 1937; Circular 30, 'Unemployment Assistance Allowances & the Cost of Living', 25 November 1937; TCJCC on 'Unemployed Associations', 15 February 1938. Our Italics.

708 ACTC Report, 28 May 1938; TUC Blackpool ACR, 1938, p118, p130 and p394. Circular 84, 'Unemployment Research and Advice Bureau', 17 March 1938.
709 ACTC May 1939, TCJCC Report by E.P. Harries.
710 W. Citrine, op cit, June 1940, quote p15; Circular 94, 'Review of Unemployed Workers', 18 July 1940.
711 Birmingham TC AR, 1940, pp8–11 and AR 1941, pp8–13; ACTC Report, 28 June 1941.
712 ACTC May 1942; TUC Edinburgh ACR, Autumn 1941, pp103–4; and Manchester & Salford TC, 27 May 1942.
713 TUC, *Trades Councils and War-Time Committees*, 1942.
714 Westminster TC, 28 June 1942.
715 TUC, *The TUC in War-Time*, February 1943, and ACTC, 1943; for the CP's enthusiasm, note W. Gallacher, The Beveridge Report, Labour Monthly, January 1943 pp7–10.
716 E. Hobsbawm *Age of Extremes: The Short Twentieth Century 1914–1991*, 1995 (2002 edition), quote p85. See also H. Baker (Birmingham TC)/V. Feather letters, 22 and 28 December 1943; TCJCC minutes, 20 August 1943, 8 December 1943.
717 Lancashire, Cheshire & North Wales Federation of TCs, June 1944 quote.
718 Leeds TC, 'Unemployed Association' Report, 7 July 1944.
719 Essential Work (General Provisions) Order, 24 July 1944; Willesden Borough LP&TC, September 1944.
720 Wolverhampton TC AR, 1944 pp1–2; TUC Blackpool ACR, 1945 p47; TCJCC Minutes, 6 October 1944.
721 Glasgow TC AR, January 1945.
722 H.E. Newbold, Manchester & Salford TC AR, April 1945.

723 Bristol TC AR, 1945.
724 Coventry TC AR, September 1945; LRD Fact Service, Service, 19 October 1945.
725 ACTC Report, 25 May 1946, quote from H.N. Harrison, TCJCC's report to this ACTC.
726 Ibid, ACTC Report, L. Fawcett.
727 LRD Fact Service, 31 May 1946.
728 LRD Fact Service, 27 September 1946 and 25 October 1946 on TCs.
729 Birmingham TC Conference, February 1947.
730 ACTC Report, 1947, Luton TC delegate quote.
731 TUC, *What the TUC Is Doing*, May 1947 pamphlet, pp25–27; ACTC Report, May 1947.
732 Penrith TC AR, 1947, Swindon TC AR, 1947.
733 Quote from Manchester & Salford TC AR, 1948 p3; LRD Fact Service, 10 October 1947; Bristol TC AR, 1947, pp1–3.
734 Coventry TC AR, 1948 (Warwick University Archives).
735 Birmingham TC AR, 1948, p6.
736 Kidderminster TC AR, 1948, see Resolution from Bristol Electrical Trades Union to V. Feather, 20 March 1948. See D. Rubinstein, *The Labour Left and Domestic Policy, 1945–50*, 1980, pp6–7.
737 London TC AR, 1948, quote; and Dartford TC letter to the TUC, July 1948 on confrontation with employers.
738 Manchester & Salford TC AR, 1932 pp4–5.
739 Mark Fisher, *Capitalist Realism: Is There No Alternative?*, 2009, p35.
740 Albert Einstein, *Monthly Review*, May 1949.
741 For example see Sue Ledwith, 'Vive la différence? Women and Trade Unions in Britain' available at available at journals.openedition.org/rfcb/1141, 2009; Rebecca Zahn and Nicole Busby, 'Women's Labour and Trade Unionism

– A Dangerous Combination?' in *Institute of Employment Rights*, available at ier.org.uk/comments/womens-labour-and-trade-unionism-dangerous-combination, 6 July 2016.
742 Zahn and Busby.
743 Ibid.
744 Lindsey German, *Sex, Class and Socialism* 1994 (Second Edition), p115.
745 Quoted in Mary Davis 'Women at Work' from *Britain at Work: Voice from the Workplace 1945–1995*, available at unionhistory.info/britainatwork/narrativedisplay.php?type=womenatwork, 2012.
746 Ibid.
747 Ledwith, paragraph 18.
748 Zahn and Busby.
749 German, p122.
750 Ibid.
751 Ibid, pp123–9.
752 Zahn and Busby, Ledwith, para. 21 and Davis.
753 Zahn and Busby.
754 Ledwith, para. 21.
755 Barbara Drake, *Women in Trade Unions*, 1920, quoted in Ledwith, para. 21.
756 Referred to in Judith Orr, *Marxism & Women's Liberation*, 2015, p98.
757 Ledwith, paras 22 and 25.
758 Orr, pp100–1.
759 German, p127 and Orr, p100.
760 German, p128.
761 Ibid, pp128–30.
762 Ibid, p130, see Sarah Boston, *Women Workers in Trade Unions*, 1980, p105.
763 German, p130.
764 Boston, pp67, p129.

765 Ibid, p150.
766 Ibid, p149.
767 Ibid, p150.
768 Orr, pp102–4.
769 Boston, p102.
770 Ibid, pp81, 215.
771 Ibid, pp87–8.
772 German, p131.
773 See Orr, pp190–91.
774 Quoted in ibid, p59.
775 Drake, p108, quoted in ibid, p192.
776 Davis.
777 Zahn and Busby; Davis.
778 Ledwith, para. 25 and Shelia Rowbotham, *Hidden from History*, 1977 (3rd edition), p130.
779 Referred to in Ledwith para. 25.
780 Ibid, para. 26 and Boston, pp212–4.
781 Orr, p192.
782 Ibid.
783 Boston, p224.
784 Ibid, p242.
785 Ibid, pp221–3.
786 Ibid, p223.
787 Ibid.
788 1947 TUC annual report, quoted in ibid, p223.
789 Boston p242.
790 Quoted in ibid p125–6.
791 German, p131.
792 Quoted in Davis.
793 Davis.
794 Ibid.
795 Ibid.
796 Ibid, our italics.

797 Ibid.
798 See Ledwith, para. 42.
799 Ibid, para. 43.
800 Ibid and Davis.
801 Ibid and Orr, pp10–11.
802 Ibid, para. 36.
803 Zahn and Busby.
804 Details at policymogul.com/library-material/648/women-and-the-uk-economy-library-material-policymogul.
805 Quote from Ledwith, para. 27; see also Davis.
806 Quote from ibid, para. 27.
807 Davis.
808 Orr, pp8–9.
809 Zahn and Busby.
810 The analysis particularly in Subsection 1 and 2 for this chapter is informed by articles from the websites of *Socialist Worker and The Socialist*, as well as the pamphlet *The Revival of Resistance* by Mark L Thomas, Jessica Walsh and Charlie Kimber (2023).
811 By radical theorist and activist Tony Cliff, quoted in Thomas et al, ibid, p37
812 Ibid, p60.
813 Paul Foot, *Paul Foot: A Tribute*, 2004, p17..
814 Thomas et al, op cit, 2023, p5.
815 Quoted in ibid, p11.
816 Quote in theguardian.com/environment/2021/sep/28/blah-greta-thunberg-leaders-climate-crisis-co2-emissions.
817 See eu.usatoday.com/story/news/2023/02/23/why-are-fossil-fuels-bad-environment-impact/10454327002/
818 Clyde Workers' Committee leaflet in the Beveridge Collection, British Library of Political and Economic Science, section 3, item 5. (our italics)
819 jrf.org.uk/report/uk-poverty-2023
820 E.P. Thompson, 'Socialist Humanism', *The New Reasoner*, 1957, p140.

821 Raphael Samuel, op cit, 1980, pp49-50.
822 E.P. Thompson, 'The Peculiarities of the English', *The Poverty of Theory* 1978.
823 Read E.P. Thompson, *Writing by Candlelight*, 1980, for inspiration.
824 Quote from D. Edwards to V. Feather, 26 February 1949; see Circular 63, 'Trade Union Publicity Campaigns', 12 January 1949.
825 Quote from Circular 145 'TUC Weekend Schools', 7 September 1949; see also TUC Bridlington ACR, Autumn 1949, p140.
826 *Labour* Journal, 'TUCs in Miniature', June 1949 pp300-1; ACTC May 1949, 'JCC Election'.
827 TCJCC Report to ACTC May 1949 'NHS; HMCs'. Nb. Circular 9, 'Tribunal Procedure', 3 March 1949.
828 V. Feather to R.T. Jenner (Oxford T&LC Secretary), 3 February 1949; TCJCC Minutes, 15 March 1949.
829 A. Compertz at ACTC Report, May 1949; Manchester & Salford TC AR, 1949, p5.
830 Sir Luke Fawcett, ACTC Report, May 1949. (our italics)
831 TCJCC Minutes, 28 June 1949; 'Growth of Local TUCs', *Labour* Journal, August 1949, p378; Circular 28, 'Hospital Management Committees – Annual Filling of Vacancies', 2 December 1949.
832 LRD Fact Service, June–September 1949; TCJCC Minutes, 28 June and 22 August 1949.
833 Quote from H.E. Newbold, Manchester & Salford TC AR, 1949, p13.
834 Quote from Manchester & Salford TC AR, 1950, pp15-6.
835 Quote H.L. Bullock, ACTC AR, May 1950.
836 Ibid. Sir Luke Fawcett, ACTC Report, May 1949. (our italics)
837 Quote from B. Burke, op cit, 1975 p6, see also pp70-82; see *Labour* Journals, July 1951, p377 and May 1952, p275.

838 Leo Panitch, 'Trade Unions and the Capitalist State', *New Left Review*, Number 125, January–February 1981, p42.
839 ACTC Conference 1944, H.N. Harrison for the TCJCC Council.
840 Alex Callinicos, *Socialists in the Trade Unions*, 1995, p39.
841 See J. Orr, op cit, 2015, Chapters 10 and 11.
842 Martha Gimenez, quoted in J. Orr, ibid, p202.
843 J. Orr, ibid, p226.
844 Immanuel Ness and Dario Azzellini, *Ours to Master And to Own*, 2011, p ix and p1)
845 On Adam Tooze's website at adamtooze.com/2020/08/28/pessimism-of-the-intellect-optimism-of-the-will-the-line-so-often-attributed-to-gramsci-was-taken-from-romain-rolland/ we see that, although this phrase is often attributed to Antonio Gramsci, it originates in Romain Rolland in a review of a novel by Ramon Lefebrve.
846 See Arundhati Roy, *Capitalism: A Ghost Story*, 2014.
847 Greta Thunberg, *The New Statesman*, 21–27 October 2022, p35.
848 Thomas et al, op cit, 2003, p58.